SULLIVAN COUNTY TENNESSEE CEMETERIES

UNKNOWN

Compiled by
Karen L. Sherman

HERITAGE BOOKS
2010

HERITAGE BOOKS

AN IMPRINT OF HERITAGE BOOKS, INC.

Books, CDs, and more—Worldwide

For our listing of thousands of titles see our website
at
www.HeritageBooks.com

Published 2010 by
HERITAGE BOOKS, INC.
Publishing Division
100 Railroad Ave. #104
Westminster, Maryland 21157

International Standard Book Numbers
Paperbound: 978-1-55613-537-8
Clothbound: 978-0-7884-8462-9

This project by no means was done single handed. It was a joint effort by Haskell(Skeeter) Morrell, Jr., his wife Debby Morrell, Ralph R. Morrell II and myself. We spent many Sunday afternoon driving, hiking and carrying on all over Sullivan County, armed with field glasses, topographical maps and hearsay about cemetery locations. We dodged angry animals, barbed wire fences, electric fences, snakes and things I'm sure we're glad we weren't aware of. We tried very hard to be very exact, if one couldn't read the stones we took a vote as to what we thought it could be. Spelling on some of the names are different, but that is not a typographical error on our part, perhaps the stone cutter was in error. Even if we knew "Betty" was spelled "Betty", but the stone says "Betyt" - that's what we wrote down. We made no attempt to second guess the stones.

I want to thank all those involved, both physically and emotionally. It was a project I started as a labor of love, and a project that needed doing. I wished it could be more complete, but it was difficult to work on given my location for the last 5 years. I hope someone picks up the ball and continues on. Sullivan County printed material is far and few between and it's too bad, it's such an important county.

Karen L. Sherman
Westbrook, Maine
1991

Sullivan County, Tennessee

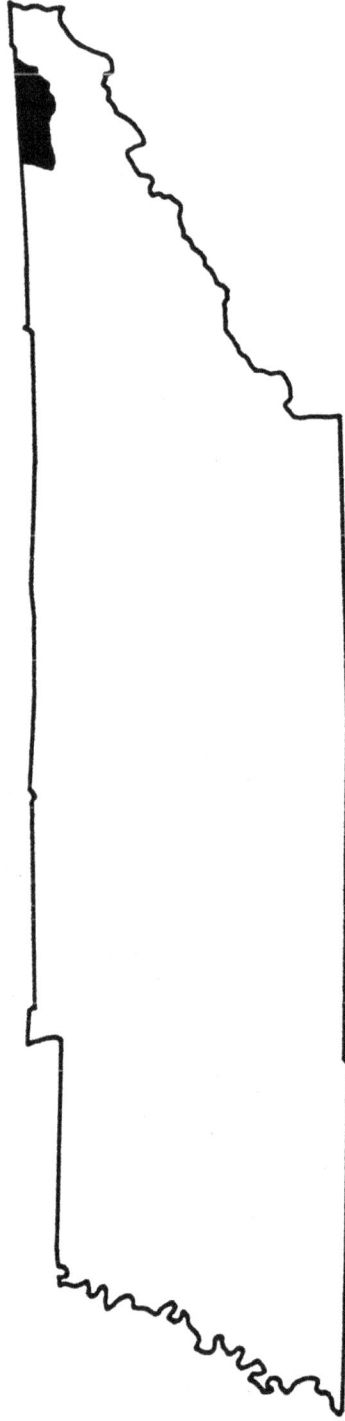

Cemetery Index

Atkinson - 9
Bachman - 24
Beidleman Presbyterian - 53
Beeler - 137
Black - 15
Blountville - 170
Boy - 13
Chinquapin - 26
Clark - 111
Cloud - 6
Cox - 116
Cross - 10
Crumley - 39
Deck, Abraham - 7
Deck, Jacob - 18
Delaney - 9
Denton - 12
Denton #2 - 36
Dishner - 3
Double Springs Baptist Church - 112
Droke - 6
Droke, Old - 47
Edgefield - 131
Fain - 49
Gaines - 25
Groseclose - 47
Harr - 24
Harr, Old - 49
Henley - 5
Hite - 119
Holston Grove Luthren Church - 198
Holt - 4
Immanuel Church - 46
Kendricks Creek Methodist Church - 117
Latture - 134
Leonard - 4
Lilley - 36
Lindamood - 4
McLaney - 1
Massengill - 62
Mauk - 38
Missionary Baptist Church - 37
Morningside - 63
Morrell - 193
Morrison Chapel Methodist Church - 59
Mottern - 3
Muddy Creek Baptist Church - 140

New Bethel Presbyterian Church - 181
Newland - 18
Old Baptist - 49
Old Methodist - 150
Old Salem Methodist Church - 48
Ordway - 19
Paperville - 126
Pemberton - 61
Peregoy-Profitt - 9
Phipps-Netherland - 18
Pleasant Grove Church - 109
Potter - 58
Presbyterian Church - 2
Rock Springs United Methodist Church,new - 120
Rock Springs United Methodist Church,old - 124
Roller's Memorial Church (Cox Chapel) - 54
Seneker-Steele - 8
Shipley - 150
Smith - 5
St. John - 8
Steele - 54
Stophel - 7
Vanover - 11
Walker's Fork Baptist Church - 50
Waterman - 25
Weaver - 94
Webb - 60
Webb-Lady - 16
Wheeler - 145
Wyatt - 59
Yoakley - 25
Zion Evangelical Luthren Church - 3

Cemetery Locations

Bachman – Along Hwy 81 between Kingsport and Fall Branch. Where Mill Creek Road crosses Hwy 81.

Clark – Hwy 126.

Cloud – Carter Valley Road out of Morrison City.

Cox – Next to East Cherokee School.

Jacob Deck – 2/3 mile SW of Johnson Chapel on old Staubus Farm.

Denton – 1/2 mile West of Zion Luthren Church.

Double Springs Baptist Church – North side of Kendricks Creek.

Old Droke – Where Blountville & Reedy Creek Road join.

Fain Family – Across from Union Church at Arcadia.

Gaines – Just off County Hwy. trunning thru Village of Orebank.

Groseclose – NW of intersection of Bloomingdale Road & Hwy 11W.

Harr – Across road from Dishner Cemetery.

Old Harr – 1/2 way from Blountville to Reedy Creek.

Holt Family & Abraham Deck – Between Zion Luthren & Immanuel Luthren Churches.

Holston Grove Luthren Church – 2 miles from Buffalo School, near mouth of Beaver Creek., 1/2 mile from North shore of Boone Lake.

Kendricks Creek Methodist Church – off Hwy 23 in Colonial Heights.

Leonard – 1/4 mile from Zion Luthren Church.

Lilley – east side of Hwy 11E., Piney Flats.

Mauk Family – 1 mile left of Bluff City bridge.

Missionary Baptist Church – Near Shavers Store and in sight of Holston Grove Luthren Church.

Muddy Creek Baptist Church – NW side of Boone Lake, near mouth of Muddy Creek.

Newland Family – Between Arcadia Presb. Church & Arcadia Methodist Church. 1 mile from Virginia line.

Phipps-Netherland – On Cannongate Road in Rotherwood Hills, Kingsport.

Pleasant Grove – 2 miles north of Bluff City on Pleasant Grove Road.

Roller – 1 mile south of Bridwell Heights, TVA says its Cox Chapel.

Old Salem – in sight of new Hwy. 11W.

Cemetery locations, cont.

Seneker-Steele - 5 mile WSW of Bristol, on headwaters of Becks Creek, a tributary of Beaver Creek.

Waterman Family - 1 1/2 mile NE of Jackson School (Kingsport).

Yoakley - 100 yards south of Hwy & 100 feet from runways of Tri-Cities Airport.

Zion Evangelical Luthren Church - Headwater fo Becks Creek.

I wish I had better directions for all the cemeteries, but after I moved from the area it was impossible to get any help with locations.

McLaney Cemetery

Bare, Geneva M.	Jan.30,1901 - Feb.21,1954
Cagle, Bill	no dates
Mattie	no dates
Isaac	June 9,1845 - Feb.15,1916
Sarah	Mar.18,1858 - Aug.3,1932, w/o Isaac
Samuel B.	Oct.12,1872 - Mar.10,1896
Carr, James	Aug.6,1846 - Sept.29,1914
Suda	d.Jan.26,1932, aged 73y,w/o James Carr
Maggie	1887 - 1935
Walter	Dec.29,1885 - Mar.14,1957
Ella	Apr.9,1890 - Dec.10,1957
Cross, Lillie	Jan.19,1919 - Sept.19,1936
Ellis, George	Feb.6,1887 - Aug.2,1970
Mollie C.	Aug.26,1895 - Oct.15,1976
Glover, Infant twin boys	d. Aug.21,1953
Gregg, Harry P.	July 3, 1896 - Mar.28,1968
Georgia	Aug.27,1903 - Nov.17,1975
Humphreys, Rosco	June 14,1894 - Mar.5,1899, s/o G.H. & Allice Humphreys.
Lillie	June 13, 1899 - Oct.26,1901, d/o G.H.& Allice Humphreys.
Ollie	Nov.16,1901 - Mar.23,1903, d/o G.H. & Allice Humphreys.
Nellie	b.& d. July 22,1912,d/o G.H. & Allice.
Hyatt, Andie	May 6,1887 - May 6, 1963
Liley, G.C.	Dec.1915 - July 30,1916
Lilley, Hester	July 30,1897 - Oct.16,1900,d/o A.J.& N.C.
Clyde	Apr.23,1906 - Nov.17,1915, d/o A.J. & N.C.
Andrew J.	May 22, 1864 - May 24,1944
Nannie C.	May 15,1868 - Feb.25,1955
MacKlaney, R.	Feb.5,1908 - Mar.2,1910, s/o J. & M.
McLaney, Infant	d.1904, d/o J.& M. McLaney.
McLaney, Infant	d.Jan.1903, s/o J.& M. McLaney.
Telitha	Apr.8,1905 - Feb.21,1920
Lena	Sept.13,1906 - Feb.11,1959
Clyde	Mar.29,1915 - Nov.8,1976
McClaney, Patrick	Mar.17,1815 - Jan.25,1892,Co.H,13th TN Cal.
T.C.	Aug.6,1841 - Jan.16,1928
McLaney, Clifford R.	Apr.15,1913 - Aug.1,1981
Rosa P.	Sept.30,1916 - Sept.23,1951
John H.	Aug.3,1882 - Sept.10,1969
Mary C.	Oct.15,1882 - Jan.6,1965
Haskel	1911 - 1914, s/o John McLaney.
Presnell, Garr H.	1870 - 1910
Jennie M.	1871 - 1957
Proffitt, Henry L.	1913 - 1975
Beulah M.	1917 - 1975
White, Talitha Cumi	1868 - 1946
Wilson, W.T.	1868 - 1946

Presbyterian Church Cemetery
In Old Kingsport

W.O.P. J.B.	Aug.10,1908, home made marker
Arnold, Emmanuel	no dates
Bear, John	July 18,1843 - Oct.24,1918,h/o Polly, Co.K., 4th TN Cav.
Brawley, Infant	no dates
Brown, Liza Heiskell	d.Oct.19,----, aged 9m15d., d/o Hugh & Mary Ann S. Brown.
Campton, Aura D.	Dec.16,1910 - May 22,1912
Castle, Laura	d.June 10,1835, aged 34y1m3d.
Cloud, Charlie	July 12,1873 - Sept.1,1887, s/o W.S.&F.
Emeline	Aug.25,1831 - Apr.14,1912
George W.	Oct.5,1896 - Nov.7,1918, 2nd Repl.Reg.
W.S.	Mar.12,1828 - Aug.13,1920
Clyce, M.E.	June 26,1820 - Jan.14,1896,w/o Wm.H.
Coletrane, Ethel	aged 7 years.
Darchrity, Allie	Nov.22,1852 - Jan.6,1909
Lenne	no date, aged 20 yrs.
Devault, Jennie	no dates
Margaret	no dates
Dishner, George	b. & d. Apr.29,1914, s/o W.A. & N.
Fink, John W.	1839 - 1900
Anna L.	1839 - 1912
Maggie C.	1861 - 1889
Goodman, J.G.	Oct.18,1880 - Apr.15,1915
Hedrick, Peter E.	Oct.16,1830 - Aug.20,1830
Jones, Fred	American Legion Marker.
Jones, Willard M.	Feb.24,1934, aged 19y6m23d.
King, Charles B.	Aug.3,1888 - Feb.20,1919
E.H.	Mar.31,1845 - Nov.28,1911
E.Nicholas	Feb.17,1893 - Aug.23,1897
John B.	June 16,1843 - Aug.23,1897
Mary A.	Mar.20,1850 - Feb.1,1909
Nancy E.	1856 - 1935
Mann, Mrs. W.H.	1859 - 1934
Moore, Jennie	Mar.15,1935, aged 1m19d.
Netherland, George W.	Mar.14,1800 - Apr.14,1869
John	Nov.12,1845 - Sept.25,1846,s/o G.W. & N.
Nancy	Mar.22,1806 - Nov.7,1845,w/o George W.
Patton, Ann A.	Feb.1830, Kingsport - May 18,1887,Bristol,TN
James S.	Oct.14,1825 - June 28,1903
Powell, Garston	Sept.11,1826 - June 6,1862
Roberson, Grace	May 30 - Apr.12,1815,d/o Nat & Jessie.
Rogan, Anne E. Gamble	Oct.28,1816 - Aug.24,1891,w/o Daniel.
Carl S.	Oct.7,1902 - Oct.6,1921
Daniel	d.Nov.28,1842, aged 71 yrs.
Ellen C. Morrison	June 12,1851 - Apr.14,1877
Fannie C.	May 2,1872 - Oct.9,1813
Rev.Daniel	May 1,1806 - Apr.5,1821
Lynn G.	July 20,1850 - July 12,1918
William Augustus	d.May 25,1843, aged 26y10d,s/o Wm.&Mary.
Skinner, Thomas	Jan.6,1828 - Oct.9,1903
Upchurch, Luella	d.Feb.17,1925, aged 22y11m1d.

Presbyterian Church Cemetery, cont.

Waterbury, Rev. Calvin	Apr.21,1809 - Jan.5,1874
Wills, Clara F.	July 20,1888 - Aug.31,1899
Mary E. Rogan	June 5,1859 - July 28,1920, d/o
	Daniel & Ann Rogan.

   In the same grave are buried two Confederate soldiers:
Kimbrough, Lt. Asa Hazan   1845 - 1864, Morgan's Cavalry.
   An unknown Kentucky Lieutenant, both fought and were killed in a battle
between Old Kingsport adn Rotherwood.

Church, Coates	no dates
John W.	no dates, Rebel soldier.
Lewis, James	no dates, TN soldier.
Nelms, Charlie	no dates
David	no dates, Federal soldier.
Nepelda, Anthony	no dates, TN soldier.
Parker, Joe	no dates.
Peltier, Bill	no dates.
Piles, Monroe	no dates, Presyb. Church Sexton.
Powell, William	no dates, old soldier.

Mottern Cemetery

Miller, Catharine	June 30,1828 - Jan.4,1871, w/o John
Elbert	Sept.4,1870 - Mar.4,1871, s/o John & C.
Freddie	Sept.17,1903 - Jan.15,1904, s/o W.J.&S.
John	July 23,1826 - May 10,1898
John H.	d.Sept.10,1895, aged 9 days.,s/o Wm. & Sallie.
Susan	Oct.12,1823 - Jan.7,1893
Mottern, Susan	d.June 5,1863, aged 71y5m
Henry	May 9,1831 - Apr.11,1904
J.S.	1866 - 1902
Nicolas	d.Sept.24,1868, aged 80y5m2d.
Teague, Franey	Dec.25,1827 - Mar.1,1900
Logan	Oct.27,1823 - May 27,1902

Dishner Cemetery

Dishner, Jackson A.	Sept.19,1839 - Feb.5,1918
Margaret A. Deck	Aug.19,1850 - July 27,1932
Jacob	Apr.20,1849 - Apr.23,1924
Amanda B.	Jan.31,1862 - Dec.14,1935
G.A.M.	Feb.11,1875 - Feb.15,1900
James L.	Mar.30,1871 - May 17,1943
Cora D.	Aug.28,1870 - Apr.6,1917
Herbert C.	Aug.9,1897 - Dec.23,1954
Infant	Sept.9,1906 - Sept.12,1906,d/o James & Cora
Paris S.	Nov.6,1910 - Sept.2,1955
Carolyn Lou	no dates

Zion Evangelical Luthren Church Cemetery
Cemetery completely destroyed.

Shaffer, John	d.Apr.27,1847 (Govt.marker),
	TN.Pvt. Benewit's Co.,Rev. War.

Lindamood Cemetery

Combs, Andrew Emmert	Oct.22,1876 - Dec.12,1937
Emma Jane Millhorn	Nov.26,1874 - Apr.9,1957
Nora Pauline	Oct.4,1911 - June 20,1924
Ida May	d.June 15,1902 - infant
Cross, Hoyle	Dec.1,1853 - Sept.20,1900
Sarah	Oct.8,1858 - Jan.10,1918
Hicks, John W.	1819 - Jan.15,1894
Susannah Emmert	Nov.24,---- - Nov.23,1899
Jones, Nancy Hicks	1837 - 1873, w/o Henry Jones
Lindamood, Charlie	Feb.26,1875 - Nov.5,1898
D.A.	May 17,1852 - Oct.6,1908
Margaret Jane	Sept.19,1851 - Mar.8,1903,w/o D.A.
Malone, Ben F.	1849 - 1850
John Kyle	1862 - 1864
Mary G.	1851 - 1870
Curtis B.Kester	1884 - 1892
Jacob	1821 - 1895
Elizabeth	1819 - 1908
Susan	1842 - 1915
Francis M.	Oct.2,1852 - July 23,1928
Sarah M.McCrary	Oct.17,1862 - Nov.2,1932
Millhorn, William B.	Mar.16,1845 - May 26,1918, CSA,Co.G.,60 Regt.TN Inf.
Elizabeth C.	Nov.29,1851 - Aug.30.1924
Morrell, Nellie N.	Nov.15,1917 - Jan.1,1966
Smith, Charlie O.	1873 - 19--
Nora D.	1880 - 1960
Roy H.	May 5,1905 - Oct.15,1923
Therman Andrew	1908 - 1974
White, Mary	Oct.3,1817 - Sept.17,1886, w/o John

Leonard Cemetery

Hickman, James Edward	1931 - 1936
Ira D.	1880 - 1938
John I.	1891 - 1940
Garrett	1897 - 1947
Leonard, Ernest Beecher	1917 - 1936
Edward G.	Aug.15,1852 - Feb.10,1916
Nancy E.	Oct.22,1850 - Sept.22,1922
Velmae	1935 - 1936
Eyvon	1933 - 1936
Georgia	1934 - 1936
William James	1879 - 1947
Rogers, Mrs. G.W.	1907 - 1935

Holt Family Cemetery

Holt, J.J.	July 13,1858 - June 18,1922
Hattie E. Stine	July 18,1858 - June 22,1938
Mary Isabel	Aug.24,1890 - June 2,1910, d/o J.J. & Hattie E. Holt.

Henley Cemetery

There are at least 40 to 50 graves with fieldstone markers or no markers at all.

Bowers, Charlie D.	June 3,1886 - Dec.18,1974,m.July 8,1908
Eliza J.	May 2,1895 - Aug.11,1962
Brown, Jamie	1933 - 1945
Billy	1934 - no date
Cole, Andrew L.	1894 - 1965
Fannie G.	1895 - 1982
Greenway, Infant	1953 - 1953
J. David	1867 - 1956
Ellen D.	1873 - 1946
John W.	1956 - 1959
Peggy Sue	1956 - 1959
Tolbert Clark	Sept.7,1895 - Apr.23,1948
W.G.	Jan.1,1835 - Mar.8,1914
Henley, Leonia	June 11, 1905 - July 24,1905, d/o M.T. & Bettie Henley.
Louesa	Sept.1852 - May 8, 1902, w/o H.Henley
Lilley, Caleb V.	1833 - 1906
Amanda E.	1853 - 1922
Chassie B.	Nov.9,1883 - Oct.4,1963
Clarence J.	Nov.14,1914 - Aug.28,1971
Jimmy D.	Nov.8,1879 - Feb.5,1880
John W.	July 18,1919 - June 7,1971
John W.	1889 - 1928
Nora G.	1897 - 19--
Lilley, Nannie P.	b. & d.Aug.21,1886
Roberty Lynn	June 19,1923 - Jun 27,1929
Sword, Robert Lee	Oct.2,1905 - Aug.31,1906, s/o H.M.Sword

Smith Cemetery

Many graves unmarked, marked with fieldstone or illegible. Cemetery in very bad shape.

Cross, John F.	1872 - 1910
Adeline	1837 - 1890
Sarah C.	1852 - 1892, d/o S.L.Cross
Samuel L.	1849 - 1921
Clint C.	1894 - 1897
Infant	d.1900, d/o S.L. & S.C. Cross.
Laura J.	1871 - 1898, w/o S.L.Cross.
Smith, John U.M.	Dec.22,1813 - Aug.6,1878
Malinda Matthews	Oct.23,1813 - July 8,1878
John	Oct.18,1786 - Mar.3,1829
Catharine Umphres	Mar.17,1787 - July 3,1881

HONORING:

Henry Smith and wife Mary, the first persons buried here, about 1820. Their son John and his wife CatharineUmphes have marker herein, and 3 of their daughters and 3 of their sons are buried here. Viz Polly, w/o James Webb, Betie, w/o Simon Deck, and Nancy, w/o John Masengill, and Mother of Dr.John David Masengill; George,David Hart; and John Umphes Smith. Mary Powell, w/o David Hart Smith and Simon Deck, Vir of Bettie, and James Webb, Vir of Polly, are buried here.

Droke Cemetery
Many graves unmarked, marked with fieldstones or illegible.

Cross, Sue	1877 - 1968
Jacob C.	Apr.9,1868 - Nov.20,1944
Sarah Lula Droke	Oct.21,1870 - Mar.15,1915
Lena	1895 - 1915
N.A.	Oct.11,1862 - June 1, 1936
Blanc Jeter	June 12,1868 - June 20,1964
Enoch	1892 - 1972
Droke, David A.	Mar.28,1843 - May 16,1923
Lydia E. Webb	June 2, 1864 - Feb.13,1890
Susan E.	Dec.21,1889 - June 2,1890
Charley M.	Sept.15,1886 - June 26,1888
James	Mar.20,1810 - Dec.7,1891
Elizabeth M.	d.Nov.11,1874, aged 65y7m23d,w/o James
Catharine	d.Sept.-,1843, aged 6y11m10d
Francis	1881 - 1962
Mary Belle	Nov.6,1883 - May 21,1908
William C.	Apr.1,1840 - Dec.20,1926, m.Mar.21,1861
Agnes J. Webb	June 12,1844 - Jan.29,1926
Hicks, Hester	1895 - 1898
Henry	1858 - 1926
Eliza D.	1862 - 1916
Jeter, H.Cliford	1910 - 1912
Cora Jane	Sept.22,1874 - Aug.30,1901, w/o George
Ledford, Bell C.	1889 - 1961
Lindamood, Samuel D.	Mar.8,1862 - May 17,1889
Elizabeth A.	Mar.12,1862 - Dec.20,1926
Droke	Mar.8,186? - May 17,1889
John	June 17, 1813 - Jan.11,1894
S.A.	Oct.22,1806 - May 17,1887
G.W.	Mar.1,1837 - July 6,1908
Malone, Family of George & Sarah	
D.E.	Sept.23,1854 - Apr.19,1903
Mary M.	Sept.4,1850 - Nov.22,1916,w/o David E.
Morrell, R.W.	Aug.27,1843 - Dec.6,1915,Co.D,63 Reg.TN.Inf.
Albert Sidney	Nov.29,1886 - Sept.3,1923
Letha Tulin	Oct.6,1891 - June 26,1965
Smith, John	Jan.13,1766 - Dec.25,1830 (?), b.Shenandoah Co.,VA.
Elizabeth	June 7,1770 - 1830, w/o John Smith
Webb, Sarah	Dec.28,1804 - Dec.19,1892
Sarah M.	Sept.13,1877 - June 16,1880, d/o B.F.&S.

Cloud Family Cemetery

Cloud, George	d.July 20,1871, aged 73y2m8d
Mary A.	Apr.24,1807 - Mar.23,1889

Stophel Cemetery

Blevins, Elizabeth	1891 - 1896
Blanche & Bertie	1896, infant twins
Perry	1892 - 1895
W.R.	1854 - 1937
E.C.	1856 - 1896
Minerra Taylor	1854 - 1956
Rebeckah J.	July 4,1829 - Jan.3,1919
Huffman H.	Apr.13,1837 - Apr.3,1903
Ugen Abit	Nov.1,1908 - Dec.1,1908
L.E.B.	no dates
Booher, Rutledge M.	Dec.23,1850 - Jan.20,1927
Mary A.	Mar.11,1850 - Oct.7,1928
Buckles, Barbra Stophel	May 3, 1838 - Mar.20,1916
Booher, Claude Lyn	1945 - 1945
Bowery, David Scott	b.&d. July 5,1962
Dodson, Ruby G.	1935 - 1935
Ferriter, James	Mar.10,1823 - Jan.1,1916
Amanda M.	Oct.18,1846 - Aug.25,1869, w/o James
Henson, Odell B.	1940 - 1961, w/o James H. Henson
Henson, Thomas J.	1938 - 1938
Miller, Louisa J.	1858 - 1940
Osborn, Isaac G.	June 1, 1848 - June 18,1912
Eliza J.	Dec.12,1862 - Feb.12,1940
Osborne, Thomas Fred	Nov.28,1920 - July 27,1954
Eula Fay	Mar.14,1914 - Aug.19,1914
Charles J.	b.Dec.1882
Lillie B.	May 10,1880 - Dec.27,1926
Anna Lee	July 8, 1922 - Aug.29,1923, d/o C.J&L.B.
Presnell, James C.	1868 - 1951
Victoria A.	1874 - 1959
Joseph	1861 - 1956
R.L.R.	d.Nov.29,1936
Richardson, Isaac	1890 - 1956
John M.	no dates
Stophel, Nora M.E.	Nov.12,1889 - Sept.7,1899,d/o E.L. & M.A.
William W.	Oct.4,1863 - Dec.7,1900, s/o Owen Stophel
Jacob R.B.	Nov.8,1867 - Apr.2,1897, s/o Owen Stophel
Jonathan M.	Apr.10,1859 - Dec.10,1884, s/o Owen
James	Mar.31,1823 - Nov.4,1860
Barbara M.	May 22, 1825 - Mar.7,1909, w/o Jacob
Elizabeth N.	July 23, 1855 - Aug.25,1857, d/o Jacob
Owen	Oct.25,1825 - no date
Emmaline	Apr.4,1832 - Oct.8,1896
Taylor, Catherine	aged 90 years

Abraham Deck Cemetery

Deck, Abraham	1800 - 1862
E. Minerva	1846 - 1863

Seneker-Steele Cemetery

Dailey, Charles W.	Dec.28,1862 - Aug.13,1886
Margaret J. Seneker	Apr.27,1830 - Feb.3,1905, w/o C.W.
Dishner, Rhoda	d.July 18,1898, aged about 82 yrs.
Fleenor, Martha E.	no dates
Margaret A.	Feb.3,1903 - Mar.22,1903
Goff/Gott, Elijah	Jan.13,1811 - Sept.10,1836
Goff/Gott, Christina	Aug.8,1811 - Aug.19,1881
King, Mickey D.	1951 - 1952 (fhm)
T.C.M .	1844 - 1933
Mrs. Cordia	no dates
Lillian	no dates
Lucy	no dates
Leonard, Vicky Ellen	Jan.18,1955, aged 5m 22d.
Nelson, ---	d.Dec.20,1924, d/o W.M.& Lizzie
Spahr, M.Ellen Spahr Fleenor	Mar.23,1866 - Mar.10,1946,1st hus. Isaac; 2nd hus. Fleenor.
Isaac J.	July 20,1836 - Feb.7,1898
Seneker, Margaret	Mar.15,1799 - July 13,1875, w/o Andrew
Andrew	Mar.17,1796 - July 4,1876
Elias G.	Apr.16,1761 - Aug.19,1834
Catherine	July 14,1771 - June 28,1839
William	June 19,1806 - Aug.15,1879
A.D., M.D.	July 1,1838 - Feb.6,1874
Spahr, Isaac J.	July 20,1836 - Feb.7,1898
P.J.S.	no dates
P.L.S.	no dates
Steele, Mary C.	Feb.17,1852 - Mar.20,1932
Dorothy E.	Mar.25,1872 - Feb.17,1947
Jacob F.	May 21,1875 - Mar.11,1931
William J.	July 9,1855 - Oct.29,1916
H.F.	July 2,1857 - Mar.2,1924
Stone, Archimedes	1891 - 1960
Daisey H.	1894 - no dates
J.T.	Dec.18,1856 - Nov.2,1927
Davie A. Dailey	Mar.31,1860 - Apr.20,1917, w/o J.T.Stone.
James	1878 - 1943 (fhm)
Charles D.	1890 - 1959 (fhm)

St.John Cemetery

St.John, C.F.	d. Feb.24,1895, aged 25 days
Infant	d. Dec.19,1924, s/o J.R.& O.R. St.John.
Margaret H.	May 10,1918 - Jan.20,1919, d/o J.R.& O.R.
Porter Lee	1897 - 1919, drowned while in Navy, WW 1.
Preston W.	Mar.8,1899 - July 16,1899, s/o W.B.& H.E.
W.B.	July 2,1852 - Dec.9,1907
Hattie Williams	Aug.24,1859 - June 15,1903

Peregoy — Profit Cemetery

Glover, Francis M.	Oct.1852 - Apr.11,1903
Frank M.	Mar.30,1885 - Nov.11,1903
Hirl W.	Dec.26,1913 - Apr. 27,1924
Luther B.	1886 - 1937
Ella P.	1888 - 1968
Milton	May 6,1889 - Sept.28,1936
Mae	June 24,1898 - no date
Robert L.	July 10,1936 - Nov.3,1936
Peregoy, Bernard M.	1876 - 1962
Callie G.	1870 - 1937
D.N.M.	Mar.20,1826 - July 5,1894
Mary	Mar.3,1906 - Nov.1,1907, d/o B.M.& C.
Sarah C.	Dec.14,1851 - Sept.30,1914
Proffitt, Andrew J.	June 4,1855 - Jan.6,1937
Austin L.	1883 - 1959
Harry P.	July 30,1916 - Mar.16,1919, s/o W.H.& M.B.
Isabelle G.	1858 - 1935
Mary B.	June 16,1882 - Mar.5,1972
Nannie E.	1886 - 1949
Robert W.	May 21,1905 - Mar.6,1960
Taylor W.H.	Nov.26,1878 - Jan.6,1937
Willard S.	1893 - 19--
Lula C.	1895 - 1969
Smalling, Soloman	June 7,1816 - Feb.23,1903

Delaney Cemetery

Very old cemetery, 50 or 60 illegible stones and field markers.

Cowen, Andrew	Feb.5,17-- - May 29,1876
Robert	June 18,1754 - Feb.16,1840, PA Pvt. 1BN., Lancaster Co., Militia, Revoluntionary War.
Delaney, J.S.	Aug.22,1848 - Oct.23,1849
J.H.	Feb.19,1851 - Mar.5,1883
J.P.T.	June 28,1839 - Sept.24,1861, 3 s/o J.R.& M.
General J.R.	June 30,1799 - Oct.27,1879
Margaret	Nov.30,1809 - Aug.10,1863
Offield, --	---20,1788 - --- --,1850
Nancy	May 30,1810 - Feb.20,1860 (?)
William D.	Oct.2,1811 - OCt.22,1870, Mexican War Vet.
Peters, Malinda	188- - ----
Rosenbalm, M.E.	Feb.7,1857 - Aug.17,1901

Atkinson Cemetery

Atkinson, William B.	1870 - 1943
Nita C.	1871 - 1946
Lilley, J. Melvin	Aug.23,1879 - Dec.5,1945
Rebecca H.	Aug.29,1874 - Jan.13,1945
Charles F.	1900 - 1968
Jewell A.	1913 - no date
Tester, Lefler L.	1899 - 1950

Cross Cemetery

Cross, Jacob H.	Apr.18,1837 - Mar.2,1897
Hannah	Mar.10,1836 - Aug.19,1902
W.D.	Jan.15,1864 - Jan.16,1908
Alma Lee	Jan.6,1911 - Feb.1,1911
Reece B.	Nov.9,1865 - May 23, 1912
Retta B.	June 6, 1874 - Dec.18,1954
Jessee A.	1904 - 1969
Lucille F.	1922 - no date
Ida H.	1868 - 1949
Martha	1834 - 1918, w/o W.A.Cross
Wm. A.	Jan.31,1833 - Oct.27,1910
Eliza	Mar.3,1864 - July 5, 1864, d/o W.A. & M.
Jesse M.	July 27,1857 - Aug.31,1862, s/o W.A. & M.
Lola V.	Jan.20,1900 - Aug.21,1975
Arleigh C.	1899 - 1973
Era G.	1897 - no date
Braxton B.	June 6, 1871 - Mar.24,1963
Sally T.	Aug.4,1878 - June 15,1971
Davault, Henry	1807 - 1876
Matilda	1812 - 1892
Catharine	Jan.3,1838 - May 4, 1871
William	June 17,1844 - Feb.24,1862, s/o H. & M.
Elizabeth	May 1, 1851 - July 6, 1856, d/o H.& M.
Mary M.	Nov.11,1841 - Jan.16,1843, d/o H. & M.
Hancher, Joseph	July 12, 1853 - May 4, 1907
Virginia D.	d. Jan.2,1903
Joseph D.	Dec.15,1906 - Mar.4,1962
Tennie M.	Mar.18,1862 - Jan.7,1949
James K.	June 24,1900 - Dec.20,1908
Rufus B.	Mar.18,1903 - Nov.30,1905
Wiley H.	June 16,1905 - Dec.17,1908
Addie G.	Mar.18,1896 - July 28, 1957
William B.	Aug.4,1889 - Mar.5,1923
Edward D.	d.Oct.8,1907
Hicks, Royston	May 25,1842 - Nov.25,1903
Eliza Catherine	Dec.29,1846 - Sept.17,1941
Jones, Hubert	July 22,1887 - Oct.24,1973
May H.	July 29,1898 - no date
Lane, William A.	Aug.10,1896 - Apr.4,1980
Barbara J.	Dec.29,1905 - no date
Morris, Jennings B.	1914 - 1981
Celine R.	1919 - 1979
Oliver, Mary J.	1881 - 1898
Martha	1842 - 1916
J.W.	Mar.3,1833 - Mar.4, 1895
L.L.	Dec.27,1868 - Dec.11,1886
Russum, Kate Cross	Feb.12,1902 - Aug.4,1970
Webb, Eliza Blanche	Feb.26,1884 - July 4,1885

Vanover Cemetery

Baker, Samuel	June 23-24,1919
David	June 23-24,1919
Carrier, Feebia I.	Mar.10,1887 - Dec.1,1943,w/o Percy
John C.	1914 - 1972
Percy	1890 - 1964
R.B.	1916 - 1920,s/o P.P. & F.I.Carrier.
Caudill, Baxter	Feb.19,1909 - Apr.6,1957
Ben	1877 - 1939
Jacqueline	1926 - 1929
Lee Roy	1930 - 1930
Sally	1919 - 1919
Sarah	1883 - 1919
Spencer	Aug.21,1906 - Jan.18,1981
Reta Hodges	Feb.25,1912 - no dates
Cole, Harriet	no dates
Johnny	Jan.21,1917 - Jan.3,1918,s/o D. & Nora
Marshel	no dates
Combs, Roy	1900 - ----, m.Jan.24,1920.
Nancy	1894 - 1965
Cox, Aaron A.	1852 - 1926
Cordella Buchanan	Feb.10,1861 - June 22,1941
David	1884 - 1900
Edward D.	Sept.18,1892 - June 3, 1967
Frankie	1877 - 1910
Joe M.	July 31,1884 - July 3,1954
Bertha E.	July 27,1912 - no date
Mack	1880 - 1955
Belle	1883 - 1959
Mary L.	July 24,1902 - May 20,1973
Mary M. Rose	1884 - 1930, w/o E.D.Cox
Nadgie	1902 - 1922
William S.	1877 - 1948
Crout, Nora B.	1910 - 1982
Daugherty, Homer	1909 - 1973
Dean, Infant	1900
Graybeal, Hughie	Feb.19,1909 - July 23,1938
Lennie Glover	Apr.8,1908 - July 14,1934,w/o J.E.
Lula E.	Oct.12,1903 - no dates
Luther K.	Sept.12,1902 - no dates
Mary A.	1869 - 1962
Walter A.	May 6,1907 - Jan.13,1982
N.Edell	Aug.12,1912 - no dates
W.A.	Apr.18,1851 - Apr.22,1938
Hilliard, Carl W.	Apr.1,1961 - Sept.1,1979
Hopkins, Argil R.	1926 - 1963
Randolph	1949 - 1949
Jenkins, Roy	Feb.15,1900 - Aug.1,1984
Ollie	Dec.15,1893 - no dates
King, Lydia H.	Oct.20,1920 - no dates

Vanover Cemetery, cont.

Linderfelt, Ellie		Apr.20,1903 - Oct.29,1906, d/o E.Z. & Sarah Lingerfelt.
	Fonze	Oct.20,1889 - Jan.16,1967
	Jess	Feb.26,1883 - Sept.--,1958
	Lorina	June 5,1919 - Aug.17,1919, d/o E.Z. & S.
	Zeke	Aug.3,1877 - Aug.15,1932
	Sarah	Dec.31,1881 - Nov.24,1958
McKinney, William		Jan.6,1832 - May 23,1904,Co.C.,13th TN Cav.
Miller, Mary Cox		1886 - 1934
Pless, George		b. & d. 1930
	Mary	1862 - 1924
	Millard	1882 - 1959
	Emma	1883 - 1974
	Leona	1907 - 1930
Potter, Clara C.		Mar.23,1830 - Feb.14,1907
Ryan, C.F.		Nov.23,1919 - May 16,1924
Sams, Delie		d.June 17,1890, aged 18 yrs.
	Etta	d.Dec.11,1890, aged 17 yrs.
	Margaret	July 1,1836 - Jan.25,1913
	Washington	aged about 62 yrs., no dates
Stufflestreet, Fannie		May 7,1905 - no dates
	John W.	Apr.27,1889 - Nov.12,1972
Waters, Suda		no dates

Denton Cemetery

Barr, Jacob A.		Sept.19,1832 - Apr.5,1891
	Alma H.	1886 - 1919, w/o N.E.Barr
Denton, Infant		Aug.13-22,1894, i/o B.G. & L.V. Denton.
	B.C.	Sept.21,1864 - May 23,1924
	Cornelia	Feb.25,1842 - Feb.28,1916, w/o J.T.E.
	Ellie	June 1847 - June 1921
Haga, Ellen		1887 - 19--
	Jack	1880 - 1942, concrete marker, H.Jack Haga,1877 - 1942.
	Hobert	May 12, 1914 - June 19,1916, s/o J.H. & E.V.
Hobbs, Eliza J.		July 3,1848 - Mar.11,1916, w/o J.A.Hobbs
	John A.	Dec.28,1848 - Nov.2,1920
Perkey, Fannie		d.Mar.1886, d/o A.M.Perkey
	Ernest	July 11, 1877 - July 18,1878, s/o A.M.
	Alice B.	June 4,1874 - July 6,1878, d/o A.M. & F.M.
Peterman, America J.		June 16,1834 - Jan.15,1877, w/o W.P.
	W.M.	June 25,1870 - May 10,1939
	Arthur	Dec.23,1874 - Dec.30,1916
	W.B.	Apr.5,1824 - Mar.6,1907
	George	Dec.25,1871 - Apr.16,1941

Boy Cemetery

Recently fenced in cemetery, about 100 gravestones were either illegible or stone field markers. There were two Scottish cairns in this cemetery, both were in very poor condition.

Boy, D.W.	1867 - 1906
Infant	Aug.2,1891, inf/o J.H. & V.T. Boy
K.L.	1864 - 1917
Louissnna Mauk	Jan.26,1826 - Sept.25,1886,w/o J.M. Boy
James M.	Apr.7,1835 - Mar.2,1906
Sarah Jane	Dec.13,1838 - June 28,1899, w/o J.M.Boy.
Eva Grace	1901 - 1914
Mattie Lee	Sept.3,1893 - Aug.3,1894, d/o R.A. & A.C.
Mary Blanche	Sept.3,1893 - May 23,1894,d/o R.A. & A.C.
F.M.	Dec.25,1825 - Jan.4,1911
Mary Ann	Mar.5,1834 - Mar.6,1891,w/o F.M. Boy
Mary E. Akard	Dec.10,1845 - Sept.25,1899, w/o P.J.Boy
Rev.John A.M.	Apr.22,1871 - Aug.19,1899
Phillip J.	Nov.30,1843 - Oct.16,1932
Francis M.	Dec.27,1882 - Oct.11,1899
Mary E.	d.Sept.2,1873
Jacob	Apr.17,1752 - May 20,1833, Rev. War, Pvt. Campbell VA. Regt.
Alfred	d. Apr.12,1850, aged 12 yrs.
Ruth	1808 - 1882
Jacob	1808 - 1892
Delia J.	1885 - 1919
James E.C.	1880 - 1943
M.E.	Nov.30,1903 - Feb.4,1904
Ellen M.	Feb.20,1838 - Dec.27,1913, w/o J.M.Boy
John W.	June 4,1847 - Feb.18,1936
Berry, Susannah	Feb.22,1822 - Nov.30,1850
Carico, Joseph	b. about 1864 - June 22,1909
Combs, Dora B.	Oct.2,1869 - Mar.13,1871, d/o J. & R.
Carrier, Vollie R.	Feb.23,1895 - Dec.1,1901, s/o D.B.
Katherine Denton	d.Aug.18,1919, aged 74 yrs,w/o Elbert
Elbert	d.Jan.19,1924, aged 78 yrs.
C.S.A.	1863 - 1865
Eads, William F.	Aug.18,1862 - July 15,1862, s/o D.C. & S.
R.E.	Feb.10,1859 - Apr.21,1863
Fleenor, Elizabeth S.	May 2,1839 - Apr.25,1905
Foster, Elizabeth	Apr.24,1862 - Oct.8,1890
Giesler, Jacob	Dec.20,1789 - Aug.29, 1865
Nancy	May 4,1816 - June 6, 1863
Martha	May 24,1860 - Apr.24,1863
Houston, Robert Boy	d.Aug.12,1901, aged 12y2m1d, s/o J.N. & F.A.
Fannie A. Boy	Feb.19,1861 - Mar.28,1890, w/o J.W.
Hicks, Reuben	July 19,1800 - Aug.2,1874
Mary	d.Apr.22,1879, Aged 73y2m9d.
Mary J.	Aug.28,1838 - Sept.24,1901,w/o H.J.Hicks
Rev.William	d.May 20, 1882, aged 71 yrs., 48 yrs. a traveling preacher,M.E.Church South.
Jacob	Apr.5,1842 - Jan.18,1867
J.E.	1848 - 1914

Boy Cememtery, cont.

Humphreys, G.W.,Sr.	May 23,1850 - Jan.30,1902
Minerva	May 8,1844 - Oct.28,1902, w/o G.W.
John M.	d.Aug.30,1874, s/o G.W. & Minerva A.
Harkleroad, Bonnie Alice	June 7,1892 - Apr.10,1894, d/o J.A.&Mary
William H.	d.Oct.12,1865, aged 43y10m28d.
Sarah H.	Dec.16,1822 - Dec.28,1887, w/o W.H.
Littleford, J.H.	Sept.26,1839 - Oct.30,1910
Anna B. Fleenor	Dec.11,1836 - Jan.16,1905, w/o J.H.
Morrell, Mary E.	July 5,1837 - Dec.1,1874
Daniel	Feb.5,1828 - June 24,1898
William R.	Sept.1,1860 - Dec.12,1884
Martha J.	Jan.17,1849 - Jan.31,1849, d/o C. & L.
Daniel L.	May 31,1862 - Oct.18,1862,s/o C.&L.
Sallie A.	Nov.7,1861 - Dec.9,1889, w/o E.J.
Hattie E.	Aug.24,1893 - Mar.16,1907, d/o E.J.& Jinnie
Hattie E.	May 2,1857 - Nov.28,1878,aged 21y6m21d.
James A.	Apr.13,1853 - June 30,1877, aged 24y2m17d.
Sarah E.	OCt.30,1827 - July 6,1896, w/o Wm.
W.M.	Mar.31,1818 - Feb.2,1900, aged 81y10m1d
Millard, Delilah E.	Dec.25,1842 - Mar.5,1895, w/o E.C.
Edward F.	Mar.28,1897 - July 22,1909
Minnick, Walden B.	Aug.8,189J - Dec.21,1909,s/o W.H.&M.Y.
Minnie Faris	1869 - 1918, w/o William H.
Miller, Daniel	Feb.15,1798 - July 27,1863
Mary	July 5,1801 - Nov.17,1874
Royston, Sie	d.Feb.18,1918, aged 41 years
George W.	d.Jan.18,1928, aged 67 years
Rebecca Glover	d.May 12,1926, aged 65 years
Lilburn	Sept.15,1884 - June 11,1915, s/o G.W. & R.
Riley, William B.	1885 - 1914, s/o W.W.Riley
Riley, Elizzie	Aug.23,1853 - Dec.11,1895, w/o James H.
Martha Crawford	Aug.4,1881 - Nov.18,1884, d/o J.M.&E.J.
Alice R.	DEc.6,1897 - Dec.31,1898,d/o W.W. & R.E.
Rebecca E.	July 28,1861 - Sept.31,1904, w/o W.W.
Rader, Nancy A.	Feb.1,1859 - May 11,1891, d/o J.&S.
Daniel	May 28,1868 - Sept.14,1883, s/o J.& S.
Robert	Oct.24,1874 - Sept.14,1883, s/o J.& S.
Charles	Dec.29,1881 - Sept.20,1883, s/o J.& S.
Susan	Mar.31,1832 - Apr.6,1908, w/o Joseph
Joseph	Apr.10,1831 - July 21,1918
Swiney, Webb	July 7,1895 - May 19,1952,Sgt.U.S.Army,WWII
Sweeney, Webb	J.B. & Eliza Sweeney
William	Our sons, no dtes.
Smith, Irena W.	d.Nov.3,1850,aged 31 yrs.,w/o Alex H.
Sarah	Aug.24,1825 - July 9,1845
Elizabeth	Sept.7,1826, aged 78y1m6d.
Major William	Jan.31,1789 - Nov.4,1858
Charles	Nov.22,1841 - June 11,1898
Wassom, Mary P.Buckles	Apr.12,1848 - Nov.11,1924,w/o W.J.
W.J.	Dec.25,1846 - Apr.13,1896
M.Carrie	May 4,1802 - Dec.3,1892, d/o W.J.&M.P.
James L.	Sept.1,1842 - Mar.3,1882, aged 39y6m8d.

Boy Cemetery, cont.

Wassom, Elizabeth Grant	Nov.1,1808 - Feb.19,1890, w/o John
Isaac G.	Feb.5,1839 - May 10,1868
J.M.	Dec.27,1825 - Mar.6,1903
Worley, Margaret H. Boy	Mar.21,1821 - Apr.1,1894, w/o James B.

Black Cemetery

Beidleman, Arthur E.	Apr.2,1898 - Nov.14,1980
Pearl D.	May 10,1902 - no date
Charlie F.	1892 - 1968
Beatrice D.	1897 - 19--
Marion L.	1881 - 1961
Jeanette H.	1894 - 1961
John A.	1906 - 1967
William Garfield	Feb.2,1886 - Jan.3,1963
Jennie Florence	June 16,1896 - Nov.28,1976
William	d.Apr.11,1944
Beidlemans, Steven	1857 - 1929
Rosa D.	1866 - 1940
Belton, Flora Helen Patton	Oct.31,1914 - Apr.27,1961
Blevins, Jerelyn	d.Nov.20,1944
James	1880 - 1934
Bessie	1883 - 1974
Brewer, Luther W.	May 15,1897 - Dec.1,1944
Coffey, Lee Roy Jr.	b. & d. July 4,1926, s/o L.R.&C.F.
Dixon, Charles H.	Dec.14,1911 - Nov.20,1966
Samuel	1915 - 1979
Fugate, Fred L.	1904 - 1968
Howard, Armond N.	d.Dec.24,1947
Hughes, Charlie	no dates
Alice	no dates
Patton, James D.,Sr.	1892 - 1929
Washingston, Frank	Aug.10,1885 - Aug.11,1927
Wisdom, Samuel King	Spet.20,1873 - Jan.29,1902
Charley	May 25,1861 - Sept.12,1910

Webb-Lady Cemetery
Probably 50 or more graves unmarked, marked with fieldstones or stones
that are illegable.

Booker, Billie B.	Nov.13,1949 - Apr.16,1985
Boone, Connie S.	Nov.2,1932 - Apr.4,1979
Bouton, Edward King	Dec.6,1897 - Nov.3,1969
Winnie	1893 - 1963
Joseph Lee	1893 - 1958
John B.	Mar.29,1855 - Mar.24,1914
Lucy Ann	July 18,1863 - Mar.23,1935
Belle	1890 - 1908
Brown, Irene McCrary	1908 - 1943, w/o H.C.Brown
Carrier, Belle Hicks	1881 - 1964
Carty, Edward B.	1914 - 1968
Coffey, Joseph R.	Oct.29,1937 - Nov.7,1937
Collins, Fannie Webb	Feb.8,1880 - Dec.23,1937
Crusenberry, Rev. Worley Lee,Jr.	1930 - no date
Doris Jean	1930 - 1978
Emmert, John G.	Apr.1,1882 - Nov.15,1893
Feathers, Infant	Aug.22,1913 - Aug.24,1913, s/o Sam & Faye
Fannie	July 8, 1890 - Sept.19,1914
Ruby J.	July 22,1913 - May 8,1914
Fleenor, Wm. Henry	1920 - 1921, s/o Ray & Elsie Fleenor
Nora Bess	Oct.25,1927 - May 20,1930, d/o W.R.&Elsie.
Fleming, Infant	June 15,1901 - July 25,1901,inf/o G.F. & Emma Fleming.
Moncy	Feb.3,1876 - Sept.26,1906
Hamilton, Joshua	Feb.19,1797 - Aug.9,1887
Sallie	Nov.1,1807 - June 20,1873, w/o Joshua
Mary J.	1839 - 1922
Hicks, John W.	July 27,1851 - Feb.3,1922
Martha Cross	Apr.20,1855 - July 19,1915
Pearl	Jan.8,1896 - Oct.22,1898,d/o A.M. & R.S.
James M.	1888 - 1934
Okie Eads	1896 - 1924
George J.	Nov.2,1866 - June 9,1936, m.May 2,1892
Laura J. Jones	May 9,1865 - June 23,1956
Hyatt, Harry D.	Jan.28,1946 - no date
Betty Irene	Sept.27,1949 - Apr.29,1981
Jones, Lavinia M.	Aug.10,1893 - Spet.30,1898, d/o E.F.&Joana.
Joana	1868 - 1916, w/o E.F.Jones
Charles H.	Mar.15,1895 - Oct.1,1898, s/o E.F.&Joana
Henry	1831 - 1917
Cordelia E. Millard	1837 - 1904
R.B.	Sept.30,1860 - Sept.20,1915
Maude Webb	1879 - 1926
McCrary, Pearl	1911 - 1929
Anna Felty	1890 - 1913
Margaret	1882 - 1939
Charlie R.	Jan.3,1884 - Apr.29,1951
Margaret J.	Feb.24,1838 - Mar.19,1912,w/o J.M.
Malone, Nellie P.	Nov.16,1902 - Feb.26,1979
Earnest	Sept.19,1896 - July 24,1975

Malone, Maude P.	1892 - 1980
Barry Andrew	1955 - 1972
Fred	July 3,1903 - May 17,1967
Melvina W.	Jan.5,1870 - Jan.19,1965
Frank C.	Apr.7,1898 - Aug.28,1971, m.Nov.18,1923,
Viola C.	June 1,1905 - no date
Emmalou	Sept.28,1946 - Sept.29,1946
Miller, Cindy Lorine	b. & d. Mar.23,1967
Thomas	1826 - 1913
Barbara	1842 - 1908
David M.	1973 - 1973
Scotty Lee	d.June 22,1984, s/o Megan & Dennis Miller
Morgan, R.L.	1845 - 19--
Martha	1849 - 1921
Myrtle E.	Dec.1,1886 - July 3,1912, d/o R.L.&M.
Morrell, Caleb R.	Aug.4,1835 - Jan.23,1903
Margaret E.	Mar.21,1843 - Aug.6,1923,w/o Caleb R.
E.A.	1838 - 1900
Sarah A. Hamilton	1845 - 1904
Jerome T.	1872 - 1922
Lola M.	1874 - 1929
Moser, James E.	1913 - 1937
Neal, Joe A.	1918 - 1983
Margaret	1925 - 1970
Odell, Father	no dates
Mother	no dates
Nora	no dates
5 stones with ODELL	
Painter, Infant	s/o Mr & Mrs Tim Painter
Taylor, Robert A.	1866 - 1938
Taylor, Millard L.	1907 - 1970
Beulah K.	1913 - 1969
Trail, Michael Kevin	June 18,1977 - June 19,1977
Weaver, Dennis Eugene	1956 - 1972
Donald Wayne	Oct.2,1919 - Nov.26,1984
Gladys Pearl	Oct.11,1920 - no date
Webb, R.C.	1851 - 1904
Susan C.	1857 - 1915
Lizzie	Nov.2,1845 - Dec.2,1914
George W.	July 13,1843 - Oct.19,1870
Samuel	Jan.23,1812 - Oct.30,1892
Elizabeth	Oct.16,1817 - Feb.2,1890
Hugh	Dec.16,1847 - Dec.23,1914
Mary A.	Feb.11,1857 - no date
Lucy T.	May 11,1877 - Aug.14,1893
David	aged 89 years
Paralee Jones	1858 - 1936
Mike	Aug.7,1893 - Feb.6,1914
Wilburn, Samuel J.	1856 - 1939
Wolf(e), Henry F.	Jan.29,1855 - Mar.29,1835
Wolf, David	no dates
Worley, Danny Lynn	1955 -1972

Newland Family Cemetery

Barker, Allison B.	1877 - 1936
Branstetter, Barbara	1785 - 1816
Dooley, William A.	Aug.16,1830 - July 11,1893
Martha A. Newland	Sept.13,1836 - Mar.3,1911
McCrary, Mary A.	Nov.18,1837 - Nov.12,1922,w/o Dr.B.D.
Dr.Benjamin D.	Jan.18,1834 - Aug.26,1890
Newland, Joseph Mitchell	Mar.26,1847 - Jan.21,1925
Judith Lessley	July 26,1842 - Feb.27,1923
Isaac Anderson	May 13,1842 - Mar.29,1922
1st wife,Mattie Lewis	Jan.25,1847 - Oct.14,1889
2nd wife,Nannie Vance	Jan.9,1853 - Jan.30,1939
Newland, Margaret Pecktal	Nov.22,1807 - Mar.9,1873,w/o Wm.
Kate L.	Sept.9,1842 - June 2,1867, w/o W.D.McGee.
William	Jan.2,1808 - Dec.11,1894
Joseph S.	1776 - 1839
Jane Anderson	1780 - 1839
Helen Brown	Mar.1,1863 - June 30,1928
Samuel Anderson	June 11,1852 - Aug.6,1939
Joseph Jr.	Nov.13,1809 - Oct.28,1867
Rebecca H.	June 2,1818 - July 23,1893,w/o Joseph
S.Allie	Feb.28,1858 - May 24,1859
Allie	May 17,1877 - Dec.10,1955
Joseph M.,Jr.	July 12,1883 - Nov.26,1946
Martha Jane	Apr.20,1881 - June 22,1926
Pence, Martha Ellen	Jan.12,1886 - June 13,1956
Elkanah D.	May 13,1836 - Feb.14,1919
Fannie Newland	Dec.3,1849 - Oct.27,1922
Shaver, William D.	Aug.19,1827 - Feb.1,1901
Taylor, Rev. Robert Hays	Oct.31,1859 - Apr.27,1949
Rebecca Newland	Mar.23,1876 - June 10,1954

Phipps-Netherland Cemetery

Cosler, Frances Phipps	Dec.15,1889 - Oct.13,1956
Mahady, Alice Ann	d.June12,1932 - infant
Netherland, Robert G.	Feb.17,1902 - Mar.1,1926
J.Phipps	Oct.10,1852 - Dec.1,1853
W.V.	July 22,1864 - May 18,1916
Phipps, Infant	1886
K.L.	1879 - 1901
Mary	1884 - 1886
J.Gaines	1881 - 1930
Ann P. Bachman	Mar.9,1827 - Nov.17,1901,w/o Joshua
Joshua	Feb.24,1801 - July 18,1861
J.M.	1853 - 1929
Mary McKinney	1854 - 1920
Charles McKinney	Oct.2,1877 - Apr.19,1959

Jacob Deck Family Cemetery

Deck, Jacob	Mar.28,1770/9 - May --. 18-9
Catherine	d.June 24,1826, aged 23y7m28d
Elizabeth	d.A--,21,1840, aged 38y10m7d

Ordway Cemetery

Ball, George D.	1888 - 1956
Pearlie A.	1889 - 1976
Charles H.	Sept.20,1916 - Sept.8,1919,s/o George
Grace May	Jan.17,1912 - Sept.8,1914, s/o G.&. P.
Lillie Kate	no date, d/o G.&.P. Ball
Mary (Peggy)	1930 - 1955
Bays, Clarence H.	June 29,1908 - Aug.24,1910, s/o C.H. & Alice
Charles H.	July 24,1868 - July 30,1912
Alice E. Spickard	Oct.4,1865 - Dec.23,1923, w/o Charles H.
Beard, Ruth Hicks	Oct.8,1842 - Dec.10,1913
Bell, Foye	1924 - 1924, s/o J.M. & Otye Bell.
Bishop, Jerry R.	1932 - 1971
Lewis E.	1918 - 1975
Eva E.	1925 - 1980
Stanley W.	1915 - 1917, s/o W.M. & T.L. Bishop.
Thomas B.	1891 - 1923
William H.,Jr.	1934 - 1935
Blevins, William	May 10,1907 - July 24,1980
Edward L.	1884 - 1926
Mittie M.	1889 - 1964
Ella	Apr.23,1896 - Mar.9,1908, d/o W.P. & B.E.
infant	b. & d. Mar.27,1907, inf/o A.W. & E.S.Blevins
Bettie E.	Jan.6,1863 - Nov.26,1911, w/o W.P.
Bowers, John H.	Apr.14,1890 - Jan.21,1978
Maggie P.	May 6,1890 - no date
Leila	June 15,1914 - Aug.1,1914,d/o V.V. & W.H.
Eunice	Aug.19,1915 - Sept.27,1915, d/o V.V. & W.H.
Branch, J.H.	1857 - 1929
Isobelle Dixon	1877 - 1932
Bray, Charlie P.	Jan.28,1882 - Nov.12,1899
Hersal C.	1912 - 1918
Alvin H.	1884 - 1914
Thomas J.	1902 - 1976
Brown, Mary ELiza	1849 - 1918
Orville Sion	1851 - 1917
Burnett, Simon	Oct.23,1847 - Sept.10,1925, Co.F.63 Inf CSA.
Elizabeth Boyd	Nov.2,1851 - June 18,1892
S.A.	Aug.7,1844 - Dec.11,1910, w/o D.Burnett.
Decatur	June 20,1838 - Jan.2,1918
Dick H.	Aug.7,1873 - no date
Ester	1876 - June 1918
Mayne	May 20,1902 - Apr.18,1928, d/o D.H.& E.
Ellen	1895 - 1918, w/o Roy Burnett
Eugene	no date, s/o Roy & Ellen Burnett
Burnette, Basil E.	1905 - 1967
Christine	1933 - 1933
Thelma M.	1910 - no date
Sarah Jane Jones	Jan.14,1857 - Apr.8,1942
John Greenbury	Feb.9,1883 - Sept.14,1949
Robert J.	Dec.13,1899 - Apr.6,1983
Sarah J.	June 6,1903 - Mar.28,1971
Cagle, Tootsie	1920, inf s/o John & Jennie E. Cagle.

Ordway Cemetery, cont.

Cagle, John L.	Mar.29,1883 - Sept.29,1960
Jennie E. Love	1887 - Apr.25,1932
Campbell, Isaac N.	Apr.4,1856 - Jan.27,1929
Marylue S.	July 30,1848 - July 20,1908
James	Mar.14,1894 - June 19,1896
Harry C.,Sr.	1913 - 1983
John H.	May 23,1877 - no date
Minnie	Jan.23,1879 - Oct.20,1942
T.Eldridge	1869 - 1908
Homer	1906 - 1908
Richardson, Martha Ann Carrier	1870 - 1929
Holt, Lucy Bell Bray	1907 - 1937
Carrier, Clarence W.	Dec.27,1895 - Jan.23,1928
Earl J.	d.May 29,1928,TN.Pvt.1 Cl.50 Reg.Coast Army.
William Joe	1870 - 1940
Ida Trinkle	1873 - 1973
Lee A.	Mar.17,1898 - May 6,1974
Robert C.	1909 - 1973
Noah (Peg)	Aug.9,1898 - June 21,1981
William W.	1916 - 1916
ALbert W.	1917 - 1920
Coffey, Elizabeth	1897 - 1929
Margaret Leona	Nov.28,1927 - Oct.8,1929,d/o B.E.Coffey.
Beeler E.	1890 - 1965
Collins, Thomas RObert	1914 - 1984
Bessie Lee	1892 - 1984
Alice Blanche	1891 - 1918
Cross, Mary Jane	Jan.18,1880 - Feb.10,1910, w/o H.H.Cross.
James J.	Oct.29,1851 - Jan.4,1924
Margaret T.	June 1,1855 - ----1936
Nannie L. Smith	1876 - 1917, w/o John C. Cross
Joseph W.	Aug.14,1883 - Sept.27,1954
Harvey W.	1911 - 1912
Fannie M.	1884 - 1912
Trula J.	1904 - 1905
Chassie T. Smith	June 22,1892 - Mar.6,1923
Chassie Grace	Feb.23,1923 - Apr.13,1923, d/o R.L. & C.T.
Belvie K.	Mar.21,1913 - Apr.13,1913, s/o R.L. & C.T.
J.C.	Mar.15,1916 - Mar.19,1916, s/o J.C. & N.L.
Davis, Annins B.	1873 - 1956
Dishner, R.J.	1903 - 19--
Marinda Eva	1897 - 1969
Doyle, Thomas D.	1870 - 1926
James P.	1904 - 1985
Lena R.	1917 - 19--
East, Mary Smith	May 9,1891 - Nov.17,1914
Emmert, Julia	1868 - 193-
Emmert, Robert S.	1897 - 1974
Minnie V.	1895 - 1976
Fleenor, Sherry Lynne	1958 - 1977
Garland, Samuel D.	June 4, 1878 - Dec.6,1953
Dicie V.	July 28,1894 - Dec.16,1967
Glover, Fennattee T.	1874 - 1932
Zebeidee	1859 - 1924
Edgar	OCt.24,1886 - July 13,1919

Glover, Verna Cathaline	Sept.25,1911 - Nov.29,1922,d/o Edgar & Maudie
Infant	no date, s/o M.F. & M.E. Glover
Mary E.	July 30,1888 - July 4,1911,w/o M.F.Glover
Sarah Evelyn	1921 - 1933
Marian F.	1889 - 1939
Myrtle S.	1891 - 1955
Callie	Apr.4,1891 - Oct.23,1913, d/o J.W. & C.
Andrew	no dates, s/o J.W.Glover
Pearl	June 5,1898 - July 3,1919
John W.,Jr.	Mar.11,1905 - June 14,1933
John W.	1872 - 1944
Catherine	1868 - 1944
J.G.	1891 - 1970
Dora R.	1888 - 1964
Infants	1913 - 1921,inf/o J.G.Glover
Godsey, Addie L. Stickley	1880 - 1916, w/o Chas. Q. Godsey.
Charles Quillen	1877 - 1918
Charles Quillen,Jr.	1911 - 1918
Jessie May	1909 - 1918
Jamie Carter	1907 - 1918
Goodman, Mary Elsie	Aug.25,1907 - Sept.1,1909, d/o A.H.&H.
Infant	b.& d. Jan.2,1902, s/o A.H. & Hasie.
Goodson, Sarah	d.June 13,1816, aged 76 yrs.
John	d.July 7,1829, aged 65 yrs.
Gorley, S.R.	APr.5,1883 - Nov.30,1934
Martha J.	July 12,1886 - Aug.12,1946
Landon H.	1917 - 1980
Griffith, Ruben	1911 - 19--
Cora	1922 - 19--
Haga, Bertie	1879 - 1966
Harkelroad, Charles Lewis	d. July 30,1925, TN.Pvt.120 Inf.30 Div.
Ollie B.	Sept.8,1921 - June 27,1922
Hart, Andrew W.	1884 - 1978
Cora M.	1897 - ----
Hawthorne, David R.	1912 - 1970
Hays, S.W.	1833 - 1913
Hempton, M.	d.May 17,1817, aged 84 yrs.
m.	d.June 1,1828, aged 89 yrs.
Henley, Rufus E.	1878 - 1972
Minnie	1882 - 1961
Roby G.	1880 - 1951
Mattie E.	1878 - 1935
Carl	1906 - 1906
Carrie Ruth	1909 - 1910
Hickman, Sherley	1932 - 1932, d/o E.L. & Ethel Hickman.
Hicks, Wm.Edgar, Jr.	1915 - 1937
Blanche K.	1921 - 1922
George K.	1920 - 1920
George W.	1883 - 1970
Nellie M.	1892 - 1978
Dave	Jan.2,1897 - Oct.5,1984, WWI.
Lizzie	1889 - 1963
J.J.	1857 - 1928

Ordway Cemetery, cont.

Hicks, Kate K.	1864 - 1935
David N.	1856 - 1948
Martha A.	1853 - 1937
G.M.	June 27,1829 - Jan.23,1907
Grace R. Cross	1894 - 1985
Hines, W.C.	1833 - 1917
James	1883 - 1911
Hostrawser, Forest W.	1897 - 1976
Birdie E.	1905 - 19--.
Hudson, John H.	1916 - 1921
Fred C.	1920 - 1926
Robert	1853 - 1927
Catherine	1855 - 1930
Johns, Horace	d. Sept.25,1929, TN.Sgt.120 Inf.30 Div.
Johnson, Harry K.	May 14,1894 - Dec.3,1901,s/o B.H. & M.J.
J.Howard	July 18,1888 - Sept.2,1910
Jones, Addie	1905 - 1929
Roxie	1902 - 1962
Ketchem, James	d.Sept.29,1918,VA.Pvt.120 Inf.30 Div.
King, Col.James	d.Aug.17,1825, aged 72 yrs.
S.	d.Dec.13,1806, aged 41 yrs.
Lambert, T.J.	Dec.15,1833 - Dec.25,1926
Mary M.	July 15,1843 - Sept.22,1914
Leonard, Willie	1901 - 1966
Lola B.	1907 - 1968
Love, James	June 23,1868 - Jan.16,1909
Amanda Cross	July 24,1866 - June 26,1946
Arthur M.	Feb.3,1899 - June 4,1917
Luttrell, Charlotte Anne	1929 - 1938
Ernest R.	1907 - 1965
McLaster, Jennie	June 13,1867 - Apr.10,1887
McMillin, Bettie H.	Sept.23,1841 - Sept.8,1907, s/o S.D.
McNutt, Infant	no date, s/o T.A.McNutt
Manis, Charles Grant	1947
Meadows, John D.	no date, Co.B.4NC Line CSA
Sarah	Feb.8,1850 - Apr.5,1935
Miller, Jasper P.	1902 - 1973
Bertha S.	1909 - no date
Mills, Cornelious	1860 - 1916
Monroe, Gladys Bowers	Aug.17,1920 - June 13,1963
Moore, W.A.	Aug.27,1862 - Oct.31,1917
Mattie Griffin	Dec.21,1858 - no date
Neal, Catherlean	Jan.5,1912 - Jan.20,1912, s/o W.H. & E.Neal.
Odell, Carl A.	1906 - 1959
Lillian Kathleen	Sept.24,1920 - Apr.10,1921,d/o H.J.& N.E.
Henry J.	1882 - 1961
Nannie E.	1888 - 1950
Paul M.	1911 - 1965
Grace, V.	1913 - 1976
Overbay, George B.	1906 - 1971
WIllie Mae	1901 - 1975
Owens, Sarah	Mar.15,1854 - July 2,1910, w/o J.E.Owens, m. Sept.1, 1875.

Ordway Cemetery, cont.

Owens, Dunk A.	1882 - 1955
Edna M.	1897 - 19--
Phelps, Samuel	1859 - 1931
Jane	1857 - 1931, w/o Samuel
J.Robert,Sr.	1892 - 1959
Phillips, Earlie A.W.	Mar.29,1909 - Oct.6,1912, d/o J.A. & L.A..
Quisenberry, Robert	Mar.9,1893 - Oct.18,1918, in France.
Johnie	June 11, 1913 - July 22,1914
---	Sept.23,1911 - Dec.4,1911
Mary	Oct.2,1909 - Dec.23,1910
John	Dec.24,1866 - Oct.4,1923
Lee	Aug.31,1895 - July 27,1923
Ray, Hazel Ellender	Feb.6,1912 - Oct.14.1980
Rhymer, Junior	May 23,1922 - Oct.30,1924
Roberts, Mary Ruth Odell	1912 - 1930
Rosenbalm, Elizabeth	1850 (?) - 1935
Ross, Nellie	1911 - 1923
Ruth, Addie L.	June 5,1880 - Jan.18,1940
Samuel D.	Apr.28,1878 - Oct.2,1951
Shelley, Robert C.	1866 - 1930
Mary E.	1870 - 1936
Dorothy M.	Nov.19,1910 - Sept.23,1912
Shelton, Harvey	1868 - 1930
Shoecraft, Rev. N.V.	1856 - 1909
Clyde E.	Mar.7,1892 - Oct.1,1918
Silvers, Magdalene G.	1919 - 1976
Sisk, Sarah A.	Jan.30,1852 - Jan.2,1921, w/o Wm. Sisk
Smith, B.I.	May 23,1854 - Oct.4,1908
Amanda Hicks	May 14,1865 - Sept.26,1925, w/o Ben Smith.
Henry T.	1906 - 1956
Allie F.	Sept.19,1879 -Apr.2,1907, w/o J.L.Smith.
Viola	Apr.10,1928 - Mar.3,1956
Infants	1913 - 1917, infs/o W.D.Smith
George M.	d.1908, Father
Josephine E.	d.1924, Mother
Frank	d.1911, Son
Carle E.	d.1924, Daughter
Snodgrass, Vilena	Aug.27,1897 - Dec.24,1920
Statzer, Walter	1880 - 1954
Lola L.	1888 - 19--
James W.	Oct.1,1908 - no date
Avery Pauline	May 15,1909 - Oct.7,1983
Steadman, James T.	Nov.3,1862 - Apr.4,1912
Stout, Rebecca	1879 - 1967
Ollie Burnett	Jan.31,1878 - Apr.27,1911, w/o Press Stout.
Strouth, Willie	1910 - 1935
Lilbern H.	1886 - 1933
Myrtle B.	1888 - 1958
Taylor, Hattie King	Mar.30,1861 - Mar.31,1950
Trinkle, Georgia H.	Oct.16,1916 - Oct.12,1920
Hattie M.	1877 - 1955
George R.	1885 - 1949
Rosa P.	1912 - 1979

Ordway Cemetery, cont.

Trinkle, Herbert Y.	1907 - 1981
John E.	1878 - 1947
Laura B.	1878 - 1960
Lee B.	Sept.6,1893 - Oct.30,1918, s/o D.T.& S.R.
Sarah Rebecca	Aug.27,1853 - Aug.13,1929
Jane S.	1810 - 1912
C.Jess	1914 - 19--
Lucille	1915 - 19--
Ward, Mary E.	Dec.5,1915 - Mar.3,1964
Weaver, Lydie E.	1913 - 1923
Eula L.	1915 - 1931
Wade P.	1879 - 1940
Elizabeth L.	1880 - 1962, w/o Wade P. Weaver
Webster, Dorothy	Jan.11,1906 - May 1, 1906
White, Thomas	Sept.27,1890 - Oct.9,1957,TN.1st.Sgt.WWI&II.
Nora B.	1909 - 1980
Martha J.	1949
George	1889 - 1929
Emma	1910 - 1976
Widner, Clark C.	1902 - 1957
Wyatt, Ben J.	1876 - 1948
S.W.	1888 - 1936
Martha E.	no date
William C.	June 4, 1920 - Aug.22,1921
Mary Lee	1900 - 1966
W.F.	Dec.28,1870 - Jan.14,1923

Bachman Family Cemetery

Bachman, Jonathan	Aug.6,1769 - July 3,1861
Martha	Aug.9,1782 - July 3,1855,w/o Jonathan
Nathan W.	Nov.28,1802 - Oct.3,1887
Mrs.Emaline T.	Feb.3,1824 - Aug.8,1883,w/o Nathan W., & d/o Sanford & Mary A. Birdwell.
Bailey, Ella Myrtle	Aug.13,1907 - Feb.9,1908, d/o Dr.R.K.& J.
James C.	Nov.19,1901 - Apr.1,1908, s/o Dr.R.K.& J.
Dr.Rufus K.	1859 - 1938
Virginia McClellan	1867 - 1959
Bond, Frances L.	Aug.7,1865 - Aug.7,1908, w/o E.L.Bond.
McClellan, Infant	June 16-26,1843, s/o W.& H. McClellan
Cora Belle	Mar.2-Apr.9,1892, d/o W.B. & L.E.
Samuel G.	Feb.17,1861 - June 17,1928
Hannah Bachman	Dec.9,1824 - Apr.20,1900, w/o William
Martha Ann	Dec.12,1849 - Feb.25,1892
Smith, L.D.	Feb.28,1828 - Apr.27,1865

Harr Family Cemetery

Harr, Thomas J.	Aug.15,1867 - Jan.23,1944, m.Oct.2,1890
Rebecca Massie	Aug.1,1871 - Oct.12,1934
James E.	Aug.1,1900 - no date
Dora A.	Dec.1,1900 - Aug.14,1959
Douglas H.	Apr.19,1932 - Oct.19,1933

Yoakley Cemetery

Ford, R.L.Bruce	Sept.11,1878 - Nov.27,1899
Sarah A.	Sept.24,1848 - May 19,1921, w/o D.J.
D.J.	Sept.30,1840 - May 4,1918
M.Jack	Jan.1,1876 - July 27,1897,s/o J.A.&F.J.
Hakes, Minnie I.	Aug.22,1873 - Oct.23,1905,w/o Wm.E.
Hester H.	Oct.5,1903 - Dec.26,1905,d/o W.E. & M.I.
Hickman, John	Dec.7,1828 - Nov.16,1874
Mary D.	Apr.4,1856 - Sept.12,1878
Roller, Rachel Olivene	Feb.17,1866 - Jan.7,1889, S.D.Roller
Lillie E.	Aug.8,1887 - May 23,1888,d/o S.D.& R.O.
Yoakley, Peter, Sr.	Sept.8,1782 - May 29,1857
Rachel	Feb.14,1789 - July 26,1855
Peter	Sept.9,1829 - June 4,1897, erected by Lizzie Yoakley.
John	Dec.5,1810 - Feb.23,1874
Eliza M.	OCt.2,1815 - Feb.16,1886,w/o John
Julia A.	Jan.13,1838 - Feb.21,1906
Eliza Jane	Apr.10,1843 - Feb.11,1844,d/o John & E.M.
Rachel Pauline	Aug.4,1841 - Feb.23,1844, d/o J. & E.M.
Peter Lafayett	Nov.25,1839 - Mar.7,1844,s/o John & E.M.
Julia A.	July 24,1838 - Apr.14,1880
M.V.	Dec.5,1836 - July 30,1896
Samuel B.	Feb.6,1861 - Sept.18,1862
Martin K.	Apr.21,1863 - July 3,1884

Gaines Family Cemetery

Brown, Walter	June 1,1888 - Dec.23,1944
Myra Gaines	Jan.23,1883 - Apr.5,1957
Maggie A. Shaver	Feb.8,1836 - Nov.30,1868, w/o Jesse N.
Gaines, Nannie C.	Apr.3,1851 - May 23,1927
Kalista V.	1925 - 1929
William A.	Dec.13,1880 - Mar.18,1946
Benjamin Franklin	Nov.13,1838 - Jan.16,1916
George D.	July 7,1890 - Oct.2,1956
Lynn, John G.	Jan.1,1839 - July 10,1908
Fannie Gaines	Dec.12,1849 - Dec.8,1939, w/o John G.
Moody, Elizabeth S.	can't read dates
Pulliam, Samuel M.H.	aged 1 day, s/o R.W.& S.M. Pulliam.
William M.	d.Jan.1856, aged 6m5d.
Susan M.	d.Dec.22,1856, aged 26y4m9d, consort of R.W.Pulliam.
Rayl, Theo C.	Sept.20,1859 - Oct.18,1863, d/o Annie J.
Wilson, Thomas E.	Jan.10,1943 - Jan.11,1943

Waterman Family Cemetery

Cleek, Anna C.	Oct.11,1857 - Mar.24,1906
Waterman, D.J.	Jan.26,1833 - July 18,1884
L.D.	Jan.27,1835 - June 10,1910

Chinquapin Church Cemetery

Barbe, John M.	1967 - 1967
Barnette, Harrison	Nov.1,1899 - July 9,1939
Baxley, Virginia S.	Apr.21,1925 - May 31,1949
Buechler, Lena Grace N.	1931 - 1979
Buchanan, Patrick H.	1953 - 1953
Riley Adam	Mar.7,1905 - July
Dewey	1900 - 1979
Una	1898 - 1952
Boling, Delia E.	1930 - 1936
Samuel L.	1873 - 1937
Daisey A.	1880 - 1966
Ernest	1907 - 1979
no name	1915 - no date
Asa R.	Jan.25,1899 - Apr.18,1958
Edith M.	June 18,1902 - no date
William B.	June 12,1884 - Oct.20,1952
Anice L.	Apr.8,1892 - June 19,1954
Elizabeth Adelia	Sept.6,1930 - Apr.6,1936
Infant	May 23,1933, s/o W.B. & A.L. Boling
Elizabeth Adeline	Dec.7,1850 - Jan.24,1928
Nellie Virginia	Nov.5,1920, inf/o J.D. & Bessie Boling
Warren J.	Sept.6,1920 - Oct.23,1920,s/o J.A. & Mary
Harry C.	Mar.20,1923 - July 16,1960
Pansy L. Mottern	Apr.13,1922 - no date
James Roy	Oct.5,1961 - Jan.23,1963
James A.	1881 - 1954
Mary M.	1896 - 1967
John D.	May 7,1878 - Feb.24,1972
Bessie R.	June 5,1885 - July 18,1960
Bolling, Millie B.	1904 - 1918, d/o S.L. & D.A. Bolling.
Bowling, Glen T.	Oct.10,1916 - Sept.1,1962
Ethel B.	Feb.24,1922 - no date
Bryan, Sallie A. Hodges	Jan.23,1847 - Jan.1,1918, w/o J.D.Bryan.
J.D.	May 1, 1842 - Dec.17,1921
Cross, Walter Elbert	1885 - 1932
Lola Crussell	1891 - 1941
Infant	d.1922, s/o W.E. & L.A. Cross
Combs, Jonathan	1853 - 1928
Adeline Watson	1853 - 1912
Carrier, Annie May	Oct.1,1896 - Feb.8,1923
Leona B.	July 16,1921 - Jan.29,1929, d/o Anna May
Ollie A.	Sept.13,1902 - Mar.19,1903, s/o T.A.& L.C.
Noah	June 4, 1907 - Mar.10,1908, s/o T.A.& L.C.
E.A.	1838 - 1930, Confederate Soldier
Elizabeth C.	1840 - 1930, w/o E.A.Carrier
Mack	Mar.3,1905 - Dec.17,1958
Mary	Dec.10,1907 - no date
Sarah Jane	May 6, 1900 - Mar.10,1919
Andy	1873 - 1957
Laura W.	1874 - 1956
Canter, Theodosia Lowrie	Aug.18,1892 - Apr.1,1920, w/o D.A.Canter

Chinquapin Church Cemetery, cont.

Carrieger,	Isaac H.	1918 - 1919
	Virginia	1876 - 1918
	Isaac R.	Co.F, 13 Tenn. Cav.
	Ada F.	1903 - 1904
	Charles Robert	Nov.14,1930 - Dec.29,1930, s/o R.E. & Elizabeth Carrieger.
Carriger,	Nannie J.	Mar.17,1885 - Aug.24,1912, w/o L.M.
	Albert Clayton	Jan.13,1906 - May 29,1968
	Lass	Feb.11,1970
	Lemuel M.	1880 - 1942
	Lola	1889 - 1929
Carroll,	Harvy C.	Oct.19,1897 - Oct.8,1902, s/o A.J. & M.M.
Combs,	Adeline Watson	1853 - 1912
	Johnathan	1853 - 1928
	John	Jan.2,1833 - Apr.4,1914
	Rebecca	Mar.4,1838 - Jan.29,1910,w/o John Combs
	John Jessie	Jan.20,1892 - Oct.16,1895,s/o A.J. & M.A.
	Elbert H.	Dec.7,1871 - Jan.3,1952
	Nannie Bertie	Aug.5,1880 - July 27,1965
Carr,	Joe	May 7,1942
	Canie	Jan.1,1967, aged 69 yrs.
	Mary	May 12,1858 - May 8,1919
	Herman	1937 - 1954
Cartright,	Albert L.	Mar.22,1886 - Apr.6,1887, s/o J.N.& A.E.
Cox,	Velma Riley	1906 - 1944
	Joseph Lynn	1925 - 1963
	Leonard Sampson	July 17,1922 - Oct.21,1923, s/o S.D.Cox
Crow,	Ritta Lyon	1870 - 1935
Danner,	Roy M.	May 10,1899 - June 3, 1966
	Lucinda E. Harmon	Jan.11,1873 - Dec.31,1911, w/o L.M.Danner
Dunn,	William C.	1870 - 1943
	Minnie E.	1872 - 1943
	Callie Sigman	1900 - 1950
	Sam Edward	1900 - 1919
Duncan,	Vona A.	Aug.25,1909 - Feb.7,1979
Ealey,	Wiley Earnest	Dec.8,1922 - Jan.1,1969
	A.W.	Sept.13,1853 - Sept.24,1924
	Martha Morrell	June 12,1853 - Jan.5,1946
	Wiley Alfred	Dec.18,1893 - Sept.7,1964
	Blanche L.	1902 - 1979
Eads,	Eugene	Aug.8,1919 - Aug.17,1932
Ellis,	Lewis James	Dec.9,1932 - no date
	Margaret Louise Estep	June 22,1937 - Oct.17,1967
	Michael Lewis	Jan.18,1967 - no date
Fowler,	Daisey	May 28,1897 - Apr.7,1901
	Edgar S.	Nov.3,1900 - Nov.6,1900
	Bessie	May 2, 1899 - Sept.4,1899
Frye,	Lucy	Dec.13,1923 - May 16,1977
Glover,	James W.	Nov.7,1912 - Dec.5,1912, s/o C. & E.T.
	Bertha	Oct.10,---- - Oct.30,1904
	Pollie	Apr.11,1895 - Jan.1,1896, d/o Richard & Martha Glover.
	Ada	Nov.1899 - Jan.1900, d/o R. &. M.
	Zack	May 6, 1896 - May 8,1897, d/o R. & M.
	Infant	inf/o C. & M.T. Glover
	Richard	OCt.15,1804 - Dec.2, 1894

Glover, William R.	1873 - 1952	
Ollie F.	OCt.19,1882 - Oct.6,1952	
Mattie M.	Apr.7,1888 - Sept.26,1971	
Edward C.	1883 - 1965	
Lily Watson	1881 - 1965	
Ralph C.	no dates	
Dorothy M.	no dates	
William G.	no dates	
William	Oct.11,1828 - June 28,1903	
Kizziah	May 10,1825 - June 25,1903	
W.M.	1851 - 1925	
Mary J.	1854 - 1925	
Rhoda E.	Aug.25,1887 - Dec.3,1896, d/o W.M.&M.J.	
D.J.	Aug.15,1839 - Oct.7,1902	
Joanna	Nov.9,1842 - June 21,1899	
Adelia	July 2,1861 - Mar.16,1927, d/o D.J. & J.	
Oscar C.	Apr.30,1875 - no date	
Mamie A.	May 10,1876 - Feb.6,1943	
Earl	May 26, 1917	
Edward	Apr.22,1924	
David B.	Feb.14,1906 - June 6,1906	
Elbert H.	1858 - 1940	
Amy C.	1851 - 1925	
Mamie W.	Nov.30,1886 - Feb.16,1899, d/o E.H.& A.G.	
Edward	1818 - 1899	
Lockie	Nov.24,1836 - Mar.14,1910,w/o Richard	
Samuel	June 4,1825 - June 26,1913,Mexican Soldier.	
Margaret	Mar.30,1848 - May 28,1935	
Sarah E.	Nov.29,1843 - July 12,1910, w/o Edward	
G.J.	June 11, 1903 - Apr.20,1920	
Richard	Sept.13,1868 - May 14,1946	
Martha Morris	Dec.5,1868 - Jan.22,1931, w/o Richard	
Lena Belle	July 7,1910 - Oct.24,1929,d/o Richard & Martha.	
Lelan F.	Nov.26,1892 - Dec.24,1911, s/o W.M. & M.A.	
W.M.	June 28,1842 - Jan.29,1917	
Maggie	Dec.9,1855 - Oct.8,1910	
John W.	Sept.2,1884 - Apr.3,1960	
Alice Combs	Nov.8,1885 - Apr.7,1967	
Oscar C.	Apr.16,1910 - July 7,1972	
Coy F.	Feb.16,1915 - July 31,1978	
Worley Michael	Feb.25,1947 - Jan.18,1982	
Gobble, J.R.	Feb.4,1900 - July 26,1901, s/o J.H. & N.E.	
Greer, Melissa E.	Sept.12,1851 - Oct.21,1926	
Green, Letha	Spet.4,1897 - Jan.23,1924, w/o M.F.Greene	
Ivory H.	Feb.27,1908 - Feb.25,1924,s/o F.M. & L.L.	
Greene, Hiram	July 15,1855 - Nov.5,1929	
Lucy A. Critcher	Oct.8,1860 - Oct.9,1935	
Ira Clark	May 13,1894 - May 10,1971	
Franke B.	Dec.23,1910 - July 21,1911,s/o F.M. & L.L.	
Marion Francis	July 7,1878 - Nov.27,1962	
Isabel Bryan	Apr.16,1876 - Nov.23,1957	
Gardner, George C.	1898 - 1960	
George G.	1897 - 1960	
Alice S.	1899 - 1978	
Garrett, Ethel Mae	1907 - 1924, d/o H.L.& Lula Garrett.	

Chinquapin Cemetery, cont.

Garrett, Iva Blanche	1921 - 1921, d/o H.L. & Lula Garrett
Hodge, L.B. (Jack)	1898 - 1958
Lena W.	1905 - 1965
Hodges, Milton L.	Dec.2,1876 - June 21,1938
Emma Augusta	Feb.21,1880 - Dec.13,1957
Haskel	1914 - no date
Winnie	1918 - no date
Hal H.	1941 - no date
Rose	Sept.2,1898 - Nov.22,1912
Hopkins, Hamp. H.	Apr.3,1904 - Aug.22,1929
Hicks, J.Walter	Feb.16,1874 - Nov.4,1911
Paul Sharp	Apr.12,1905 - Feb.2,1971
H.J.	Nov.10,1836 - Dec.24,1912
Mary Eleanor	Jan.20,1923 - Feb.4,1923,d/o J.E.& N.E.
John Elbert	1895 - 1979
Nora Combs	1897 - 1980
Glenna Rhea	July 13,1940, d/o Mr & Mrs C.B.Hicks.
Robert L.	1869 - 1945
Rebecca	1876 - 19--
Oscar L.	Mar.30,1875 - June 6,1959
Emily D.	Mar.5,1878 - Apr.9,1965
Huffman, Haze Carriger	1925 - 1972
Harman, John A.	1857 - 1940
Mary E.	1869 - 1936
Harmon, Ivan Lee	1912, s/o J.A.&M.E. Harmon
Walter H.	Mar.18,1886 - Nov.9,1909
David D.	Mar.18,1888 - July 24,1908
Wiley A.	Oct.3,1846 - Aug.9,1929
Mary A.	Nov.11,1849 - no date
Hart, Ben F.	June 18,1884 - Oct.30,1926
R.J.B.	June 26,1915 - July 12,1929
Nannie	1859 - 1943
Hinkle, Maggie	d.Dec.29,1959
Johnny A.	1934 - 1979
Cecil	1893 - 1971
Jarrett, David J.	1870 - 1936
Festa J.	1903 - 1955
C.Rabe	1896 - 1969
Fannie S.	1899 - no date
Samuel	1907 - 1924
Polly	1878 - 1955
Justice,Amanda Hope	May 11,1976, infant
Terah Suzanne	Feb.12,1981 - Sept.9,1981
Jones, Thresa Lynn	1964
Tracey Ann	1964
Jenkins, James R.	1906 - 1906
James Rufus	1908 - 1908
Emmert	----- - 1919
Nannie E.	1875 - 1949
Charlie	Sept.26,1878 - May 24,1935
Harrison	Mar.15,1908 - Mar.18,1909
Worley	1913 - 1921

Chinquapin Cemetery, cont.

Jenkins, T.N.	May 11,1846 - Feb.19,1906
Emily	Feb.19,1834 - Oct.24,1899
Robert J.	1851 - 1916
Ellen	1860 - 1944
Charles A.	Nov.1,1882 - Oct.9,1947
Sallie E.	Sept.28,1893 - Aug.23,1954
Raymond	Jan.30,1910 - Nov.12,1966
Emma	Sept.5,1882 - May 14,1955
Dewey	May 3,1904 - Feb.27,1963
Kastner, Rebecca Anne	Aug.14,1891
Kaylor, Kathleen	1953 - 1953
Lewis Aaron	May 5,1930 - Nov.27,1969
William J.	1884 - 1954
Gracie E.	1891 - 19--
King, Gladys W.	1912 - 1957
Kuhn, J.R.	June 27,1834 - Jan.14,1914
Lyon, Agnes	May 24,1853 - May 2,1889, w/o Alvin
J.C.	Oct.19,1887 - July 15,1888, s/o A. & A.
Stanton S.	1861 - 1930
Julia A.	1867 - 1941
S.J.	1869 - 1944
Virginia H.	1872 - 1926
Jennie Eads	1867 - 1916, w/o D.N.Lyon
David N.	Apr.24,1858 - Aug.20,1928
H.T.	Sept.6,1878 - Jan.11,1905
Samuel B.	Feb.22,1829 - July 23,1892, 59 Regt. TN.Inf. L.S.A.,1861 - 1865.
Adeline Ellis	June 13,1838 - Aug.2,1885, w/o Samuel B.
Thomas S.	Nov.9,1832 - Mar.20,1903
Jane P.	Nov.7,1835 - Dec.19,1894, w/o T.S.Lyon.
Infant	Jan.7,1902 - Jan.9,1902, d/o D.N. & J.E.
Ollie L.	May 13,1899 - July 4,1903, s/o S.S. & J.A.M.
Rhoda M.	OCt.5,1887 - July 12,1905
Minnie	Oct.22,1888 - Nov.19,1889, d/o A,M. & Nanie.
Nanie Smith	Apr.23,1866 - Aug.19,1893, w/o A.M. Lyon
Infant	b. & d. June 27,1943, s/o R.T.& Martha.
Florence	1928 - 1929
Alvin M.	Dec.9,1859 - Apr.3,1932
Mattew H.	1867 - 1927
Addie G.	1870 - 1957
Paul	May 25,1927 - May 25,1927, s/o H.E.& S.C.
Carl E.	June 25,1906 - Mar.31,1977
Ethel Slagle	July 2,1906 - May 9,1952
Harlan T.	June 25,1929 - Apr.30,1963
Mildred S.	1933 - no date
Alvin Collins	July 13,1891 - July 10,1967
Elizabeth	Mar.1,184- - Apr.3,1893, w/o H.C.Lyon.
Fannie W.	July 15,1874 - May 7,1898, d/o L.A. & M.C.
Minnie V.	Feb.27,1903 - Apr.26,1903, s/o G.W. & Sallie

Chinquapin Cemetery, cont.

Lyon, Bulah M.	June 13,1906 - Nov.2,1909, d/o N.L.&N.A.
Cecil V.	Oct.6,1911 - Nov.28,1974, m. Apr.12,1941
Viola	May 3, 1921 - no date
S.E.	Apr.6,1930 - Apr.7,1930
Stanton Clyde	1934 - 1944, s/o Mr & Mrs W.H. Lyon.
Oscar Worley	May 24,1873 - Mar.30,1935
Landon	Oct.23,1839 - June 30,1910, m.Aug.25,1872 to Mary C. Carr.
J. Maynard	1897 - 1969
Cordie A.	1897 - 1974
Katheren	1855 - 1925
Elizabeth	MAr.1,1894- - Apr.3,1893, w/o H.G.Lyon
Lyons, Earl Edward	d. Feb.3,1960, aged 2m15d.
Infant	b. & d. 1958
Grace	1913 - 1921
Herman J.	1911 - 1946
Hazel Carr	1916 - 1941, w/o Herman J. Lyons.
Fred Herman	1938 - 1939, s/o Herman & Hazel.
Manuel W.	Mar.13,1884 - Mar.19,1932
Mary M. Stanfield	Aug.16,1893 - Aug.2,1935
Charles W.	Sept.20,1877 - Feb.7,1963
Sallie Roberts	Nov.10,1884 - Mar.16,1951
Lane, Infant	1951
Leonard, Earl W.,Jr.	Oct.23,1941, infant
Lowrie, Minnie Alice	Mar.30,1894 - Nov.30,1896, d/o J.H. & C.L.
Geneva	May 23,1891 - Dec.11,1832, d/o J.H. & C.L.
J.H.	Feb.15,1853 - Oct.18,1930
Charlotte Lyon	June 18,1864 - Apr.20,1923
Oscar L.	Mar.8,1902 - June 20,1934
Mary Helen	APr.7,1935 - May 25,1935, d/o H.C.Lowrie.
David	June 9,1886 - Jan.2,1940
Mary Riley	May 10,1890 - no date
Adelia Ann	1883 - 1951
Lingerfile, James Newton	1946 - 1981
Lewis, Emery	May 26, 1910 - Dec.7,1962
McElyea, B.F.	1864 - 1917
Minton, Ollie J.	Nov.3,1878 - Mar.1902, w/o C.O.Minton.
Mays, Andrew	May 23,1891 - Sept.4,1944
May, Susan F.	May 5,1847 - Jan.21,1894, w/o F.M.May
Elizabeth	Oct.15,1866 - Oct.23,1902,w/o F.M.May.
Elbert Albert	May 16,1892 - Aug.31,1968
Frances A.	June 15,1895 - no date
Lizzie	Apr.8,1918 - no date
Mays, Dorothy Mae	1920 - 1985
Mayes, William Baxter	Apr.9,1870 - Dec.2,1939
Rindia	June 22,1861 - Dec.29,1936
Moody, Lillie B.	June 25,1888 - July 26,1913
Minnie	Nov.18,1890 - Dec.21,1912
Millsap, Walter	1874 - 1929
Fannie	1881 - 1916, w/o W.R.Millsap
Mottern, Maggie A.	Aug.27,1881 - Aug.14,1889, d/o W. & E.J.
Joseph L.	Sept.12,1891 - Nov.28,1922, s/o W.M. & E.

Chinquapin Cemetery, cont.

Mottern, William	MAr.17,1853 - June 19,1926
Elizabeth	Sept.17,1848 - Jan.2,1927
Ella	Aug.10,1877 - Jan.22,1940
LuEmma	June 28,1884 - July 20,1954
James E.	1855 - 1934
Louisa J.	1858 - 1936
Infant	1920, inf/o W.J. & J.E. Mottern.
Norman G.	Oct.31,1904 - Dec.13,1907,s/o M.B.&M.V.
Rev. Samuel Dayton	Sept.10,188 - Feb.3,1969
May Blackburn	July 19,1894 - Feb.7,1923,w/o S.D.Mottern.
Henry	JAn.15,1895 - Apr.27,1972
Ruby B.	May 10, 1900 - Nov.8,1933, w/o Henry
Miller, Infant	July 28,1940 - July 28,1940,s/o Jonnie & Bessie May Miller.
Irene	Sept.4,1914 - Feb.6,1932
David	1916
Rebecky E.	1883 - 1916, w/o Clark Miller
Violey	d. 1910
Sallie	Nov.25,1897 - Mar.5,1922
Bessie May	Oct.14,1914 - July 28,1940, w/o Jonnie
Montgomery, James Lee	1949, infand s/o Willard & Lavada
Myers, Rachel	1815 - July 4,1900
Morse, John B.	July 10,1874 - Dec.12,1933
A.B.	1839 - 1917
Sarah	Aug.31,1848 - Aug.12,1910, w/o A.B.Morse
Maines, Bruce C.	May 10,1910 - July 9,1952
Fred O.	MAr.20,1907 - Jan.12,1959
Charles B.	1930 - 1950
Nelson, Robert H.	1899 - 1957
Virgie S.	1902 - 1945
Gary C.	1945
James A.	May 23,1884 - Apr.11,1957
Maggie S.	Mar.30,1897 - Oct.15,1961
Nidiffer, Clyde Theodore	Aug.31,1904 - Dec.5,1906, s/o James & Rena
Mary Ann	OCt.13,1843 - Nov.10,1911, w/o Galvan
Pyle, Nancy Ann	1847 - 1927
Peeks, Adelia	Jan.2,1862 - May 21,1895, w/o R.L.Peeks
Poe, J.Albert	Nov.17,1890 - Sept.6,1892
Pippin, Roxie Boling	Oct.27,1900 - May 19,1974
Reed, Bill	no dates
Richards, Eddie L.	Mar.31,1896 - Mar.17,1979
Millie J.	Jan.12,1894 - Aug.22,1966
Infant	b. & d. Feb.18,1908, d/o Keen & Lena
Lena R.	Mar.5,1879 - Feb.19,1907
J.Keen	1869 - 1957
Orlena	1886 -
Ollie C.	1904 - 1934
M.T.	1864 - 1942
Amanda	1864 - 19--
W.Columbus	Jan.16,1861 - no date
Anna Cole	Dec.30,1861 - Mar.23,1947

Chinquapin Cemetery, cont.

Richards,	Clyde	Feb.3,1934 - Oct.16,1953
	Paul	June 20,1939 - Apr.5,1940
	Evelyn L.	Sept.8,1935 - Sept.16,1935
	J.T.	May 23,1885 - July 30,1895, s/o W.C.&D.A.
	Samuel E.	1892 - 1936
	Bertha	
	Samuel Joseph	June 26,1876 - Apr.18,1942
	Lillie Belle	MAy 29,1894 - May 27,1938
	Emma	Feb.2,1891 - Dec.20,1911, w/o H.E.
	Elaxander	1835 - 1916
	Martha	July 16,1839 - May 17.1910
	J.A.	Jan.15,1862 - Apr.12,1888
	William	Aug.21,1861 - Oct.13,1894
	H.	Dec.11,1858 - Mar.17,1895
	Alvin	1883 - 1970
	Princess M.	1885 - 1971
	T.C.	1910 - 1960, killed in a train wreck in Natural Tunnel, VA.
	D.J.	1881 - 19--
	Lula L.	1892 - 19--
	Carl W.	Apr.1,1903 - May 13,1904
	William Carl	June 23,1907 - Sept.27,1979
	Edith Salley	May 10,1910 - no date
Richardson,	Allen C.	1867 - 1951
	Margaret V.	1872 - 1949
Riley,	James	Aug.4,1815 - July 23,1900
	Sarah	June 14,1824 - Nov.7,1889, w/o James
	Infant	inf/o J.M. & M.A. Riley
	Robert J.	June 3,1884 - Apr.29,1888, s/o J.M. & M.A.
	J.M.	1859 - 1918
	Alice	1860 - 1929
	Wendell Lee	1903 - 1922
	Billy	1926 - 1926
	Velma Cox	1906 - 1944
	William E.	1879 - 1960
	Maggie M.	1885 - 19--
Royston,	Laura B.	Apr.27,1888 - Aug.22,1899
	W.Bruce	Aug.15,1892 - Feb.26,1912
	Susan	1859 - 1924, w/o J.M.Royston
Roberson,	M.E.	Oct.30,1844 - Feb.21,1906
	M.P.	d.Apr.20,1911, 13 TN Cav., Co.H.
	Roy Alexander	Jan.15,1902 - Nov.21,1904
Smith,	George D.	May 9,1867 - May 19,1949
	Fannie Pyle	Jan.21,1878 - Feb.19,1958
	Dorothy Sue	June 3,1928 - June 4,1928, d/o Fleenor & Mamie Smith.
	Rhoda A.	Feb.28,1864 - Sept.5,1915, w/o G.D.Smith
	Tommie	Nov.15,1895 - Sept.26,1908, s/o G.D.& R.A.
	Edell	Sept.3,1902 - Jan.28,1903, d/o G.D. & R.A.
	Infant	Oct.3,1903 - Oct.6,1903, d/o G.D. & R.A.
	M.L.	Mar.23,1873 - June 24,1897

Chinquapin Cemetery, cont.

Smith, Jacob H.	Oct.12,1834 - May 21, 1895
W.E.	Mar.23,1871 - Mar.7,1886, s/o J.H.Smith.
Sam D.	Oct.11,1898 - Feb.14,1972
Rosalee	1937
G.D.	Nov.5,1890 - June 23,1930
A.N.	1852 - 1930
Elizabeth	1863 - 1933
James F.	Mar.25,1892 - Nov.17,1947
J.Henry	Mar.20,1887 - Nov.8,1924
J.S.	1833 - 1918
Edgar	Apr.30,189- - June 29,1894
Taylor	June 9,1869 - Oct.11,1945
Martha Roberson	Feb.7,1870 - Jan.23,1958
Nell Marie	Apr.16,1927 - July 4,1929
J.T.	Aug.22,1930 - Mar.15,1932
Charlie R.	Sept.1,1901 - July 26,1901, s/o A.N.& N.E.
Nancy A.	May 1934 - Aug.1908
William Alford	Aug.18,1902 - Apr.14,1910
Evelyn	Dec.23,1922 - Jan.1,1923, d/o E.W. & Dollie
William G.	July 11, 1860 - Sept.17,1911
John Freeman	May 9, 1909 - Oct.10,1930
John M.	Aug.31,1860 - Nov.30,1924
Olive T.	1867 - 1955
Herbert T.	1926 - 1974
Fleenor W.	1900 - 1971
Mamie G.	1905 - no date
John W.	Mar.31,1862 - Jan.29,1947
Sarrah Ann	June 9,1870 - Oct.22,1945
Swanner, Kate Ealey	Mar.16,1878 - Jan.23,1901, w/o John
Scalf, Marvin	1916 - 1964
Lucinda Carr	July 6, 1850 - Aug.21,1926, w/o Isaac
Samuel J.	June 28,1874 - May 5,1906
Sheets, Brownlow	Mar.22,1892 - Dec.20,1964
Daniel	Apr.11,1897 - Mar.11,1912, s/o Joe & S.F.
Bobie	May 2, 1907 - Mar.17,1912, s/o Joe & S.F.
Riley W.	May 11, 1888 - July 23,1926
Sarah F.	1858 - 1934
Sigman, L.D.	1869 - 1932
Mary	1869 - 19--
L.D.	1869 - 1931 2 stones
Mary	1867 - 1958
Martha N.	1936
Amy C.	Jan.13,1905 - July 10,1979
Naomi	1947
Norman D.	Dec.20,1907 - Sept.2,1982
Agnes W.	Aug.22,1911 - Feb.7,1952
Caleb M.	1891 - 1968
Elizabeth L.	1898 - 1974
Elizabeth	d. May 1,1896, w/o L.H.Sigman.
Stevens, Cindy Sigman	Jan.13,1905 - Jan.16,1979

Chinquapin Cemetery, cont.

Sams, Anna Lyons	July 23,1922 - Dec.1,1944, w/o Winston
Infant	Apr.9-16,1916, inf/o R.M. & Carrie Sams
Infant	June 23,1915, inf/o R.M. & Carrie Sams
Dellie	Jan.3,1908 - July 5, 1909
Slagle, Mollie G.	1873 - 1909
James D.	1904 - 1979
Charlotte C.	1910 - no date
John P.	Jan.13,1901 - Oct.9,1970
Rev. H.R.	Jan.16,1863 - Dec.2,1946
Carrie I. Oliver	Sept.30,1879 - Aug.17,1973
Sallie A.	Apr.5,1867 - Apr.25,1902, w/o Rev.H.R.
Bell Trusler	1894 - 1914 Mother
Bell	1914 - 1935 Daughter
Stanfield, Hattie	1867 - 1953
Robert Jr.	1940 - 1940
Annie F.	1898 - 1936
Glenn W.	1918 - 1919
W.Fletcher	1871 - 1956
Mattie L.	1879 - 1979
Frank A.	1908 - 1979
Wesley	1903 - 1951
Alice	1896 - 19--
Spary, John E.	Sept.30,1940 - Sept.30,1940
Taylor, E.T.	June 1, 1844 - Aug.9,1903
Nora B.	May 7, 1891 - Feb.7,1893
Elizabeth	Feb.15,1890 - June 26,1890
Joseph P.	July 29,1885 - Aug.3,1886
Tester, Edward	1945 - 1947
Eureka K.	1918 - 1947
Vita	Jan.19,1940 - Jan.24,1940, d/o Denver
R.Conley	Nov.8,1930 - Dec.6,1930, s/o D.C.& M.K.
Nolia Harmon	Dec.8,1883 - Dec.25,1925, w/o George W.
Orris	June 10,1904 - Oct.25,1910
Denver	Sept.28,1906 - no date, m. Nov.13,1927.
Maulta K.	Sept.11,1908 - Dec.24,1980
Millard F.	Feb.15,1881 - Nov.19,1970, m. Nov.1,1903
Minnie E.	Dec.21,1881 - Mar.14,1977
Toolie, W.S.	1897 - 1936
Townsend, George T.	Nov.2,1907 - July 21,1975
Watson, Virgil D.	1913 - 1949
Ennis H.	1916 - no date
S.J.	1869 - 1930
Rosabelle Lowrie	1885 - 1963
Watson, Anna Dayton Elizabeth	Sept.18,1894 - June 22,1909
W.M.	Sept.26,1867 - Jan.5,1885
Infant	b. & d. Nov.20,1885, s/o J.W. & M.E.
John H.	June 26,1890 - Dec.17,1890
Susan	Mar.11,1820 - Dec.4,1892,w/o Jonathan
Rev. John W.	Oct.8,1847 - Oct.24,1914
Mary Elizabeth	July 23,1848 - Oct.31,1912
Edgar Maynard	1874 - 1916
Wiley Gaines	1879 - 1936
Jennie Moss	1888 - 1963
Vernon C.	July 17,1906 - Nov.4,1947

Chinquapin Cemetery, cont.

Watson, Nathan Loyd	Spt.28,1877 - Sept.16,1952
Jennie S.	Nov.21,1889 - Dec.13,1959
Elbert E.	1845 - 1925
Nancy Jane	1837 - 1928
Winston E.	1914 - no date
Lawson L.	1909 - 1966
Zella Mae	Mar.10,1921 - Mar.8,1924, d/o W.G.&Jennie
Guy	1903 - 1972
Mollie	1886 - 1936
Noah	1876 - 1963
Alvin E.	1907 - 1965
Myrtle H.	1910 - 1982
Sherry Lynn & Terry Lynn	1961, d/o Dean & Treva Watson
Wassom, Jimmy Allen	Dec.6,1962 - Jan.25,1967
Woods, Marshall L.	1882 - 1959
Jennie A. Lyons	1890 - 1927
Carl H.	1922 - 1940
Luster P. Lyon	Aug.29,1867 - Mar.4,1942
Webster, Leota Maines	Dec.22,1913 - Jan.6,1975
Wilson, Edith Lynn	1957 - 1958

Lilley Cemetery

Lilley, James D.	Nov.8,1867 - May 5,1890
Dollie	June 28,1883 - Sept.12,1886, d/o
	John S. & E.B.Lilley.
John S.	Jan.17,----
ELizabeth R.	Dec.15,1893, aged 29 yrs.

Denton Cemetery #2

Denton, William W.	1928 - 1954
Blanche B.	1929 - no date
Paul	1901 - 1950
Annie	1908 - 1974
William G.	July 15,1882 - Oct.16,1956
Mrs. Oma	Sept.16,1879 - Feb.26,1942
Callie	1905 - 1908
Lilla Bella	1879 - 1921
Leek	1858 - 1936
Lula Payne	1876 - 1949
Main, Harry L.	Apr.30,1917 - Nov.4,1920, s/o C.F.& M.D.
Maine, Dovie S.	Sept.17,1897 - Mar.31,1913

Missionary Baptist Church Cemetery

Carroll, Thomas	Oct.19,1814 - Feb.6,1910
William R.	June 2,1909 - June 1,1936
Rachel O.	Sept.26,1870 - no date
Robert	d.June 19-6 (fhm)
Cole, P.A.	May 8,1827 - Oct.2,1907, w/o John Cole
Martha Ellen	Oct.2,1863 - Dec.24,1929
Addaline	Sept.11,1852 - Feb.10,1937
Collins, Fuller H.	1876 - 1947
Catherine T.	1882 - 1955
Cotter, Janice Lorraine	May 28-29,1949
Emmett E.	July 19,1872 - June 11,1919
Lizzie Glover	July 16,1884 - no date
John B.	d.Oct.31,1937
Barbara A.	Jan.30,1840 - July 17,1912
G.W.	Jan.22,1840 - Jan.19,1907
Cross, Wilbert R.	1939 - 1943
Ethel K.	May 27 - June 18,1909
Rev.R.B.	Jan.7,1829 - Sept.16,1902
---W.	d.1935
Samuel W.	d.Sept.1953, aged 73y7m.
Crussell, Knicely H.	1922 - 1933
Arnold Claude	Jan.6,1913 - Oct.21,1955
Henry M.	June 16,1866 - Feb.17,1933
Sarah E.	May 20,1872 - June 6,1947
Glover, Bettie	Sept.19,1859 - June 24,1913, w/o J.N.
Hoover, Wilsie	June 27,1899 - Nov.27,1935
George	d.May 1917
Jones, James B.	1888 - 1955
Nannie E.	1896 - 1928
Robert L.	1885 - 1954
Jennie E.	1883 - 19--
King, Sarah Effa	Oct.9,1895 - Aug.26,1942
Edward Oliver	Oct.5,1858 - May 2,1945
Nancy Jane	Nov.18,1866 - Oct.30,1946
Malone, Bonnie Kate	no date (fhm)
Chas. P.	1953 (fhm)
Mink, Thomas David	July 24,1952 - Aug.26,1952, s/o Janme & Willie
Phillips, Sudie R.	May 19,1869 - Feb.5,1894
Sarah C.	Feb.14,1845 - May 9,1913, w/o J.E.
J.E.	Aug.27,1841 - Mar.30,1928
Jennie A.	Jan.22,1880 - May 15,1899
Will M.	1869 - June 28,1953, aged 83y11m13d.
Cora E.	1880 -19--
Rutledge, J.W.	1853 - 1935
Smith, Ray Herbert	d.Feb.14,1921
Ida B.	1877 - 1944
John	1874 - 19--
Brenda Lee	Dec.5,1952 - Jan.3,1957
Randy Wayne	May 22,1956 - Jan.3,1957
William D.	1871 - 1950
Nora M.	1878 - 1935
James A.	1873 - 1940
Margaret E.	1879 - 19--
Tester, Ulysses	1908 - no date
Ruby S.	1911 - 1957

Mauk Family Cemetery

Denton, John D.	Apr.26,1894 - May 11,1896
Ethel B.	July 25,1890 - Sept.29,1891
Geisler, James A.	Mar.5,1874 - May 24,1889
Landon Haines	Oct.16,1848 - Jan.21,1929
Mary A. Mauk	July 2,1846 - Nov.2,1913, w/o L.H.
Mahoffey, Infant	b. & d. Apr.22,1910, s/o C.L. & L.B.
Malone, Charles W.	1873 - 1943
David	1841 - 1916
Mary C.	1841 - 1921
Chas. V.	Oct.24-Dec.19,1897, s/o J.T. & M.E.
David E.	Oct.29 - Dec.25,1898,s/o J.T.&M.E.
John T.	1867 - 1946
Mary E.	1878 - 1954
Mauk, Lenna Kate	Apr.13,1892 - Sept.15,1893,d/oH.A. & M.A.
Mrs. M.Emma	Aug.10,1851 - Oct.30,1899
Wm.	July 1, 1823 - Dec.16,1896
Melinda	Feb.13,1818 - Apr.14,1894, w/o Wm.Mauk
George W.	d. June20,186-, aged 2y5m16d,s/o Wm.& M.A.
Infant	couldn't read
Infant	couldn't read
Mary	1830 - 1863
Margaret	Jan.6,1840 - Apr.1,1851
Mahany	1814 - May 27,1863
Infant	d. Oct.19,1879, inf/o E.T. & E.
Emily	d. Oct.24,1879, aged 42 yr.,w/o E.T.Mauk
E.T.	Jan.3,1814 - Apr.25,1879
David	1839 - 1870
Joseph	1835 - 1865
Henry	1786 - 1851
Henry	1826 - 1864
Catherine	1854 - 1899
Miller, E.Kate	Apr.5,1856 - May 20,1886, w/o D.H.Miller
Shipley, Glennie	1888 - 1889
Bruce	1887 - 1890
Rebecca	June 17,1831 - Nov.13,1899
Infant	Feb.22 - Mar.11,1900, d/p J.V.Shipley
Raymond	1885 - 1918
John V.	Jan.13,1857 - no date
Mary C.	Aug.14,1862 - Mar.24,1937
Stanfield, D.J.	Aug.28,1859 - Dec.12,1925
Elbert F.	1896 - 1913
Sarah C.	May 4,1832 - Feb.7,1907, w/o W.M.
W.M.	Dec.13,1828 - OCt.13,1912
Grace E.	Feb.15,1888 - Feb.15,1889,d/o D.J.&H.S.
Mary E.	Nov.8,1861 - Nov.26,1886, d/o Wm.& S.C.
Margaret R.	June 25,1857 - July 3,1887, d/o W.M. & S.C.
Stewart, Joseph H.	OCt.15,1846 - Mar.13,1917

Crumley Cemetery

Still in use, well taken care of.

Adams, Alice Crumley	Sept.7,1903, w/o Isaac Adams
Infant	Sept.26 - Oct.14,1902, inf/o I.A. & A.
William	Oct.11,1900 - Oct.22,1901, s/o I.A. & A.
Birdia A.	June 4,1898 - Feb.20,1900, d/o I.A. & A.
Samuel C. Thurman	Oct.11,1890 - June 23,1891, s/o I.A. & A.
Anney, Rubene	Sept.13,1919 - Sept.4,1906
Andis, John W.	Oct.1,1914 - Mar.23,1959
Lelia M.	Oct.17,1917 -
Archer, Elizabeth J.	1890 - 1963
Boyd, Andy Lee	Mar.28,1899 - Oct.21,1976
Grace Simerly	Feb.7,1905 - Dec.2,1977
Sollie F.	1918 - 1978
Lorena M.	1920 - no date
Paul Donald	Dec.13,1933 - Aug.6,1964
Robert A.	May 24,1874 - Aug.18,1948
Julia Ellen Green	Dec.20,1874 - June 17,1933,w/o S.A.Boyd
Bouton, Cecil	1909 - 1966
Robert T.	1876 - 1955
Jennie A.	1878 - 1924
Infant	Dec.21-23,1910, s/o R.T. & J.E.Bouton.
Wiley C.	MAr.16,1891 - Nov.14,1895, s/o J.M.&F.
Florence	Nov.8,1868 - Dec.21,1894, w/o J.M.
Arthur L.	May 31,1894 - Nov.20,1895, s/o J.M.& F.
John Matthew	May 19,1861 - Dec.9,1939
Charles H.	1917 - 1975
Elizabeth M.	1922 - no date
C.A.	Feb.5,1887 - Dec.24,1910
Buckles, Mary L.	1878 - 1965
James H.	1853 - 1933
Margaret J.	1852 - 1932
Charlie E.	July 6,1899 - Sept.9,1903/5(stone chipped)
Elmer L.	Apr.18,1891 - Aug.30,1900
Broyles. Gene E.	Aug.30,1937 - Dec.26,1937
Nellie R.	July 16,1909 - Oct.10,1983, m.Mar.24,1928.
Thomas C.	1869 - 1948
Laura C.	1877 - 1936
Margie E.	1924 - 1925
Luther	1875 - 1962
Sonia	1893 - 1936
Bowman, Earnest Lee	Feb.19,1923 - Mar.13,1965
Arley H.	Oct.5,1908 - no date
Freda B.	Dec.12,1913 - Nov.20,1969
John J.	Co. L 8 TN.Cav.
Bowery, Trossie M.	1921 - 1967, Mother
Louisa N. Vance	Oct.10,1916 - Feb.1,1982
Berry, Stanley L.	May 16,1887 - Dec.8,1926
Susan N.	June 24,1889 - Sept.8,1968
Barnett, Guy	1898 - 1967
Johnnie	1907 - no date

Crumley Cemetery, cont.

Baker, Robert S.	Nov.18,1883 - Dec.1,1956
Lillie Cox	July 14,1888 - Feb.12,1964
Walter	1887 - 1953
John I.	Mar.21,1919 - July 3,1944
Sylvia	1897 - 1940
Edith	1922 - 1933
Elizabeth	Sept.9,1861 - Aug.11,1930
Jessie	Nov.8,1858 - Dec.3,1929
Elbert	Mar.4,1887 - June 22,1907
Barnett, Margie Lou	1930 - 1930
Buchanan, William E.	1906 - 1970
Maggie W.	1919 - no date
Lafayette	d. Jan.2,1891
Blevins, Mary C.	1860 - 1959
Booher, I.M.	1848 - 1920
Mary C. Crumley	1847 - 1920
Bolling, William Frank	1871 - 1916
Rose Ella	1883 - 1966
Cox, Baby boy	Nov.21-23,1926, s/o Clyde & Nena Cox
Billie Joe	Sept.1,1936 - Sept.4,1951
Clyde	Sept.25,1902 - Mar.11,1971
Nena	June 24,1907 -
Alice D.	1957 (Infant)
Floyd	June 17,1925 - Sept.29,1979,PFC WWII,US Army.
Charles Ernest	1917 - 1972
Combs, W.Arthur	1906 - 1976
Annie P.	1910 - 1984
Coffey, Infant	s/o E.F. & M.E.Coffey
Margaret E.	Dec.11,1876 - May 11,1932
Cornett, Martha D.	1911 - no date
Fred A.	1905 - 1956
William C.	1907 - 1969
Nannie Kate	1909 - 1973
Cawood, Phillip W.	1939 - 1968
Pearl L.	1945 - no date
Alex	July 18,1873 - Sept.26,1935
Ida	Mar.10,1887 - June 29,1968
Donald C.	1936 - 1944, our son
William J.	May 23, 1959, Idaho, Sgt.
Crumley, Sarah Ann	1849 - 1922
Sarah Ann	1848 - 1918
J.Worley	Sept.21,1889 - July 27,1911
W.L.	Sept.20,1888 - June 23,1889,s/o Harm & S.L.
Harmon	Apr.26,1867 - Nov.21,1923
Sarah louise Cornett	July 4,1868 - May 18,1922
Sarah E.	1861 - 1938
J.L.	1851 - 1924
A.Ross	1886 - 1955
J.Carr	1892 - 1925
Martin L.	1898 - 1952
Fred W.,Sr.	1900 - 1974
Martha H.	1898 - 1974
Phillip H.	Oct.14,1827 - Oct.9,1878

Crumley Cemetery, cont.

Crumley,	William C.	Sept.20,1847 - Apr.12,1876
	Isaac D.	d.1876
	Charles T.	July 7,1881 - Mar.21,1885
	Effie B.	Mar.10,1880 - Apr.29,1885
	Joe M.	Mar.17,1883 - May 19,1885
	Lillie E.A.	Apr.18,1888 - Nov.7,1891, d/o J.L. & S.E.
	Gertie M.	Dec.23,1889 - Jan.19,1894,d/o J.L. & S.E.
	Jacob L.,Jr.	July 17,1898 - Feb.19,1900,s/o J.L. & S.E.
	Sarah Ann Jones	Nov.15,1827 - July 16,1890,2nd w/o George
	George	1862 - 1865, s/o George & Sarah .
	William Jacob	1795 - 1865
	Catherine Greer	1792 - 1874, members of Luthern Church.
	George	May 5,1826 - Feb.14,1895, s/o Jacob
	Louisa Jones	Feb.12,1826 - Aug.4,1858,1st w/o George.
	George	Nov.2,1813
	Jane (?)	d.Nov.1,1813, d/o D?W? & Stacey Crumley.
	Joseph L.	MAr.18,1857 - June 23,1858, s/o J.R. & S.
	Henry J.H.	1857 - Dec.14,1857, s/o R.E.& M.
	George Jr.	b.Penn.1769 - 1851
	Selphera	b. NC 1785, member of Lutheran Church.
	George,Sr.	1789, Pioneer Settler of Sullivan Co.,NC/TN.
	Elizabeth	Member of the Lutheran Church.
	Daniel	1766 - 1859, b. in Germany, Lutheran Church, 60 years.
	William	Oct.15,1821 - Mar.20,1887
	Eliza J.	Aug.8,1823 - July 5,1888, d/o Wm.Crumley.
Carrier,	Garrett E.	1897 - 19--
	Vadie Lee	1916 - 1964
	Worley	1941, aged 3 weeks, s/o C.E. & Vadie.
	Calvin	Aug.29,1860 - Nov.12,1933
	Callie	Mar.18,1859 - May 3,1929, w/o C.V.Carrier.
	Joe	1911 - 1980
	F.A.	1928 - no date
	Herchel G.	1916 - 1975
	Bessie V.	1921 - no date
	Lindergh	Sept.21,1927 - Jan.8,1952,TN PFC Co.A.33 Inf. Star of David on gravestone.
	Gertie	Aug.12,1888 - Sept.5,1953
	Cyrus	Jan.29,1884 - Feb.6,1977
	Douglas Glen	Aug.28,1932 - Dct.6,1974
	Lena M.	1896 - 1913
	Andy	1867 - 1942
	Ella	1873 - 1963
	John	Feb.14,1807 - Jan.25,1894
	Mary Morton	Apr.14,1809 - Oct.26,1884
Cole,	Cordelia A. Vance	Oct.8,1875 - May 26,1908, w/o C.A.Cole
	Nancy	1854 - 1922
Carr,	Ralph G.	1904 - 1906
	Cora A.	1893 - 1893
Dean,	George L.	Nov.4,1885 - Oct.12,1927
	John K.	Jan.29,1875 - Mar.1,1924
	Nancy Aleta Cox	Aug.13,1879 - Dec.26,1973
Dunn,	Bruce F.	Mar.26,1896 - Feb.8,1980.PFC US Army WWI.
	Myrtle C.	June 7,1904 - Feb.21,1980

Crumley Cemetery, cont.

Ealey, Infant	b. & d. Jan.4,1909, s/o T.J. & Mattie.
Farley, Robert S.	July 9,1866, aged 3m11d,s/o J.A.&M.C.
Farthing, Mary Riley	Feb.25,1895 - June 29,1957
Green, Juda Simerly	Apr.22,1886 - Feb.24,1919, w/o W.C.Green
H.H.	d.July 28,1907, stone broken.
Ben H.	1888 - 1916
Infant	b. & d. May 16, 1916, s/o S.I.Green.
S.I.	June 13,1873 - Jan.22,1919, age 41y3m9d.
Greene, Neola	Apr.12,1917 - June 24,1918
Jessie E.	Sept.4,1893 - Aug.10,1972
Ossie Lee	June 16,1893 - Apr.18,1980
Larkin M.	Aug.28,1878 - Jan.7,1902
John	OCt.15,1851 - June 11,1909
Sarah F.	Feb.20,1852
Lucinda Trivett	Nov.22,1825 - Nov.12,1917, w/o Larkin Green.
Callie ELiz.	1916 - 1932
Veona I.	1934 - 1934
Armena	1928 - 1938
Ora Lena	1933 - 1936
Virginia Belle	Apr.11,1923 - Mar.27,1959
Claude L.	Nov.8,1897 - Feb.9,1972
Virgie B.	June 15,1899 - Feb.13,1979
Stephen C.	1890 - 1970
Bessie L.	1892 - 1968
Toy M.	1929 - 1930, s/o J.E.Greene.
Solomon	1867 - 1921
Betty	1865 - 1945
Glover, Ethel	1898 - no date
Gene Clifton	Sept.24,1939 - June 3,1961
Thelma S.	1944 - 1984, age 39 y.
James	July 16,1891 - Mar.12,1965
Virgie	May 14,1901 - Jan.21,1981
James	July 16,1892 - May 12,1965
Landon	May 11,1879 - Feb.28,1959
Lula	Aug.13,1886 - no date
Mildred Oleda	1948 - 1981 (fhm)
Earl S.	Dec.28,1905 - Nov.27,1950
John	1848 - 1916
Loyd	June 1,1883 - Feb.5,1908
Lee	Sept.5,1881 - May 29,1906
Nannie	July 10,1874 - Mar.25,1887,d/o John & Sarah
Sarah	1850 - 1937
Thelma	1920 - 1922, d/o Landon & L. Glover.
L.C.	1937 - 1938, s/o Brownie & Ula
Scott E.	Feb.29,1922 - Apr.4,1980
Millie Sweet	Dec.11,1901 - Sept.6,1981
Charlie	June 24,1870 - Mar.24,1940
John	Apr.10,1894 - Jan.20,1961
William P.	1905 - 1972
Lissie	1903 - 1981
Graybeal, Mary Deborah	Dec.8,1955 - Jan.10,1956

Crumley Cemetery, cont.

Guffey, Hugh J.	1908 - 1982 (fhm)
Gentry, William & wife	died Jan.28,17--
Harman, Martha Bouton	Feb.25,1859 - Oct.28,1924, w/o B.F.
Hicks, William E.	1907 - 1980
Ida B.	1912 - 19--
Hartley, Claude L.	1903 - 1967, married Apr.27,1929
Pauline G.	1911 - 19--
Hyatt, Charlie C.	1889 - 1972, m. Nov.15,1921
Lillie Mae	1903 - 19--
James Vernon	1916 - 1964
Hendricks, David H.	Feb.22,1885 - Sept.21,1968
Fannie	Oct.28,1890 - Apr.24,1956
Hatcher, --	1853
Hays, Isabella L.	July 21,1864 - Oct.21,1876, d/o F.M.&C.
Hayes,F.M.	Oct.11,1832 - Oct.1,1900
Charlotte J.	1834 - 1925
Henson, Ellender McBride Harman	1844 - 1924
Harmon, Elder J.M.	June 18,1855 - Oct.2,1917
Martha J.	Mar.7,1853 - Apr.15,1929
John	1880 - 1938
Clara	1880 - 1961
Jenkins, Infant	May 28,1917 - May 28,1917, s/o W.D.Jenkins.
Homer E.	Feb.1,1913 - Oct.26,1918,s/o W.E.&M.E.
Mary E.	Feb.2,1878 - Sept.16,1964
W.Edward	June 6,1878 - Feb.6,1955
Judy Rose	1903 - 1960
Jacob L.	1886 - 1962
J.Monroe	June 8,1842 - Apr.28,1965
Susan L. Godsey	July 8,1850 - Nov.10,1923, w/o J.M.
John	June 22,1879 - May 24,1959
Nannie	May 20,1885 - Nov.16,1957
William David	Nov.5,1880 - Mar.26,1942
Amanda Jane	Jan.20,1888 - Nov.28,1954
James D.	1915 - 1972
Pauline G.	1921 - no date
Howard	Aug.6,1908 - Apr.27,1975
Lucille	Dec.18,1918 - Jan.18,1974
Rosa C.	1900 - 1920
Jones, R.L.	June 6,1865 - Dec.25,1945
Parks Worley	1916 - 1978, PFC US Army WWII.
James E.	1908 - 1979, m.Mar.10,1929
Annie Mae	1911 - 1985
Jack	Feb.15,1936 - Aug.10,1981
Eliza	June 8,1852, aged 43y9d.
Amana G.	1854 - 1926
Susan Northington	Feb.24,1844 - June 18,1880,w/o S.M.Jones.
S.M.	Sept.18,1835 - Dec.28,1905
Lyon, Lillie J.	Dec.18,1892 - Aug.23,1914, w/o A.C.Lyon.
Lingerfelt, Jeffery Dale	Aug.24,1957 - June 30,1976
Ralph	Oct.2,1935 - Aug.3,1937
Elick	Apr.26,1908 - Nov.21,1980
Nannie	Feb.1,1908 - July 23,1962

Crumley Cemetery,cont.

McKinney, Cecil C.	1921 - 1978
Jacob H.	1876 - 1922
Kate T.	1878 - 1950
McQueen, Martha Cawood	1863 - 1940
Morris, Louise N.	1916 - 1982
Miller, Noah	b. & d. 1818, s/o N.M.& Mary Miller.
Mary A. Peters	July 17,1857 - Mar.13,1940, w/o Nathan M.
Nathan M.	Sept.20,1853 - May 2,1941
A.Clark	1888 - 1970
Lillie M.	1891 - 1970
Herbert S.	1913 - 1984
Ruby L.	1913 - no date
W.Edgar	Mar.23,1894 - Dec.17,1961
Celia J.	May 5,1899 - no date
Jennie	Nov.27,1875 - Nov.13,1945
Frank B.	June 27,1874 - Feb.9,1943
Virgie B.	May 12,1907 - Sept.26,1908
Teddie B.	Oct.8,1900 - Aug.17,1901
Mays, Nathaniel N.	1875 - 1931
Martha V.	1875 - 1931
Mottern, Larry Joe	June 12,1952 - Nov.4,1978
Nave, Isaac	Mar.20,1811 - Apr.11,1865
Henry C.	Dec.9,1807 - Apr.9,1865, murdered by so called Union Soldier.
Newton, Will B.	Nov.25,1855 - June 29,1901
Dorcus E. Cornett	Apr.27,1871 - Apr.16,1916,w/o J.M.
K.A.Tennie	May 28,1904 - Feb.10,1923
Willie H.	Nov.29,1897 - July 28,1898, s/o J.M.&D.E.
Eddie	Feb.9,1898 - Jan.23,1985
John M.	1870 - 1946
Vada Ann	1897 - 1978
Robert Lee	Dec.21,1919 - Feb.12.1925
Nichols, Elbert Stewart	Oct.1,1932 - June 27,1933
Duard Andrew	Oct.1,1932 - June 21,1933
John N.	1892 - 1974
Samuel C.	Feb.26,1895 - Apr.12,1983
S.Gladys	Dec.29,1906 - May 17,1979
Charles Wayne	Sept.5,1929 - July 30,1930
B.Bert	Mar.2,1898 - Jan.5,1971
Nellie V.	1901 - 1971
William P.	1887 - 1977
David E.	Nov.8,1929 - June 3,1956,TN A1C USAF WWII.
Julie E.	Apr.11,1954
Steven G.	Oct.26,1958
Jennie B.	July 24,1889 - Feb.24,1978
Martha E.	Oct.25,1884 - Jan.5,1959
Mary E.	Aug.7,1881 - Aug.24,1955
George Bryan	Aug.8,1900 - Nov.14,1902, s/o Elbert & Nannie Nichols.
Elbert	Sept.15,1853 - May 29,1908
Nannie M.	Sept.25,1862 - Jan.11,1921,w/o Elbert.

Crumley Cemetery, cont.

Nickels, David F.	May 31,1848 - Aug.3,1901
Sarah	May 8,1844 - Apr.7,1911
Mary	June 28,1883 - Apr.20,1885, d/o A.& A.C.
Mary	d. July 24,1875, aged 64 yrs.
Andrew	May 18, 1854 - Sept.25,1901
Odell, John M.	1877 - 1937
Nora C.	1881 - 1961
Peny, Infant	b. & d. June 21,1939, s/o George & Thelma.
Reece, Fraher	June 2,1900 - Nov.2,1900, s/o J.I.&S.E.
Richards, D.Arthur	Mar.30,1883 - June 25,1984
Rosa S.	June 15,1888 - Aug.20,1981
Roark, David W.	Oct.3,1892 - May 10,1970, TN Mech US Army.
Rogers, Susan A.	Sept.17,1850 - May 4,1910, age 60
Rogers, Joseph	1883 - 1884, age 18m, s/o J.C.& Susan.
James C.	Dec.19,1858 - Mar.18,1916, age 68
Riley, James Frances	Sept.30,1896 - Nov.25,1966
John A.	Apr.12,1873 - Dec.16,1930
Mary J.	Nov.19,1867 - Feb.16,1947
Jane T.	Dec.11,1845 - Mar.21,1922
Harriet Crumley	Nov.15,1844 - May 8,1905, w/o James T.
Mary E.J.	Dec.25,1868 - Mar.12,1882
Simerly, David M.	1838 - 1903
Judah C.	1843 - 1938
James B.	1885 - 1934
Ernest	1894 - 1918, age 24 yrs.
Clarance	Mar.23,1901 - Oct.13,1918
Cecil	Nov.10,1900 - Feb.22,1920
Leon	Sept. ,1902 - Feb. ,1920
W.B.	Dec.18,1863 - Aug.20,1920
Mollie E.	1878 - 1934
David M. "Dee"	May 21,1916 - Dec.21,1976
Ronald Earl	Mar.4,1905 - Mar.21,1964
Shore, Victor Clifton	1872 - 1952
Sarah Jane	1873
Smith, Charles R.	Nov.25,1904 - Sept.24,1959
June	June 25,1910 - Mar.2,1960
Edgar W.	1896 - 1978, PFC US Army WWI.
Dollie Susan	1903 - 1983
Infant	d.Dec.2,1925,d/o H.V.& Eva Smith
Edell C.	1895 - 1944
Sarah	Jan.31,1824 - Jan.6,1897
Stepp, Wilbie "Jack"	Aug.30,1914 - June 4,1977
Sutter, G.Kaye J.	Mar.3,1938 - Nov.16,1982
Stophel, Elizabeth	Feb.10,1837 - June 16,1919,w/o R.H.Crumley.
Tolbert, Linda Jayne	Aug.15,1945 - May 4,1959
Turner, George	1858 - 1908
Elizabeth	1849 - 1919
Turner	name painted on a wooden cross.
Samuel	1874 - 1932
Vance, Samuel M.	1931, infant.
William L.	1877 - 1940
Cornettie E.	1871 - 1944

Crumley Cemetery, cont.

Vance, Dexter Earl	Jan.14,1906 - Mar.25,1956
Samuel Leander	Jan.19,1859 - July 5,1954
Sarah Ellen	Feb.8,1864 - Nov.12,1940
Sarah L.	Oct.13,1873 - Mar.30,1893
Susan C.	May 27,1851 - May 10,1914, w/oJ.L.Vance.
Jacob	Dec.2,1848 - Jan.4,1882, age 33 yrs.
Infant	s/o Susan C. & Jacob L. Vance
Isaac	1822 - 1899
Susan V.	1834 - 1913
Webb, Susannah	Dec.3,1833 - Feb.23,1916, w/o Benjamin F.
Benjamin F.	Aug.27,1831 - Jan.5,1915
Chara L.	Apr.15,1895 - Aug.2,1896, d/o M.E.& L.C.
Infant	b. & d. Jan.20,1904, d/o M.E. & L.C.
Fred Raymond	Sept.16,1901 - Aug.22,1902, s/o M.E.&L.C.
Ruby Lynn	July 18, 1910 - Feb.20,1916,d/o M.E.& L.C.
Mike E.	Aug.23,1870 - Aug.24,1957
Louisa Odell	Nov.25,1874 - Nov.24,1925
William A.	1864 - 1934, aged 70 yrs.
Elizabeth E.	1866 - 1927, aged 61 yrs.
Walter J.	Jan.18,1900 - Mar.31,1983
Maxie L.	Jan.6,1898 - no date
William M.	May 5,1961, infant
Novella J.	Aug.10,1924 - May 21,1984
Fred Thomas	1934 - 1949
Walsh, Lillie	Sept.16,1891 - Oct.20,1911
Wenny, Martha E.	d.Aug.19,1851, 16y 6m 3d.
Woodring, Daniel	Feb.12,1852 - May 11, 1924
Julia	Jan.30,1871 - Dec.21,1921

Immanuel Church Cemetery

Booher, Catharine E.	Jan.11,1829 - Mar.22,1893
Cassidy, Margaret E. Hodge	1879 - 19668, w/o Dr.H.H.Cassidy.
Droke, Alice J.	1858 - 1927
Jacob S.	1864 - 1929
Gaines, W.H.H.	July 16,1836 - May 14,1910, Erected to his memory by the Sullivan County Sunday School Association whom he faithfully served as its Secretary from 1870 to 1910.
Gena Isabel	1889 - 1893, d/o W.H.H.& A,M.Gaines.
Harr, Martin	1813 - 1902
Seneker, Amanda Maria	1853 - 1934, w/o W.H.H.Gaines
Wolford, Elkanah D.	Oct.25,1832 - Nov.27,1910
Frances V. Cain	Apr.13,1842 - Jan.9,1931
Amanda M. Bushong	Jan.16,1833 - Jan.8,1897
Wolfford, William J.	Dec.12,1861 - Oct.26,1938
Amanda E. Steele	Mar.25,1863 - May 14,1937
Joseph I.	May 17,1870 - June 21,1888
Rev. W.G.	Sept.4,1842 - July 31,1919
Susan P.	June 2,1841 - Sept.10,1902, w/o W.G.

Old Droke Cemetery

Akard, Lucy Emily	Dec.13,1865 - Nov.28,1874, d/o John & E.M.
Joseph Hancher	Dec.11,1882 - Feb.17,1883, s/o A.B. & N.B.
Barr, Ester Droke	May 13,1866 - May 19,1920, w/o S.E.Barr.
Isaac Edward	Aug.10,1902 - June 7,1904, s/o S.E.& Ester.
Clark, Emaline C. Rodefer	Sept.26,1844 - Jan.11,1886, w/o J.H.
Benjamin E.	Feb.12,1877 - Mar.13,1877, s/o J.H.& E.C.
Droke, Susannah E.	Apr.24 - 29, 1885, d/o A.J.& S.D.
Sarah Catherine	Aug.26,1844 - Mar.4,1887, w/o A.J.Droke.
Susan C.	Jan.7,1863 - June 28,1880, d/o I.D. & E.G.
Isaac D.	May 27,1838 - Feb.13,1923, m. Mar.9,1862
Emaline G. Horne	Feb.6,1842 - Mar.1,1923
Infant	d.Jan.3,1863, d/o J.M. & S.M. Droke.
Harr, Infant	d.Aug.30,1877, d/o S.W. & L.C. Harr.
John S.	Jan.25,1791 - Feb.2,1852
Lydia	Feb.14,1789 - Apr.25,1860, w/o John S.Harr.
Joseph	d.Nov.9,1822, aged 23y7m15d.
John	Apr.25,1800 - Dec.25,1871
Elizabeth	Sept.2,1808 - Dec.9,1892
Smith, N.T.D.	Nov.30,1860 - Aug.16,1882
Susie E.	Dec.14,1858 - Oct.31,1859, d/o G.W. & M.S.
Snapp, Infant	d.Mar.28,1888, s/o J.B. & L.C. Snapp.

Groseclose Cemetery

Bolton, Martha	d.June 3,1863, aged 43y10m.
Catherine	Oct.26,1780 - Apr.2,1842, w/o Noah
Cleek, Mary	July 20,1801 - Aug.9,1884, w/o J.J.
Dillard, D.D.	1868 - Apr.8,1910
Gibson, Jeremiah	Jan.11,1841 - Oct.4,1888
Margaret Elizabeth Kinkead	Sept.15,1841 - Aug.27,1912
Green, J.W.	d.Apr.15,1864, aged 1y17d., s.o J.N.& A.
Groseclose, Susan Cassell	Apr.16,1827, b. Mythe Co.,VA,w/o Joseph.
Joseph	Oct.2,1816 - Aug.8,1890, b. Smyth Co.,VA.
James Wythe	June 14,1902 - Apr.15,1903, s/o J.W. & L.A.
Hamblin, Margaret	June 8,1840 - Feb.17,1913, w/o J.H.
Lamkins, Margaret	Sept.15,1848 - June 14,1905, w/o Samuel
Lamkins, Samuel	Jan.9,1841 - Dec.10,1914
McCluer, Lucinda Margaret	d.Jan.4,1847
Neil, James C.	Sept.12,1866 - Jan.27,1919
Nelms, Anna W.	Nov.19,1818 - Apr.5,1865
Pierce, Judith	d.May 24,1830, aged 64y.
Sumner, Lizzie	June 8,1878 - Dec.19,1896, d/o A.L.& S.A.
Vaughn, Marie A.	Aug.15,1849 - Sept.25,1916, w/o Harmon

Old Salem Methodist Church Cemetery

Anderson, Reeve S.	1894 - no date
George A.	1880 - 1940
Samuel L.	May 29,1873 - Sept.19,1886, s/o J.R.& R.
James H.	Nov.13,1868 - Sept.26,1895, s/o J.R.& R.
Alzada E.	July 10,1876 - Oct.19,1934,d/o John R. & Rebeca L. Anderson.
Rebecca Lessley	Nov.4,1844 - Jan.1,1926, w/o John R.
John R.	Mar.26,1846 - July 25,1895
Barr, Isaac A.	Jan.19,1850 - Jan.15,1928, m.Aug.8,1872
Mary A.	May 6,1848 - May 14,1932
Fannie Elizabeth	Aug.26,1880 - Oct.7,1919, d/o I.A. & M.A.
Manerva Smith	May 24,1824 - July 9,1906, w/o James E.
James	Aug.2,1883 - June 24,1931
Bear, James E.	Jan.30,1824 - Aug.23,1887
Byrd, S.C.	Sept.13,1857 - Apr.27,1894, w/o Rev.S.K.
Rev.Samuel K.	Sept.27,1854 - June 8,1923
Horace E.	Aug.9,1878 - Apr.17,1897, aged 18y8m8d.
Carter, Mary Salley	Aug.20,1843 - July 30,1886, w/o E.H.
George H.	July 5,1870 - Mar.17,1891,s/o E.H.& Mary
Clark, ---	no dates
Clark, ---	no dates
Cole, J.A.G.	Aug.9,1835 - Aug.15,1909
Naomi A.Smith	Sept.18,1843 - Mar.2,1917
Elizabeth Folkner	May 7,1865 - Feb.7,1929, w/o John H.
Joseph J.	Dec.14,1891 - Apr.1,1942
John H.	May 22,1867 - Feb.27,1948
Droke, Mary C.	Feb.18,1863 - Aug.26,1890, w/o E.M.Droke.
Nancy A.	Apr.22,1822 - Aug.3,1894, w/o E.L.Droke.
E.M.	Oct.27,1851 - Jan.4,1913
Goforth, Easter Eatmon	Aug.25,1833 - Jan.1,1906, w/o David
Hamilton, Elizabeth Bear	Aug.23,1851 - Feb.10,1911, m.June 3,1894, w/o H.H.Hamilton.
Harvey H.	Jan.1,1872 - Sept.22,1926
Hicks, Wm.Henry	Dec.11,1848 - Jan.10,1906
Alzader E.	June 9,1847 - July 26,1890, w/o W.H.Hicks.
Huffman, Noah A.	1876 - 1949
William D.	Apr.19,1844 - May 25,1919
Rubin	July 17,19-- , aged 8y11m6d.
William D.	Apr.19,1844 - May 25,1919
Hutchens, Mary O.	Oct.4,1852 - Aug.10,1929, w/o W.D.Huffman.
Jackson, Mary Mauk	Nov.18,1788 - July 8,1824, aged 35 yrs., m.Dec.4,1808, w/o J.J.Jackson.
Jordan, Gilmar W.	July 4,1897 - Jan.30,1918, s/o Shan & Sallie.
Keys, Henry Spurgeon	Sept.27,1884 - Apr.28,1948
Hazel Lessley	Dec.2,1898 - no date
Lessley, Mollie E. Smith	Feb.2,1868 - May 1,1931, w/o John J.
John J.	Dec.16,1852 - Jan.14,1911
Andrew, Sr.	Sept.21,1796 - Feb.23,1858
Catherine	Jan.5,1813 - Dec.29,1893, w/o A.Lessley,Sr.
Andrew, Jr.	Feb.8,1818 - Oct.17,1871
Mary Jane	Feb.13,1833 - July 30,1903, w/o Andrew,Jr.
Lewis Augustus	Mar.28,1858 - Oct.4,1862,s/o A. & M.J.
Lewis H.	1840 - 1926, s/o Andrew & Catherine Shaver Lessley.
McGhee, Lydia A.	Nov.7,1889 - Apr.18.1957

Old Salem Methodist Church Cemetery

Morrell, William T.	Dec.3,1870 - Sept.8,1891
Samuel R.	June 23,1872 - July 31,1958
Margaret E.	Sept.26,1873 - Apr.11,1922
Harold Davis	b. & d. Feb.16,1944
Jonathan	Aug.17,1814 - Aug.8,1891, aged 82y11m21d.
Joe Willard	Feb.8,1937 - Feb.6,1947
Patton, Ellen L.	Mar.28,1861 - Sept.5,1890
Pope, George W.	Mar.27,1849 - Dec.5,1929,m. Nov.11,1883
Barbara P. Winkles	June 5,1860 - June 29,1927
Salyer, Maude C.	1903 - no date
Roy D.	1898 - no date
Slaughter, N.	Sept.9,18-- - ---31,1936
Smith, W.Henry	May 10,1860 - Oct.25,1895
Welsh, Claude Stanley	Dec.21,1900 - Feb.14,1901, s/o J.D. & Nannie A.
Wilson, J.E.	1857 - 1930
Juda A.	1858 - 1917
Juda A.	May 23,1858 - May 17,1917, m.Oct.1,1882, w/o J.E.Wilson, d/o A.J. & Malinda Smith.
Mary L.E.	1886 - 1932, aged 46yrs.
Thomas O.	July 31,1883 - Aug.7,1949
James C.	1932, aged 22 days.

Old Harr Cemetery

| Hancher, Rev. Wm. | d.Sept.5,1870, aged 82 yrs, less 2 days |
| Sarah | July 25,1792 - Mar.4,1833 |

Here lies 3 infant sons of W. & Elizabeth Hancher and an infant daughter of
W. & Sarah Hancher.

Surrounded by an iron fence-

Harr, Mary J.	Mar.17,1822 - July 27,1865, w/o David
David E.	Aug.31,1853 - Aug.29,1867, s/o David & Mary.
E.H.	Nov.4,1847 - Sept.6,1884
Lane, J.E.	Nov.29,1866 - Apr.23,1936
Cora Lee	May 27,1873 - June 16,1905, w/o J.E.Lane.
J.Frank	Jan.24,1900 - June 8,1901, s/o J.E. & C.L.
Infant	b. & d. Aug.7,1888, d/o J.E. & C.L.
Lane, Georg F.	1871 - 1915
Ada M.	1876 - 1944
Susan G.	July 8,1839 - Apr.1,1895, w/o Wm.J.Lane.
Wm.J.	May 17,1832 - Sept.11,1898
Wolford, Mary A.	d.July 4,1848, 17y3m, w/o David Wolford.

Old Baptist Cemetery

Galloway, Marshall	Apr.28,1813 - May 25,1867
Holt, S.F.	Jan.2,1870
Hull, Lavina L.	Dec.27,1816 - Sept.27,1886

Fain Family Cemetery

Marble Memorial Marker:

In memory of Thomas & Rachel Fain, who came to this section in 1840, naming
it Arcadia, set aside this spot for the family cemetery. Erected by Mack L.
& Mary Fain Hicks.

Fain Family Cemetery , cont.

Fain, Thomas	July 31,1809 - Mar.25,1891
Rachel	May 27,1814 - July 10,1884, w/o Thomas
Hugh Lot	Apr.20,1879 - July 1,1903
Ellen E.	July 27,1876 - Feb.9,1905
John R.	d.Apr.13,1930, TN Sgt.321 Inf 81 Div.
Samuel Perry	Dec.19,1892 - Jan.22,1919, s/o Samuel Anderson & R.Jennie H. Fain.
Samuel Anderson	May 25,1847 - Dec.24,1906, s/o Thomas & Rachel A. Fain.
Rachel Jennie	Dec.31,1854 - July 14,1928, d/o Henry C. & Sarah J.Hicks.
Hugh	Jan.20,1844 - Feb.18,1896, s/o Thomas & Rachel Anderson Fain.
Hannah A.	July 26,1849 - Mar.25,1887
Amelia Elizabeth	July 7,1854 - Feb.6,1855, d/o Thomas & Rachel Fain.
Thomas George	Aug.4,1856 - Mar.16,1862, s/o Thos. & Rachel Fain.
3 infants	no dates, inf/o S.A. & R.J. Fain.
Lella Jane Lynn	Mar.7,1880 - Oct.6,1884, d/o Will. H. & Alice Spurgeon Fain.
Thomas	Aug.23,1877 - Sept.2,1878, s/o W.H. & A.S.
Gunning, Infant	no dates, great grandchild of Thom.& Rachel.
Hicks, Mack Lynn,Sr.	June 26,1876 - Sept.14,1949, s/o Wesley Fletcher & Caroline G. Hicks,m.Nov.28,1903.
Mary Rachel Fain	Mar.22,1882 - Mar.26,1957, d/o Samuel Anderson & R.Jennie Fain.
Lynn, Mattie J.	June 26,1860 - Jan.1,1883, w/o Dr.J.M.Lynn.
Ellen R.	Mar.24,1838 - Apr.21,1876, w/o John G. Lynn, d/o Thos. & Rachel Fain.
Smith, Stephen	Oct.3,1826 - June 20,1860

Section reserved for family slaves:

"Aunt Beck"	colored	Ben	colored
"Uncle Jack"	colored	"Uncle George"	colored

Walker's Fork Baptist Church Cemetery

Copied by James Thomas Dykes, 9 March 1985. The Church was established in 1847 and is still used.

Arnold, Thomas Arter	Nov.14,1884 - Apr.4,1959
Beady E. Phillips	Mar.24,1880 - Feb.17,1942
Barrett, Joseph N.	1887 - 1949
Minnie Pearl	1892 - 1959
Roy T.	July 27,1931 - Aug.30,1981
Martha W.	Mar.9,1935 - no date
Benton, Jack	1962 - 1962 (fhm)
Boyd, Tommy E.	1950 - 1950 (fhm)
Michael	1958 - 1958 (fhm)
Bragg, Robert M.	May 31,1892 - July 29,1975
Mellie P.	Jan.8,1905 - Jan.9,1979
Peggy E.	May 8,1938 - Sept.17,1980
Sam C.	Dec.17,1908 - June 2,1974
Ethel J.	Sept.6,1916 - no date
Jerry R.	Oct.4,1941 - Sept.9,1980
Robert Franklin	Nov.30,1866 - Nov.9,1955

Walker's Fork Baptist Church

Bragg, Sallie Light	Jan.5,1873 - June 30,1947, m. Nov.7,1889 to R.F.Bragg.
Tom	Nov.26,1903 - Aug.1,1973
Carlton M.	Oct.5,1914 - Aug.18,1953
Colin K.	Jan.15 - Feb.8,1942
Geneva	Jan.6-June 1,1940
Jeannette	Jan.6 - 21,1940
Mary E. Hickman	Feb.3,1859 - Feb.8,1940
Leman	Feb.3,1872 - May 10,1880, s/o G.W. & Nancy Bragg.
James A.	Feb.11,1887 - Sept.6,1899,s/o G.W.& Nancy.
George Huston	Aug.25,1883 - July 25,1906, s/o G.W.& N.
William H.	Mar.3,1854 - Nov.1860, s/o T.&.B.Bragg.
Rachel	Feb.22,1817 - Dec.2,1903
Guy	1900 - 1954
Flossie	1910 - no date
Chase, Clyde E.	Dec.9,1913 - Aug.20,1955,TN.Cpl. 1 Depot Unit AF WWII.
Clark, Connie Lue	July 17,1952, d/o Frank & Lena Clark.
Frank	Jan.17,1921 - Mar.30,1976, US Army WWII.
Lena P.	1918 - no date
Coates, Henry Wesley	1871 - 1955
Collins, Mary Grace	Oct.22,1928 - June 12,1956,w/o Will Collins, d/o Norman & Lora Lucas.
Conkin, Patsy Sue	July 12,1951
Bighie H.	1908 - 1981
Stella O.	1911 - 1955
Samuel Jeff	June 30,1913 - no date
Lydia Babb	Jan.30,1923 - Mar.5,1966
Carson F.	Aug.13,1914 - Dec.22,1980
Mary D.	Feb.12,1913 - no date
Samuel Houston	1867 - 1952
Mary Jane	1872 - 1955
Lillie Lee	May 5,1916 - July 31,1950
Major C.	1911 - 1961
Ollie G.	1911 - no date
Connie June	June 6,1946 - Mar.29,1947
Sena Nelson	Dec.29,1867 - Apr.20,1954, w/o J.K.P.
Earnest	Mar.13,1922 - June 15,1944, PFC, Co.C, 120 Inf. 30th Div.WWII
Rosie Lee	May 5,1932 - June 5,1932
Clara Lucile	Nov.13 - Dec.26,1930
Noah H.	June 16,1879 - May 10,1960, m.Dec.25,1907,
Martha H.	Apr.1,1889 - Oct.15,1979
John Noble	1877 - 1942
Sarah Annie	1878 - 1959
Daisey	Mar.7,1913 - Aug.29,1919, d/o N.C. & A.
Glen Rufus	Aug.4,1916 - July 3,1918,s/o N.C.& A.
Lida	Spet.19,1908 - Apr.7,1909
Thomas	Jan.18,1867 - Sept.17,1868
Ramon	Sept.24-29,1907
George W.	Dec.17,1871 - Mar.2,1939
Leeaner	Oct.21,1881 - June 5,1928

Conkin, W.J.	Apr.30,1841; enrolled Nov.15,1861, Co.B,4th Reg.TN Cav.
Elizabeth J.	Jan.7,1840 - May 25,1911
Cox, Patsy Ruth	1934 - 1981 (fhm)
Crawford, William (Bill)	July 1,1905 - Aug.7,1971
Lena C.	May 18,1911 - no date
Byrd	1901 - 1968 (fhm)
Ellis Ira	Apr.25,1913 - Jan.2,1973
Edith Marie	May 20,1921
George Rice	1882 - 1953 (fhm)
Altha	Apr.15,1965 - Nov.19,1907, w/o W.M.
Pvt. Harry	Oct.5,1922 - July 17,1944
Depew, Conrad Jerome	1954 -1956
Duncan, Nancy E.	Oct.15,1850 - July 6,1919, w/o S.P.
Dykes, Lisa Rena	Oct.19,1965
Flanary, Mamie C.	Apr.25,1902 - June 14,1937
Hickman, Joseph	Dec.5,1855 - Apr.24,1897
Thomas	Jan.15,1886 - Sept.13,1915, s/o J.& L.
Mandy J.	Jan.15,1886 - Mar.18,1893
Jobe, Floyd	May 11,1920 - July 11,1980
Lola B.	Oct.8,1917
Roy C.	Aug.28,1913 - Apr.8,1978
Ruby B.	May 14,1916
James B.	Oct.4,1867 - Dec.9,1936, Masonic Emblem.
Rachel Ann	May 22,1874 - Mar.24,1940
W.M.	Apr.12,1873 - Jan.30,1936, Masonic Emblem.
Clyde T.C.	Oct.28,1895 - July 26,1919, s/o W.M. & R.C.
Kyle	Aug.9,1913 - July 17,1918,s/o W.B.Jobe.
Mack	July 10,1877 - Feb.10,1927
Minnie B. Hickman	Dec.2,1895 - Mar.10,1917, w/o Mack Jobe, d/o J. & M.E.Hickman.
Light, Bill	1904 - 1984 (fhm)
Lucas, Norma Jean	1932 - 1937
G.Norman	Sept.18,1901 - Mar.10,1968
Lora B.	Nov.26,1905 - Mar.8,1968
Melear, Rev.William Elbert	Nov.10,1867 - Feb.20,1952, An Ordained Minister for 64 yrs.
Miner, Danny Michael	Nov.20,1955 - Mar.4,1973
Morelock, Ellis C.	1888 - 1965, m. Nov.22,1911
Etta S.	1893 - 1970
Mullenix, Quillen H.	1918 - 1949
Stacey J.	1913 - no date
John H.	1890 - 1891
Mullins, Alma R.	Apr.1,1909 - Feb.4,1955
Rossie	1910 - 1976 (fhm)
Glen T.	July 16,1921 - May 11,1979,Cp.US Army WWII, mar. Dec.30,1944
Evelyn M.	May 19,1925 - no date
Mary C.	Jan.18,1905 - Feb.8,1934

Walker's Fork Baptist Church Cemetery, cont.

Overbay, Rose	1915 - 1958 (fhm)	
Oscar	1906 - 1962 (fhm)	
Delbert K.	Apr.24,1901 - no date	
Fannie C.	Oct.14,1913 - Apr.6,1983	
Infant Loyd J.	Apr.20,1932	
Overbey, Joe J.	1878 - 1957	
Loucreaty Ward	1866 - 1933, w/o J.J.Overbey.	
William Thomas	1876 - 1938	
Laura Murrell	1867 - 1939	
Patterson, Annie J.	1913 - 1980 (fhm)	
Phillips, Onnie	Sept.1,1901 - Mar.30,1960	
Georgia	July 8,1909 - no date	
George W.	1878 - 1951	
Nancy E.	1881 - 1969	
James	1887 - 1976	
Edna	1884 - 1952	
G.K.	Mar.14,1927 - Sept.20,1946, Enlisted US Navy-Oct.1,1945,Disch. Aug.6,1946.	
George W.	Aug.6,1896 - June 30,1966, Veteran WWI.	
Ora K.	Feb.26,1901 - no date	
Victoria V.	May 22,1916 - Feb.4,1936	
Rosie B.	Sept.10,1911 - Nov.14,1914,d/o J.M. & N.E.	
Mary	Dec.4,1908 - Nov.11,1909, d/o G.W.&N.E.	
Oma May	June 3,1895 - Apr.6,1900	
W.J.	July 19,1856 - June 9,1926	
Rachel	Aug.15,1856 - Apr.9,1915, w/o W.T.Phillips, d/o T. & Rachel Bragg.	
Stout, Virgil	Jan.14,1933 - Nov.6,1954, TN.PVT.HO Co., 502 ABN Inf.	
Yakley, Larry Gene	1947 - 1975, SP 5 US Army	
Lynn	May 22,1953 - Dec.5,1954	
J.W.	July 30,1945 - Nov.16,1951	

Beidleman Presbyterian Cemetery

Bebber, Franklin M.	Apr.13,1909 - May 31,1940
Booher, Ruth	1940 - 1945
Campbell, Flora E.	1888 - 1956
Duncan, Enoch M.	1882 - 1959
Ona I.	1886 - no date
Gammon, Minnie	Apr.17,1878 - Sept.8,1939, w/o Charles W.Witcher.
Horner, Mary Edith	July 2,1926 - Oct.10,1946
Moore, Martin M.	Aug.6,1861 - Mar.3,1941
Osborne, Abbot A.	1884 - 1939
Ollis, M.Perlo	1898 - 1942
B.Pearl	1903 - 1946
Rosenbalm, Martha	1882 - 1963
William Isaac	1878 - 1942
Stophel, Elbert W.	1857 - 1949
Rosa Belle	1867 - 1945
Susan & Lucy Jane	1873 - 1960
Owen A.	1870 - 1949
Smith, Lucy Jane	1883 - 1963
Watkins, William E.	1875 - 1954
Margaret M.	1887 - 1966

Steele Cemetery

Booher, Benjamin P.	June 3,1844 - Mar.27,1936, Conf.Soldier imprisoned in Maryland, walked home.m. Feb.23,1871.
Martha A. Crumley	Nov.14,1849 - Apr.14,1928
Lee R.E.	d.Feb.13,1876, aged 3y11d,s/o B.P. & M.A.
Robert W.	June 11,1927 - Nov.14,1932, s/o Jim & Roxie Booher.
Sarah A. Steele	July 16,1822 - Feb.24,1900, w/o James.
James	Aug.26,1818 - June 15,1905
Crawford, Anna	July 23,1841 - Mar.25,1916
Charlie	Dec.7,1866 - Jan.29,1893
Nettie	Apr.25,1875 - July 15,1893
Dishner, S.L.	1877 - 1944
Gibson, Penelope M.E.Moore	Mar.9,1854 - Jan.17,1902, w/o L.B.Gibson.
Haga, Clint	Aug.6,1905 - Apr.9,1906, s/o J.W.& M.
Dewey	July 17,1900 - Apr.27,1912,s/o John & Minnie.
Therman	July 17,1899 - Aug.19,1899, s/o J.W. & M.
Hunt, Lila Kate	Oct.23,1907 - June 24,1908, d/o M.L.&E.J.
Lemons, Marva Lanter	Apr.4,1835 - Oct.18,1906, m. Dec.1,1859, w/o A.Lemons.
Moore, Martha Maud	May 23,1882 - June 28,1922, w/o George E. Moore, d/o J.T. & Althea Moore.
Leonidas Levi	June 4,1883 - Apr.5,1918, s/o J.T.&Althea.
James T.	Feb.19,1859 - Jan.3,1903
Althea E. Gibson	Jan.18,1863 - June 15,1953, w/o J.T.Moore.
Levi	Nov.3,1831 - Oct.15,1904
Martha A. Denny	Aug.22,1833 - July 5,1904, w/o Levi Moore.
Steel, David	d.Dec.23,1849, 65 yrs.
Mary	Oct.25,1788 - Apr.12,1864
Steele, Henry	d.Mar.10,1857, aged 40y1m23d.
Elizabeth J.	Sept.21,1830 - Mar.28,1895, w/o Henry.
Wolford, Edwin L.	Oct.11,1878 - Aug.23,1960
Jennie B.	Apr.28,1881 - July 12,1968, d/o B.P.& M.A.

Roller's Memorial Church Cemetery
also known as **Cox Chapel.**

Aiken, Abraham	July 12,1797 - Apr.26,1876
Barger, Annie C.	May 1,1870 - July 5,1937, w/o J.T.Barger.
John Thomas	June 25,1870 - Feb.13,1945
G.J.	July 21,1867 - Nov.23,1924
Susan A.	Apr.12,1872 - Aug.31,1920, w/o G.J.Barger
Annie Mae	Jan.22 - 24, 1923, d/o E.G.&P.P.Barger.
Goldie A.	1904 - 1905
Cordelia Barker	1879 - 1905
William W.	1877 - 1950
Infant	b. & d. Apr.8,1899, s/o S.E.&F.E. Barger.
Mary E. Fleenor	July 30,1863 - July 29,1929,w/o J.W.Barger.
Jacob W.	July 26,1872 - Oct.12,1943
Samuel E.	1876 - 1926
Flora E.	1877 - 1957
Charles H.	1881 - 1945
Bettie C.	1879 - 1959

Barger, Anna Hickman	Oct.29,1799 - Oct.7,1876, w/o John Barger,Sr.
John, Sr.	Nov.1,1797 - Sept.15,1859
F.W.G.	Jan.28,1835 - Aug.29,1880, m.July 11,1858.
Adeline	June 22,1839 - Nov.26,1927
Amanda	Sept.25,1845 - Nov.25,1883, w/o Geo. W. Barger, d/o G.&. E. Roller.
Nancy	Mar.24,1824 - Aug.20,1901
Charlotte H.	Feb.16,1819 - May 16,1881
George W.	Mar.25,1841 - Dec.13,1920
Booher, Nancy Belle Rodgers	Feb.10,1867 - Dec.20,1929
Bridwell, Jesse Elbert	1868 - 1933
Mary Elizabeth	1872 - 1947
Sarah Holt	Jan.31,1834 - Jan.26,1924, w/o Sanford
Sanford, Jr.	Dec.2,1831 - Oct.22,1900
Norvella M.	May 1-9, 1903, d/o R.J.& I.B.Bridwell.
Mary E.	July 19,1866 - June 20,1888
Bullis, Ida R. Susong	Dec.18,1879 - Mar.14,1910, w/o J.D.Bullis.
Bessie C.	Mar.24,1901 - Oct.29,1909, d/o J.D.& S.E.
Sarah E.Susong	July 5,1868 - Jan.31,1906
Cox, Florence E. Holt	Jan.5,1857 - May 8,1890
Gracie	Oct.21,1889 - Nov.26,1892, d/o Wm.& F.Cox.
William	Dec.15,1849 - Sept.13,1905
Mellie M.	d.Jan.9,1906, aged 61 yrs.
Dixon, Rachel	no dates.
John	no dates
Eakins, Eliza E.	Apr.7,1819 - Mar.10,1883, w/o Abraham Eakins.
Erwin, Juletta H.	Jan.19,1817 - Oct.20,1854
James	Jan.5,1813 - Jan.30,1885
Ford, James	Apr.10,1834 - Feb.6,1902
Galloway, C.Richard	Feb.1838 - Dec.1910
Hauk, Nancy	d.Nov.20,1862, aged 58 yrs.
Andrew	d.Jan.31,1887, aged 81y4m17d.
Robert	Jan.17,1830 - Mar.26,1884
Sarah Ann	Feb.17,1835 - Feb.7,1887, w/o R.R.Hauk.
Edith V.	May 1,1886 - Nov.5,1894
Edna E.	Mar.20,1885 - no date
James S.	Mar.11,1858 - Jan.19,1941
Francis E.	Nov.12,1853 - Aug.8,1862
Hawley, Elizabeth	d.Aug.7,1841, aged 44y3,6d.,w/o William.
Eldridge B.	Mar.10,1849 - June 27,1850
Margaret E.	Feb.11,1847 - Sept.28,1918, d/o John & Barbara Hawley.
John	Feb.27,1819 - May 24,1884
Barbara C.	May 10,1822 - Oct.24,1895, w/o John.
Hays, Infant	d.June 14,1910, s/o G.C.Hays.
Edward H.	Jan.10 - 13,1915
Robert G.	Aug.17-19,1916
Robert R.	Sept.17,1835 - Mar.4,1902
Elizabeth J.	May 25,1837 - June 23,1886, w/o Robert R.
Hendrickson, Ann E.	Jan.27,1877 - Sept.1,1878, d/o J.M.& L.E.
Hickman, Charles B.	Sept.1,1940 - June 9,1941

Roller's Memorial Church Cemetery, cont.

Holt, John N.   July 24,1887 - May 15.1954
      Maxie M.   no dates
      George J.   Spt.6,1879 - Jan.15,1919
      W.A.   May 13,1849 - Mar.6,1910
      L.E.   May 4,1854 - Mar.2,1910
      Sarah F.   June 2,1875 - Jan.4,1876, d/o W.A & L.E.
      Margaret E.   Apr.13,1818 - Mar.1842,, w/o Jacob Holt
      George W.   July 20,1860 - Dec.4,1891
      J.B.   Jan.12,1859 - May 12,1920
      J.   aged 62 yrs.
      C.D.   aged 35 yrs.
      Martha A.   d.Sept.27,1856, aged 5y9m5d., d/o Jacob Holt.
      Elizabeth   July 10,1826 - Jan.22,1899, w/o John Holt
      John   Spet.13,1820 - Feb.27,1898
      Barbara   May 31,1835 - Aug.7,1895, w/o James Holt.
      James,Sr.   Dec.22,1826 - Jan.8,1893
      M.E.   Mar.8,1889 - Nov.11,1892,s/o J.W. & L.I.
      John Wesley   Oct.1,1853 - July 6,1898
      Lavenia I.   Oct.31,1858 - Oct.25,1909
      Amanda C.   May 15,1850 - May 12,1851,d/o Jno. & E.
      James E.   Oct.19,1861 - June 16,1928
      Mary C.   1863 - 1939
      James H.   Sept.6,1840 - Feb.18,1899, m. Jan.23,1867.
      Mary A. Horn   Aug.21,1847 - Feb.9,1922
Holts, Elizabeth M.Lots   Sept.3,1832 - Sept.6,1898,w/o George,Sr.
Isley, Donnie Gene   1957 - 1958
      Emma   1849 - 1908
Lamberth, W.C.   July 13,1846 - Sept.14,1900
        M.Ella   June 16,1881 - June 25,1902
        Mollie A. Lanter   Dec.8,1844 - July 16,1925,w/o W.Z.Lamberth
        E.D.   Mar.24,1860 - Sept.14,1930
Necessary, Timberlake   1939
        Imogene   b. & d. Sept.4,1948
Nuckols, Mary Alice   July 6,1855 - May 10,1902
Nuckolls, Richard   May 9,1831 - Aug.28,1910
        Mary A.F.   Feb.19,1831 - Apr.18,1897, consort of Richard
Peoples, Elizabeth M.   Nov.8,1843 - July 12,1872
Rainey, Jess   1869 - 1953
        Laura B.   1875 - 19--
Robinson, Lula Belle   1880 - 1960
        Gregory Allen   1959 - 1959
        Infant   1953 - 1953
Rodgers, Edgar L.   Jan.5,1921 - Jan.7,1921,s/o E.S.& S.P.
        James B.   Apr.20,1922 - Jan.12,1923
        Rev.John Barger   July 9,1854 - Dec.20,1929
        Mellie A. Watkins   July 29,1857 - no date
        Margaret Ann   Dec.16,1862 - Apr.3,1936
        Emanual S.   1877 - 1957
        Sophia P.   1877 - 19--
        Emery Lee   Dec.19,1890 - Jan.15,1891, s/o P.K.& E.C.
        George A.   June 28,1868 - Feb.12,1889, s/o Jos.& Margaret
        David   Apr.1,1857 - Dec.26,1860, s/o Jos. & Margaret
        Joseph S.   Apr.17,1858 - Oct.15,1862,s/o Jos.& Margaret

Roller's Memorial Church Cemetery,cont.

Rodgers, Polly C.	June 19,1865 - May 9,1866, d/o Jos.& Marg.
Joseph	Dec.20,1828 - Nov.18,1909, m. Oct.13,1853
Margaret Barger	Sept.9,1832 - Nov.22,1906
James N.	1860 - 1938
Roller, Samuel W.A.	1881 - 1948
Margaret	Apr.1,1788 - Apr.11,1858
David	Apr.14,1832 - Jan.7,1863
Lucinda	no dates
Sarah	no dates
Joh,Sr.	no dates
Maryan	no dates
Elizabeth Hughes	1812 - 1849, w/o George Roller.
George	d.MAy 11,1868, about 62 yrs.
Rebecca	d.Spet.15,1832, aged 3y5m.
George	d.July 15,1821,a ged about 5-? yrs.
James M.	1858 - 1937
Mary E.	1860 - 1941
Mary B.V.	Aug.28,1886 - June 15,1908,d/o J.M.& M.E.
Susan Alvirda	June 5,1884 - May 9,1911, d/o J.M.& M.E.
Solomon	Dec.13,1839 - Feb.8,1901, m.Mar.18,1861
Percy E. Horn	Aug.17,1844 - Dec.9,1900
Martin	d.Mar.8,1848, aged 94y9d.
Martha V.	Oct.2,1893 - Sept.15,1894, J.M.& M.E.
Rebecca J. Dulaney	Dec.20,188 - May 9,1890,d/o J.M.& M.E.
James M.	May 20,1878 - Apr.12,1894
Stacie E.	June 8,1884 - Nov.22,1887
Wesley B.	Aug.4,1870 - Aug.11,1893
Noah	Feb.16,1837 - May 18,1905
Elizabeth C. Morrell	July 13,1849 - May 19,1922
Lillian E.	Nov.14,1893 - Nov.16,1896,s/o W.C.& Sue R. son of -- is what is on the stone.
W.C.	Aug.29,1861 - Apr.15,1926
Sue R. Hawley	July 29,1864 - Sept.18,1920
Jacob W.	1876 - 1948
Louise Yonce	1889 - 19--
Shipley, Jacob M.	Jan.13,1865 - no date
Mary J.	July 20,1859 - June 7,1934
Ida Blanche	June 25,1894 - Sept.23,1913,d/o J.M.& M.J.
John Ray	Dec.20,1895 - June 17,1896, s/o J.M. & M.J.
Adam C.	Nov.2,1835 - Apr.20,1916
Sarah C. Erwin	Oct.28,1838 - Oct.28,1885, w/o A.C.
Benjamin	Mar.12,1800 - July 27, 1870
Margaret Miller	Apr.5,1806 - Mar.12,1881, w/o Benjamin
Suesong, James B.	Nov.29,1803 - Sept.13,1864
Nancy	Mar.26,1812 - Aug.19,1894
·John A.	June 19,1841 - Nov.2,1891
Margaret	Dec.18,1833 - Apr.2,1881
Welsh, John D.	1875 - 1932
Ida M.	1875 - 19--
Sarah Ida	b. & d. June 15,1916, d/o J.D. & I.M.
Okla Marie	1915 - 1936
Yonce, Conley A.	1894 - 1907
Polly L.	1867 - 1958
David L.	1865 - 1930

Potter Cemetery

Arnold, Charlie A.	1888 - 1974
Maggie	1888 - 1978
Jerry W.	1958 - 1958
Daniel M.	1862 - 1942
Alice C.	1870 - 1944
Atkins, Mary	Aug.22,1840 - Sept.9,1899,w/o Lewis Atkins.
Cooper, Robert F.	June 4, 1890 - Sept.11,1944
Dollar, Rachel L.	Jan.6,1882 - Apr.2,1953
Greer, Infant	b. & d. July 15,1928, s/o Robert & Bertha.
Gregory, J.P.	1877 - no date
Maude A.	1889 - 1955
Dora B.	1871 - 1938
Hillard, Laura	1890 - 1963
Susie Inice	Mar.26,1894 - Sept.1,1961
Charles R.	1912 - 1975
Jones, Clarance W.	Aug.30,1905 - Oct.26,1907, s/o M.M.&C.E.
M.M.	1858 - 1949
C.E.	1861 - 1951
McNew, John Roby	Aug.1,1944 - Oct.18,1973
Martin, Delia	Feb.27,1863 - July 17,1927
Maye, Danna, Vesta, Ruth, Marie, Myrtle, Vergie, & Helen:	
	Dec.2,1942
Mayne, Frank	Aug.15,1893 - Sept.23,1972
Lelea T.	Sept.3,1896 - July 14,1913, d/o H.S. & R.T.
Henry S.	Dec.21,1860 - Apr.30,1920
Rachel T.	June 7,1861 - Oct.30,1922
Phillips, Floy	Apr.12,1891 - Jan.29,1923, s/o J.F.Phillips.
J.H.	Sept.17-19,1921, s/o J.F. & F.M. Phillips.
Potter, Susan E.	Aug.1837 - Feb.1916
Conley R.	Aug.30,1910 - July 26,1962
Osborne, Sarah	1869 - 1942
Rush, David	1924 - 1971
Rutherford, Walter Lee,Jr.	Nov.14,1928 - Feb.22,1960
Infant	June 11-12,1909, d/o W.R. & Ida R.
Snyder, Daniel	1862 - 1949
Lottie	1872 - 1949
Stewart, Earnest Gray	July 25,1925 - Oct.28,1930
Charles W.	Sept.8,1930
Webster, Victor L.	1903 - 1967, m.Jan.16,1946
Stella M.	1924 - no date
White, Rev.Benjamin F.,Sr.	Aug.25,1837 - Mar.10,1920
Sarah E.	Apr.30,1841 - Jan.18,1908
Edgar Lee	Dec.15,1889 - Dec.15,1904
Wilson, Vicie	1930 - 1974
Wyatt, Robert Milton	Feb.19,1895 - Oct.16,1918
Vanover, Leighton S.	May 23,1907 - Oct.19,1924

Wyatt Cemetery

Arnold, Clint A	Dec.9,1911 - Oct.27,1972
Samuel R.	1955 - 1957
Infant	no dates, moved from Davenport Cem.6-4-42.
Bentley, Peggy	no dates
Jones, Angela Renee	1974 - 1974
Norris, Floyd (Joe)	Mar.6,1896 - Feb.9,1961
Phillips, James B.	1884 - 1942
Sarah M.	1888 - 1952
Poore, Ethel A.	July 30,1914 - Nov.26,1981
Frank Albert	June 1,1918 - Jan.14,1955
Rush, Charles F.	July 18,1924 - Jan.4,1979
Beatrice L.	June 27,1933 - Dec.18,1974
Infant	1958
Claude William	May 20,1925 - Dec.20,1977
Daisey Myrtle	1900 - 1973
Ryder, Arthur T.	Aug.21,1888 - Dec.14,1956
Lula May	1894 - 1962
Stone, Edward	July 16,1895 - Apr.15,1958
Michael Lynn	1976 - 1976
Wood, C.J.	no dates, moved from Davenport Cem.,6-4-42.
Woods, Kate M.	May 20,1904 - Mar.15,1953
Wyatt, Mamie L.	no dates
Robert Lee	1900 - 1941
Delmar Clay	1923 - 1927
Andrew Franklin	1900 - 1941
Mary Ellen	1876 - 1947
Virginia Lue	1904 - 1981
U.	1908 - 1968
Conniel	1961 - 1961
Alice Marie	d.Dec.17,1948

Morrison Chapel Methodist Church Cemetery

Bellamy, Wliza E.	Mar.5,1885 - Aug.22,1942
William H.	Oct.22,1876 - Jan.13,1956
Nancy P.	1859 - 1935
Bishop, Monnie S.	1898 - ----., w/o W.J.Bishop.
William J.	1889 - 1968
Brickey, Charlie E.	1901 - 1969
----	Sept.16,1921 - July 28,1939
Mary B.	1902 -
Carter, Annie Lee	Feb.22,1933 - Sept.18,1933
Infant	May 20,1937, d/o J.L. & Lena Carter.
James L.	Mar.10,1890 - Aug.27,1960
Lena B.	Sept.17,1907 - Apr.28,1963
Davidson, Blanche Anne	Nov.17,1907 - Mar.22,1913
Charlie D.	May 10,1868 - May 15,1936
Julia A.	Aug.25,1897 - Mar.14,1974
Maxie Lee	May 21,1903 - Jan.16,1948
Nahoma	May 13,1878 - Feb.8,1921
Nahoma	Aug.12,1924, inf/dau/of J.F. & G.M.
Fields, Judy C.	MAr.1862 - Sept.1950
Freeman, Joseph A.	1878 - 1962
Susannah A.	1877 - 1958
Gilliam, Sally Low McKenzie	Jan.20,1914 - Oct.16,1947, w/o Geo.W.
Hammonds, John B.	1883 - 1943

Morrison Chapel Methodist Church Cemetery, cont.

Hicks, Ronald	May 24,1917 - Dec.31,1929
Jennings, Glen	1926
Loring Basel	1895 - 1934
Mattie	Jan.23,1903 - May 17,1932
Patton Gale	d. Mar.3,1880
Paul	1931
Sarah Ida J. Arnold	1898 - 1965
Johnson, Peggy K.	Nov.7,1935 - Aug.20,1941
Lane, Bert W.	1885 - 1932
Bertha	Jan.25,1917 - July 1,1919
Canzada	Mar.25,1910 - Jan.16,1941
Donnie & Darlene Quillen	twins, Feb.15-Mar.3,1938
Floyd W.	Apr.23,1883 - Sept.24,1964
Infant	Sept.1940
Jethro W.	July 13,1912 - Aug.12,1965
Joe R.	May 23,1955 - July 17,1919
Pearl S.	1881 - 1965
Sarah G.	Apr.17,1875 - Apr.24,1940
Larkin, Robert R.	July 22,1835 - Aug.21,1903
McDavid, Dennie G.	Jan.27,1895 - Aug.8,1918
Mary E.	May 20,1860 - Mar.24,1941
Patton, Rev.Samuel D.D.	1797 - 1854, Centennial Memorial erected by Holston Conference Methodist Episcopal Church South, 1925.
Sanders, Grace R.	1916 - 1936
Shelton, Mark	1959 - 1967
Spears, J.M.	1860 - 1936
Wilson, Mary C.	Oct.18,1875 - Jan.5,1947

Webb Cemetery
Over 200 graves unmarked or with fieldstones.

Brushingham, Cornelious	d. Dec.30,1902
Carr, Jarry	Dec.1,1872 - Aug.27,1909
Carr, Samuel	Mar.11,1848 - Aug.20,1913
Daniel	Aug.9,1857 - Feb.20,1880
Infant	b. & d. June 11,1886, inf/o Samuel & Mary Ann Carr.
Infant	Feb.17,1879, inf/o S. &. M.A. Carr.
Lilvorn	Feb.18,1874 - July 9,1893
Matilda	1888 - 1898
Maudie	1885 - Apr.8,1889, d/o Abe & Bettie Carr.
Carolyn	1887 - 1889, d/o Abe & Bettie
Maggie	1890 - May 10,1892, d/o Abe & Bettie
Bettie	1861 - July 18,1899, w/o Abe Carr
Maggie	Apr.30,1894 - Jan.22,1895, d/o Johnson & Nannie Carr.
Augusta	Apr.8,1891 - OCt.8,1910, d/o Johnson & Nannie Carr.
Nannie	Nov.5,1865 - Jan.1,1905, w/o Johnson.
Davis, D.D.	Dec.25,1854 - Apr.5,1909
Floyd, W.F.	no dates, Co.,F., 2nd TN Inf.
Frazier, David	1818 - 1898
Martha Hodge	1818 - 1898, Honored Pioneer School Teachers.
Glover, Ella	Oct.9,1895 - Aug.9,1895, d/o J.W. & C. Glover. (This is the way the stone reads)

Webb Cemetery, cont.

Glover, Becky — d.July 4,1902, aged 52 yrs.
        Irson — d.Nov.29,1883, aged 70 yrs.
Gross, Rosie Ann — Dec.23,1915 - Sept.12,1916, d/o S.L. & L.V.F.
Lane, Rhoda Carr — 1883 - 1901
Perry, George — Aug.1852 - May 3,1921
        Martha — 1862 - Sept.15,1894
        William — July 16,1845 - June 3,1917
Sams, Evort — Mar.16,1918 - Mar.17,1918
        Infant — b. & d. May 7,1889, inf/o A.G.& M.S.
        Rye — Jan.4,1913 - Jan.19,1913, s/o E.G. & M.A.
        Ken M. — May 23,1915 - May 6,1916, s/o E.G. & M.A.
Shipley, Robert Eldridge — MAy 27,1900 - Sept.21,1918
        Fred — Oct.29,1910 - July 5,1916, s/o J.M. & M.L.
        Cora — Jan.25,1894 - July 16,1896, d/o J.M. & M.L.
        Infant — b. & d. June 8,1891, inf/o J.M. & M.L.
        Ellen — Feb.17-20,1890, d/o J.M. & M.L.
        Gaines — Feb.21,1881 - Spet.15,1889, s/o J.M. & S.L.
        Bessie — Nov.30,1886 - Feb.29,1887, d/o J.M. & S.L.
Webb, Infant — 1915, inf/o C.G. & U.U. Webb.
Woods, Isaac — 1836 - Aug.9,1888
        Rachel A.Senth — 1844 - 1914
        Mildred — Jan.9,1922 - Jan.9,1922
        Hazel — 1908 - 1918

Pemberton Cemetery

Booher, Alice S. — Sept.21,1870 - June 19,1878, d/o N.C. & E.C.
        Elizabeth Wassum — Jan.4,1833 - Feb.29,1908, w/o N.C.Booher
        Louisa — Sept.24,1824 - Feb.24,1894
        Martin — Dec.16,1775 - Feb.3,1869
        Mary V. — Sept.15,1869 - Jan.14,1896, d/o N.C. & E.C.
        Noah C. — Aug.2,1845 - Dec.28,1919
        Ollie — Mar.8,1788 - June 5,1861, w/o Martin Booher.
        Peter — Apr.16,1846 - Dec.21,1912
Duncan, James J. — Co. M 13th TN Cav. (govt.marker)
George,Elizabeth — July 18,1779 - June 4,1802/9
        Frances — Jan.9,1776 - Apr.11,1798
Hawkins, Jennie McQueen — Oct.29,1860 - May 20,1937
        Joe — Feb.14,1888 - Oct.21,1918, Died in service of his country.
        Sue Annie — June 12,1897 - Apr.23,1904, d/o J.F.& Jennie.
Morrell, Samuel Andrew — Dec.26,1851 - Mar.21,1912
        Florence Amelia — Apr.16,1859 - Mar.6,1920
O'Dell, David A. — Aug.3,1865 - June 14,1868, s/o J. & J. O'Dell.
        Col.James J. — June 2,1827 - Sept.27,1877
        Jeanette Tate — June 2,1823 - June 29,1909, w/o Col.J.J.
Oldfield, Mary Catherine — July 23,1833 - Jan.9,1892
        William — Nov.16,1832 - Jan.16,1914
Pemberton, Elizabeth — July 17,1749 - Aug.7,1819
        Ezekial — Aug.1,1781 - Sept.1,1857
        James — Dec.16,1767 - Nov.25,1815
        John — Oct.12,1742/9 - Oct.25,1819, Rev. War - Pemberton Oak namesake.
        Thomas — Jan.29,1775 - June 1848
Pile, George F. — 1851 - 1917

Pemberton Cemetery, cont.

Rhodes, George W.	Aug.22,1858 - July 28,1917
Jennie T.	d.July 6,1884, aged 1 yr,d/o G.W.& T.E.
Rogers, Melvina A.	Mar.26,1818 - Mar.9,1911, w/o Robert
Robert	June 10,1810 - Mar.15,1888
Rohr, Ann Eliza	Aug.22,1822 - Nov.30,1891, w/o W.H.Rohr.
William M.	May 29,1808 - Apr.18,1887
Rosenbalm, John	1829 - Dec.10,1901
Mary	1832 - Dec.3,1897, w/o John.

Massengill Cemetery

Hyder, George T.	1863 - 1941
Emma T.	1866 - 1940
Annie	Feb.26,1901, aged 2d., d/o G.T.& E.T.Hyder.
Willie M.	Jan.8,1899 - Nov.30,1900, s/o J.B. & F.L.
Fannie L.	Oct.28,1876 - Oct.26,1905, w/o J.B.Hyder.
J.B.	June 4,1868 - Apr.4,1930
Neppie	Oct.8,1865 - Jan.4,1907
H.H.	Jan.9,1825 - July 16,1902
Sallie Massengill	Feb.15,1835 - Jan.4,1889
McFall, Jennie Massengill	Jan.7,1873 - Mar.7,1901, m.July 29,1900 to Charles H. McFall.
McMackin, Hannah Hyder	Jan.22,1871 - Jan.20,1929, w/o A.J.McMackin.
Massengill, Penelope	d.Sept. 4,1810, aged 49 yrs.,w/o Henry.
Deborah	d.Sept.7,1833, aged 46y11m, consort of Wm.
Alecy	d.Aug.14,1809, aged 11m.
Elizabeth	d.Sept.28,1875, aged 85y7m14d, w/o Henry.
Henry	1758 - Sept.25,1837, VA Pvt.NC Troops,Rev.War.
John	Sept.1816, aged 78y5m
Mary	d.June 20,1909, aged 83 yrs.,w/o John.
Lucinda Evaline	1842 - 1902, d/o Michael & Hannah Torbett Massengill.
William Allen	1849 - 1896
Deborah Lucinda	1855 - 1943
Sally Blanche	Jan.17,1878 - May 3,1889,d/o W.A.& D.L.
Deborah	d.Mar.28,1874, aged 63y9d, w/o F.D.
Felty Devault	Apr.30,1815 - Mar.30,1894
Martha	May 1,1844 - July 3,1890, w/o F.D.
Louise B.	d.Jan.10,1870, aged 28y11m16d.,w/o Michael.
Hannah	Aug.29,1807 - May 17,1887, w/o Michael.
Massengill, ---	no dates, d/o M. & L.B. Massengill.
Robertson, Calvin Allen	Feb.16,1904 - July 4,1904, s/o E.E. & Lula.
Stuart, Devid	d.Arp.12,1827, aged 32y4m.
Wolfe, Joe M.	July 11, 1865 - Aug.25,1868. s/o T.H. & L.S.
T.H.B.	Jan.31,1843 - June 21, 1863
Priscilla	June 15,1813 - Sept.17,1897
John	Oct.16,1810 - Aug.19,1891
T.C.	Mar.31,1865 - July 20,1888
Woolf, Maggie Massengill	Dec.22,1880 - Dec.1,1906, w/o Buford Woolf.
Mary D.	Feb.13,1904 - Feb.17, 1904, d/o B.B. & M.A.

Morningside Cemetery

Adams, Charles B.	June 2,1891 - June 2,1933
Cleo Bryson	Jan.13,1896 - Feb.6,1981
Eileen	May 27,1891 - Aug.10,1891,d/o J.Q.& B.
Belle Lindamood	Apr.8,1867 - July 21,1910, w/o J.Q.
John Quiney	June 27,1865 - Apr.5,1951
Nannie E.	1892 - 1920, w/o W.A.Adams.
Wiley A.	1888 - 1971
Mollie B.	1900 - 1971
Allen, Viola L.	Feb.18,1889 - Feb.10,1909, w/o B.P.Allen.
Marshall Francis	Jan.9-10,1912, s/o B.P. & Nora Allen.
Dana Lyon	Feb.4-July 20,1909, w/o B.P. & Nora.
Anderson, John H.	July 4,1857 - June 2,1940
Kate	Mar.13,1872 - May 15,1906
Jennie R.	Mar.13,1881 - Dec.10,1924
Margaret Tinsley	1923 - 1982
John T.	Mar.29,1946 - Aug.19,1946
George Rhea	Apr.14,1902 - May 15,1973
Hessie B.	June 24,1906 - no date
Arnold, Robert M.	Oct.30,1880 - Sept.5,1958
Mattie L.	Mar.29,18191 - May 18,1965
Tommy R.	Apr.2,1931 - June 21,1983
Betty G.	Nov.16,1932 - no date
Arrants, Lola Smith	May 21,1892 - June 23,1930, w/o W.J.
J.B.	1872 - 1914
Catherine	1841 - 1921
Blanche Woods	Jan.10,1883 - Sept.3,1924,w/o W.J.
May Nell	Feb.3,1924 - June 26,1924
Austin, Samuel L.	Jan.1,1888 - no date
Dallas J.	Apr.29,1904 - no date
Bachman, Charles W.	1899 - 1985
William Bruce	Nov.25,1852 - Sept.9,1922
Lula May Peterson	Mar.21,1870 - June 24,1958
James	Mar.1,1896 - July 3,1931
S.B.	May 1884 - Apr.1914
Robert B.	1894 - 1979
Gladys H.	1905 - no date
Baird, Noah S.	July 22,1875 - Apr.17,1959
Myrtle E.	July 15,1885 - Nov.14,1971
Infant	no dates, inf/o Doyle G. & L.Lucille.
William J.	1887 - 1925
Baker, Thomas G.	Oct.3,1895 - Apr.10,1966
Bare, Brenda M.	1949 - 1970
Roby	June 5,1893 - Jan.27,1968
Odell	Apr.12,1896 - Dec.2,1966
Sula Mae	Mar.7,1916 - no date
Barnett, Bobbie,Jr.	Feb.20,1931 - July 14,1931
Henry E.	1923 - 1955
Mary H.	1886 - 1977
John C.	1881 - 1935
Bartle, Emeline	June 2,1831 - Aug.27,1863
Bates, Herman Ryden	Oct.18,1909 - Mar.14,1983
Clarice Wiles	July 4,1915 - no date
Dr.Robert	1843 - 1924
Anna B.	1848 - 1909

Bates, Nannie Blanche	1884 - 1981
Marshall	1882 - 1953
Anna M.B.	1910, d/o R.M.&N.B.Bates.
Earl Ryden	1891 - 1970
William T.	1880 - 1942
John H.	1889 - 1915
James C.	1868 - 1948
Beach, Wade C.	Mar.8,1889 - Oct.21,1971
Myrtle C.	Mar.1,1892 - no date
Willow Grey	June 19,1925 - Feb.19,1926
Faith	b. & d. Mar.7,1956
Beard, W.N.	Oct.13,1852 - no date
Sarah E. Harr	Sept.25,1858 - Oct.6,1928
Bellamy, Haskel	Nov.10,1917 - June 21,1936
Bennett, Ernest F.	1902 - 1955
Jason	1981
Berry, Jennie	1865 - 1933
Harry William	July 26,1893 - May 3,1966
Margaret Ellen	Aug.9,1894 - Jan.16,1938
Eliza	1858 - 1943
Adison	1850 - 1918
Birdwell, C.Akard	Feb.1,1897 - Sept.10,1975
Bishop, Joseph K.	Apr.16,1878 - Apr.25,1949
Black, Walter	d.Feb.19,1938
Blair, Robert Frank	1879 - 1946
Blankenship, Louise Dempsey	1922 - 1960
Blaylock, Georgia Mae	June 29,1905 - Jan.7,1971
William R.	Nov.13,1907 - Sept.19,1980
Boling, Donald	June 15,1908 - Aug.10,1967
Hazel	Apr.22,1915 - Feb.24,1938
William	Apr.3,1902 - Aug.8,1966
Frank S.	Apr.27,1912 - Apr.19,1952
Bouton, George E.	June 23,1872 - Oct.26,1891
James E.	1847 - Mar.7,1926
Maggie	Mar.3,1848 - no date
Daniel M.	Jan.19,1874 - Oct.31,1902
Susan Lilly	1912 - 1915
Roby A.	Jan.26,1908 - Nov.8,1960
William E.	1876 - 1930
Sarah E.	1878 - 1947
Charles F.	Feb.19,1906 - Oct.13,1965
Earlene H.	Jan.10,1916 - no date
Herman	1920 - 1953
Bowers, Andrew	Aug.14,1898 - Mar.13,1962
Boy, Wm. Alford	1888 - 1933
Robert A.	1896 - 1978
Robert A.	1865 - 1932
Amanda C.	1870 - 1952
Nora	1897 - 1978
John A.	1848 - 1920
Jacob Lee	1895 - 1923
Harriet E. Geisler	1861 - 1924

Morningside Cemetery, cont.

Boy, Lula Anne	1885 - 1971
Bradley, Lillie L.	1921 - 1963
Brown, Mary M.	Apr.12,1859 - Mar.2,1903, w/o J.C.Brown.
Carrie Mae	1917 - 1919, d/o R.A. & L. Brown.
Broyles, Thomas A.	1913 - 1969
Ruby P.	1914 - 1955
Brumit, Harold Ryden	Aug.14,1907 - Apr.9,1941
Robert A.	Dec.2,1880 - Dec.30,1950
Georgia L.	1908 - 1982
Iris D.	1929 - 1958
Mayme R.	Mar.28,1883 - Mar.21,1981
Bryan, James B.	May 15,1873 - Nov.12,1963
J.Myrtle H.	Sept.25,1879 - Nov.18,1968
Ruth	1919, s/o Mr.& Mrs. J.B.Bryan.
Esther	1913 - 1916, d/o J.B.Bryan.
James G.	1907 - 1907, s/o J.B. & J.M. Bryan.
Benjamin K.	Apr.15,1899 - May 22,1955
Billy L.	1925
Harlan L.	Aug.26,1923 - Oct.23,1944
William J.	Nov.30,1896 - Dec.10,1971
Edward Worley	Mar.5,1916 - July 6,1965
Margaret Odell	June 7,1917 - no date
Bryson, Amelia	Apr.1815 - Apr.1899
J.M.	1856 - 1922
Nannie E. Mantz	1858 - 1928
Buckles, Dora Cawood	1875 - 1957
JoAnn	Dec.13,1950 - Dec.17,1950
Toy W.	Nov.27,1893 - Jan.3,1968
Grace M.	Feb.24,1893 - May 6,1968
Beulah E.	June 24,1919 - Aug.3,1984
Buckner, Elva J.	Aug.14,1850 - Aug.14,1869,w/o D.L.Buckner.
Gettie L.	Apr.6,1867 - Sept.23,1867, s/o D.L.& E.J.
Bunn, Joseph A.	1874 - 1938
Sallie Webb	1880 - 1980
Burnette, Clifford E.	1894 - 1963
Margaret W.	1902 - no date
Burnett, Emert C.	Sept.27,1882 - Apr.4,1951
Charles A.	Aug.26,1908 - no date
Gladys O.	Oct.21,1907 - Feb.2,1970
Edward H.	July 29,1880 - June 23,1958
Fanny A.	Feb.22,1885 - Jan.26,1959
Edward Ted	1919 - 1977
Opal E.	1918 - no date
John B.	1928 - 1929
Lucy Ruth	Mar.28,1916 - Jan.8,1932
Edward T.	Sept.29,1919 - Aug.14,1977
Lanny Ike	1952 - 1952
Bush, Infants	2 children of E.S.& F. Bush.
Effie Myrtle	Apr.21,1878 - Feb.15,1879,d/o E.S.& F.C.
Elbert S.	Sept.11,1855 - Sept.10,1880
Callahan, Kyle Dean	Oct.16,1941 - May 9,1985
Campbell, W.R.	Dec.29,1869 - Jan.29,1910
Gayle Virginia	1902 - 1983

Cannon, Patricia E.	1950 - 1983
Cantor, Bonnie B.	July 25,1933 - Aug.15,1972
Carmody, Martin M.	Aug.5,1877 - June 19,1950
Zona Bell	June 11,1878 - Dec.26,1969
Sylvia Lee	Aug.15,1905 - Aug.13,1906
Buster Raymond	Apr.24,1909 - Jan.26,1938
Roy M.	Aug.17,1907 - Jan.20,1956
Claude	Feb.6,1896 - June 24,1932
Infant son	Sept.14,1935
Joseph Melvin	1901 - 1976
Carr, Sarah E.	1863 - 1944
Samuel C.	1863 - 1944
Carrier, Carl P.	1890 - 1935
Verna Henry	1888 - 1974
Jacob C.	1860 - 1931
Ellen Pucket	1864 - 1950
Nellie D.	1892 - 1920
Homer R.	1883 - 1885, s/o Ellen & Jacob C. Carrier.
Nathaniel	1844 - 1929
Emmaline	1846 - 1907
Emma F.	1878 - 188-, d/o I.L. & G.A. Carrier.
Oscar A.	1877 - 1877, s/o I.L. & G.A. Carrier.
Frank H.	May 17,1880 - Dec.9,1894
J.P.	1844 - 1928
Martha J.	1851 - 1932
Ethel M.	1890 - 1978
S.M.	1851 - 1906
Louise	1850 - 1932
William D.	Mar.3,1807 - Jan.3,1900
Raney	May 10,1835 - Sept.1887
Maude E.	1886 - 1972
K.M.	Dec.14,1876 - May 11,1905
Catharine	Dec.31,1838 - Feb.26,1906, w/o J.H.
Harley K.,Jr.	June 12,1909 - Nov.19,1971
Stella Dempsey	Feb.19,1912 - Feb.15,1982
William C.	Aug.18,1864 - Sept.26,1948
Mittie Ryden	Sept.10,1876 - Sept.5,1942
Infant	Feb.22-23,1914, d/o W.C. Carrier.
Jack R.	Sept.17,1919 - Sept.12,1958
Neppie L. King	Apr.12,1903 - Apr.29,1924, w/o Glen W.
Sudie Hicks	Jan.17,1893 - Apr.24,1942
Joseph L.	June 27,1896 - June 27,1967
Leander	1853 - 1933
Georgia A.	1856 - no date
Arthur L.	1881 - 1956
Blanche W.	1888 - 19--
Cora H.	1893 - 1978
Albert E.	1890 - 1938
Stella Rowe	Aug.19,1960 - June 26,1981
Anna Mae	May 3,1889
Martha Mae	Jan.17,1918 - July 31,1918
Robert L.	Sept.29,1908 - May 14,1925
James Stewart	1910 - 1978

Morningside Cemetery, cont.

Carrier, James M.	Sept.11,1887 - Apr.15,1970
Hubert L.	July 18,1892 - Apr.9,1938
Azlene Hicks	Mar.28,1895 - Feb.23,1983
W.Cecil	Oct.1,1905 - no date
Emma Dyche	Aug.2,1912 - no date
Anna Ruth	Nov.8,1937 - Dec.10,1983
Fred H.	July 9,1895 - Apr.22,1964
Nathaniel F.	Feb.25,1914 - Dec.1,1982, m. June 27,1939
Mary E.	Feb.6,1920 - no date
Alma	Jan.18,1893 - Oct.3,1893, d/o C.D. & Dora
Charlie D.	1868 - 1929
Dora B.	1871 - 1941
Willie	Sept.7,1886 - Aug.14,1887
Charles R.	1898 - 1898, s/o I.L. & C.A. Carrier.
Anna L.	1886 - 1889, d/o I.L. & C.A. Carrier.
Dulaney	1824 - 1899
Amanda	1828 - 1891
Bo---y, (?)	May 15,1862 - June 10,1884,s/o D.& A.
Carriger,Ella C.	Sept.17,1884 - Dec.6,1887, d/o I.R. & M.E.
Infant	no dates, inf/o I.R. & M.E. Carriger.
A.T.	Sept.27,1869 - Nov.14,1897,s/o I.R.& M.E.
M.I.C.	Dec.27,1850 - Sept.4,1893, w/o I.R.
Gatha	1878 - 1945
Ed.	1877 - 1944
Robert E.	1900 - 1953
Belle R.	1881 - 1962
Wendell A.	Aug.29,1923 - Dec.11,1970
Carter, James	1860 - 1915
Paul	1897 - 1954
Catron, Callie	1861 - 1918
Cawood, Jacob C.	1881 - 1951
Nannie	Oct.2,1872 - July 25,1957
Grant	Apr.12,1892 - Sept.2,1970
Infant Grace	June 15,1922
Earl A.	Dec.27,1900 - Dec.1,1967
Bertie B.	Sept.12,1901 - no date
Lettie J.	1844 - 1916
Mary F.	1886 - 19--
Cawood, ?	1882 - 1939
Alaxander	1814 - 1894
Chamberlain, J.H.	Feb.7,1826 - Jan.6,1903
C.L.	Mar.27,1877 - July 1,1906
G.G.	Jan.8,1833 - Dec.9,1906
Clark, Margaret S.	May 6,1889 - Aug.11,1970
Clinton, Marshall	July 22,1873 - Sept.3,1943
Collins, Mary	d.Dec.21,1915, aged 65 yrs.
Jesse	1850 - 1917
Martha	1845 - 1923
Mary Ann Smith	d.Feb.24,1925, w/o A.C.Collins.
Lucille Isabelle	Feb.24,1922 - Dec.28,1932, d/o Jas. Franklin & Sue Massengill Collins.
Walter	Feb.13,1883 - Sept.21,1921
Randall	Oct.19,1927 - Oct.1927
Eugene	Feb.26,1925 - Mar.7,1931
Wilam Sue	1928 - 1950
Corbett C.	1899 - 1976

Morningside Cemetery, cont.

Collins, Pearl C.	1903 - 1984
Combes. John E.	Apr.26,1884 - Oct.27,1886, s/o W.W.& E.J.
Combs, J.L.	1858 - 1908
Jennie F.	1853 - 1912, w/o J.L.Combs
J.S.,Jr.	June 14,1914, s/o J.S.& Launa Combs.
Docia	June 7,1890 - Sept.5,1908
W.W.	May 20,1860 - Feb.27,1906
Emma Harkleroad	Nov.12,1864 - Dec.8,1954
Ida M.	d.Oct.8,1902, aged 18 days, d/o W.W.& E.J.
Sherman J.	May 25,1887 - Nov.24,1918
Bill	June 5,1923 - Sept.23,1971
Edward K.	Apr.21,1939 - May 7,1979
Cook, John Oscar,Jr.	Aug.1,1918 - Feb.8,1983
Elizabeth S.	Nov.5,1840 - Aug.21,1917
Leona Mills	Jan.17,1888 - May 1,1964
Coolsby, Robert R.,Jr.	Dec.31,1895 - Aug.29,1954
Cope, Dulcenia	Dec.--,1874 - Feb.4,1954
Cowan, Phoebe Rebecca	May 12,1872 - Aug.16,1948, w/o George Cowan.
George S.	1866 - 1931
Rebecca	1893 - 1911, d/o Geo. & Rebecca Cowan.
Bulah	1900 - 1911, d/o G.&. R.Cowan.
Gracie	1891 - 1911, d/o G. & R. Cowan.
Infant	no dates, s/o Winston Cowan.
Cox, Walter G.	Sept.18,1874 - Feb.3,1882
James G.	Mar.18,1848 - Dec.16,1908
Clara Frank	1937
Carter Wightman	no dates
Louise Henry	no dates
Crabtree, B.F.	1857 - 1917
Kittie G.	1848 - 19--
Crawford, Theodore R.	Dec.17,1917 - July 1,1977
Dolores	Sept.24,1956 - inf d/o C.J.& Evelyn.
Crockett, Mollie	1875 - 1937
Mary E.	Mar.31,1871 - Sept.5,1872, d/o O.P. & A.E.L.
Emma	1866 - 1923
James	1862 - 1925
David M.	d.Apr.9,1857
Charles S.	Oct.14,1878 - Apr.28,1960
Alma B.	Oct.17,1889 - no date
Cross, Bradley Justin	Apr.7,1882
Crowder, William Fred	1879 - 1920
Carl M.	1903 - 1923
William F.,Jr.	Sept.21,1909 - Jan.31,1960
Crowe, Larry Raymond	June 19,1949 - Aug.25,1949
Silas P.	Mar.26,1910 - Aug.19,1983
Virginia M.	Sept.6,1917 - no date
Crumley, Henry H.	1914 - 1984
Jake	1894 - 1972
Sarah D.	1901 - 1979
Mabel L.	Dec.17,1923 - Jan.6,1980
Crussell, Sarah E.	Aug.22,1850 - Feb.20,1928
Mattie	no dates
Johnie	no dates

Morningside Cemetery, cont.

Crussell, R.H.	June 2,1877 - Nov.9,1906
Eliza	no dates
Bessie	no dates
Curtis, Anna Mae	1921 - 1983
Jennie	Aug.21,1911
J.C.	1930 - 1970
Nannie L.	1864 - 1950
Clark M.	1896 - 1953
Czoka, David Ladd	Feb.26,1936 - Aug.7,1978
Davis, James	1838 - 1884
Robert	June 14,1863 - Jan.18,1937
Minnie E.	d.Oct.18,1872, 4y4m8d, d/o James & Ann.
Ann M.	d.Mar.20,1875, aged 36y8m19d, w/o James.
Hannah E.	d.Apr.19,1922
A.R.	1854 - 1920
Lydia M. Hawk	Oct.4,1864 - Mar.2,1901,w/o A.R.Davis.
Infant	1885, d/o A.R.& Lydia Davis.
Adaline E. Hicks	1859 - 1918, w/o R.G.Davis
James Roy, Sr.	Dec.10,1894 - Oct.17,1974
Dean, Rev.John Kerr	Aug.18,1892 - Nov.17,1970
Alice Vivian Snead	Dec.31,1894 - Sept.22,1978
James Lamar	Oct.13,1929 - Nov.5,1941
Delaney, Paul A.	1919 - 1981
Minnie M.	1890 - 1980
Bill	1880 - 1942
Dempsey, J.R.	1915 - 1930
Robert A.	1901 - 1918
William F.	1875 - 1929
Josie M.	1886 - 1976
Imogene	1917 - 1918
Paul Conley	1911 - 1929
George M.	May 10,1887 - Dec.24,1954
Addie Louise	July 12,1888 - May 23,1970
Denny, Grace Lee	Sept.7,1884 - Jan.6,1970
Jacob W.	Jan.1,1855 - Mar.4,1932
Mary Lucy Rhea	Feb.12,1868 - Sept.27,1897,w/o J.W.Denny.
Dorak	July 1897 - Sept.1897, d/o J.W.& M.L.
John L.	1883 - 1942
Denton, Charles H.	Mar.8,1870 - May 29,1943
Henry Edward	Apr.19,1876 - Nov.23,1945
Mary Edna Williams	Dec.26,1880 - July 3,1959
J.E.	May 12,1848 - Apr.20,1913
Martha J.	Sept.30,1845 - Feb.15,1922, w/o J.E.
John A.	1878 - 1939
Jacob	July 23,1810 - Apr.28,1890
Catherine	Mar.23,1832 - Feb.6,1891
E.C.	Sept.12,1858 - July 1, 1936
Dewey E.	1898 - 1920
Claude H.	1906 - 1975
Nannie E.	1870 - 1956
John L.	1861 - 1939
Bernice	1909 - 1913
Johney	1902 - 1912

Morningside Cemetery, cont.

Denton, Albert E. "Doc"	Aug.6,1900 - Apr.2,1978
Maude L.	Aug.24,1912 - no date
William N.	Sept.23,1896 - Aug.20,1932
Bertha M.	Aug.22,1902 - Nov.30,1978
Eva	June 12,1916 - Feb.9,1957, w/o J.Forrest Thomas.
C.B. (Buster)	Nov.7,1892 - Dec.28,1965
Martha C. (Duckie) Sams	Nov.18,1898 - May 2,1961, w/o C.B.
Dickson, James E.	1895 - 1939
Beatrice G.	Feb.2,1895 - Feb.4,1979
Dishner, D. Arcil	1920 - no date
Virginia M.	1924 - 1979
Doan, James Edward	Oct.10,1875 - Nov.30,1943
Retta Crussell	May 7,1875 - Apr.27,1958
Rev.Robert H.	Mar.25,1907 - no dates
Geraldine R.	Oct.22,1913 - no dates
Dodd, Steven Wayne	Jan.23,1969 - Dec.9,1974
Donigan, George O.	Mar.4,1901 - Mar.9,1970
Etta J.	Jan.11,1900 - Sept.18,1922
Lt.James M.	Mar.4,1920 - July 20,1944, buried at Arlington National Cemetery.
Doss, Everett Matthew	Oct.7,1926 - Apr.22,1984
Doughterty, James Rolfe	Aug.3,1925 - May 27,1947
Dowell, Allen Ellsworth	Sept.8,1955 - Jan.8,1963
Larry W.	Jan.26,1951 - Jan.30,1951
William E.	Mar.4,1953 - Apr.10,1954
Droak, Frank	Jan.26,1857 - Oct.1,1883
Dunn, Joseph F.	1906 - 1972
Dutton, John E.	1855 - 191-
Roie Lee	1858 - 1899
Dyche, Infant	Nov.24,1924, s/o James L. Dyche.
Clara Ellen	1871 - 1947
John B.	1879 - 1936
Margaret E.	1881 - 1934
Jane I.	1844 - 1919
J.L.	1841 - 1919
Sudie A.	Apr.16,1881 - Sept.23,1886
James L.	Sept.8,1904 - no date
Anna Sue	Oct.30,1904 - no date
Eads, Lucile	Jan.13,1902 - Jan.22,1902,d/o D.N.& H.M.
Robert W.	Aug.25,1893 - Mar.12,1894
Amanda T. Lipps	Aug.5,1870 - Nov.24,1893, T.A.Eads.
Hassie Webb	Nov.7,1881 - Nov.20,1953
Charles Henry	no dates
David Nathan	June 4,1878 - Nov.3,1964
Charles H.	1871 - 1949
Margaret Lou	1869 - 1954
M.D.,Jr.	1932 - 1932
Frank A.	1902 - 1914
Thomas A.	Feb.2,1867 - Mar.9,1946
Nora B.	Feb.8,1884 - July 25,1924
David C.	1837 - 1915
A.K.	1838 - 1924
Arthur	1882 - 1963
Bessie	1888 - 1943

Morningside Cemetery, cont.

Eads, Robert C.	1834 - 1920
Eliza J.	1850 - 1923
Marjorie Kate	1925 - 1934
Johnney C.	b. & d. Nov.14,1905, s/o C.H.& M.L.
Dora B.	May 30,1907 - Dec.17,1909, d/o C.H.&M.L.
Billy E.	May 14,1929 - Mar.15,1985
W.Howard	1926 - 1967
W.Dillard	1886 - 1967
William R.	Jan.14,1896 - Aug.3,1976
Pansy R.	July 17,1897 - Nov.1,1972
Ealey, Infant	1929
Elva A.	1920 - 1920
Sue N.	1921 - 1923
William W.	1891 - 1939
Nannie	1903 - 1974
Early, William Frank	1931 - 1985
Eaton, Dock	1903 - 1984
Ora	1911 - no date
Edwards, Edith Lillian	Aug.18,1890 - July 11,1892, d/o A.W.& J.C.
Elliott, Delphia	1817 - Feb.25,1894
Emery, Amy Catherine	Mar.9,1858 - Sept.24,1936
James A.	Mar.4,1881 - Jan.4,1951
William H.	1889 - 1952
Rittie L.	1882 - 19--
John L.	1884 - 19--, m. Feb.11,1911
Ethel J.	1890 - 1967
Warron W.	Mar.4,1890 - Jan.5,1957
Emmert, Lizzie Hicks	Dec.30,1863 - May 6,1896
A.C., M.D.	Feb.1,1843 - Aug.29,1900
Louisa	d.Oct.23,1882, aged 40y, w/o Dr.A.C.Emmert.
Jas. W.	1878 - 1936
Mary Lucille	1914 - 1918, d/o J.W. & Gertrude Emmert.
Ewing, Henry Wood	b.Sept.1,1822,Scott Co.,VA.
	d.Mar.12,1901, Bluff City, TN.
Laura E.	May 23,1863 - Oct.3,1863, d/o H.W. & E.P.
Alonzo D.	Apr.25,1861 - Apr.4,1862, s/o H.W.&E.P.
Henry W.	Jan.6,1884 - Oct.20,1893, s/o L.M. & Dora E.
Dora	Dec.28,1863 - Aug.24,1894,w/o L.M. Ewing.
Vica G.	1851 - 1914
Mattie E.	1856 - no date
Fain, Thomas H.	1872 - 1902
Anice Y.	1878 - 1955
Gertrude Worley	Apr.29,1871 - Jan.20,1909, w/o John M.Fain.
John M.	1861 - 1950
Margaret Carr	1854 - 1949
Faison, Garnett	1982
Fauver, Andrew W.	June 4,1920 - Jan.26,1924
Joseph H.	Nov.3,1875 - Nov.4,1925
Rose E.	July 12,1880 - May 12,1953
Charles H.	June 26,1907 - Aug.27,1967
J.William	1905 - 1971
Maudie L.	1910 - no date
John W.,Jr.	Nov.12,1936, infant
Anna M.	June 14,1934 - Aug.17,1936
Faw, Walter	Nov.22,1900 - June 17,1901, s/o C.P. & B.H.
Tom and Jul	Jan.7,1893 - June 14,1893;twins/o C.P. & B.H.

Faw, Frank W.	Jan.5,1871 - Sept.19,1891
Feathers, Virginia B.	Oct.7,1914 - no date
Wiley James	June 23,1910 - Aug.28,1892
Feazell, Margaret Bune Bates	Sept.3,1892 - May 21,1962
Elbert A.	1884 - 1934
Fenner, Joseph	June 16,1890 - Jan.14,1966
Susie Swift	Aug.20,1890 - Dec.28,1884
Fleenor, Ancel Howard	d.Jan.15,1877, aged 8m2d.,s/o C & R.Fleenor.
A.D.	1875 - 1919
Virgie L. Giesler	1883 - 1926
Baby	b. & d. Feb.17,1903, s/o A.D. & Virginia
Joseph Isaac	Jan.18,1924 - May 10,1945
William C.	June 9,1921 - July 8.1981
William C.	1872 - 1932
Mettie McClelan	1896 - 1927
Fleming, Florence Shell	1909 - 1981
Roy Franklin	1897 - 1968
Teddy F.	Sept.24,1929 - July 30,1963
William Franklin	1878 - 1942
Robert Lee	1869 - 1945
Fannie O. Morgan	1876 - 1945
Ford, Thelma Bunn	1916 - 1937
Foust, Mary E.	Mar.27,1897 - Nov.4,1898
James H.	Mar.16,1890 - Mar.11,1891,s/o S.J.& M.L.
John R.	1879 - 1959
Susan L.	1876 - 1951
William K.	Apr.28,1857 - Aug.26,1925
Elizabeth A.	Jan.1,1873 - Jan.28,1957
Frazier, Albert Sidney	1865 - 1917
Mollie Catherine	1882 - 1906,w/o Albert S. Frazier.
Freeland, Emma Raper	Mar.28,1886 - Sept.26,1901,d/o R.H.& V.J.
Freeman, Clydene S.	1939 - 1970
Mary C.	1890 - 1980
Thomas B.	1893 - 1936
Helen Carrier	1926 - 1974
Friebel, Clara S.	Dec.4,1905 - Dec.26,1971
Friesland, Hal Douglass	Sept.29,1941 - Sept.29,1941
Galloway, C.H.	Apr.16,1906 - Sept.2,1906,s/o J.R.& R.A.
Robert	Dec.5,1870 - May 7,1960
Roxie H.	Apr.16,1869 - July 24,1964
Gammon, Maxie B.	1920 - 1985
Geisler, Charlie H.	Aug.30,1900 - Jan.14,1959
Litha Mae	Feb.14,1902 - Jan.16,1925
Howe	Oct.22-25, 1915, s/o Ed & Nannie Geisler.
Sarah A. Thomas	1853 - 1894
Amanda D.	1861 - 1934
Hugh E. Giesler	1851 - 1920
Charlie M.	1874 - 1898
Noah H.	1886 - 1957
Mary M.	1882 - 1965
Will H.	Mar.30,1880 - Sept.14,1914

Morningside Cemetery, cont.

Gentry, Smith B.	1895 - 1979, m.Dec.26,1933
Opal	1912 - 1961
Robert B.	Nov.11,1920 - Aug.5,1944
Gerstle, Katie	Mar.19,1876 - Aug.31,1877
Gibson, Infant	no dates, s/o C.L. & F.S. Gibson.
Gibson, Fannie Sells	1888 - 1918
Giesler, A.J.	Oct.16,1848 - Oct.20,1932
Haynes Earnest	Aug.27,1895 - Jan.8,1911,s/o A.J.&M.A.
Margaret A. Mauk	Dec.19,1858 - Mar.25,1912, w/o A.J.
Jacob	July 6,1832 - Mar.22,1900,m.Sept.11,1842
Clemma	Aug.27,1821 - Dec.14,1908
W.C.	Mar.9,1878 - July 11,1904
Martha B. McAmis	Aug.22,1875 - Aug.5,1898, w/o
	W.A.C.Giesler, Aug.1,1897.
Henry	Aug.31,1818 - Sept.16,1900
Nancy A. Mauk	Nov.19,1829 - Feb.28,1911, w/o Henry.
Beulah A.	Feb.15,1884 - Dec.12,1885
Giles, D.N.	1844 - 1924, Co.C.59 Inf. CSA.
Emma F.	Feb.17,1838 - Feb.9,1907, w/o D.N.Giles,
	w/o T.W.Jenkins.
Gilley, James McCoy	Apr.23,1874 - Oct.29,1945
Mollie Inez	Aug.12,1879 - no date
Gilreath, Charlene R.	Oct.11,1931
Glover, Raymond F.	May 1,1907 - Sept.26,1953
Frank M.	Feb.7,1867 - Dec.14,1948
Sarah T.	Oct.16,1873 - Feb.20,1956
Earl Lee	Apr.26,1891 - June 27,1980
William M.	1877 - 1970
Tonie Webb	1877 - 1940
Albert A.	Jan.9,1902 - Oct.31,1984
William B.	Nov.24,1905 - Oct.11,1978
Ethel L.	Mar.4,1910 - no date
Worley C.	Oct.27,1909 - Aug.27,1954
Mollie C.	Oct.22,1872 - Dec.25,1957
Andrew J.	May 1, 1854 - Jan.23,1929
Godsey, Blanche Haun	Sept.6,1872 - Apr.24,1949
Thomas F.	May 8,1900 - Aug.29,1962
Grace F.	Dec.12,1907 - no date
Paul P.	Nov.16,1915 - Apr.18,1964
Novella C.	July 30,1919 - no date
Good, Annie Bates	June 8,1876 - Nov.15,1948
Goodwin, Elbert A.	1876 - 1934
Infant	Mar.28,1927 - Mar.31,1927, s/o E.A. & Ruth.
Gorman, Charles Ed.	Aug.1,1904 - Feb.8,1976
Green, Riley & Ann	no dates
Greenway, Albert A.	Oct.22,1909 - Dec.4,1979
Ruth C.	Nov.18,1914 - no date
Griffith, Robert H.,Jr.	Oct.28,1910 - Jan.31,1979
Margaret E.	1878 - 1967
Robert H.	1877 - 1944
A.	Apr.12,1890 - July 2,1891
Nannie L.C.	Jan.20,1873 - Jan.6,1897
Bertha	1915 - 1984
Patrick	1920 - 1980

Morningside Cemetery,cont.

Grimsley, Lucy Anderson	Feb.26,1904 - May 29,1962
Guthrie, Landon	1860 - 1924
Charles C.	Apr.12,1889 - Nov.25,1952
Mattie R.	1899 - 1952
Russell T.	Aug.14,1894 - May 22,1950
Clarence	June 14,1891 - Aug.13,1945
Hall, Robert Y.	Aug.20,1866 - Feb.14,1940
Clara Atkinson	Nov.29,1870 - May 18,1921
Basil	June 6,1903 - June 24,1956
Lutz Earl	Nov.25,1897 - Dec.18,1979
Hamilton, P.H.	1835 - 1922
Nannie M.	1850 - 1921
Charles K.	1888 - 1942
Ina B.	1906 - 1966
John M.	1866 - 1935
Lucy V.	1863 - 1944
Thelma	July 3,1905 - Oct.7,1905, d/o J.M. & L.V.
Infant	b. & d. Jan.14,1887, s/o P.H.& N.M.
Hammer, George Wilbur,Sr.	May 6,1896 - Apr.3,1967
Barbara Henley	Feb.19,1929 - June 18,1983
Dorothy	1915 - 1920, d/o G.W.& M.F.Hammer.
Maxie Denny	Mar.10,1894 - July 20,1965
Hampton, Ina B.	Sept.12,1935 - July 4,1971
Hansford, J.G.	Dec.12,1869 - Jan.5,1904
Mary M.	1842 - 1916
Harkleroad, Elzira	Mar.12,1840 - June 4,1889, w/o J.I.
Florence U.	Mar.24,1873 - Feb.18,1907, 2nd w/o J.I.
Emaline	Dec.9,1826 - Dec.18,1883
Henry	Oct.7,1829 - Feb.16,1884
Mary E.	Jan.21,1889 - Oct.19,1883, d/o D.M. & M.M.
Willis	Aug.18,1881 - Feb.15,1891,s/o W.D. & Irene.
W.D.	1841 - 1929
Irena	1846 - 1903
Andrew R.	July 20,1834 - Apr.20,1880
Katie L.	Mar.17,1857 - July 9,1885, w/o T.J.
Walter E.	1881 - 1955
Joseph Franklin	1874 - 1929
Elizabeth N.	1886 - 1965
Daniel Miller	Jan.9,1863 - Sept.19,1936
Maggie Glover	Jan.24,1871 - Jan.19,1950
Robert C.	Oct.6,1904 - no date
Sue Jones	July 8,1902 - no date
Landon D.	1861 - 1910
Andrew J.	1882 - 1916
Cecil	1914 - 1918, s/o L.E.& F.E.Harkleroad.
Infant	May 4,1908, inf/o D.M.& M.M.
Fredie	May 8, 1891, s/o I.M. & M.E.Harkelroad.
Isaac M.	Dec.31,1872 - no date
Mary E.	Mar.15,1873 - Nov.20,1947
Emma	Oct.8,1900 - Nov.3,1900, d/o I.M.& M.E.
Roy B.	1893 - 1949
Clyde	Dec.26,1896 - Mar.20,1897, s/o I.M.& M.E.

Morningside Cemetery, cont.

Harkleroad, George W.	no dates, Co.K. 26 TN Cav. CSA.
John W.	1864 - 1932
Julia	1870 - 1936
Andrew J.	1913 - 1980
Bashie H.	Jan.25,1887 - Dec.29,1967
J.I.	Nov.22,1837 - Jan.13,1924
Pauline	1910 - 1914, d/o J.I. & B.Harkleroad.
Shelby Delores	1936, d/o Pearl & Tom Harkleroad.
William H.	1851 - 1913
Mattie J.	1864 - 1941
Infant	Apr.21,1919, d/o L.E. & D.K.
Andrew P.	Apr.2,1889 - Feb.19,1971
Maxie Geisler	Sept.7,1888 - no dates
Willie J.	1897 - 19--
Bessie Lee	1899 - 1971
Logie E.	Oct.5,1887 - July 31,1962
Dora K.	Apr.4,1888 - May 12,1960
Henry J.	1875 - 1961
Mary E.	1872 - 1961
Clyde S.	1900 - 1948
Jacob H.	Feb.9,1871 - Apr.26,1934
Florence C.	Aug.30,1877 - Dec.27,1961
Jesse J.	1893 - 1977
Alice Rutledge	1901 - no date
Barbra	1936 - 1936
Jessie	1930 - 1930
Evelyn Hull	Aug.21,1902 - Aug.20,1978
Arthur E.	Sept.26,1903 - Aug.24,1977
John Willis	Mar.15,1900 - Jan.20,1948
Pearl Ethel	Aug.13,1905 - no date
Helen M.	Jan.1,1927 - July 18,1929, d/o John & Pearl.
George D.	1891 - 1950
Maude C.	1890 - 1948
William E.	Aug.21,1862 - July 17,1947
Ruth	June 10,1865 - Aug.13,1924
A.R.	1869 - 1912
Charles	Dec.20,1895 - Feb.11,1902, s/o C. & A.
Infant	Sept.8,1899 - Oct.22,1901,d/o C. & A.
Harmon, Will	1890 - 1974
Mae	1891 - 1926
Lynn W.	Aug.12,1918 - Sept.23,1976
Virginia P.	1921 - no date
Myrtle Lyon	Oct.12,1894 - Aug.23,1974
Hurley C.	Aug.28,1894 - June 25,1940
Susie K.	Apr.28,1894 - June 28,1962
Harrigan, Lester T.	July 31,1897 - Apr.26,1966
Margaret E.	Apr.29,1898 - June 23,1975
John Anderson	1871 - 1941
Eliza Dyche	1875 - 1960
Hawk, James	no dates
Eliza L.	Apr.1,1835 - May 30,1905
Della	Feb.24,1866 - Jan.22,1898
Hawkins, Gordon M.	1971 - 1971
Hendrix, Nannie Gertrude	Jan.25,1897 - Oct.10,1902, d/o J.H. & S.
Vonnie V.	Aug.14,1904 - Nov.4,1904

…irix, Aetna   190⌇ - 1963
    Sudie R.   187⌇ - 1946
    Erful D.   190⌇ - 1971
…iley, Roy C.   191⌇ - 1982
    Harlan   191⌇ - 1980
    Fannie S.   1874 - 1949
    S.G.   1865 - 1934
    Opie S.   1902 - 1927
…enry, Hattie Gertrude   1893 - 1976
    Nora Josephine   1868 - 1912
    Earl Erwin   July 16,1895 - Dec.9,1971
    Blanche Henton   Feb. 17,1902 - June 27,1979
Henson, Charles P.   1858 - 1942
    Sallie L.   1860 - 1915
    Frances E. Sells   July 29,1850 - Aug.12,1917
    Rittie L.   Dec.9, 1895 - Jan.18,1975
    Helen   May 7, 1923 - May 9,1923
    Bobby   June 22,1932 - May 1,1934
    Harvey McCoy   Jan.5, 1890 - July 15,1955
    Thomas J.   Oct.4, 1893 - Sept.25,1954
    Lucy Lee   May 25, 1895 - Nov.3,1945
Hickman, Robert C.   July 22,1922 - Sept.2,1971
Hicks, Emma A. Fickle   Oct.2, 1854 - July 30,1886, w/o A.F.
    Ben   Apr.24, 1865 - Dec.19,1892
    J.P.   Dec.12, 1826 - Jan.30,1902
    Elizabeth   Oct.20, 1827 - Feb.16,1889,w/o J.P.Hicks.
    Della   May 8,1872 - Apr.16,1886
    H.L.D.   Dec.15, 1887 - July 5,1888, s/o J.N.&M.C.
    N.H.   Aug.29, 1880 - Oct.18,1881,d/o J.N.& M.C.
    James B.   Sept.28,1822 - Feb.23,1891
    Agnes C.   Aug.1,1828 - Apr.14,1903
    Fannie G.   1865 - 1923
    Albert H.   1901 - 1977
    Grace L.   1901 - no date
    Albert Edwin   Oct.13,1942 - Oct.18,1942,s/o A.H. & Grace.
    Joe Lee   June 10,1879 - Feb.21,1911
    Buford   Oct.16,1904 - July 7,1907
    Joseph S.   Oct.24,1846 - July 4,1923
    Hazel Lee   Oct.20,1943 - Dec.17,1943
    Thomas   Feb.21,1905 - no date
    Lela L.   Feb.29,1904 - Oct.26,1981
    George J.   1892 - 1969
    Nora E.   1884 - 1946
    G.James   Feb.27,1852 - May 14,1924
    Mary   Nov.7,1860 - Oct.22,1891, w/o G.J.
    Florence A.   Feb.8,1932 - Aug.25,1985
    Blanche M.   Sept.1905 - Mar.1974
    Toy N.   1897 - 1942
Hobbs, Harrison H.   Aug.1,1833 - Nov.15,1923
    Eliza Ann   July 21,1846 - Aug.5,1933
Hodge, Mary L.   June 18,1875 - June 4,1961
    Lassie   Aug.18,1910 - Sept.26,1973
    Marcus   Nov.6,1876 - Jan.3,1925
    Maggie Ellen   July 16,1881 - Feb.21,1975

Morningside Cemetery, cont.

Hodges, Elizabeth Combs	Feb.4,1835 - Nov.5,1906,m.A.R.Harkleroad
	Sept.21,1856. m. C.A.Hodges,Feb.26,1893.
Henry H.	Apr.28,1854 - Sept.5,1913
Jennie V.	Sept.23,1859 - Jan.30,1930
J.M.	Sept.15,1847 - Jan.20,1910
O.P.	June 16,1870 - July 4,1899
Addie E.	Aug.19,1847 - Feb.26,1907, w/o J.M.
Wanda Mae	Jan.11,1885 - Jan.12,1885,d/o H.H.& J.V.
John M.	1910 - 1971
Ethel	1911 - 1973
Holley, A.J.	1875 - 1969
Holt, John Wesley, Jr.	Aug.4,1941 - Apr.27,1945,s/o J.W.& L.M.
Hood, John D.	May 19,1871 - June 20,1951
Nancy Tate	Feb.14,1900 - June 3,1973
Houston, J.P.	Mar.16,1869 - July 16,1926
Mary Hannah	Jan.18,1883 - no date
J.N.	1861 - 1919
Nannie C.	1867 - 1944
Edward Dallas	Oct.12,1898 - Dec.31,1946
Howard, W.F.	1855 - 1899
Mollie Richmond	1855 - 1923
Hull, A.Frank	Feb.2,1881 - Feb.7,1963
Ruth M.	1928 - 1928
Humphreys, Georgia Lee	June 22,1924 - July 23,1955
Hunt, Phillis J.	Sept.9,1941 - July 5, 1942
Hutchins, Harry W.	1915 - no date
Eva Ruth	1920 - 1980
Hyatt, John	1927
John W.	1903 - 1966
Nora M.	1900 - 1975
Hyder, Carrie Morrell	1873 - 1955
Inscho, William L.	Aug.10,1915 - Sept.11,1968
Jacobs, Michael Lynn	Aug.31,1951 - June 25,1982
James, Evelyn	1983
Jarvis, Linda	1910 - 1911
Jenkins, Stannie L.	July 13,1870 - Jan.25,1871, s/o S.L. & E.A.
Delia C.	Mar.17,1867 - July 19,1891, w/o C.A.
Charles A.	d. Apr.18,1936
Lena Bates	d. Apr.13,1953
Samuel	1895, s/o C.A. & M.L.Jenkins.
Charles C.	Nov.19,1881 - Jan.9,1906,s/o I.A.&L.A.
Berlin	June 29,1887 - Jan.18,1913
Stanford L.	June 29,1828 - Sept.5,1908
Frances A.	Sept.18,1829 - Feb.13,1906,s/o S.L.Jenkins.
William Ensor	1897 - 1977
Wanda Mae	Oct.20,1891 - Sept.18,1952
Helen R.	Feb.2,1919 - Oct.4,1921,d/o J.A. & N.E.
Emma Sams	1878 - 1961
G.Edward	1878 - 1922
Loval	Oct.31,1895 - Sept.16,1952
Johnnie	1903 - 1944
Emma S.	1863 - 1941
Thomas	1861 - 1929

Morningside Cemetery, cont.

Jenkins, L. Bernese	19-- - 19--
L. Charles	1906 - 1948
Nema Durham	1913 - 19--
T.B. "Brack"	Nov.13,1888 - Oct.14,1947
Tommy	1906 - 1970
Frank	1909 - 1945
Nora N.	1901 - 1977
Johnson, Tommie	Apr.27,1872 - July 13,1885
Daniel	Aug.28,1870 - Sept.20,1889
John	d. June 18,1891, aged 54yrs.
Catherine	d. Sept.22,1918
Johnston, Earle C.	1899 - 1975
Nellie R.	1902 - no date
Rev. H.S.	1867 - 1936
Fanny S.	1874 - 1953
Joe H.	1903 - 1982
Ada B.	1906 - 1979
J.L.	1858 - 1929
N.T.	1863 - 19--
Gaynell	no date
Jones, M.Luther	July 7,1869 - Feb.11,1951
Lettie Jane	Aug.21,1877 - July 29,1962
Luther A.	Sept.18,1909 - Aug.10,1977
Florence L.	1901 - 1927
Annie	d.June 2,1894, w/o E.S.Jones.
Thomas B.	1902 - 1963
Mary H.	1908 - 19--
Oscar L.	Apr.5,1892 - Oct.9,1943
Dolly C.	1901 - 1964
Infant	May 21,1938, d/o Oscar & Dolly Jones.
Clarence "Casey"	Sept.14,1902 - Sept.20,1965
Arthur Ray	May 25,1852 - Jan.9,1976
Justice, William Lee	b. & d. Mar.9,1927
Kaywood, Alexander	1870 - 1953
Elsie	1901 - 1955
Kaylor, Arnold H.	June 13,1911 - May 20,1965
Kensinger, Dr. E.C.	1886 - 1930
Ketron, Joseph	1866 - 1935
King, John P.	Jan.12,1820 - July 26,1882
Mary J.	Aug.12,1829 - June 9,1907
Rittie	b. July 18,1875, w/o J.W.King
J.W.	Nov.6,1854 - June 19,1926
Martha Alice	Apr.9,1857 - Jan.3,1920
Arlie	1900 - 1915
Jeffrey Scott	Oct.22,1963 - Oct.22,1963
Cora Belle	no dates, w/o Dr.E.S.King.
Dr. E.S.	1864 - 1922
Ann Pemberton	no dates, d/o Dr. & Mrs.Edward Stanton King.
Kirkpatrick, James C.	July 9,1933 - Aug.26,1955
Mary Ada	Dec.28,1904 - Oct.1,1957
Kyte, John W.	1945
Lambert, Mollie M.	1876 - 1954

Morningside Cemetery, cont.

Landers, Jimmy Lee	1964 - 1966
Latture, Charlie T.	Jan.24,1879 - Apr.22,1953
Mary Blanche	Mar.13,1888 - Dec.3,1947
Lee, Robert L.	July 10,1910 - Apr.18,1938
Edna L.	1904 - 1914
Ed	1869 - 1934
Nancy A.	1872 - 1925
Leonard, Marcel C.	1943 - 1967
James D.	July 10,1893 - July 23,1974
Rhoda C.	Sept.23,1889 - no date
Lewis, Anna M.	1898 - 1955
I. Fielden	Oct.18,1862 - June 28,1909
Lilley, Ivan H.	Nov.27,1917 - Sept.29,1981
Stella M.	Aug.2,1910 - Aug.24,1978
Lindamood, W.C.	June 16,1877 - Oct.3,1910
M.W.	Feb.22,1838 - Apr.27,1923
Sallie B. Millard	Feb.17,1847 - Aug.7,1914
Lingerfelt, William E.	Feb.22,1923 - Oct.1,1983
Lions, James Tipton	1882 - 1946
Lipps, Geo. K.	Mar.20,1832 - Aug.16,1901, Co.C.,13th TN Cav.
Michael M.	1856 - 1927
Alice E.	1862 - 1942
Little, J.Henry	no dates
George F.	1890 - 1971
Lena S.	1890 - 1954
Wiley Graves	Feb.17,1923 - Nov.25,1946
William A.	Sept.2,1867 - July 3,1937
Fannie L. Hall	Sept.9,1864 - Dec.4,1931
Andrew	Sept.12,1898 - May 27,1980
Fay	Nov.9,1898 - June 18,1976
Catherine Harkleroad	1844 - 1920, w/o G.W.Little.
G.W.	Feb.9,1843 - Mar.29,1906
Laura E.	1892 - 1914
Jacob H.	1870 - 1947
Martha V.	1872 - 1953
Uncle Charley	May 8,1884 - Nov.6,1956
Kate B.	Apr.10,1884 - Jan.14,1966
Joseph W.	Jan.25,1878 - Feb.25,1953
Sarah E.	Jan.27,1877 - May 30,1963
Littleford, Charles R.	1876 - 1947
Love, Mary E. Greelee	1871 - 1918, w/o D.W.Love.
Beauford L.	Dec.11,1907 - Aug.13,1908, s/o D.W. & M.E.
Lovelace, Tommy David	June 16,1957
Lyon, Curtin	1887 - 1963
Nora	1890 - 1979
Samuel T.	June 19,1872 - Mar.4,1940
Maggie L.	Aug.11,1873 - Apr.23,1943
John A.	Nov.26,1906 - May 10,1961
John E.	Dec.3,1915 - June 3,1916
five infants	no dates, W.D. Lyon.
Grace Miller	1891 - 19--
Effie Cawood	1890 - 1942
William David	1864 - 1947

Lyon, Nannie Eads	1864 - 1921
John S.	1834 - 1912
Margaret Ellis	1834 - 1917
Infant	1954 - 1954, s/o R.L.Lyon.
Alfred J.	1890 - 1962
Josie B.	1888 - 1957
David Lee	Sept.19,1882 - Nov.3,1966
Mollie W.	Aug.15,1889 - Oct.23,1975
Infant	Jan.26,1948 - Jan.27,1948,d/o Bailey Lyon.
Joseph H.	July 9,1946 - July 10,1946
Hubert H.	Oct.14,1918 - July 31,1948
Samuel A.	Apr.26,1896 - Mar.31,1970
?	Jan.3,1900 - Jan.8,1977
Lee L.	1898 - 1933
Margaret C.	1862 - 1929
Myrtle N.	1885 - 1963
Elizabeth	1871 - 1938
Thomas E.	1880 - 1946
Ada M.	1884 - 1972
Raymond Allen	Mar.26,1937 - Dec.6,1971
McBroom, Christopher C.	Oct.16,1979 - May 17,1980
McClellan, Jonathan B.,Jr.	Nov.22,1900 - Nov.19,1975
Bettie E. Wyatt	d.M r.24,1901, aged 37y5m9d,w/o A.McClellan.
Capt. D.	d.Apr.25,1862, aged 47y8m4d
Elizabeth	Jan.21,1874, aged 56y6m15d.
J.B.	1854 - 1901
Harriet Isadore Briscoe	1873 - 1948
Dora Belle Carter	Aug.15,1869 - Feb.24,1892, w/o J.B.
Mary E.	Oct.22,1849 - May 7,1882, w/o E.A.
A.	1843 - 1915
Mary	Sept.27,1804 - Dec.19,1884
Oliver	May 9,1903 - Jan.8,1957
Sarah N.	1861 - 1930
Simpson Wolf	1856 - 1948
Francis Sue	1920 - 1926
Florence Louise	1912 - 1927
William M.	1882 - 1929
Belle Glenn	June 30,1881 - June 8,1968
McClelland, Elizabeth M.	Nov.26,1865 - Aug.19,1948
Jacob H.	1852 - 1916
John Page,Sr.	Mar.13,1894 - Mar.19,1944
Mary Clemma	Sept.15,1898 - Apr.22,1980
McGhee, Eugene	Apr.2,1904 - Mar.17,1958
McGalamary, Rhoda M.	no dates
McGuire, John G.	1868 - 1929
Florence	1875 - 1941
McKamey, R. Frank,Sr.	1870 - 1932
Melissa C.	1873 - 1947
John R.	1892 - 1959
Lily B.	1897 - 1977
McKinney, Robert Franklin	Apr.21,1946 - Aug.25,1959
Oscar A.	1893 - 1924
Maggie Ray	1890 - 1975
John S.	1870 - 1931

Morningside Cemetery, cont.

McKinney, Martha Ann	1874 - 1953
William P.,Jr.	Dec.25,1922 - July 5,1930
William P.	July 12,1896 - Nov.15,1967
Dewey D.	May 10,1898 - no date
John H.	1924 - 1982
Nellie Marie	Feb.26,1943
Linda Lee	July 18,1944
William O.	June 11,1919 - July 2,1948
Madison, Donald Rey	Sept.20,1955 - Jan.14,1982
Claude	May 23,1917 - Sept.29,1984
Dan S.	Apr.15,1921 - Jan.8,1977
Mahaffey, William J.	1872 - 1942
Rusha M.	1872 - 1955
John J.	Nov.19,1874 - Apr.30,1923
James E.	1837 - 1919
Hannah Francis St.John	1850 - 1879,whose remains lay at Green Springs, Virginia.
Infant	1920
Blanche M.	1886 - 1959
Charles L.	1876 - 1948
Charles L.	1924 - 1933, s/o C.L. & L.B. Mahaffey.
Ruby	1912 - 1938
Malone, Martin S.	Oct.20,1881 - Nov.16,1962
Effie B.	1884 - 1926
Dorothy Jane	1922 - 1923
Robert F.	July 14,1924 - May 31,1928
James E.	Jan.20,1928 - July 14,1928
Phillip K.	Oct.2,1938 - Oct.10,1953
Robert L.	July 18,1905 - Dec.21,1982
Bobby L.	Sept.5,1945 - Sept.6,1945
L.C.	1904 - 1976
Bessie I.	1898 - 1974
J.D. "Dick"	1892 - 1968
Roscoe R.	May 15,1896 - Apr.4,1962
Mattie M.	1882 - 1960
Sallie E.	1856 - 1934
Robert R.	1850 - 1904
Billy B.	May 10,1936 - Oct.10,1953
Jacqueline Louise	Feb.1,1938 - Feb.18,1950
Mary E.	1910 - 1976
Manes, George Dewey	Mar.16,1898 - July 20,1899,s/o W.A. & S.E.
Marion, R.L.	1879 - 1926
Myrtle A.	1879 - 1961
Marion, Emery C.	June 30,1906 - Apr.15,1907, s/o R.L.& M.A.
J.Frank	1857 - 1936
Rachel E.	1857 - 1943
Ora Elizabeth	1880 - 1954
Charles	1909 - 1932
Eddie	1895 - 1964
Marley, N. Pauline	Nov.10,1927 - Nov.11,1935
Mary R.	Dec.16,1924 - Feb.12,1928
George F.	Apr.16,1893 - Apr.11,1962

Morningside Cemetery, cont.

Masengill, Fannie Deborah	June 1883 - July 1902
Infant	Feb.28,1882, s/o G.D. & M.E.
George D.	July 1844 - June 1897
Lilly Flora	d. Jan.1,1880, aged 8m4d, d/o J.T.&M.A.
Ruby	Aug.31,1885 - Sept.16,1887, d/o J.T.& Mary.
Joseph F.	Apr.19,1838 - Jan.11,1906
Susan C. Thomas	May 8,1838 - Sept.11,1905
Massengill, Roy Clifton	1876 - 1948
Cora Myrtle	1874 - 1966
Evan Porter	1879 - 1954
John Lynn	1922 - 1922
Lissie Burnett	1886 - 1922
Helen Regina	1912 - 1913
Mary Evans	1853 - 1922
Frederick M.D.	Aug.8,1874 - Feb.28,1938
Eulalia I. Logan	Feb.2,1880 - Sept.18,1972
Felty D.	1870 - 1942
Ollie Cox	1876 - 1951
Joseph Cox	1917 - 1919, s/o Ollie Cox & F.D.Massengill.
J.B.	1890 - 1956
Nellie S.	1891 - 1978
Mast, Jason C.	May 9,1900 - Nov.14,1966
Maxine	Oct.16,1894 - no date
Matthews, Wilbur W.	May 22,1871 - Jan.21,1893,s/o F.H. & M.C.
Mauk, Herry A.	1854 - 1939
Maggie Alice Miller	1860 - 1932
Metzger, Sue E. Curtis	Nov.4,1903 - Jan.1,1981
Milhorn, Sam J.	1887 - 1978
Sallie L.	1893 - 1967
J.W.	1915 - 1933
Andrew E.	1917 - 1919
James F.	1854 - 1921
Rebecca	1860 - 19--
Fred	Mar.28,1900 - Apr.28,1923
Eugene	Mar.4,1916 - June 7,1960
John O.	Jan.24,1907 - Sept.16,1964
Richard H.	1861 - 1944
Laura	1878 - 1948
Walter L.	July 31,1891 - Jan.17,1977
Ethel S.	Feb.4,1896 - July 29,1931
Edward Ralph	June 22,1918 - Oct.18,1984
Pauline G.	Jan.12,1926 - Aug.29,1967
William J.	1896 - 1962
Repha F.	no dates
Everett J.	Oct.1,1909 - May 18,1977
Jewel Richard	Aug.19,1940 - Mar.26,1970
Carol June	May 12,1935
Barbara A.	1941 - 1979
Winfred	no date
Eva	1978
Millard, Donzella S.	no dates
John W.	1869 - 1949
Martha C.	1870 - 1924

Millard, Ollie Sue	1874 - 1938
James I. (Bruce)	July 4,1904 - Feb.6,1978
Linnie Mae	1902 - 1976
Miller, Nannie M.	Feb.16,1872 - June 26,1908
C.W.	Oct.3,1865 - July 23,1949
Sallie I.B. Pile	May 10,1862 - Aug.2,1901
Vicy	1852 - 1938
James M.	1842 - 1909
Walter E.	Jan.8,1882 - Nov.11,1968
Lucy A.	July 4,1889 - Jan.27,1961
Hettie R.	1874 - 1925
S.L.	1855 - 1912
William Toy	Sept.18,1892 - May 10,1931
Louise H.	no dates
Daniel Henderson	1855 - 1929
Ellen Frances Anderson	1858 - 1915
John Thurman	Mar.20,1890 - May 31,1954
Robert Abe	June 16,1901 - Aug.10,1980
William G.	Dec.25,1911 - Dec.27,1958
P.H.	1863 - 1923
Martha	1878 - 1919
E.Dewey	1898 - 1962
Maggie S.	1897 - 1975
Oleta	Apr.24,1927 - May 10,1927
J.L.	May 5,1923 - July 1,1926
James Bentley	1896 - 1934
John B.	1860 - 1939
Harriet Jones	1869 - 1946
Earl C.	Apr.29,1907 - Sept.9,1970
Ida D.	1906 - 1977
Chester	Feb.22,1934 - Oct.30,1970
Rose M. Franklin	Oct.2,1941 - Mar.29,1973
James Elbert	1875 - 1945
Mary Nelson	1881 - 1947
Roy Ernest	1907 - 1939
W.Harrison	Aug.5,1892 - Apr.6,1972
Ethel S.	Dec.8,1897 - no date
Bertha	d.Dec.18,1961
Hazel Helena	1914 - 1946
S.Jones	1859 - 1951
Mary Eliza	1868 - 1943
Richard	1857 - 1934
Francis	1859 - 1914
Susan Effie	Nov.9,1884 - Nov.29,1887, d/o R.& F.I.
Matilda Wright	d.June 17,1878, aged 74yrs.
William J.	Dec.14,1867 - Jan.12,1935
Sallie K. Mottern	1868 - 1943
Harmon	1895 - 1943
Wolford W.	June 21,1909 - July 25,1961
Adam Trigg	1905 - 1977
Mills, E.A.	June 27,1847 - Jan.16,1906
Maggie J. Hicks	Apr.9,1851 - Mar.11,1932, w/o E.A.Mills.
Lula Margaret	Apr.5,1878 - Mar.12,1952, d/o E.A. & Margaret Hicks Mills.

Morningside Cemetery, cont.

Mills, Harry L.	Nov.21,1884 - Dec.31,1947
Sallie Ann	Dec.3,1889 - Dec.1,1952
Minnick, William H.	Apr.8,1967 - Dec.23,1929
Glen E.	Aug.18,1908 - Sept.28,1964
Moody, Malissa A.	d.Sept.6,1899, aged 77y11m8d.
Dr.Earl H.	1897 - 1944
Rosalind Hyder	1916 - 1977
Johanna H.	1869 - 1959
Wm. T.F.	1863 - 1951
Morgan, Fannie Lynn	1923 - 1984
Morrell, Mary E.	Feb.28,1904 - Mar.16,1904
Nancy E.	Feb.7,1867 - Dec.7,1921
Joseph A.	Apr.15,1864 - Aug.31,1946
Clara Gay	Mar.30,1890 - Sept.20,1900
Edith K.	Feb.6,1901 - Feb.11,1985
Alice	1887 - 1915
Sallie	1865 - 1894
Albert M.	1862 - 1934
Bessie	1904
Infant	1905
Jennie	1880 - 1937
Frank C.	no dates
Alice H.	1898 - 1981
George A.	Nov.5,1914 - Aug.12,1943
Albert	1880 - 1934
Richard P.	1966 - 1966
Fairy Lee	d.Mar.5,1955, aged 1y1m.
Infant	July 20 - Aug.12,1894, s/o S.G. & L.J.
Emma F.	Aug.12,1886 - Jan.9,1888, s/o S.G.& L.J.
Edith	1901 - 1903
Infant	June 5,1904 - Nov.10,1906, s/o C.E.& Dora.
Johnnie A.	1947 - 1949
Clifford L.	1946 - 1946
Rev. Woodrow	1916 - no date, m. Feb.15,1937
Iva Mae	1919 - 1983
J.E. "Jody"	Nov.3,1883 - Oct.3,1953
Infant	Apr.6,1921, d/o J.E. & A.B. Morrell.
Eulalia	1894 - 1918
Thurman	June 13,1924 - Aug.10,1929
J.D.	Oct.28,1922 - no date
Irene	Apr.16,1925 - Jan.26,1975
Henry	July 22,1890 - no date
Mary Jane	July 24,1885 - Sept.29,1969
Lonnie D.	Apr.6,1940 - June 24,1962
Bobby Kay	Nov.19,1952
Gary C.	Oct.11,1947
Annis Thomas	May 8,1858 - May 7,1942
John Harvey	Nov.25,1851 - Nov.19,1938
Bertha V.	Apr.24,1879 - Oct.2,1964
Charles V.	1896 - 1930
N.Pearl	1890 - 1926
Charles Edwin	July 1932 - July 15,1932
Samuel C.	1858 - 1948
Laura J.	1869 - 1932

Morningside Cemetery,cont.

Morrell, Kenneth W.	1933 - 1968
E. Luanne	1933 - 19--
Carl H.	Feb.13,1908 - May 24,1978
Myrtle F.	Mar.17,1911 - no date
Mary Dyche	Jan.19,1910 - Apr.11,1984
Elva Marie	1905 - 1978
William J.	June 6,1908 - Nov.1,1965
Mae S.	Feb.5,1899 - May 13,1978
Andrew Albert	Jan.6,1888 - May 8,1959
Robert Earl	Mar.12,1888 - Oct.12,1962
Hattie B.	Nov.17,1888 - Jan.16,1965
Frank H.	June 14,1890 - Oct.9, 1963
Beulah Mae	Feb.17,1894 - Apr.26,1956
Mattie A.	Aug.27,1867 - Aug.31,1925
Marshall	1844 - 1922
Susan C.	1847 - 19--
Morris, Marion Virginia	Jan.4,1919 - June 28,1979
Moss, John Curtis	Mar.24,1959 - June 25,1982
Mottern, John S.	1889(?) - 1978
Maude T.	1891 - 1979
Murphy, Cordie	May 11,1873 - May 25,1902, d/o T.J.&Ibby.
Murry, Jimmy A.	1970 - 1970
Myers, Mary	1850 - 1923
Birdie	1918 - 1968
Garland B.	1892 - 1965
Hattie H.	1897 - 1982
Neal, Sarah J.	1833 - 1919
Elmer K.	1903 - 1957
Bernie O.	1903 - 19--
Necessary, Eugene R.	Oct.5,1915 - Aug.9,1982
Nelson, Bob	Feb.22,1879 - Nov.7,1951
Eliza M.	June 15,1884 - ---,19--
Hubert Martin	1921 - 1952
John H.	1878 - 1955
Ella V.	1890 - 1967
John Paul	May 23,1923 - Dec.22,1975
Martin L.	May 10,1949 - Sept.21,1966
Newman, Mary	1902 - 1984
Newton, W.E.	Mar.9,1848 - July 9,1923
Lizzie E.	Apr.5,1870 - Apr.10,1963
Sarah B.	1839 - 1919, w/o James Newton.
R.L.	1875 - 1910
J.Guy	Mar.8,1904 - Nov.26,1921
Anna Pearl	Nov.4,1916 - Nov.26,1921
Infant	July 25,1909
Mary M.	July 6,1907 - Dec.15,1908
Jennie M.	Sept.18,1875 - Mar.9,1960, w/o Charles S.
Charlie S.	Jan.9,1869 - Dec.1,1930
Arkie Akers	Dec.13,1873 - Mar.20,1900, w/o C.S.Newton.
Nick D.	1910 - 1962
Glenna M.	1916 - 1965
Nichels, Robert	Apr.10,1910 - June 3,1911

Morningside Cemetery, cont.

Nichols, Acie	1896 - 1961
Eva	1891 - 1949
Ray	1891 - 1969
Lonie	1881 - 1960
Richard	1881 - 1939
Fred	d.June 26,1930
Grace S.	Oct.26,1897
Jonathan	Oct.26,1853 - June 8,1923
Eliza	Oct.22,1864 - Mar.6,1927
Sallie	no dates
Wm. T.	1872 - 1961
Eliza J. Elliot	Apr.6,1874 - Jan.31,1947
James A.	July 12,1905 - Dec.2,1942
Gay	no dates
Ava	no dates
Gilla	no dates
twins	no dates
Ama R. Smith	Feb.23,1913 - Feb.4,1984
Nickels, Henry E.	Nov.13,1880 - Apr.3,1954
Mary E.	July 16,1885 - ----, 1977
P.W.	Oct.9,1913 - Oct.11,1918
Alive Weaver	June 20,1854 - Jan.16,1940
K.Treola	1912 - 1938
Gladys P.	1903 - 1963
Veda L.	Feb.3,1906 - July 1,1929
Elbert R.	1878 - 1927
Bessie O.	1880 - 1941
Lula M.	1911 - 1912
Ethel	d. 1975
Frances Mae	1958 - 1958
Curtis Lynn	Mar.20,1953 - Sept.4,1979
Mark R.	Aug.7,1980, s/o Doug & Kathy Nickels.
Jinnie	d.1958
Bonnie	d.1966
Guy D.	d.1967
Odell, Martha Ella	Dec.7,1896 - Oct.16,1973
John Edward	Nov.13,1874 - Mar.20,1969
Ollie B.	July 5,1877 - Dec.15,1957
Oliver, Glen S.	1915 - 1945, buried in Metz, France.
Walter P.	1885 - 1954
Cordia E.	1892 - 1972
Andy Snyder	Aug.31,1917 - no date
Vena Mae McCrary	May 23,1918 - Apr.10,1981
John	June 9,1894 - Feb.22,1936
Lillie B.	July 8,1900 - Apr.23,1977
Lonnie	Nov.11,1905 - June 13,1928
William J.	1879 - 19--
Rhoda	1882 - 1957
Owens, Ruth B.	Jan.17,1911 - June 25,1982
Parks, Nina Kate	1912 - 1943
Alfred Grant	1884 - 1959
Martha R.	1885 - 1969
Raleigh F.	Aug.9,1908 - Aug.28,1979
Ida C.	July 18,1903 - no date

Morningside Cemetery, cont.

Patton, Viva Hodge	Nov.9,1897 - Nov.13,1980
Mary Thomas Denny	1895 - 1918, w/o R.S.Patton.
Patterson, Norman E.	Apr.20,1918 - Dec.1,1978
Mary Ellenor	Nvo.20,1918 - July 12,1981
Sy A.	1867 - 1949
Sina Sine	1877 - 1947
Sine, Maria	1836 - 1934
Pennington, Howard	1913 - 1951
Roby Ambrose	1836 - 1965
Perry, Gleason Earl	1926 - 1926
Etta Bell	1929 - 1930
Peter, Rosa T.	Sept.29,1902 - Feb.28,1918
Theodore	May 8,1912 - May 27,1912
Infant	Dec.16-21.1904, s/o C.N. & M.M. Peters.
Minnie Clinton	Apr.30,1907 - Dec.3,1910, d/o C.N. & M.M.
Pearl Winona	Dec.18,1899 - Oct.2,1968
Cornelius N.	Sept.18,1866 - Feb.15,1937
Mollie M. Geisler	Oct.14,1877 - Nov.18,1966
Peterson, Orpha J.	Nov.1838 - Dec.1918
Phillips, Dorothy	1921 - 1923, d/o I.H. & T.M. Phillips.
Tracy M. Ryden	1897 - 1923, w/o J.H. Phillips.
Pierson, Carson D.	1943 - 1982
Worley L.	July 12,1907 - Aug.7,1983
Plank, Dr.G.L.	Aug.24,1864 - Aug.6,1906
Rutha	1869 - 1920, w/o G.L.Plank.
John Edward	Dec.22,1900 - Oct.15,1971
Virgie Hicks	Jan.28,1902 - June 21,1963
Prater, Lenah Newton	June 26,1892 - Nov.2,1979
Preston, Emmet D.	Nov.27,1874 - Jan.9,1943
Lodemia Jane Anderson	May 17, 1844 - Mar.31,1924, w/o John T.
Charles W.	1884 - 1973
Katherine C.	1894 - no date
Walter H.	Dec.16,1922 - Sept.12,1944
Puckett, Lynn	1950
Rankin, Rex R.	Aug.26,1900 - May 2,1975
Redfain, Lula	d. Oct.2,1941
Mary	d. Sept.16,1943
Reece, Charles E.	1902 - 1965
Beatrice W.	no dates
Reed, Susie	1907 - 1955
Reedy, Bess L.	1905 - 1937
Nannie E.	1874 - 1964
Reeves, Michael Lynn	May 27,1976 - Apr.24,1979
Ben Lee	Aug.3,1937 - July 8,1981
Reynolds, Lillian Crowder	July 26,1911 - Apr.27,1948
Repass, Jerry E.	May 22,1964 - May 24,1964
Rhea, Lucy J. Williams	1830 - 1916, w/o Samuel Rhea
Samuel	Sept.11,1830 - Jan.13,1902
Fanny McElwane	July 7,1879 - Nov.8,1899
Dr. J.A.L.	Mar.23,1869 - Oct.15,1948
Emma Mills	Oct.7,1874 - Dec.15,1954
Richmond, Shannon	1905 - 1982
George	1881 - 1958
Albert G.	Oct.9,1912 - Mar.10,1940

Richard, Nannie	1875 - 1962
Retha	1909 - 1921
Richards, Rutha A.	July 8,1837 - Oct.27,1913
B.H.	Feb.8,1834 - Sept.25,1909
Addie	May 30,1865 - July 5,1909
Lee D.S.	1862 - 1937
Ann R. Miller	1856 - 1935
F.M.	Sept.26,1866 - Dec.11,1870
Lee	Aug.1840 - Feb.11,1862
Stacy	1811 - Dec.27,1885
Herbert P.	Dec.11,1898 - Apr.28,1982
Mary H.	Jan.22,1901 - Sept.29,1974
Richardson, Nora	1896 - 1969
Lee L.	1891 - 1972
Riddle, Oscar	1975
Riden, William M.	Mar.2,1878 - July 15,1903
Riley, Ella Lucille	Jan.4,1905 - Nov.18,1907, d/o J.A. & M.A.
John M.	Apr.10,1859 - Dec.18,1934
Emma J.	1852 - 1929, w/o John M.Riley.
Minnie S.	May 21,1884 - Dec.25,1964
James A.	Feb.2,1884 - Nov.18,1945
Ralph	1925 - 1970
Charles David	1882 - 1942
William Harold	1925 - 1927
William W.	Jan.21,1852 - June 3,1938
Jennie E.	June 27,1888 - Dec.7,1965
Roy Akard	Apr.17,1895 - Dec.4,1972
Ina Smith	June 28,1905 - no date
Ritchie , Isaac R.	1875 - 1945
Ollie S.	1880 - 1938
Harold B.	1912 - 1918
Cileta M.	1905 - 1908
Silas M.	1841 - 1890
Mary Bishop	1846 - 1918
Roark, Jessie J.	Mar.17,1919 - Jan.25,1974
Vivian Francis	1955 - 1969
Roberts, Garrett H.	1916 - no date
Mary Jane	1921 - 1968
Charles O.	1907 - 1970
Nellie T.	1913 - 19--
Roden, Earl White	Dec.8,1896 - no date
William Herbert	Apr.8,1893 - Mar.18,1979
Roe, William Clay	Mar.12,1902 - July 18,1902
Andrew Johnson	June 16,1860 - Dec.15,1928
Nannie H.	June 29,1861 - Dec.25,1938
Henry C.	Jan.17,1857 - Jan.24,1927
Parlee B.	1859 - 1934
Freeman F.,Sr.	1891 - 1969
Clarence G.	d.Nov.8,1942
Fred	1896 - 1971
Franklin G.	1848 - 1917
Nancy E.	June 29,1849 - Sept.18,1925
Virginia	1881 - 1918
Oscar R.	1891 - 1974

Morningside Cemetery, cont.

Roe, J.L.	1869 - 1918
Adeline Smithton	no dates
Edgar L.	1896 - 1919
Elizabeth	Apr.30,1824 - Jan.11,1899
John Henry	1888 - 1890, s/o A.J. & Nannie
Lawrence	1875 - 1961
Chassie Mae	1883 - 1967
Ada Fields	Sept.17,1899 - Oct.25,1978
Rush, Etta Jenkins	1867 - 1920
Robert W.	1868 - 1940
Rutledge, James T.	May 6,1926 - June 22,1946
Gertrude	Sept.16,1906 - Apr.13,1942
Emerald R.	Apr.28,1902 - Aug.19,1983
Samuel T.	1867 - 1940
Louisa A.	1872 - 1954
Joe Allen	Feb.22,1928 - Mar.26,1929
Marvin D.	July 31,1935 - Mar.11,1936
William R.	Aug.31,1893 - May 12,1976
Ryden, Charles Thomas	1886 - 1945
Evelyn Ruth	1919, d/o C.T. & R.I. Ryden.
David Thomas	1850 - 1926
Nanney Smith	1856 - 1929
J.W.	1874 - 1955
E.L.	Oct.19,1880 - Nov.21,1966
Lena	Nov.4,1883 - Feb.29,1984
Salts, Cora Bell	Feb.10,1874 - Nov.4,1963
Mary J.	Mar.10,1856 - May 28,1942,w/o Thomas J.
Goscar B.	Dec.22,1897 - June 24,1899
James H.	July 21,1940 - May 29,1960
Sams, Evelyn L. Crowder	Dec.10,1882 - Feb.7,1938
Geneva	July 29,1898 - May 8,1925, d/o E.G. & Maggie.
Swanson	Mar.12,1910 - Aug.21,1936
Edward G.	Aug.1873 - Jan.1946
Maggie W.	Dec.14,1979 - Jan.6,1969
Viola	Oct.12,1902 - Feb.8,1978
William Randolph	Oct.14,1907 - July 25,1979
George Landon	1875 - 1928
Pearl	1876 - 1921
George L.	July 13,1904 - Sept.11,1966
James Murray	d. Oct.28,1922
Ruby I.	1924 - 1972
Isham H.	1895 - 1928
Charmie E.	1899 - no date
Savage, Herbert Jesse	Feb.1,1893 - Dec.29,1962
Ida Lee	Mar.10,1901 - Jan.26,1963
Scott, Conley S.	July 23,1881 - Nov.1,1943
Mary J.	Jan.30,1845 - Apr.19,1900
Sells, James Rodney	Aug.5,1923 - Nov.30,1923, s/o J.W. & O.B.
James W.	1893 - 1927
William Rodney	1852 - 1924
Nannie McClellan	1856 - 1929
Guy McClellan	1882 - 1901
Abraham David	1890 - 1929

Morningside Cemetery, cont.

Sharp, Edward S.	Jan.18,1937 - Apr.28,1962
Betty L.	Mar.1,1932 - Oct.5,1932
Henry Vance	May 9,1897 - May 23,1962
Isabell Dyche	Oct.20,1900 - Feb.27,1970
Shell, Fannie	Apr.13,1881 - Nov.27,1881, d/o Aaron & Anna.
Shelley, Jessie C.	1903 - 1980
Eliza H.	1911 - no date
Shepard, Joe L.	1897 - 1933
Lilliam	1903 - 1933
Shepherd, H.C.	d. Oct.17,1904
Silver, Lawrence A.	June 13,1916 - Apr.16,1918, s/o H.E. & E.K.
Eva Kate	1885 - 1956
Sims, George E.	d. June 15,1950
Stewart	d. Aug.18,1946
Hyder	Sept.20,1898 - May 4,1912, s/o David S.
David S.	Mar.7,1870 - July 18,1924
Slaughter, James D.	Sept.14,1905 - Mar.20,1972
Violet M.	Apr.2,1914 - Aug.1,1982
Smalling, Ann Crockett	1847 - 1936, w/o A.G.Smalling.
Smith, Elbert J.	Apr.23,1853 - Oct.30,1884
Jackson M.	Mar.9,1827 - Oct.25,1873
Catherine	1833 - 1979
David E.	May 12,1821 - Sept.9,1893
G.L.D.	Feb.10,1863 - Mar.31,1899
Elmer	1894 - 1940
Hubert Z.	Jan.10,1910 - July 12,1977
Ella L.	1869 - 1939
W.J.M.	1859 - 1923
William O.	Mar.11,1900 - Apr.11,1980
Milburn	Aug.20,1851 - Jan.31,1928
Permelia H.	1831 - 1912
James W.	June 2,1865 - Oct.14,1950
Theodocia Combs	Apr.11,1874 - Nov.12,1942
Wiley Samuel	May 21,1900 - Jan.23,1965
John L.	1895 - 1896
Roy T.	1893 - 1895
W.Walter	1872 - 1920
Clemmia	1870 - 1951
William	Jan.20,1824 - June 20,1894
Elizabeth	Aug.22,1825 - Aug.8,1906
John Aldine "Al"	June 22,1913 - Dec.22,1974
Hannah Worley Massengill	May 27,1915 - no date
Venice Thomas	Mar.24,1892 - Dec.4,1976
W.C.	1863 - 1919
Maude Aileen	July 1892 - Oct.10,1927
Belle M.	Jan.7,1884 - Sept.8,1965
Oscar R.	May 21,1901 - Aug.1,1912
Charles H.	May 18,1905 - Feb.16,1910
William C.	Dec.25,1875 - Mar.4,1939
J.C.	May 22,1916 - Nov.23,1934
Emmett E.	Mar.26,1892 - Mar.7,1958
James C.	Feb.16,1864 - Jan.13,1949
Carrie Lyon	Nov.18,1868 - Nov.20,1937

Morningside Cemetery, cont.

Smith, Augustus T.	1880 - 1926
Mabel R.	1882 - 1952
Charles B.	1884 - 1926
James Lee	no dates
Martha L.	1878 - 1963
Minnie F.	1894 - 1963
Elbert C.	Mar.23,1890 - Aug.8,1947
Harry Lee	Oct.19,1892 - June 29,1966
Ella A.	Dec.25,1891 - Oct.26,1855
Ralph S.	Nov.23,1895 - Nov.26,1952
Inez Miller	Dec.10,1901 - Nov.11,1967
Betty Lynn Hemphill	July 6,1930 - Mar.5,1970
Sobolewewski, Albert J.	Aug.14,1894 - July 12,1956
Spears, John H.	1882 - 1946
Emma H.	1880 - 1973
Sproles, B.F.	June 24,1873 - June 26,1952
Carrie N.	June 19,1885 - Sept.2,1972
Gold Catherine	Dec.9,1911 - Feb.12,1912, d/o B.F. & Carrie.
Stafford, Margaret Roe	1884 - 1938
Stanley, Nellie Doan	Aug.15,1897 - Oct.18,1933,w/o N.C.
Staples, J.H.C.	Sept.25,1875 - Mar.24,1954
Pearl H.	Feb.9,1873 - Dec.3, 1950
John	Oct.9,1908 - Aug.14,1972
R.Clarence	Mar.9,1873 - Mar.30,1950
Lola H.	Aug.27,1867 - Feb.4,1909
Mary Lynn	June 1,1898 - July 18,1934
Stapleton, Ralph J.	Aug.18,1913 - Dec.8,1946
S.P.	1908 - 1951
Lloyd L.	1883 - 1949
Robert L.	Mar.19,1911 - June 23,1969
Stewart, Betty	Aug.16,1897 - Oct.10,1974
Stine, William T.	Oct.3,1894 - Sept.8,1962
Nell B.	Feb.15,1895 - July 7,1970
John Abraham	1871 - 1940
Mary Ann	1871 - 19--
Charles F.	Jan.28,1900 - Mar.23,1959
John	Aug.25,1911 - Oct.7,1970
Verna B.	d.1922
Joseph E.	1894 - 1982
Rhelda G.	1898 - 19--
Stokes, Carson K.	July 22,1907 - Apr.7,1980
Kate G.	Dec.10,1910 - no date
Stone, Horton J.	Jan.24,1898 - Jan.14,1970
Ruth B.	June 14,1909 - Mar.7,1978
Stout, Terrance Michael	Feb.4,1947 - Mar.10,1947
Tate, William	1897 - 1948
Bessie A.	1908 - 1979
Elizabeth Harkleroad	Feb.26,1872 - Mar.18,1969
Taylor, James Rod	Apr.4,1892 - June 17,1978
Leila N.	no dates
Lee L.	Sept.20,1890 - no date
Kate	July 14,1897 - Nov.30,1968
Ricky Allen	1950
Ollie	1894 - 1979

Morningside Cemetery, cont.

Terry, Mary	Apr.14,1855 - Sept.5,1889, w/o J.S.Terry.
Tester, Sarah J.	1887 - 1966
Thacker, Cora L.	1874 - 1954
Thomas Adam	1823 - 1892
Frances E. Hunt	1836 - 1921
Dr. S.G.	1868 - 1923
Fannie St.John	1882 - 1967
Hazel P.	July 12,1909 - Dec.26,1925
Jaems A. "Bert"	Jan.27,1880 - Oct.8,1958
Noah W.	July 30,1851 - Sept.28,1932
Louise Mauk	May 30,1852 - Feb.22,1931
Charles J.	1872 - 1940
Etta Bell	1872 - 1956
Amanda	1954 - 1954
Noah Preston	no dates, s/o C.J. & E.B.Thomas.
Thompson, Robert L.	Sept.16,1906 - July 28,1927
Tinsley, Linnie Capps	1899 - 1980
Fred Milton	Oct.10,1921 - Dec.2,1967
Tittle, Alice B. Hicks	Sept.15,1862 - Feb.15,1902, w/o M.H.Tittle.
Todd, Hugh W.	Nov.18,1914 - Dec.16,1957
Tollie, MAude G.	Sept.9,1897 - July 25,1971
Torbett, Mollie	1961
Trivett, Maud Smith	Mar.4,1897 - Apr.11,1968
Turner, Luther J.	Dec.26,1896 - Aug.27,1977
Upchurch, William	Mar.25,1874 - Oct.5,1899
Vance, Charles Roy	Mar.19,1877 - Apr.23,1948
Cleta S.	July 13,1894 - June 30,1982
Mack	1903 - 1974
Lynn D.	1912 - 1957
Verna	1919 - 19--
Vanover, Lilliad K.	July 9, 1912 - no date
Alice L.	July 26,1922 - no date
Vaught, Myrtle Lee	1893 - 1944
Vickers, William T.	Sept.7,1880 - June 19,1970
Mattie W.	Aug.9,1886 - Oct.31,1973
Waddell, Cecil Howard	July 30,1914 - Jan.7,1972
Frances B.	Apr.27,1912 - no date
Victor A.	Oct.18,1949
Infant	June 1952
Walter S.	1880 - 1949
Carrie A.	1892 - 1975
Margaret Nell	June 29,1937 - Feb.4,1977
Hazel Gertrude	May 26,1912 - Apr.7,1978
Mildred Elizabeth	Feb.27,1916 - June 16,1976
Wagner, Mamie W.	Feb.22,1882 - July 23,1902
Fannie E.	1880 - 1944, w/o J.H.Wagner.
J.H.	1874 - 19--
Sarah Elizabeth	1871 - 1924, w/o J.H.Wagner.
Waldron, Isaac	Dec.13,1878 - Feb.10,1940
Dora	Sept.23,1882 - July 28,1929
Walker, Mary	Oct.16,1845 - Apr.25,1922
W.H., her son	July 31,1870 - Sept.14,1914
Ervin A.	1895 - 1939

Morningside Cemetery, cont.

Wallace, Wm. B.	d.Aug.3,1881, aged 52y6m16d.
Harriet M. Wood	Jan.25,1833 - July 22,1921,w/o Wm.B.
Ward, Jewel Shannon	June 13,1969 - June 23,1981
Warren, Thomas C.	May 12,1879 - Nov.1,1964
Ethel B.	July 1,1885 - Nov.23,1952
William C.	July 7,1907 - Dec.23,1938
Washington, James	1968
Washow, Alda Webb	1916 - 1966
Wassom, Arthur T.	July 26,1883 - Mar.12,1947
Lula Mae	Aug.18,1880 - Jan.3,1955
John T.	July 21,1877 - Apr.29,1941
William B.	May 1,1886 - May 7,1961
Evelyn S.	May 2,1907 - no date
Mary P.	Dec.23,1927 - May 29,1929
Watson, Mary N.	Sept.9,1876 - July 17, --?, w/o L.R.
George F.	Feb.6,1894 - Dec.10,1956
Madelene H.	Oct.12,1898 - July 29,1982
George	Feb.6,1894 - Dec.10,1956
Webb, Mamie Hermon	Dec.25,1892 - Aug.18,1893,d/o J.& P.H.
Ped Haynes Gammon	Apr.10,1838 - Oct.10,1894, w/o John Webb.
John	Oct.8,1845 - July 7,1911
Fannie C.	Aug.18,1860 - Feb.19,1890, w/o J.B.Webb.
Lola V.	1894 - 1916, w/o H.D.Webb.
James S.	Sept.2,1844 - Mar.22,1926
Ruth C.	Jan.23,1855 - Sept.3,1894
John B.	1857 - 1910
Herbert L.	Feb.28,1885 - June 7,1905, s/o J.B.& F.C.
Sam B.	1884 - 1969
Anna Miller	1902 - 1977
Guy W.	July 17,1879 - Dec.27,1953
Infant	1935
Infant	1932 - 1933
Edward K.	1891 - 1970
Bessie L.	1891 - 1960
Wilma J.	1928 - 1929
Dorothy N.	1926 - 1929
Marvin L.	1914 - 1939
Roy L.	Sept.17,1880 - Mar.11,1936
Ada M.	June 15,1886 - Apr.21,1959
Wells, Samuel M.	Sept.9,1957
Deadrick W.	Apr.7,1890 - Mar.11,1964
Lizzie M.	Sept.7,1892 - Feb.21,1973
Lucinda	1904 - 1943
Whitaker, Nicky	July 25,1957 - July 9,1979
White, Homer	Sept.4,1895 - Dec.9,1967
Loray	May 1,1866 - July 4,1947
Susie R.	no dates
W.Carl	Apr.8,1895 - July 8,1975
Virginia D.	Aug.4,1897 - Aug.4,1974
Blanche E.	May 9,1893 - Jan.27,1980
Clifton Clark	Jan.19,1892 - Nov.23,1968
Susan Frances	1861 - 1934
John K.	1855 - 1942
Pauline Demsey	1911 - 1941

Morningside Cemetery, cont.

Whitlock, Infant		1926, s/o C.M. & Mae Whitlock.
	Infant	1923, d/o C.M. & Mae Whitlock.
	Harry	1895 - 1921
Wiles, Frank M.		1846 - 1904
	Mary	1849 - 1922
	Paul M.	July 26,1906 - Nov.21,1976
	G.Herbert	1875 - 1954
	Maude Alena	1880 - 1937
	Eva Winnifred	Aug.8,1902 - Oct.12,1903
	Charles Francis	Feb.23,19211 - Aug.1,1921
	Doris	Nov.5,1923 - July 29,1924
	Arthur H.	1870 - 1900
	Sarah Emmert	1869 - 1966
	Infant son	July 31,1897
Williams, Raquell Alena		Oct.13,1970 - inf d/o Ronald & Roxie.
	E. Eugene	1914 - 1932
	George W.	1875 - 1952
	Lulu M.	1881 - 1978
Williamson, Minnie E.		1880 - 1954
	C.M.	1874 - 1932
Wishon, Carrie N.		d.1977
	Thomas F.	June 8,1892 - Aug.13,1960
Witcher, Alice Ann		Jan.19,1870 - Jan.--,1933
Witt, William H.		1838 - 1925
	Sarah A. Lindamood	1849 - 1936
Woods, William		d.1903
	Susan	1830 - 1908
	Samuel G.	Apr.10,1883 - Feb.23,1955
	Gertrude L.	Aug.8,1891 - Apr.9,1947
Worley, Virginia E.		Oct.2,1851 - June 3,1915
	Carrie E. Wiles	Oct.10,1877 - July 1,1903, w/o W.W.Worley.
	Mary Ella	Mar.28,1903 - June 8,1903, d/o W.W.& C.E.
	James Parks	1873 - 1921
	Elizabeth Hickerosn	1921 - 1972
	Charles E.	Aug.21,1890 - Nov.11,1943
	Infant	d. May 29,1878, s/o E.S. & M.E.
	E.S.	Oct.6,1847 - Dec.22,1905
	Martha Ella Faw	Dec.26,1847 - July 5,1913, w/o E.S.Worley.
Worhsam, Samuel		Sept.24,1906 - Aug.19,1907, s/o W.L.& Ella.
	Mattie U.	1910 - 1912, d/o W.L. & Ella Worsham.
	Ruby	1902 - 1913
	May	Dec.31,1900 - Jan.24,1901, d/o W.L. & Ella.
	Infant	b. & d. June 23,1897, d/o W.L. & Ella.
	Charles Thomas	June 19,1908 - Mar.8,1980
	Wm. H.	1904 - 1984
	Ella M.	Sept.29,1874 - June 28,1946
	William L.	May 8,1866 - June 2,1942
	Nancy Ann	Aug.20,1833 - Jan.8,1908
Wright, David Oliver,Sr.		Mar.11,1888 - Aug.30,1967
	Bessie Denton	Dec.26,1888 - Aug.7,1957
	Kenneth	Feb.27,1919 - Nov.17,1931
Wyatt, M.		d. Oct.18,1898
	A.	d. Nov.20,1891

Morningside Cemetery, cont.

Yamashiro, Harry Lee	Feb.26,1950 - Feb.27,1950
Yost, J.M.	1834 - 1911
Rebecca	1838 - 1916
Youst, Bettie G.	1866 - 1948

To the Unknown Confederate Dead.

Weaver Cemetery

Anderson, A.	d.Apr.5,1818, age 33 yrs.
Audley	1785 - 1818
Akard, James B.	1876 - 1945
William P.	Sept.1,1919, TN Corp. 117, Inf 30th Div.
Price	1900 - 1919
Rebecca Weaver	1875 - 1957
Allmon, John C.	1891 - 1913
Robert	Apr.30,1877 - June 7,1954
Mollie V.	Sept.21,1879 - July 29,1955
George W.	Mar.22,1864 - July 19,1886
James Otious	Apr.9,1867 - May 17,1887
Wesley	1859 - 1921
Ayers, Joel Oliver	1876 - 1950
Bales, James H.	1868 - 1925
Kathleen Cable	1874 - 1958
Ball, R.Clayton	May 23,1887 - Oct.19,1961
Catherine Godsey	Sept.5,1876 - July 5,1931
Levi	May 17,1864 - Sept.11,1935
Barnett, Addie Cole	1862 - 1940
Martin	Sept.16,1850 - Dec.11,1926
J.G.B.	Dec.11,1810 - Jan.21,1893
Barr, William F.	Sept.18,1875 - Dec.21,1930
Amanda A.	Apr.1,1877 - Jan.16,1955
William F.	Oct.4,1903 - Oct.2,1957
George Edward	1931 - 1933
George Samuel	1884 - 1960
Ollie Mae	1884 - 1962
Beidleman, Henry C.	June 17,1829 - Apr.21,1919
Elizabeth M. Delaney	Jan.22,1837 - Oct.22,1920
Jane Gammon	1910 - 1959
Bishop, Milligan B.	1896 - 1959
Ida D.	1897 - 19--, w/o Milligan B. Bishop.
Ruth E.	1926 - 19--, d/o M.B. & I.D. Bishop.
William W.	1932 - 19--, s/o M.B. & I.D. Bishop.
Blevins, Robert P.	Nov.26,1926, TN Cook 68th Inf. 9th Div.
Infant	b. & d. AMy 18,1947, s/o E.K. & Beaulah Rhea.
William H.	Jan.9-29,1884, s/o A.W. & Rebecca Blevins.
John M.	1878 - 1944
Samuel C.	Oct.4,1893 - Feb.18,1894, s/o A.W. & Rebecca.
Alfred W.	1853 - 1912
Rebecca A.	1862 - 1927
George Lee	Mar.19,1895 - May 27,1963, TN Pfc US Army WWI.
Booher, Juno P.	1871 - 1953
Hugh	July 3,1908 - Aug.9,1965

Weaver Cemetery, cont.

Booher, Mike P.	June 30,1879 - Apr.6,1946
John M.	Apr.23,1879 - Sept.23,1935
Harriet A.	Aug.28,1867 - Nov.5,1928
Lucille M.	1922, age 13 mons.,s/o Noah Booher.
Mary	1885 - 1886
Mary	1860 - 1885
A.C.	July 3-14,1927
William B.	June 26,1827 - Apr.4,1903
Sarah J.	May 7,1839 - July 19,1920
Margaret V.	Sept.24,1917 - Apr.3,1919
William Samuel	July 26,1900 - July 7,1902,s/o D.O.& J.P.
Benjamin	Nov.24,1781 - July 14,1860
Harriet	Aug.25,1832 - Aug.10,1869
A.M.	Jan.30,1830 - Oct.15,1867, aged 37y2m16d.
Benjamin F.	Feb.13,1856 - Dec.15,1873,aged 17y10m2d.
Edgar	1910 - 1926, s/o M.L.& C.E.Booher.
David O.	1864 - 1913
John B.	1886 - 19--
Sallie Pet	1890 - 1931
Virginia S.	1857 - 1927
Jess M.	1881 - 1963
Becca S.	1887 - 19--
Eugene H.	1907 - 1951
Evelyn	1932 - 1935, age 3, d/o S.I.& Tobie
William Scott	Feb.13,1906 - July 5,1928
Ben Oliver	Aug.31,1891 - Oct.9,1955, Tn Pfc Co.11 Mech. Regt. As WWI.
Mrs. Chatham	1878 - 1952
Joseph Alexander	1871 - 1940
Anna E.	1937 - 1937
Clyde E.	1912 - 1963
Bertha J.	1916 - 19--
Bill Cole	1876 - 1955
Noah	Oct.8,1898 - no date
William L.	1882 - 1959
Carrie W.	1892 - 19--
Bowen, Ina A.	1938 - 1947
Daniel C.	Mar.25,1915 - Feb.10,1958, Tn Cpl. 519 Air Svc.,Gp.AAF,WWII.
Bowers, Bob	1885 - 1943
Susan	1887 - 1959
David	1863 - 1934, aged 71 yrs.
Juley	1869 - 1939, aged 70 yrs.
John W.	1890 - 19--
Kittie E.	1896 - 1954
Nick	May 15,1901 - Jan.5,1962
Bowry, A.Wiley	1874 - 1944
Breden, Elizabeth Dysart	d.Oct.4,1828 - Aged 91 yrs.,w/o John Breden, died in Ireland.
Broyles, Amelia M.	Dec.17,1876 - July 13,1962
Donald Wayne	May 21,1951 - July 14,1952
J.W.	Oct.16,1930 - Oct.28,1935
John O.	May 4,1867 - Apr.27,1947
L.S.	1838 - 1914
Charity C.	1847 - 19--

Weaver Cemetery, cont.

Broyles, George	Oct.19,1868 - Apr.10,1910
Drucilla Florence	Sept.27,1871 - June 1,1948
Robert Floyd	Apr.6,1880 - Oct.12,1912
Mattie McKamey	May 19,1885 - Nov.11,1959
Mertie C.	June 6,1900 - Apr.1,1943
Brown, Mary Irene	May 26,1875 - Oct.6,1948
John W.	1850 - 1927, Father.
Florence	1865 - no date, Mother.
Dan F.	1875 - 1939
Hiram	1848 - 1916, aged 68 yrs.
Rhoda	1847 - 1914, w/o Hiram Brown.
John	1886 - 1927
Mary	Sept.21,1876 - Sept.14,1891
James William	1917 - 1918
James Robert	June 15,1881 - June 19,1953
Richard E.	Feb.15,1881 - Feb.26,1955
Mary K.	Apr.21,1881 - Feb.7,1961,w/o Richard E.
Elizabeth Hicks	July 27,1849 - May 21,1911
William	Aug.10,1845 - Nov.1,1918
Cynthia	Mar.5,1872 - Apr.14,1893
Buckles, John F.	1910, infant
Dollie Mae	1908 - 1909
Daughter	July 4,1902 - Mar.21,1908,d/o J.F.& M.J.
Frank	1880 - 1935
Mary Jane	1876 - 1914
Isaac L.	Jan.31,1882 - July 9,1883, s/o L. & L.
Lee B.	June 16,1858 - Oct.8,1929
Isabella	Jan.10,1861 - Dec.21,1888,w/o L.B.
V.Gertrude Blevins Barker	Jan.29,1884 - Apr.27,1951
Bullock, Margaret S.	1908 - 1915
Thelma	1905 - 1915
John A.	Oct.4,1870 - Nov.25,1939
Sarah E.	Aug.29,1843 - May 8,1890, w/o A.H.Buckles.
Adam Henry	1839 - 1910
John A.	Oct.4,1870 - Nov.25,1939
Clyde M.	b. & d. 1899, dau/o A.H.& S.E.Bullock.
Albert S.	May 27,1857 - May 10,1926
Sarah J.	Dec.26,1858 - Apr.5,1941
James	Aug.7,1843 - Oct.5,1919
Letta Jane	July 7,1945/8 - Jan.1,1914
William A.	Sept.14,1852 - June 3,1926
Henry A.	1895 - 1924
John A. & Edward A.	1898 - 1899
Louisa	---1821 - Mar.4,1887
Henry	Feb.14,1807 - May 10,1883
Charlie Lee	1866 - 1947
Dixie Alice	1892 - 1964
Fannie H.	June 5,1884 - May 23,1895,d/o A.H.&S.E.
Mattie Potts	1901 - 1965
Lucy J.	d.Sept.1,1890, d/o A.H.& S.E.
Samuel	May 29,1859 - Feb.1,1862
Flora Melissa Collins	Oct.31,1870 - June 6,1928, w/o John A.
Marie Arrants	1865 - 1945, w/o Charlie Lee Bullock.
Bushong, Grace R.	Jan.30,1874 - May 27,1906,w/o J.W.
J.W.	MAr.12,1867 - Sept.14,1935, s/o David & Mary C.

Bushong, Ada Eleanor	Apr.17,1895 - Mar.12,1943
Cable, Henry A.	1883 - 1957
Lucy M.	1884 - 19--
Charles B.	Mar.4,1838 - Apr.3,1912
Charles	b. & d. Jan.10,1920, s/o H.A. & Lucy Cable.
Martha E.	Sept.27,1842 - Jan.31,1913
Campbell, Thomas J.	Jan.16,1843 - Mar.28,1900
Edward	Dec.29,1869 - Feb.9,1941
Louisa A.	Dec.31,1851 - Jan.3,1940
M.Y.	June 15,1846 - Jan.23,1885
M.Y.Buford	Dec.19,1835 - May 18,1877
John E.	1900 - 19--
Zealy	1884 - 19--
Grace Dugger	Mar.15,1895 - Dec.21,1932
Liege L.	Mar.9,1891 - Dec.1,1958
Ellen P.	Feb.20,1897 - no date
Julia Hayes	Apr.1,1871 - Jan.8,1951
J. Drum (?)	Mar.30,1867 - Sept.28,1943
Sallie Stacey	Jan.3,1908 - June 28,1925
E.E.	1874 - 1930
J.Marshall	Mar.5,1886 - June 23,1919
Carrier, Daniel Hershel	1952 - 1952
Cawood, Randolph M.	1913 - 1931
Connie S.	1889 - 19--
John H.	Oct.21,1833(?) - June 26,1897
Annas C.	Feb.24,1843 - July 29,1913, w/o John H.
Addie M. Thomas	Oct.28,1884 - Apr.3,1904
Chapman, Jennie Green	Sept.30,1866 - July 5,1928
Clark, Ernest	1914 - 1938
Cole, Adelaide Smith	1871 - 1963, w/o W.J.Cole.
F.P.	June 14,1837 - May 26,1892/7
James Simon	Sept.2,1859 - July 2,1889
Mary Cawood	1866 - 1890
Collins, Ezra Tyler	1934 - 1966
Charles Lee	1886 - 1966
Hogan L.	1929 - 1953
Clinton R.	1924 - 1940
Combs, Mary	Nov.14,1840 - Jan.18,1920
Vergie May	May 29,1906 - May 10,1924
Julie	1873 - 1955
Copehaver, J.L.	Oct.19,1885 - Mar.11,1898
G.S.	Oct.29,1887 - Dec.31,1914
Mary Groseclose	1858 - Jan.3,1940
S.E.	Sept.18,1879 - Sept.27,1965
C.E.	June 26,1854 - May 26,1933
L.H.	May 25,1842 - Jan.2,1921
M.E.	Aug.27,1881 - Nov.21,1965
Cook, William A.	June 12,1924 - Oct.8,1962
Cowan, Thomas H.	Dec.4,1877 - Dec.17,1945
Carmack	May 21,1869 - June 12,1948
Crockett, Charlotte	Nov.19,1819 - Oct.15,1890
Croft, Amanda	no dates
Cross, Eliza	d.June 24,1905, aged 61 yrs.
Crumley, Sarah J.	d.Sept.28,1879, aged 33y5m11d,w/o D.J.
Elizabeth Hatcher	June 16,1843 - July 2,1919,w/o D.J.

Weaver Cemetery, cont.

Crumley, William O'Dell	Apr.22,1864 - Apr.20,1912
Laura Greenlee	July 2,1869 - Mar.19,1958
John Truman	May 10,1905 - Feb.28,1964,
	TN Pvt. 1570 Serv. Unit WWII.
Davis, Ida Bell	May 27,1886 - Dec.17,1922
Joe	d.June 28,1917, aged 62 yrs.
Delaney, Elizabeth M.	June 17,1829 - Sept.21,1919
Dickens, Robert E.	May 31,1900 - Dec.1,1965
HAzel C.	Dec.13,1906 - no date
Dickson, Albert Myers	d.May 14,1967, aged 59y5m13d.
Dugger, Emanuuel M.	Apr.29,1853 - Jan.6,1928
Callie D.	June 7,1856 - Dec.29,1926
Elkins, Alvin A.	b. & d. 1836, s/o Daniel M. & Eliza.
Sarah	b. & d. 1851, d/o Daniel M. & Eliza.
Emerson, J.W.	1860 - 1941
Sarah M.	1865 - 1927
R.N., Jr.	1916 - 1941
Feagins, Nellie Morton	no dates
Feathers, Dorcus	July 18,1822 - May 9,1887
Fred	May 26,1911 - Mar.3,1918
Levi F.	1870 - 1934
Mary A.	1876 - 1934
Grover C.	1888 - 1951
Elizabeth J.	1887 - 1954
Nancy A.	1846 - 1923
Elkanah	1830 - 1923
Eli	July 4,1829 - Apr.30,1902
Rachel	June 18,1843 - Apr.4,1914
Douglas B.	July 17,1872 - May 9,1887
Elizabeth	July 13,1875 - Sept.12,1883
Laura E.	July 18,1876 - July 14,1877
Julie B.	June 1,1880 - Sept.10,1883
Sarah	Aug.2,1882 - Oct.4,1883
Fannie L.	Apr.3,1885 - Oct.10,1886
John J.	b. & d. 1884
Tommie J.	May 18,1915 - Feb.26,1948
Pearl	1905 - 1933
Arthur Lee	Aug.28,1894 - Oct.7,1963,
	Tn Pvt. Co.K. Inf.WWI.
Minnie K.	Sept.29,1893 - Jan.20,1953
Viola	Aug.8,1904 - Sept.11,1962
John M.	1868 - 1941
Sarah E.	1873 - 1954
Ida Lynn	July 31,1909 - Mar.11,1965
Fields, Joseph Cecil	1960 - 1962
Fine, Chester V.	1885 - 1936
Mary L.I.	Aug.9,1880 - Sept.14,1883, d/o N.L.& M.E.
Newton L.	June 27,1857 - Apr.9,1894
Galliher, Walter C.	1879 - 1928
Lena M.	1880 - 1946
W.C.,Jr.	1915 - 1918
Galloway, Rufus M.	1865 - 1916
Lucy H.	1865 - 1923

Weaver Cemetery, cont.

Galloway, C.W.	1837 - 1919
S.C.	1840 - 1929
Infant	Sept.10,1900 - Dec.11,1908,d/o C.H. & S.
Sallie W.	1878 - 1918
George H.	1873 - 1939
Leah J.	Mar.3,1906 - Aug.13,1921
Audrey D.	1898 - 1934
Gammon, Hillie Seneker	1876 - 1952
William C.	1871 - 1936
George Seneker	1914 - 1933
Garrett, Rose Ann	Aug.23,1867 - Mar.18,1977, d/o Francis & Sarah Garrett.
Glover, Arthur J.	1899 - 19--
Ida R.	1900 - 19--
Arthur Wayne	Sept.14,1939 - Feb.9,1964, Tn.Sp4 3 Rad RSCH Unit Vietnam.
Goddard, Vergie Mae	1921 - 1960
Godsey, Bessie	1859 - 1942
Monroe	1902 - 1918
Mary C.	Feb.9,1854 - Mar.10,1923, s/o Hamilton.
Hamilton	May 10,1844 - Nov.27,1912
William F.	Sept.2,1859 - Feb.21,1932
Ella A.	Oct.16,1867 - Jan.26,1929
Goldstein, Ira	July 10,1895 - Oct.25,1957
Ella	Nov.2,1894 - no date
Goodwin, Edward E.	Dec.22,1898 - Feb.7,1920, Pvt. 1st Class Co.E.,117 Inf.WWI.
Gray, Valentine B.	Mar.15,1885 - Aug.29,1892
Eldridge Preston	Nov.28,1904 - June 27,1928
Joseph Charles,Sr.	Nov.19,1871 - Nov.26,1941
Hattie Bushong	Oct.2,1876 - July 23,1947
Eldridge Hoard	Jan.23,1835 - May 1,1918
Mariah Elizabeth Beidleman	Mar.31,1844 - Jan.22,1929
James Alexander	Mar.2,1876 - June 28,1947
N.B.	1886 - 1936
Maggie E.	1879 - 1957
John Harlan	May 19,1869 - Sept.3,1940
Carrie E.	Feb.2,1875 - June 5,1912/8
Green, James	Dec.25,1883 - Mar.9,1904, s/o S.R.&S.E.
Rufus	Nov.21,1834 - Apr.6,1869
Jane Walling	Apr.27,1840 - Sept.18,1871
Walter	Nov.24,1885 - Mar.17,1889,s/o R. & E.
Greenlee, Sarah Fine	Feb.5,1851 - Sept.7,1923
W.W.	1842 - 1919
Maggie Lee	b. & d. 1885, d/o W.W. & Sarah Fine Greenlee.
William G.	MAy 11,1888 - Mar.6,1889,s/o W.W. & S.F.
John L.	Jan.19,1858 - May 7,1859,s/o W.W. & S.F.
Greeson, Montie Everett	Oct.19,1940 - May 23,1941
Groseclose, Lavinia Virginia	1874 - 1921
John L.	1883 - 1947
Lelia E.	1887 - 1960
Gross, Lee E.,Sr.	1904 - 1966
Zora E.	1909 - no date
Guffey, Mary C.	June 19,1869 - Feb.6,1949,w/o William H.
William H.	Jan.17,1861 - no date
Guffy, Edell	Mar.11,1912 - May 21,1946

Weaver Cemetery, cont.

Harrigan, Anna E.	Nov.29,1863 - Nov.3,1885, d/o T. & E.
Edgar M.	May 4,1878 - June 8,1962
Harrington, Josephine	1891 - 1918
William H.	1859 - 1929
Mary P.	1857 - 1920
Rhea	1892 - 1954
Florence	1891 - 19--
Albert Rhea	Oct.10,1925 - Apr.17,1926
Lula I.	May 17,1875 - July 9,1937
James H.	Aug.15,1865 - Feb.7,1939
James C.	Dec.19,1888 - Apr.18,1961
Sudie I.	Mar.6,1902 - no date
Joseph Lee	Aug.2,1937 - Feb.4,1954
Hattie E.	1899 - 1943
William J.	1921 - 1935
Hatcher, Eliza E. Millhorn	1856 - 1914, w/o S.L.Hatcher.
Sam Looney	Aug.10,1848 - May 9,1937
William B.	Jan.6,1841 - Feb.2,1909
Alice	Jan.31,1895 - Aug.4,1914
Robert L.	no dates
Mrs. R.L.	1867 - 1945
Katie B.	Oct.31,1908 - Oct.18,1918,d/o J.P. & Maggie.
Sidney	Dec.12-22,1919,s/o J.P. & Maggie Hatcher.
Stayce	Mar.28,1906 - Oct.20,1910, d/o M.W. & H.E.
J.A. & G.G.	Feb.11,1889 - Nov.5,1890
Mary A.	July 6,1853 - June 3,1903, w/o George
George W.	Sept.2,1862 - Jan.26,1928
Stacey	Aug.4,1848 - Oct.15,1915,w/o William B.
James M.	1889 - 1964
Hather/Hatcher, Mollie V.	1888 - 1958
Lula B. Feathers	1900 - 1928, w/o Edgar C. Hatcher.
Marshall W.	1871 - 1951
Hattie E.	1877 - 1951
Hawk, John A.	Oct.18,1861 - Feb.5,1944
Sarah E.	Aug.27,1859 - May 24,1912
Hawthorne, Sylvester F.	1886 - 1954
Carrie L.	1890 - 19--
Hayes, Mae Cordella	May 1,1892 - Sept.15,1947
Ronald Eugene	Apr.11,1924 - Oct.5,1926
Hicks, John C.	Oct.6,1876 - June 22,1963
Nancy Garret	1872 - 1942
Dr.Harry, Sr.	1884 - 1945
Hill,Pauline Richards	1915 - 1942
Hopkins, John	1861 - 19--
Frances A.	1869 - 1943
Hopkins, Denver	no dates
Harold M.	Jan.19,1924 - Nov.25,1959
Horner, Samuel O.	1895 - 1956
Fred E., Jr.	b. & d. Feb.2,1928, s/oF.E.& M.L. Horner.
Houser, J.H.	1879 - 1937
Franklin K.	Dec.2m1904 - Jan.5,1906, s/o J.H. & L.B.

Weaver Cemetery, cont.

Houser, Lena Belle	1878 - 1940
Huggins, James J.	Nov.5,1932 - Jan.10,1956, Sgt. Co.G., 3Bn 2 Marine Div.
Hughes, Sam	1847 - 1910, aged 63 yrs.
Irena	1815 - 1889
Jenkins, Mrs.H.T.	1884 - 1944
Charles Chover	1927 - 1930
Jones, Mary Jane	1868 - 1936
M.E.Fine	Apr.8,1853 - Apr.2,1912,w/o E.S.Jones
Elbert S.	1850 - 1940
A.J.	1855 - 1937
Mrs. Lida	1862 - 1928
James	Sept.25 - Nov.23,1898,s/o T.V.& M.A.
Frank P.	1831 - 1933
T.W.	Nov.29,1922 - Feb.14,1910
M.A. Newton	Apr.18,1863 - Oct.6,1898, w/o T.W.Jones.
Effie L.	Mar.20,1882 - Nov.5,1904
Frnacis P.	Feb.9,1931 - Jan.22,1933
Luther	Dec.27,1891 - July 16,1958
Evelyn	Jan.11,1931 - Feb.27,1934
Alice	June 5,1827 - Aug.22,1901, d/o D.W.Jones.
Nellie	d.1935, aged 1 mon.,d/o W.A.Jones.
Joseph T.	1882 - 1960
Betty J.	1893 - 19--
Annie	1900 - 1934
Darellas	1930 - 1949, d/o Roy & N.E. Jones.
Samuel L.	1876 - 1946
Olive K.	1882 - 19--
John M.	Aug.29,1851 - Dec.24,1930
Robert L.	1889 - 1959
Blanche	1877 - 19--
Daniel Calvin	Sept.27,1894 - Sept.10,1965
Nellie Edith	Mar.30,1900 - Aug.20,1914
Jordan, Walter J.	1889 - no date
Fannie R.	1893 - no date
Walter J.,Jr.	May 24,1921 - Oct.21,1957, TN.Pfc.Inf.BSN WWII.
Kesner, Infant	July 30-31,1903, s/o H.L. & S.L. Kesner
King, Mary J. Ellis	Apr.23,1829 - Feb.21,1914, w/o A.J.King.
Rufus M.	Aug.21,1895 - Jan.28,1921,AWWS,Co.,A 325 82 Div.
Kyte, Laura	Feb.3,1896 - Oct.14,1963
Lane, Martha C.	June 30,1835 - Dec.9,1900
Laughter, Robert L.	1871 - 1945
Nannie L.	1875 - 1954
Thomas L.	Aug.26,1874 - Aug.11,1903
Leonard, Edward R.	1892 - 19--
Sallie A.	1883 - 1956
Lewis, Rener Matilda	1884 - 1958
Littleford,Amanda M.Sharp	June 23,1867 - Aug.21,1932,w/o H.H.
Infant	Nov.10,1950, inf/o Mrs. Littleford.
James R.	Nov.3,1894 - Nov.9,1898, s/o H.H.& A.M.
Infant	b. & d. Feb.21,1939, d/o J.F. & Ruth.
John W.	1891 - 1958

Weaver Cemetery, cont.

Littleford, Bessie R.	1899 - no date
Joseph F.	Aug.21,1893 - May 30,1961, TN Pvt Med Corps WWI.
Lyon, Bular	Jan.9,1901 - Oct.23,1910,d/o D.W.& Martha.
McCall, A.J.	Oct.2,1858 - July 8,1908
McCleelan, Hon. A.	d.May 6,1866, aged 22y10m1d/
McCorkle, Forest Lynn	1939 - 1939
McCrory, Colonel Thomas	d.June 1819 (?), DAR marker.
McGhee, Thomas	May 13,1878 - Oct.16.1917
McNeill, Myra Brown	1861 - 1943
Madgett, Infant	Jan.12,1934, s/o R.E. & Hattie Madgett.
Mann, Mabel P.	1904 - 1944
Marsh, Lizzie M.	Aug.20,1873 - Aug.2,1905
Mason, Macharmie	b. & d. 1945
Meredith, Joseph L.	May 29,1858 - Oct.1,1884
William E.	Jan.21,1841 - Oct.21,1861, died Centercille,VA, in camp.
Margaret	Nov.23,1814 - Jan.26,1894, w/o Joseph.
Joseph	June 5,1815 - June 17,1877
J.L.	d. June 26,1904, aged 53 yrs.
Mary E.	aged 34 yrs.,d/o J.E. & C.S.Meredith.
Milhorn, Adellia H. Jones	Mar.19,1864 - July 22,1897,w/o R.H.Milhorn.
Nancy A.	Aug.19,1819 - Aug.8,1894
Mattie L. Brown	d.Aug.30,1903, age 28y3m2d, w/o D.B.Milhorn.
Millard, Edward C.	1871 - 1917
Mary L.	June 17,1856 - Sept.14,1912
Thomas	b. & d. 1845, s/o G.& E. Millard.
Samuel L.	d.May 9,1862 of wounds received in Battle of McDowell, aged 19y1m11d.
George W.	Oct.18,1831 - June 25,1908
Capt. Samuel	d.SEpt.20,1850, aged 51y9m14d.
Kitty M.	Jan.7,1855 - Feb.7,1859, d/o D.J. & E.F.
Hannah	May 5,1812 - Nov.21,(?) 1891
Thomas	Dec.5,1806 - May 19,1876
Sallie	Dec.20,1809 - Jan.22,1944,w/o Thomas.
Sarah J.	July 22,1829 (?) - Feb.21,1879,2nd/o Thomas.
Samuel	d.Feb.10,1862, aged 75y7m.
Alice	d.June 10,1866, aged 79y.,w/o Samuel.
Alfred J.	Dec.1,1810 - Oct.7,1894.
Abia	Mar.22,1812 - Oct.17,1852, consort of Pamelia.
Pamelia	d.Nov.18,1850, aged 34y10m28d.
Abia	Mar.2,1789 - Jan.11,1846, Soldier of 1812, Member of the Lutheran Church for 24 yrs.
Martha	Jan.5,1811 - stone sank.
Mary Weaver	d.Mar.23,1884, aged 92y5m3d, w/o Abia.
Captain Levi	Feb.1816 - 1874 (?)
Elizabeth	Jan.7,---- - May 11, ----(?)
Miller. Easter C.	Aug.16,1839 - Apr.25,1931, w/o Samuel R.
James W.	Oct.20,1813 - Aug.2,1883
William J.	1869 - 1962
Laura E.	1874 - 1952
Martha Barrett/Burnett	May 20,1842 - Apr.4,1924
Edward Frankiln	Apr.6,1864 - Apr.11,1888
Millhorn, Ben	Dec.25,1850/9 - Oct.21,1906
Maggie H.	1851 - 1941
Oscar	Sept.23,1874 - Feb.27,1958

Weaver Cemetery, cont.

Millhorn, Shoral	Oct.30,1931 - Nov.4,1931
Eliza O.	Oct.1,1885 - Feb.16,1925
Floyd Clinton	1918 - 1919, s/o S.G.Millhorn.
Millsap, J.W.	1879 - 1948
Lula	1892 - no date
Mitchell, Sonny	b. & d. 1946
Montgomery, Henry A.	Dec.20,1884 - Apr.14,1904,s/o D.K. & S.F.
D.J.	Dec.1,1861 - Dec.11,1936
Moore, Mrs. Ida F.	1906 - 1955
Morrell, J.E.	Apr.11,1855 - Apr.28,1947
Jennie Buckles	Aug.16,1872 - Nov.21,1932
Jacob C.	Nov.12,1855 - Aug.23,1887
Nathan O.	June 2,1828 - Dec.10,1907
Rosannah Millard	July 24,1830 - Nov.8,1909
Samuel L.	Sept.2,1858 - Aug.21,1863,s/o N.O. & R.
Elizabeth	May 18,1831 - Oct.23,1869, w/o James B.
Alice Isobelle	Nov.30,1855 - Aug.28,1857, d/o J.B. & E.
John S.	1884 - 1954
Lilliam Riley	1891 - 1947
Walter Eugene	1874 - 1953
Mollie Belle	1878 - 19--, w/o Walter Eugene Morrell.
William M.	June 16,1887 - Nov.12,1964
Morse, Nannie	Oct.15,1880 - Apr.17,1902,d/o A.B.& S.A.
Morton, Henry S.	Aug.6,1873 - Mar.9,1962
Julia C.	Mar.5,1875 - June 12,1963
E.Carmack	1907 - no date
Avery M.	1905 - no date
Ruth (daughter)	1930 - 1931
John Adam	1862 - 1930
Laura Arants	1867 - 1945
Harmon J.	1894 - 1947
Johnathan M.	May 6,1837 - Dec.13,1910
Sarah B.	Feb.12,1844 - Apr.18,1917
George A.	Oct.7,1874 - Mar.31,1963
Mattie A.	Oct.20,1882 - no date
Sarah Ann	1930 - 1930
Sadie A.	1908 - 1913, s/o W.M. & M.E. Morton.
Rosella H.	Sept.28,1892 - no date
Charles Lee	Dec.15,1889 - Aug.31,1965
Martha E.	Nov.3,1891 - Feb.9,1924
Harold W.	Aug.12,1923 - Aug.18,1924
Hattie Jane	May 23,1913 - July 4,1920, d/o H.S. & Julia.
Robert L.	Jan.22,1871 - Nov.8,1952
Annie C.	July 5,1872 - Dec.7,1957
Randall	Jan.10,1912 - May 7,1913, s/o H.S. & J.E.
Murphy, Eleanor	July 21,1828 - Sept.2,1905,w/o Dr.J.A.
John A.,M.D.	Aug.15,1823 - Nov.3,1915
Nelson, Elvira	Sept.3,1861 - Sept 24,1907, aged 46y11d, w/o J.D. Nelson.
O'Dell, Parks	1909 - 1965
Lorena	1910 - no dates
Offield, Sarah Ellen	1872 - 1946
Oliver, Samuel	no dates
Marvin J.	Feb.2,1935 - Mar.5,1938

Weaver Cemetery, cont.

Patrick, George T.	1941 - 1945
Peaks, Freddie L.	July 22,1907, s/o W.E. & B.C.Peaks.
Jessie Mae	June 4,1907 - June 24,1948, w/o Joseph T.
Mary E.	May 19,1903 - Nov.2,1908, d/o A.J. & M.C.
Infant	May 3,1928, inf/o A.J. & M.C. Peaks.
Andrew J.	Oct.4,1875 - Aug.15,1953
Minnie C.	1880 - 1953, w/o Andrew J. Peaks.
Peoples, Joseph	May 2,1881 - Sept. 2,1881
Elizabeth M.	Dec.27,1843 - Oct. 22, 1882
Rutledge	Aug.22,1845 - July 7.1930
Lizzie	Oct.22,1882 - July 1,1892
William	May 2,1881 - Sept.6,1881
Henry N.	Oct.24,1886 - July 4,1914
Susan H.	Aug.19,1854 - May 8,1927
Perry, George W.	d. Dec.22,1932
William E.	July 20,1894 - Feb.16,1965
Martha J.	Aug.4,1894 - no date
Peters, Jennie L.	1863 - 1936
William J.	1888 - 1967
Elizabeth Booher	Nov.20,1841 - Sept.29,1924, w/o M.S.Peters.
Fannie C.	Oct.6,1898 - Dec.4,1899, d/o L.L. & S.E.
John R.	1855 - 1933
William C.	Jan.22,1922 - Apr.27,1924, s/o Hunter & Berdia.
Oscar C.	1888 - no date
Bertie Alice	1885 - 1937
Joseph D.	Oct.12,1889 - Dec.22,1958
Frances Alice	Aug.12,1896 - no date
William B.	1864 - 1937
Mariah B.	1875 - 1952
Martain C.	Jan.4,1896 - Sept.13,1898, s/o J.R. & J.L.
Phillips, Jimmy A.	1947 - 1955
Phipps, Preston L.	June 13,1955
Johnathan M.	1848 - 1935
Bruce B.	1875 - 1895
M.Elizabeth	1849 - 1909
Plummer, Roscoe	Apr.28,1877 - Feb.17,1960, Tn.Pvt. Co. H.,2 Regt. Inf,Spanish Am.War.
Preston, John	d.Sept.1,1776/96, aged 35y.
Price, Martha Matilda	June 26,1879 - Oct.4,1965
Rod Butler	Mar.11,1869 - Feb.7,1947
Profit, Millard F.	Nov.18,1877 - Apr.1,1953
Glen	1912 - 1932
Quailes, Irvin M.	1891 - 1940
Rader, Mary E.	1889 - no date
Billy	1843 - 1951
Louise E.	1878 - 1957
James	1872 - 1942
Barbara Ellen	1870 - 1950
William	1860 - 1912
Eliza R.	1863 - 1936
John	Apr.26,1866 - Sept.22,1950
Julia Ann	Aug.29,1873 - Mar.25,1946
Charles C.	1889 - 1957

Weaver Cemetery,cont.

Rhea, Jane Preston	d.Nov.1800, aged 42 yrs.,w/o Matthew Rhea.
Matthew	d. 1816,a ged 61yr.,in Revol. War.
Samuel	d. Oct.17,1840, aged 19y, s/o Joseph M. & Catherine Myers Rhea.
Rev. Joseph	1715 - Sept.20,1777, buried Piney Creek,MD.
Elizabeth McIlwaine	1732 - Dec.19,1793,this family came from Ireland in 1769.
Dr. J.P.	Feb.6,1872 - Apr.27,1916
Adah Carmack	Aug.10,1876 - Jan.4,1924
Major Robert	d.Aug.23,1841, aged 65yrs.
Elizabeth	1767 - Mar.13,1821, w/o Maj.Robert Rhea, d/o Rev.Joseph & Elizabeth Rhea.
Joseph	Oct.24,1762 - Feb.24,1825
Frances Breden	Mar.17,1764 - Apr.13,1850, w/o Joseph Rhea.
John	d.1793, s/o J. & F. Rhea.
John Preston	d.Sept.1,1796,a ged 70 yrs.
Eleanor Fairman	d. Jan.6,1820
Robert Orestes	May 3,1864 - Dec.28,1938
Barsha Gamon	Oct.7,1867 - Nov.14,1945, w/o Robert O.
Margaret Gammon	no dates
Richards, Clarence	July 9, 1902 - Nov.29,1906, s/o J. & S.
Joseph L.	d. July 10,1927, aged 74 yrs.
Bonnie B.	1902 - no date
Albert E.	1896 - 1950
Roma G.	b. & d. Mar.28,1940
Earl W.	Jan.16,1915 - Dec.22,1929
Ramsey, Samuel P.	Dec.8,1894 - no date
Clara B. Rhea	July 22,1893 - Apr.19,1954
Reece, Abel L.	Sept.7,1897 - Feb.21,1956
Richard, Dea V.	1894 - 1941
Edith Leta	1917 - 1923
Annie C.	1877 - 1963
Richards, James T.	Dec.11,1875 - Oct.30,1952
Samuel A.	1882 - 1965
Minnie H.	1883 - no date
Eliza Gathern	Apr.26,1857 - May 22,1889, w/o Joseph
Riffey, Mrs. Bessie	1906 - 1966
Donald Richard	Jan.28,1947 - May 22,1964
Riley, Sarah Cawood	1871 - 1932
Ringley, Bessie Mae	1896 - 1938
Rogers, Frances Cawood	1876 - 1919
Royston,James	Mar.10,1847 - Apr.24,1924
T.B.	Mar.5,1879 - Sept.29,1954
James Henry	b. & d. 1912, s/o T.B. & M.L. Royston.
Minnie Alice	b. & d. 1920, s/o T.B. & M.L. Royston.
Maggie R.V.	1915 - 1916, d/o T.B. & M.L. Royston.
Rutherford, V.V. (Jack)	1898 - 1957
Rutledge, Charles A.	Oct.30,1844 - Jan.20,1864
Robert M.	Feb.26,1850 - May 12,1883
Elzira C.	Dec.16,1818 - Feb.3,1886
William R.	June 12,1801 - July 12,1861
George W.	Feb.2,1855 - Mar.4,1903
Cornelia C.	Apr.2,1845 - Dec.22,1917

Weaver Cemetery, cont.

Rutledge, Wade Presley	Aug.2,1841 - June 22, 1903
Lucy Fry	1856 - 1937
William	1885 - 1891, aged 6 yrs.
Thomas R.	1850 - 1907
Mary V.	1854 - 1911, aged 57 yrs.
Rev. William H.	Oct.6,1894 - Dec.7,1951
Ida M.	Feb.14,1900 - June 25,1943
James Samuel	1883 - 1962
Catherine	Dec.25,1839 - no date
Infant	Oct.6, 1918
Infant	May 20,1920
Nellie	1909 - no date
Samuel	1808 - 1891, aged 83 yrs.
Elsie	1810 - 1885, aged 77 yrs.
Thomas R.	1883 - 1907, aged 18 yrs.
George D.	1887 - 1911, aged 24 yrs.
Infant	b. & d. May 1920, d/o Wm. H. Rutledge.
Adria C. Bushong	Sept.18,1896 - Apr.9,1962, w/o J.B.
Rymer (?), John E.	Apr.23,1863 - May 28,1936
Rymer (?), Barbara J.	Aug.17,1873 - Oct.16,1966
Sames, Martha	Mar.6,1851 - Dec.29,1924
Sams, Lillie Bertha	1879 - 1880
David M.	July 17,1916 - Feb.7,1935
Wilse V.	June 11, 1884 - June 21, 1944
Elizabeth E. Weaver	Jan.29,1846 - Oct.1,1880
George Washington	Dec.18,1832 - Oct.22,1915
Scott, Thelma Pauline	May 25,1899 - Nov.17, 1903,d/o E.Y. & Belle B.
Edward Y.	1871 - 1960
Belle B.	1874 - 1942
Sedgley, William T.	May 25,1894 - Mar.10,1959, Va.Sgt.Q M Corp.WWI.
Frances K.	July 2,1892 - no date
Seneker, John B., M.D.	Oct.27,1874 - Mar.11,1903
John Hill ·	Dec.24,1828 - Aug.26,1908
Sharp, James A.	Apr.22,1873 - Feb.6,1966
Viola M.	July 10,1879 - Oct.26,1965
Sharpe, John F.	Oct.1838 (?) - Mar.27,1882
Jennie	Aug.3,1879 - Mar.21,1956
Nancy E.	Dec.15,1868 - Oct.19,1931
Harriet	Aug.27,1842 - June 26,1910
Sam T.	Dec.17,1871 - Sept.24,1951
Hattie	Dec.31,18881 - no date
Robert A.	1877 - 1953
Irena L.	1881 - 19--
Shields, John Russell	Aug.11,1918 - May 15,1954, Tn. Pvt. Co.101, Mil. Police, WWII.
Simerly, Amanda Jane	June 30,1900 - Feb.14,1909
Lafayette P.	Sept.24,1870 - Aug.19,1955
Flora Mary	June 19,1878 - no date
Bessie Marble	Jan.10,1902 - Dec.7,1918, d/o L.P. & F.M.
Sizer, Harry A.	d. June 20,1943, Tn 2nd Lt. 6 US Vol. Inf.
Ethel	1906 - 1945
Slaughter, William Harvey	d. Nov.17,1915, aged 82 yrs.
Sloan, Leslie Winton	1897 - 1955
Nettie Offield	1903 - 1953

Weaver Cemetery, cont.

Smith, Arthur J.	1886 - 1958
Nettie B.	1896 - no date
J.L.	Apr.6, 1817 - Nov.21,1876
Esther	Nov.15,1821 - Mar.30,1881,w/o Joseph L.
William M.	1860 - 1926
Elmer Lee	Sept.14,1887 - May 3,1949, Tn. Pvt. 149th Inf. 39 Div., WWI.
Irene	1890 - 19--
Noah H.	1889 - 1958
Etta V.	1897 - 19--
Mary Alice	1868 - 1904, w/o J.M.Smith.
James L.	Apr.9,1838 - Mar.28,1922
Mary E.	Oct.5,1842 - May 5,1913,w/o James L. Smith.
Esther M.	Jan.5,1878 - Mar.8,1935, d/o J.L. & M.E.
Sarah Jones	Aug.30,1855 - Jan.5,1897, w/o B.I.Smith.
David B.	b. & d. 1900, s/o J.L. & A.F. Smith.
Snow, M.C.	Jan.4,1856 - Apr.3,1925
Sallie Galloway	Mar.17,1868 - Mar.28,1948
Snyder, Rodrick Hamilton	d. June 28,1964, aged 63 yrs.
Lula May	Sept.26 - Nov.1,1920,d/o R.H. & Celia J.
Stafford, William T.	Apr.25,1889 - June 24,1950, Pvt. 61th INf. 5th Div. WWI.
Stout, Hazel	b. & d. Oct.1906, d/o A. & E.D. Stout.
Strouth, John H.	Oct.10,1879 - Oct.28,1928
Mrs. J.H.	1888 - 1935
Ida N.E.	Oct.26,1910 - Dec.28,1914
Addie B.	Apr.20,1908 - Mar.12,1923
Taylor, Charles E.	1896 - 1924
Isaac L.	1851 - 1925
Cordelia V.	1856 - 1900
Thomas, Amanda	Mar.28,1868 - Feb.21,1941
Lillie Mae	May 3,1922 - Oct.15,1962
Thompson, Robert Lee	Nov.18,1927 - Jan.27,1952
Helen Marie	Sept.8,1928 - Dec.23,1928
James C.	1865 - 1955
Annis S.	1869 - 1919
Trusler, Jennie	Aug.25,1880 - Dec.9,1898
Vance, David G.	no dates
Charlie	1885 - 1951
Mary	d. June 25,186-, aged 71y3m,consort of John.
C.A.	1861 - 1925
Bessie	1893 - 19--
Walter	1889 - 19--
Dora	1896 - 19--
Mary G.	1880 - 1904
Mildred	1854 - 1919
David	1850 - 1886
Harriet Elizabeth	June 20,1865 - Aug.26,1943
Helen E.	1918 - 1926
Willie W.	b. & d. 1919
Sallie T.	1877 - 1902
John	1853 - 1942, aged 89 yrs.
Eliza Ann	1859 - 1932, aged 73 yrs.

Weaver Cemetery, cont.

Vance, John	Apr.12,1782 - Nov.6,1865
Jessie L.	Nov.17,1855 - June 11, 1911
Elizabeth	1862 - 1937
R.C.	1906 - 1922
David	Jan.20,1824 - July 18,1904
Mollie B. Merritt	d.Jan.15,1922, aged 74 yrs.
John	1853 - 1942, aged 89 yrs.
Eliza Ann	1859 - 1932, aged 73 yrs.
Mary E.	Dec.3,1896 - no date
Van Devort, Raymond	Feb.11,1908 - Jan.8,1954
Celia Warren	Nov.19,1904
VanHoy, Roy Winston	Apr.25,1852 - Feb.1,1943
Vires, Sarah Elizabeth	d. Aug.15,1875, aged 9m11d.,d/o James & Nancy.
Wampler, Grace Kathleen	Feb.5,1817 - July 17,1918,d/o C.S.Wampler.
Hugh C.	1898 - 1947
David	July 14,1863 - July 14,1922
Margaret Ann	1874 - 1936
William D.	1872 - 1930
Elizabeth Booher	Jan.19,1853 - Jan.24,1919
Susan A.	Jan.30,1869 - July 20,1890
Oscar C.	Nov.28,1906 - Oct.23,1961,
	Ga. Pvt. 203 Q M Corp. Co., WWII.
Charles S.	Aug.4,1883 - Mar.19,1943
Gray R.	May 20,1908 - June 1, 1909, s/o S.J.& Mary.
Rachel A. Gray	July 30,1877 - June 16,1908, w/o S.J.
Laura Rose	1877 - 1949
Martha Edna	Sept.18 - Oct.6,1913,d/o S.J. & Mary.
Martha J.	May 5,1867 - May 19,1940
Henry David	Nov.5,1893 - July 25,1958,
	Tn Cpl. 4th Co. 2 Div. B N WWI.
J.C.	1903 - 1922
Samuel J.	July 28,1883 - Dec.19,1958
Rosanna	Aug.24,1840 - Apr.26,1891
David	May 16,1834 - Nov.17,1907
Warren, Hugh Michael	Feb.24,1852 - Feb.1,1943
Eligugh	Apr.2,1907 - July 12,1919, s/o H.M. & C.S.
Georgia	1888 - 1917, w/o J.E. Warren.
Campbell	1881 - no date
Blanche R.	1884 - 1956
Campbell E.	Feb.9,1818 - Feb.18,1895
Martha M. Millard	Mar.14,1814 - July 30,1908, w/o Campbell E.
John K.	1886 - 1945
Weaver, Lydia L.	1856 - 1943
Isaac	Aug.17,1817 - Jan.23,1905
Albert D.	1885 - 1934
Byrd W.	1884 - 1948
Miss Dora K.	1884 - 1966
Ruby Lee	d. Nov.15,1910, inf/o A.D. & B.A. Weaver.
Martin David	Mar.17,1896 - Oct.24,1962,
	Tn. Chauffeur 487 Aero Sq. WWI.
Jacob E.	May 9, 1870 - Dec.9,1909, m. May 9,1894,
Lula Belle	Oct.6,1874 - July 6,1961
Jacob E.	May 25,1849 - Oct.17,1919
Rutha Ann	Mar.27,1844 - Mar.3,1915

Weaver Cemetery, cont.

Weaver, Henry	May 6,1853 - Apr.30,1906
Lydia E. Turner	Mar.10,1883 - Feb.2,1943
Hester A.	Dec.25,1857 - June 5,1899,w/o David.
White, Frank L.	1857 - 1917
Jessie L.	1911 - 1967
Hazel	1906 - no date
Mary E.	1866 - 1948
Sarah C.	Jan.25,1815 - Aug.19,1841
Wilkerson, Sarah E.	1867 - 9149
Alice Jane	Apr.25,1876 - Nov.17,1955
William E.	1834 - 1915
Mary	Sept.10,1842 - Aug.3,1894
Willis, Danny	no dates
Wilson, Carrie Belle	1888 - 1944
Mary J.	Oct.15,1830 - Feb.18,1903
John H.,Jr.	May 15, 1915 - Mar.26,1959
Wise, Robert	1952, s/o Dorothy & H.H.Wise.
Witcher, George A.	1887 - 1937
Darrell Lee	1958 - 1959
Samuel D.	Oct.29,1884 - Mar.16,1961
Lillie M.	Jan.11,1889 - no date
William R.	1855 - 1939
Mrs. W.R.	1860 - 1939
Carl Lee	1916 - 1955
J. Ernest	1904 - 1938
Crockett Andrew	Oct.16,1880 - Mar.27,1959
John T.	Oct.10,1958 - Mar.8,1861, s/o J.V. & M.J.
Alice M.	Apr.10,1881 - Mar.10,1936
Robert	Oct.5,1857 - Jan.17,1885
Katerine	1872 - 1939
Charles D.	Mar.17,1868 - Nov.18,1906
Ellen M.	Mar.8,1846 - Nov.25,1912, w/o Dudley C.
D.C.	1850 - 1918

Pleasant Grove Church Cemetery

Adams, Germie	1909, s/o J.H. Adams.
Arrants, Margaret Amner	1864 - 1913
Elizabeth M.	1833 - 1924
William Sharp	1860 - 1878
Harmon Monroe	1833 - 1884
Corinthia Susan	1873 - 1974
Booher, Flora Williamson	Aug.23,1891 - Dec.20,1915, w/o W.G.Booher.
Burkey, Mary Rhea	May 10,1858 - Mar.1,1902, w/o E.J.Burkey.
Burnett, A.J.	Apr.7,1849 - Nov.10,1911
Burnett, John A.	1840 - 1920
Ellen M. Miller	1849 - 1903
Catron, Maxie B.	Apr.15,1907 - July 9, 1910, d/o J. & V.V.
Chmabers, Ethel L. Fleenor	Mar.19,1885 - Jan.28,1903, w/o J.B.Chambers.
Dalton, Bridget Jane	d. Mar.11,1863, aged 2y5m5d.,d/o Jas.& Martha.
James Murphy	d.Dec.29,1867, aged 1y2m22d.,d/o Jas.& Martha.
Davidson, Susan C.	Nov.15,1827 - May 18,1893, w/o L.W.Davidson.
Dykes, Elihu Rhea	b. & d. Sept.1902, s/o Elihu & Margaret Dykes.
Fleenor, Isaac	1834 - 1913
Martha L. Seneker	1845 - 1922

Pleasant Grove Church Cemetery, cont.

Fleenor, Ora Leah	1877 - 1913
Fleming, Cleo P.	Oct.22,1871 - Oct.12,1877,d/o J.B. & Amanda E.
John A.A.E.	Nov.10,1867 - Mar.31,1887,s/o J.B. & Amanda E.
J.B.	1838 - 1913
Amanda E.	1843 - 1919
Greer, Jacob	Mar.24,1831 - June 7, 1899
Sallie	Nov.25,1825 - Jan.12,1903,w/o Jacob Greer.
Grier, M.E.	d. Oct.12,1889,a ged 33y9d.
Grier, W.L.	May 6,1854 - July 4,1896
Hamilton, William	1832 - 1914
Catherine Hawk	1839 - 1898
M.W.	Dec.23,1870 - Apr.7,1884
Ensor	Mar.20,1869 - July 31,1896
Annas	1869 - 1950
Henderson, Alice L. Miller	Mar.28,1870 - Mar.13,1895, w/o E.C.
Hopkins, Isaac B.	Oct.12,1852 - Feb.1,1946
Maggie R. Miller	Feb.13,1861 - Sept.22,1896
Charles C.	May 17,1890 - Nov.21,1946
Jones, Mary V.	Sept.28,1862 - May 15,1904
William H.	Aug.20,1820 - Nov.6,1903
Margaret A. Crockette	1832 - 1918, w/o William Jones.
Bettie	Aug.5,1870 - May 3,1904
John C.	Jan.11,1860 - May 24,1878
Longacre, Joseph A.	Apr.7,1807 - Dec.13,1883
Mary Edward	June 18,1811 - Feb.18,1865, w/o Joseph A.
I.W.	Feb.19,1819 - Nov.8,1903
Sarah Ann	Mar.21,1825 - Dec.23,1882,w/o I.W.
Luck, Freddie A.	June 4,1902 - Feb.22,1904, s/o E.A. & G.A.
Ossie L.	Feb.19,1892 - Oct.12,1894, d/o E.A.& G.A.
Lyon, Lillian K.	Aug.25,1898 - Nov.23,1893
Lettie B.	Apr.20,1872 - Aug.25,1898
Millard, Nancy Margaret	July 8,1865 - Feb.3,1952
James Abia	May 6,1870 - Nov.26,1959
Mary E.	Apr.25,1860 - July 16,1861, d/o Dr.J.& E.F.
Dr. John	Feb.21,1828 - July 20,1911
Eleanor Rhea	Oct.14,1828 - Apr.16,1901
Miller, S.R.	Sept.2,1834 - Apr.15,1911
Gerda M.	June 20,1887 - Oct.7,1898
David S.	Apr.22,1860 - Sept.14,1883
Julia A.	Jan.2,1858 - Oct.22,1883
Adam F.	Jan.15,1863 - Dec.25,1883
Adam T.	May 17,1822 - June 25,1895
Susan	Sept.12,1828 - Dec.27,1911,w/o A.T.Miller.
Luther M.	b. & d. Sept.15,1854
Julia	Feb.10,1861 - Dec.7,1861
Maggie	Feb.10,1861 - Sept.22,1896
Gideon	Aug.10,1855 - Jan.21,1862
Josiah T.	Jan.30,1863 - Jan.3,1869
Jessee B.	Aug.26,1815 - Jan.9,1894
Elizabeth Morgan	Sept.26,1826 - Apr.3,1908
Jane C.	1858 - 1918
Morris, Margaret	Mar.8,1925, d/o W.T. & Margaret Morris.

Pleasant Grove Church Cemetery, cont.

Nelson, William H.	Mar.29,1850 - Dec.19,1914
Catharine Mottern	Oct.31,1848 - July 18,1913,w/o Wm.H.
Charlie	July 16,1878 - July 12,189-
Rhea, Elizabeth Henderson	Nov.25,1824 - Mar.28,1899
Joseph M.	May 14,1787 - Aug.14,1860
Kitty	July 29,1788 - Feb.25,1868, w/o Joseph M.
Dr. John Preston	Aug.20,1829 - Mar.13,1896
Matilda Longacre	1834 - 1922, w/o Dr.John Preston Rhea.
Dr. Mat. B.	Jan.20,1862 - May 17,1891
Robert P.	June 28,1791 - Mar.31,1872
Nancy	Mar.3,1801 - Oct.4,1875, w/o Robt. P.
James D.	July 4,1802 - Nov.29,1886
Margaret Jane	d. May 17,1880, w/o James D. Rhea.
Margaret E.	d. Sept.27,1878, aged 25 yrs.
James W.	Mar.2,1876 - July 10,1876, s/o J.T.& Mary.
Matthew Belmont	Feb.22,1863 - May 27,1863, s/o Marg.&J.D.
Rodgers, Sarah A.	1828 - 1914
Roe, Hollie K.	Mar.24,1903 - Aug.13,1905, s/o L. & M.C.
Sells, John W.	Apr.14,1822 - Jan.12,1908
Rebecca	Mar.8,1826 - Oct.2,1881, w/o J.W. Sells.
Shelton, Ida F.	no dates
Jeston F.	no dates
Taylor, Martha C. Miller	Feb.1,1872 - Mar.31,1913, w/o John B. Taylor.
Thomas, William	d. Mar.4,1872, aged 52y7m7d
S.G.M.	1876 - 1914
H. Ogden C.	Mar.5,1868 - June 20,1871, s/o Saml. & A.E.
Adam	1794 - 1866
Elizabeth	1797 - 1855
Fannie Catherine Webb	July 10,1882 - Jan.3,1945, w/o S.G.M.Thomas.
Whillock, L.F.V. Thomas	Feb.3,1862 - Sept.13,1887, m. Aug.3,1879, w/o A.G.Whillock.
Woods, Elsie Morrell	May 6,1820 - Nov.22,1913, w/o Levi Woods.
R.L.	July 29,1861 - June 22,1890
Levi	Feb.5,1813 - Dec.1,1873
Agnes	Nov.12,1777 - Oct.17,1868
Martha	Feb.5,1846 - June 20,1858
Agnes	d. July 18,1862, aged 6 yrs.
Pheba J.	d. July 23,1862, aged 4 yrs.

Clark Cemetery

Clark, John B.	1882 - 1958
Elizabeth H.	1884 - 1957
Bill	1855 - 1929
Ellen	1850 - 1931
J.T.	Dec.15,1873 - Jan.22,1931
Foster, Annis C.	Nov.13,1861 - Dec.27,1936
Cicero	1886 - 1949
Finnie Droke	1887 - 1970
Haga, John W.	Dec.18,1865 - May 25,1949
Minnie C.	July 27,1877 - Aug.14,1947
Hickman, George N.	1900 - 1943
Myrtle S.	Oct.10,1905 - July 5,1968
Jones, William Noah	1910 - 1969
Srah Ellen	1898 - 1969

Clark Cemetery, cont.

Newton, John Emory	1934 - 1935
Infant	1930
Emory W.	1897 - 1973
Nancy J.	1904 - 1972
Shoemaker, B.H.	Oct.26,1881 - no date
Kate	Sept.12,1879 - Jan.5,1967
Alex	July 1,1883 - Dec.4,1940
Slagle, James A.	Sept.13,1873 - Apr.23,1944
Rebecca A.	Jan.14,1878 - no date
Edith E.	Jan.23,1906 - Mar.4,1958
Steele, Clarence (Billy)	Mar.26,1921 - Jan.27,1937
John Henry	Oct.22,1882 - June 22,1947
Robert L.	1878 - 1940
Myrtle M.	1879 - 1971
Stewart, Nellie M.	1897 - 1972
Willard, Cecil B.	1903 - 1962

Double Springs Baptist Church Cemetery
Upper Cemetery.

Clark, Paul	May 31,1902 - Dec.15,1922, s/o C.M.& E.K.
J.Gerald	1933 - 1933, s/o Vincent & Margaret Clark.
Ella K.	Spet.22,1877 - no date
Cox, Mary C.	June 16,1848 - May 7,1928, w/o Rev. L.E.Cox.
Crouch, Jonathan	Oct.14,1808 - June 2,1872
Ruth	Nov.11,1810 - June 3,1898
Ferguson, George E.	Feb.16,1868 - May 19,1935, m. Jan.1,1890
Lydia E. Taylor	Apr.26,1873 - May 14,1926
Fink, Lillie Ryans	Apr.30,1902 - Dec.6,1940, w/o Herbert Fink.
Marvin R.	Aug.5,1938 - June 1,1939, s/o H. & L. FInk.
Kincheloe, Dicie Ann	Feb.22,1872 - Nov.9,1914, w/o J.J., d/o E.K. & Nancy A. Hunt.
John J.	Mar.5,1868 - Sept.7,1922
Lady, Beryl A.	July 30,1910 - Jan.31,1939
Willie G.	July 28,1905 - Sept.16,1921,s/o W.M. & Nettie.
William	1869 - 1951
Nettie Brunner	1870 - 1951
Infant	d. July 28,1918, s/o R.C. & Pearl Lady.
Sherfey, Lona Ferguson	Apr.1,1891 - May 13,1922
Joseph	Feb.14,1886 - May 30,1954

Double Springs Baptist Church Cemetery
Lower Cemetery

Bacon, Lillie M.	Feb.6,1879 - Feb.27,1928
Barnes, Salley Cox	1877 - 1940
Blakely, Laura	Nov.13,1906 - Dec.9,1908, d/o J.E. & Elvira.
Emma Jones	Apr.18,1873 - Dec.30,1951, also fhm: Lou Emma Blakley, 1873 - 1951.
William	May 16,1879 - Feb.8,1939
Blakeley, Jacob Ellis	1869 - 1948
Elvira Guinn	1876 - 1952
James C.	1924 - 1961 (fhm)
Charles Andrew	1895 - 1942

Double Springs Baptist Church Cemetery, cont.

Bruner, Elenore C. Childress	Sept.17,1880 - Sept.3,1934,w/o W.D.Bruner.
William D.	1879 - 1960
Flora A.	1885 - 1953
Bond, Nannie E.	Dec.25,1850 - Feb.16,1927
Carberry, George W.	Sept.17,1884 - Nov.29,1929
Infant	b. & d. Sept.16,1942 (fhm)
Paul B.	b. & d. 1958 (fhm)
Infant	b. & d. Oct.16,1950 (fhm)
Nana Gray	Aug.25,1927 - Nov.23,1950, w/o Carl.
Basil L.	Oct.2,1919 - Mar.25,1959,
	TN. Tec.5, H.Q., Det.Station Com.,WWII.
Thomas	1887 - 1928
Oma Bruner	1884 - 19--, w/o Thomas.
Robert T.	Dec.3-9,1921, s/o T.M. & Oma Carberry.
Bernard	Infant grave, no dates.
Carroll, Lona F.	Jan.5,1884 - Oct. 14,1942,w/o Alfred Carroll.
Chase, Irene N.	1903 - 1928
Luther C.	1909 - 1909
Richard D.	1877 - 1946
Virginia W.C.	1878 - no date
Mrs. Sarah	d. Jan.3,1942, aged 90 yrs. (fhm)
Childress, James M.	May 30,1851 - Nov.13,1909
Mary Jane	Nov.27,1849 - Feb.11,1929
Jesse D.	Apr.13,1878, s/o James M. & Mary Jane.
Clark, Robert S.T.	June 16,1861 - 1863, s/o J.B. & Hannah E.
Oscar T.	June 22,1880 - July 26,1906
Cythnia Ann	July 22,1842 - July 17,1913, w/o John B.
Thomas J.	Nov.15,1818 - Jan.22,1888
Theuhama F.	1815 - 1884, w/o Thos. J. Clark.
John B.	May 9,1821 - July 25,1899
Hannah E.	Feb.26,1840 - Jan.30,1874,w/o John B.Clark.
Cox, William F.	July 11,1849 - Mar.31,1922
Nancy J.	June 21,1853 - Jan.23,1928
Grover C.	Aug.12,1882 - July 11,1936
Ida May	Nov.28,1890 - no date
Infant	May 17,1915 - May 29,1915, w/o G.C. & May.
Ezekiel D.	1874 - 1960
Sarah Ida	1880 - no date
Rev. L.E.	June 10,1848 - Mar.11,1900
Cordelia	Jan.23,1876 - June 18,1890, d/o Jas. & Delcena.
Delcena	Feb.1,1844 - Apr.10,1896, w/o Jas. H. Cox.
Jas. H.	Aug.11,1836 - Mar.27,1883
Martha E.	Aug.1,1855 - June 12,1902
G.F.	Mar.1,1846 - Aug.8,1890
Mary Louemma	Dec.16,1877 - Sept.12,1915
Samuel Payne	May 11,1875 - Mar.22,1951
Infant	b. & d. May 31,1917, s/o V.T.& L.B.Cox.
Martha	Apr.11,1849 - Mar.2,1915, w/o C.M.Cox.
Kenneth S.	Feb.17,1935 - no date
Bobbie D.	June 14,1942 - no date
Floyd A.	June 24,1883 - Aug.24,1887, s/o Rev.L.E.& M.C.
Melvin P.	1855 - 1920
Marry A.	1861 - 1930
Charles	Apr.20,1810 - Feb.10,1887
Malinda	Nov.10,1811 - Mar.12,1880,w/o Charles Cox.

Double Springs Baptist Church Cemetery, cont.

Cox, Charles S.	Feb.29,1847 - July 16,1913
Elizabeth	d. Apr.10,1919
Bradie N.	June 22,1907 - Feb.12,1946
Nathan Kermit	1907 - 1955 (fhm)
James F.	Dec.8,1913 - Aug.31,1917, s/o C.M.& O.M.
Ollie M.	1888 - 19--
Charles M.	1868 - 1946
Cross, Alice C. Matherly	May 28,1885 - Jan.11,1919, w/o J.A.Cross.
James Arthur	1882 - 1960 (fhm)
Charlie L.	June 13,1922 - Aug.28,1944,
	TN. Pvt. 116 Inf., WWII, P.H.
Samuel C.	1880 - 1935
Maggie Cox	1886 - 19--
Duncan, James E.	1866 - 1930
Annie E.	1868 - 1954
Basil E.	1896 - 1939
Ferguson, J.M.	1871 - 1944
L.L.	1900 - 1951
Newman B.	1897 - 1957 (fhm)
Betty Ruth	1934 - 1936 (fhm)
James Lee	Nov.20,1897 - Oct.27,1958,
	Tn. Pvt. Co.B.,66 Pioneer Inf. WWI.
Esteel Blaine	1852 - 1953 (fhm)
Infant	(fhm)
Elbridge	Co.A,1st TN Cav. (Govt marker & VFW marker)
E.E.	Dec.24,1847 - Sept.24,1895,Co.I,8th TN Cav.Vol.
John W.	1862 - 1933
Nannie E.	1878 - 1938
Howard P.	Dec.21,1930 - Feb.21,1931
Myrtle F.	1912 - 1930
Fink, W.E.	Feb.18,1866 - Feb.24,1932
M.H.	Jan.6,1815 - Aug.5,1866
Jesse M.	Jan.22,1860 - July 29,1927
Ford, D.M.	Sept.30,1915 - Oct.3,1915,s/o J.T.& Sallie.
Junior Harold	1933 - 1958 (fhm)
Virgie Eleanor	1890 - 1958 (fhm)
Gibson, Kiziah	Mar.6,1816 - Oct.12,1896
David L.	Nov.20,1822 - Feb.11,1864
David	June 30,1786 - Apr.13,1851
Jane	1861 - 1932
James	Jan.6,1859 - Nov.11,1864
Jessee M.	1881 - 1941
Nora	1884 - 19--
Jane B.	Sept.7,1816 - July 12,1892
Francis	Feb.26,1813 - May 31,1884
Golden, Patsy	June 9,1806 - Feb.2,1844,consort of Abraham.
E.F.M.H.	24 1817 (lettered fieldstone)
Harshbarger, C.D.	Sept.16,1862 - Sept.8,1932
Maggie B. & Infant Belle	Sept.26,1872 - July 19,1906,w/o & d.o. C.D.
Hannah A.	1871 - Dec.1891
Hawk, John R.	d. Dec.18,193-, aged 72y1m, (fhm)
Vergie E.	dates covered by earth.
Hickman, George	Sept.2,1860 - Sept.2,1903
Hilton, Dissa G.	Apr.19,1850 - June 24,1875, w/o John M.
George K.	Sept.21,1873 - Sept.9,1875, s/o J.M.& D.G.

Double Springs Baptist Church Cemetery, cont.

Hulse, Willey	1880 - 1943
William E.	1892 - 1955
Amanda E.	1899 - no date
Jones, J.W.	1861 - 1943
James Ronnie	Sept.14,1940 - Nov.10,1942, s/o J.D. & F.
Oscar M.	Aug.12,1879 - Aug.4,1922
Kincheloe, Roxie	Feb.26,1884 - Sept.2,1907, w/o R.T.
Mary C.	Jan.20,1846 - Aug.8,1917, w/o J.H.
James H.	May 13,1834 - Sept.25,1900
Cynthia Ann	Apr.8,1840 - Mar.23,1881,w/o J.H.
Lady, Henry	Aug.1,1820 - Mar.23,1890
Rhoda	June 2, 1825 - Sept.18,1860
Elbert	Apr.7,1884 - July 5,1884, s/o J.D. & Eliz.
Elizabeth	Dec.22,1848 - June 2,1903
J.D.	1852 - 1931
Mary S.	1869 - 1934
W.D.	Spet.6,1847 - Aug.10,1933
Amanda J.	1866 - 1945
John P.	1865 - 1943
Leedy, Edwin S.	1878 - 19--
Maggie R.	1888 - 1943
McCrary, Arthur	1879 - 1941
Emma Lady	1882 - 19--
McCulley, John R.	Nov.20,1880 - Apr.3,1905
Robert F.	Dec.11,1837 - Apr.29,1914
Almira V.	July 14,1846 - no date
McDonald, Melissa	Mar.18,1864 - Aug.21,1941
Martin, Carolyn Sue	b. & d. Feb.6,1940,d/o Carl & Charlcie
Nora Ethel Moody	Jan.30,1892 - Feb.1,1935
Infant	Nov.13-15,1912, inf/o Henry & Nora Martin.
Infant	Jan.7-12,190-, s/o Henry & Nora Martin.
Masingale, Robert F.	1904 - 1963 (fhm)
Matherly, Mary Ethel	Mar.21,1887 - Dec.7,1906, d/o G.W.& M.P.
George W.	June 1,1848 - Dec.13,1918
George A.	July 11,1888 - Jan.8,1912, s/o G. & M.P.
Mrs. J.W.	d. Aug.9,1934, aged 78y2m10d, (fhm)
Mitchell, James	July 27,1852 - June 6,1905
Luecreatia Ellen Lady	Jan.5,1867 - Aug.12,1937
Mary E.	1870 - 1955 (fhm)
Miles M.	Nov.18,1923 - Nov.4,1944, #34922505, he died in France, TN Pgvt.7th Inf.3rd Div.WWII.
Robert T.	1889 - 1940
Dona	1895 - 19--
Mary C.	Apr.14,1848 - July 5,1890
Thomas	Sept.4,1826 - June 15,1897
Moody, Clara Mitchell	1857 - 1923, w/o D.C.Moody
Moore, Johnnie	Nov.16-20,1949
Nancy E.	1951 - 1956
Pickens, Eliza Jane	Mar.17,1886 - Feb.24,1907, w/o David E.
Riggs, Rev. Jesse	Aug.22,1792 - Jan.27,1869,40 yrs.a Bap. Min.
Jackson C.,Jr.	Dec.25,1888 - Oct.17,1918
Paul J.	June 19,1916 - Apr.23,1917, s/o J.C. & Lorena.
Jackson, Sr.	Aug.13,1851 - Aug.23,1891
Evelyn	Oct.14,1857 - Sept.18,1920
Charlie Roy	Apr.17,1885 - Oct.28,1903

Double Springs Baptist Church Cemetery, cont.

Riggs, Walter C.	Jan.1,1882 - Oct.27,1912
Rigsby, Jacqueline	July 3,1943 - Dec.29,1943
Robinson, Jacob	Dec.3,1773 - Feb.19,1840, consort of Eliz., mar. Sept.19,1794.
Elizabeth Wheelock	Dec.16,1777 - May 7,1855
Shanks, ELizabeth	Feb.15,1817 - July 17,1886, w/o James.
Sherfey, Infant	Aug.17-18,1916, s/o John & Mattie.
Infant	Apr.7-20,1915, inf/o John & Mattie.
Mattie	July 24,1887 - Nov.13,1924
John T.	1878 - 1950 (fhm)
Shipley, Julia Annis	July 13,1847 - Nov.9,1907, w/o James.
Jas. H.	Feb.22,1840 - Nov.13,1913
Simmons, Jackson C.	May 10,1839 - May 3,1904, Killed at Jonesboro,Tn.,by a train.
Sarah J.	b. Nov.1,1837
Smith, ----B.	Mar.22,1846 - July 14, 1847
Thomas J.	Aug.28,1847 - June 9,1848
Smith, Newton C.	July --- - Mar. ---- (dates gone)
Calvin	1786 - Sept.10,1869
Nancy	Oct.26,1789 - July 9,1862
Speers, Mary C.	1863 - 1949
Dorsey E.	Nov.9,1892 - Jan.13,1923
Stanford, Laura J.L.	May 20,1856 - June 24,1874,d/o R.L. & Mary.
Jonathan F.	June 16,1848 - Jan.6,1882
Nancy E.	Mar.11,1845 - Dec.28,1874, d/o R.L.& Mary.
Mary	Feb.4,1819 - date gone, w/o Dr.R.L.
Robert L.,M.D.	May 9,1816 - Apr.16,1867
Sarah E.	Aug.18,1847 - Jan.17,1873, d/o R.L. & Mary.
John Lee	Mar.8,18-- - ---30,1862 (dates gone), s/o R.L. &. Mary Stanford.
Steadman, Zora E.	June 23,1883 - June 14,1906
Watkins, Margaret	May 15,1840 - Dec.1900
Wells, Clive C.	1899 - 1941
Johnnie D.	1906 - no date

Cox Cemetery

Brown, Samuel H.	no dates, Co.K.,1st Ohio L.A.
Cox, Jerry M.	1845 - 1917
Orphy C.	1851 - 1913
Jackson, John C.	Mar.4,1842 - Aug.3,1914
Martha M.	Mar.3,1842 - Oct.28,1918
Maye, Paul L.	1918 - 1938
Birdie L.	1891 - 1935
Ellen J.	Sept.29,1941 - Oct.22,1941
Landon C.	1932
Nancy A.	1934
Roy Dean	Apr.12,1944 - July 14,1985
Edgar D.	Oct.22,1916 - Aug.26,1971
Ralph C.	July 22,1950 - Apr.26,1971
John H.	1891 - 1954
Potter, Robey P.	Sept.7,1900 - Nov.9,1952
Sarah C.	Sept.15,1902 - no date

Cox Cemetery, cont.

Potter, Onnie H.	1912 - no date
Elsie D.	1916 - 1974
William Jefferson	1880 - 1942
Myrtie A.	1892 - 1979
Sluder, Thomas L.	Nov.5,1885 - Apr.28,1969
Delphia S.	July 11,1888 - Jan.4,1970
James Glenn	1911 - 1973

Kendricks Creek Methodist Church Cemetery

Andarson, Minnie P.	1866 - 1952
Bailey, Grover H.	May 4,1948 - Jan.7,1949,s/o Alex & Anna.
Lochiel N.	Oct.2,1904 - Jan.26,1933
Perry H.	Feb.24,1907 - May 11,1909, s/o Sam'l & Kate.
S.P.	1876 - 1955
Kate	1876 - 1959
Bell, Vernon D.	Jan.9-13,1918, s/o C.R. & Alice V.Bell.
Nancy R. Hite	Aug.11,1918 - Jan.5,1948
Bennett, William Amos	Feb.20,1900 - Apr.22,1958,Tn.Pvt.HQ TC WWII.
Boyer, J.W.	Sept.1,1886 - Aug.11,1887, s/o G.W. & L.E.
Bradley, Sarah Zimmerman	1874 - 1942
Calton, Charles E.	Feb.6,1943 - July 9,1943, s/o V.O.Calton.
Cecil, James Pensin	1953 - 1953 (fhm)
Cox, C.W.	Apr.28,1941
William B.	Feb.3,1862 - Sept.14,1935
Sarah Jane	May 23,1863 - June 27,1911
Depew, Roy	1941 - 1941 (fhm)
Fannie	1904 - 1952 (fhm)
Mary Copas	Dec.26,1864 - Sept.13,1927, w/o J.D.Depew.
Jake D.	1867 - 1935
Devault, Minnie M.	Dec.13,1881 - Mar.3,1900, w/o J.W.
Sally C.	June 2,1860 - May 19,1889, w/o J.W.Devault.
Dillow, John N.	June 16,1874 - Apr.7,1907
Thomas J.	Aug.8,1841 - June 7,1915
Myrtle	Apr.27,1890 - May 23,1890
Joseph R.	1859 - 1942
Jonnie E.	1863 - 1944
T.Nelson	1859 - 1913
Henry A.	1834 - 1911
Mary J.	June 18,1827 - Oct.14,1889, w/o Henry.
Emma L.	Oct.15,1855 - Apr.12,1922, w/o H.A.
Easley, Mamie W.	June 18,1886 - July 29,1887, d/o E.J. & R.
Nannie C.	Apr.25,1886 - Aug.18,1887, d/o P.N.& A.
Farmer, Mary Crandoll	b. & d. Mar.1,1937, d/o Kent & Bessie.
Ferguson, Wilson	Jan.12,1884 - Oct.5,1906
Lou Emma	Sept.16,1887 - Jan.15,1906, w/o Wilson.
Mary A.	Nov.1,1880 - Feb.24,1903, d/o J.J. & Sarah.
J.W.	Nov.11,1948, aged 82 yrs., (fhm)
James H.	Oct.29,1899 - July 17,1900, s/o J.W. & S.A.
Maude	1898 - 1952 (fhm)
Fulkerson, Jerry A.	1872 - 1944
Minnie H.	1885 - no date
Thomas J.	Dec.18,1861 - Mar.30,1927
Florence Devault	July 25,1873 - Jan.12,1913
Infant	Sept.16,1941 (fhm)

Fulkerson, James H.		1876 - 1939
	Mannie A.	1891 - no date
	Mary V.	Feb.16,1901 - Sept.23,1911
	Jesse	Mar.7,1896 - Dec.20,1941
Galloway, Edgar L.		Apr.30,1883 - Dec.30,1939
	W.J. "Bill"	Oct.12,1902 - Aug.23,1956
Golloway, Elijah C.		June 6,1856 - Feb.12,1923
	John C.	Mar.4,1879 - June 22,1904
	Infant	Nov.9 - 10,1898, s/o John C. & E.M.
Hargis, T.S.		d. Nov.2,1906, aged 52y.
	Mary E.	Mar.9,1859 - Jan.12,1905
Herron, Walter C.		Feb.20,1916 - May 23,1917
Hite, S.Fred		1880 - 1958
	Elizabeth R.	1883 - no date
	Bethel Grace	Jan.3-May 6,1916, d/o W.T. & Nora Kate Hite.
	Lula K.	1889 - no date
	William T.	1887 - 1946
Hood, William H.		1920 - 1944
	Samuel D.	d. June 21,1921,aged 28 yrs.
Hudson, William E.		1884 - 1957 (fhm)
Isbel, Bulah M.		b. & d. July 17,1922, d/o H.L.& E.L.Isbel.
	Nannie Kate	Mar.16-27,1919, d/o H.L. & E.L. Isbel.
	Vera Dollie	1920 - 1952 (fhm)
Jones, Alice M.		1897 - no date
	Opie Ernest	1887 - 1954
	Onetia Zelfa	Feb.25,1905 - Jan.2,1908, d/o G.W.&E.M.
Light, Kathryn		1943, infant
	Nora May	Nov.6,1882 - Mar.31,1916, w/o W.T.White.
	Bessie M.	1899 - 1932
	Edward V.	1878 - 1958 (fhm)
	Roy Oscar	Dec.28,1884 - Apr.30,1943
Litz, Wanda		1926 - 1930
	Charles W.	Mar.26,1881 - Dec.31,1947
	Almer J.	Mar.11,1893 - no date
Moody, D.C.		1853 - 1920
Oler, James Matterson		May 28,1853 - July 13,1939
Overbay, Maude		1894 - 1956 (fhm)
	Ava Louise	Jan.13-15,1938
	Shelby Rae	Jan.14,1942 - Aug.17,1943
	,---	d. 1953 (fhm)
	Lonzo	Feb.17,1906 - Dec.3,1919, s/o Ed & Lula.
	Danzel	Mar.1,1922 - Aug.10,1924, s/o E.L.
	Edward L.	1877 - 1955
	Lula E.	1878 - 1947
	Billie R.	Jan.26,1940 - Nov.2,1941, s/o E.C.& C.E.
	Eddie	Apr.19-28,1948
	Ancel R.	1931 - 1958, s/o Eddie Overbay.
	Rutha Rebecca	1877 - 1952 (fhm)
	Thomas A.	1874 - 1950 (fhm)
Perry, Jane		Mar.20,1786 - July 18,1848
	David, Jr.	Mar.5,1783 - May 1,1867
	Thomas R.	May 8,1820 - Jan.10,1863
	Virginia Everitt	June 14,1822 - Apr.7,1903, w/o Thomas R.
	Wm.	Aug.5,1807 - Oct.14,1892
and	Leah	Sept.4,1808 - July 30,1862
wives	Eliza	Nov.15,1827 - Apr.16,1896

Kendricks Creek Methodist Church Cemetery, cont.

Pickens, Infant	Oct.4,1906 - Oct.17,1906, d/o N.M.
Evelyn E.	July 6,1917 - June 27,1919,d/o N.M.
Mary H. Ferguson	d.June 9,1913, aged 71 yrs.,w/o G.W.
R.K.	Jan.20,1867 - Apr.11,1941
Sarah E.	1881 - 1959 (fhm)
Thomas U.	1872 - 1950 (fhm)
Audrey	1899 - 1956 (fhm)
James B.	1876 - 1957 (fhm)
Powell, Behethland Childress	July 12,1806 - Jan.11,1892, w/o Job.
Richardson, Sarah Coin	Mar.4,1830 - May 12,1911, w/o S.Richardson.
Rev.S.	July 7,1816 - Aug.20,1896
Anna	May 30,1820 - Dec.6,1874, w/o S.Richardson.
Samuel C.	Nov.6,1862 - Sept.3,1879
"Our Children"	
Hannah	June 10,1844 - Dec.10,1874
Theadocia	Jan.4,1842 - Oct.18,1875
Sarah J.	Mar.30,1858 - Dec.17,1875
Cornelia A.	June 17,1850 - July 18,1877
Rutherland, Thomas P.	May 20,1856 - Oct.20,1918
Taylor, Claude B.	May 7,1924 - May 12,1946
Thompson, A.E.	1880 - 1955 (fhm)
Vanzant, Hugh P.	1900 - 1948
Vaughn, Betty June	Dec.30,1934 - Oct.10,1943
Verlin McKinley	May 8,1928 - Feb.8,1929, s/o Lou & Nellie.
Ward, James Harless	Oct.8,1940 - Feb.3,1943, s/o Arthur & Pauline.
Wagner, Anna Mae	1904 - no date
Perry	1910 - 1949
Wexler, Nellie Nora Devault	Aug.29,1883 - Oct.10,1918,w/o A.G.Wexler.
Willard, Ernest Dulaney	Apr.13,1900 - Nov.12,1920, s/o H.D.& Alice.
Zimmerman, Daniel	1851 - 1916
Polley B.	1856 - 1916
Abijah M.	Oct.27,1878 - July 23,1933
Corinthia M.	d.May 6,1892, aged 12y7m16d.,d/o Daniel & Polly B. Zimmerman.

Hite Cemetery

Albright, Rachel A.	May 22,1872 - Feb.6,1969
Blakely, Charley	May 5,1865 - May 2,1929
Nancy C.	July 1847 - Nov.15,1942
Crawford, Gussie Hyatt	June 11,1885 - May 15,1926, w/o Charles.
Bertha	1904 - 1945
Fair, M.L.	Aug.3,1911 - Feb.19,1912
Ford, John	Sept.17,1866 - Mar.28,1911
Roda Hite	July 12,1877 - Oct.4,1954
Gagaway, Inez M.	Sept.11,1898 - Jan.3,1921
Hite, Fleming C.,Sr.	1888 - 1971
Taylor	no dates
Jack	no dates
Annie	no dates
J.W.	May 1,1922 - Mar.15,1942, s/o Everett & Mary.
Leona Ferguson	1909 - 1938
James Howard	Sept.1,1933 - Aug.30,1952
J.Fred	b. & d. 1931, s/o Clifford Tip & Leona Hite.

Hite Cemetery, cont.

Hite, J. Jackson	1822 - July 14,1892
Mary E.	1924 - 1955, w/o J.J.Hite.
Mary C.	Mar.4,1893 - Dec.19,1967
Elizabeth	Sept.22,1856 - Jan.9,1928
J.W.	July 4,1849 - Mar.15,1921
Floyd	Sept.12,1881 - Dec.4,1942
Everett	Aug.25,1881 - Apr.25,1953
Lucinda	June 9,1880 - Sept.4,1884, d/o W.A.& H.M.
W.A.	Feb.20,1854 - Apr.11,1903
Hannah S.	Sept.30,1852 - June 18,1913
David J.	Dec.19,1875 - Sept.20,1925
Ruth Elizabeth	1877 - 1940
Rosa L.	Apr.25,1914 - Nov.13,1936
New, Polly	d. Dec.10,1944
Willie M.	d. Mar.2,1927
Sherfey, Melvin	Mar.17,1856 - July 13, 1927
Rebecca	Oct.20,1848 - Jan.1,1902
Short, Ray C.	June 21,1878 - Feb.8,1955
Mary H.	July 8,1889 - Nov.15,1969
Mary A.	1935 - 1947
Jack	1920 - 1973
Haskell	1910 - 1965
Paul A.	Dec.26,1912 - Feb.1,1970

Rock Springs United Methodist Church Cemetery
New Cemetery.

Bacon, Clifford	Feb.27,1922 - Oct.9,1961
Beaman, Robert Raymond	June 5,1957 - Oct.20,1963, s/o Robert & Ruth.
Charles S.	1890 - 1955
Eldridge C.	1918 - 1966
Blakely, Addie	June 28,1889 - June 16,1913, w/o T.R.
Cpl.James E.	July 27,1947 - Feb.27,1973
Jackson	Mar.6,1844 - July 5,1929
Harriet	Nov.9,1853 - Sept.14,1939
Florence S.	1883 - 1954
Sam R.	Jan.30,1890 - May 13,1952
Synthia Hobart	Nov.24,1896 - Nov.11,1945
Henry C.	Dec.22,1854 - May 3,1927
Sarah E.	Nov.5,1855 - June 14,1932
Sarah V.	Nov.20,1928 - May 20,1929
William W.	May 15,1882 - May 31,1940
Stella Fleenor	June 22,1882 - Oct.11,1940
Infant	b. & d. Aug.18,1924, inf/o W.W. & Stella.
Blevins, Cynthia Grills	Dec.23,1956 - Apr.1,1970
Boyd, Paul	b. & d. Mar.28,1910, s/o W.C. & A.P.Boyd.
Charlie N.	1864 - 1909
Elizabeth	1872 - 1952, w/o Charlie N. Boyd.
Charlie N.	1864 - 1909
Elizabeth	1872 - 1952
Simon	1898 - 1964
Wilder C.	Jan.25,1870 - July 26,1938
Addie Easley	Jan.5,1873 - Aug.9,1961,w/o Wilder C.Boyd.
Bracken, Leonard Dale	June 18,1936 - Dec.16,1943

Rock Springs United Methodist Church Cemetery, cont.

Campbell, Nannie E.	Feb.28,1856 - Nov.17,1831
A.L.E.	Oct.21,1850 - Mar.9,1911
Carroll, Starling M.	1900 - 1968
Alfred K.	1900 - 1971
Alfred Leroy	Jan.17,1948 - Jan.19,1952
Sarah A.	Feb.10,1871 - Aug.26,1953
John E.	Sept.5,1959 - Apr.13,1927
Edward Lee	Aug.9,1896 - Oct.14,1918, Co.B.,6th Inf., Killed in action,France.
Thomas J.	Jan.11,1898 - Jan.24,1956
Nellie Galloway	Jan.24,1899 - Apr.1,1960
Carter, Nicky Wayne	b. & d. Dec.18,1966, s/o Bert & Linda.
Caywood, Joe Mack	1897 - 1965
Chase, Lola Kathleen	Apr.4,1919 - May 10,1919,d/o Robert C.& Bessie.
Dorothy Marie	Mar.24,1925 - Jan.21,1941,d/o R.C. & Bessie.
Gentry M.	Aug.15,1882 - Mar.4,1961
Hattie E.	Apr.3,1883 - Oct.20,1967
Cox, Leola P.	Oct.26,1904 - Feb.5,1967
Edith Light	Oct.24,1920 - Aug.17,1951
James Golden	b. & d. Aug.4,1951
Rev. I.L.	Apr.22,1878 - Mar.6,1940
Nora Elliott	June 11,1883 - Feb.20,1971
Lowell, Hayden	Feb.4,1942 - May 25,1962
Chagar Acon	May 27,1898 - Dec.26,1953
Rachel A.	Nov.2,1862 - July 1,1911, w/o John P. Cox, d/o J. & M. Blakely.
Marshall Lynn	May 7,1930 - Sept.11,1951, Co. C,38th Inf.Reg., Killed in the service of his country in the military operations in Korea.
Crawford, J. Wesley	1861 - 1919
S. Amanda	1865 - 1944
William Matt	Jan.25,1894 - Oct.13,1947
Davenport, Marvin F.	1907 - 1959
Depew, Walter A.	Feb.14,1866 - July 15,1913
Fred V.	Mar.12,1899 - Oct.26,1907, s/o L.D.Depew.
Sarah	d. May 10,1899,a ged 60 yrs.
James R.	d. July 20,1900, aged 70 yrs.
Infant	July 26,1911 - Sept.10,1911, s/o J.J.& C.M.
Eades, Carl B.	Nov.9,1891 - Aug.10,1925
G.C.	b. & d. May 20,1924, s/o C.B. & Ina Eades.
Easley, Jennie	June 5,1893 - Nov.22,1908, w/o Edward L.
William W.	1863 - 1938
Ida Lisenby	1878 - 1954
William V.	1911 - 1940
Emmert, Eugene C.	June 12,1932 - Dec.10,1958
Fink, Ida	1903 - 1970
Samuel A.	Oct.9,1969 - Aug.19,1947
Fleenor, Sarah J.A.	Feb.25,1864 - Feb.2,1918
John Q.	Feb.15,1827 - Nov.23,1898
Sarah A.Gobble	Aug.25,1841 - Mar.12,1912, w/o John Q.
Pauline	Oct.16,1870 - July 29,1887
Will T.	Oct.25,1890 - Oct.14,1910
Emma J. Pearce	Nov.22,1856 - Oct.2,1916, w/o W.B.Fleenor.

Ford, Ted A.	1908 - 1970
Galloway, Patricia A.	1950 - 1957
Dora Eleanor	1886 - 1965
Arthur K.	Apr.8,1886 - May 18,1956
Paul E.	Jan.22,1907 - Mar.11,1958
Orgie O.	Mar.18,1901 - Dec.18,1953
Samuel	June 6,1875 - June 29,1955
Martha Jane	1875 - 1966
Grills, Noah R.	Sept.11,1884 - Dec.25,1934
Ella Hood	Aug.31,1894 - Mar.22,1948
Hinkle, Charles E.	Sept.24,1900 - Feb.23,1962
Judy Patircia	Nov.6,1943 - Nov.7,1943,d/o Lillian & James.
Hite, Robert Fred	1923 - 1963,TN.Tec.5,US Army, WWII.
Leamon T.	Dec.4,1905 - Sept.16,1972
J.Frank	1849 - 1900
Mary C.	1862 - 1891
Henry S.	Mar.4,1887 - June 25,1887
Willie	Nov.25,1851 - Nov.25,1856
Ella	Apr.25,1887 - Nov.4,1903,d/o R.T.& M.J.
Andrew	July 7,1831 - Apr.15,1902
Francis A.	Oct.29,1850 - Mar.25,1944
John	Nov.16,1824 - Aug.14,1897
Polly Trevitt	July 5,1822 - Jan.25,1887, 1st to be buried in this section of cemetery.
R.T.	Oct.20,1853 - Oct.26,1907
Mary J.	Apr.8,1854 - Sept.14,1908, w/o R.T.Hite.
J.Raymond	May 17,1896 - June 19,1952
Elbert C.	Nov.22,1875 - Apr.5,1955
Mary J.	Dec.22,1881 - Apr.23,1961, w/o Elbert C.
Henry Rowe	May 30,1906 - Dec.25,1962
Floyd Armentrout	Sept.12,1908 - Mar.24,1946
Paul Wayne	1912 - 1913
Charlie W.D.	Apr.12,1861 - Apr.22,1926
Maggie E. Ketron	Jan.31,1860 - Aug.11,1926
Fleming S.	1917 - 1958
Fleming Krumbly	Feb.25,1916 - Dec.13,1957, Tn.Pvt., Co.C., Isp Training WWII.
Laura Alice	1890 - 1961
Glover H.	1893 - 1970
E.K.	b. & d. Mar.29,1929, s/o G.N. & Fannie.
Rebecca Jane	1856 - 1952
Brenda Sue	b. & d. May 8,1943, d/o George & Mabel.
Columbus B.	Nov.7,1875 - Jan.7,1948
Mollie Fleenor	June 21,1892 - July 17,1957
Baxter	1870 - 1952
Vergie	1887 - 1964, w/o Baxter Hite.
Oscar C.	Mar.13,1879 - Jan.8,1953
Eunice Lodox	July 18,1863 - July 6,1899
Sarah Rebecca	Feb.9,1870 - Sept.1,1944
Theodore Hix	Apr.26,1856 - Aug.31,1912
Melceney	Jan.31,1864 - Nov.13,1891
Virgie	1887 - 1903
Maggie L.	Feb.23,1890 - Jan.17,1910
Zala Deone	Mar.28,1911 - Oct.4,1915
Frank, Jr.	Oct.9,1922, infant.

Rock Springs United Methodist Church Cemetery, cont.

Hood, Fred H.	Mar.4,1906 - July 28,1960
Hunt, John N.	1872 - 1943
Wilkie L.	1881 - 1956
Ingle, Ellis B.	Feb.6,1848 - Mar.10,1917
Mary	Sept.1,1892 - Oct.9,1896, d/o E.B.& N.E.
Nannie E.	Dec.18,1858 - Feb.22,1898, w/o E.B.
Mandy D.	Jan.2,1897 - June 12,1914, d/o E.B.& N.E.
Jackson, Matilda Fleenor	Mar.26,1871 - Nov.9,1929,w/o J.H.
Jones, Raymond L.	Jan.6,1888 - Mar.9,1927
Elbert B.	May 9,1859 - Mar.16,1927
Arbanna Hite	1872 - 1915
King, Jacob Lee	June 24,1860 - Nov.8,1933
Ella King	d. Aug.22,1952
Gladys V.	Spet.3,1915 - Sept.15,1915
Charles W.	b. & d. June 30,1944, s/o W.S. & Martha.
Kishpaugh, Alice J.	1871 - 1956, w/o William.
Kestner, Conward G.	Mar.13,1876 - July 15,1931
Charles E.	1883 - 1959
Beulah	July 23,1916 - June 5,1922,d/o C.E.& Ruby.
Lacey, John Edward	Feb.13,1887 - June 18,1958
Martha Ellen	Jan.6,1869 - Apr.16,1950
W.J.	Mar.14,1861 - Dec.17,1927
Marion	Sept.30,1888 - Jan.9,1889, s/o W.J.& Ellen.
Lisenby, Fred	Oct.28,1884 - June 23,1950
Fitz Gerald	Sept.25,1916 - May 26,1970
Lockhart, Arie D.	1897 - 1965
Martin, G. Talmadge	1900 - 1965
Moody, Haynes	Oct.25,1907 - Mar.11,1913
John E.	Feb.2,1856 - Feb.6,1924
Addie	Mar.21,1856 - Oct.31,1938
Morefield, Thomas R.	June 25,1882 - Nov.12,1962
Rebecca E.	July 15,1873 - Mar.24,1954
Perry, Edda B.	June 17,1931 - no date
Posten, G.D.	no dates, stone broken.
Nancy	May 25,1830 - Aug.26,1917
Quillen, Hubert Elmo	Apr.22-28,1948, s/o Hubert & Pauline.
Ramsey, Rev. P.E.	Mar.14,1880 - Aug.13,1952
Ethel E.	Oct.5,1887 - Jan.20,1960,w/o Rev. P.E.
Riggs, Thomas K.	May 1,1879 - June 12,1949
Elmina	Jan.11,1883 - Jan.31,1969, s/o Thomas.
Nathan "Nat"	1902 - 1972
Robeson, Hugh V.	Mar.12,1891 - Dec.30,1892,s/o Wm.A & A.L.
Eula E.	MAr.26,1897 - June 27,1897,s/o W.A. & A.L.
Sizemore, Lori Ann	1972
Slaughter, George W.	Aug.28,1860 - May 7,1944
Nickatie Bell	Oct.29,1870 - Mar.14,1956
Smiley, Miranda Starnes	Oct.24,1840 - Aug.10,1911,w/o Sam Smiley.
R.H.	Apr.16,1871 - Mar.21,1910
Sam	Feb.11,1846 - Feb.27,1915
Spears, Walter J.	1896 - 1970
Tedrow, Mabel Hite	Dec.29,1910 - Jan.11,1957

Rock Springs United Methodist Church Cemetery
Old Cemetery.

Blakely, Labon A.	Sept.9,1903 - Sept.8,1935
Thomas R.	Oct.26,1876 - Feb.4,1959
Retta M.	Aug.20,1881 - Apr.26,1910, w/o T.R.
Booher, John M.	May 20,1860 - Oct.5,1925
Boyd, Arbelle	1857 - 1929
Elizabeth Bell	Nov.12-16,1925, d/o Clay & Nell Boyd.
Carl	May 16-19, 1875
Elizabeth Paxton	Aug.4,1818 - Aug.6,1902, w/o J.A.Boyd.
Infant	b. & d. 1879, s/o J.W. & Vina Boyd.
Infant	b. & d. 1890, s/o J.W. & Vina Boyd.
Gilbert	May 19,1871 - Feb.6,1915
J.W.	Feb.25,1842 - May 12,1920
William Dailey	Dec.19,1871 - July 21,1893,drowned.
G.W.	Nov.29,1838 - Mar.27,1911
Mary E.	Dec.28,1843 - Nov.23,1925, w/o G.W.Boyd.
James A.	Apr.14,1814 - MAy 7,1900
Small stone, no name	Feb.16,1890 - Feb.10,1891
Boyd, Edna M.	Apr.10,1867 - Mar.5,1902
Fannie Eliza	Apr.2,1866 - June 5,1948
Paul H.	Oct.24,1912 - June 27,1933
Joseph Montgomery,Sr.	Jan.21,1868 - Dec.10,1951
Byers, Mark	May 11, 1871 - Apr.12,1928, Woodsman of the World Memorial.
Catlon, Orva U.	1922 - 1972
Carroll, A. LaFayette	Nov.11,1878 - May 31,1960
Mary Bell	Mar.20,1874 - July 10,1944
Clyde	Dec.16,1897 - Mar.11,1989,s/o A.L. & Mary B.
Muriel J.	Aug.10,1900 - Nov.22,1907, s/o A.L. & Mary B.
Denver Paul	Dec.20,1934 - Dec.20,1934, s/o Richard.
Roma Gean	b. & d. Dec.16,1940, d/o Richard.
James F.	June 8,1870 - Dec.10,1945
Miss Edna J.	Nov.30,1866 - Oct.12,1922
Steve Wesley	Mar.16,1892 - May 28,1951
Maggie Cox	June 25,1867 - Apr.19,1947
Mary Viola	Aug.28,1897 - Oct.14,1923, d/o Jim & Maggie.
Elizabeth	July 8,1834 - Oct.1,1905, w/o W.R. Carroll.
W.R.,Esq.	Oct.7,1838 - Mar.1,1896
Noah B.	1853 - 1929
Hannah S.	1848 - 1925
Infant	b. & d. 1921, d/o Arthur & Ethel Carroll.
Arthur E.	1887 - 1961
William Thomas	May 3,1860 - Nov.30,1921
Addie C.	Nov.15,1861 - Mar.25,1924,w/o Wm.Thomas.
Childress, Infant	Nov.5 - Dec.5,1905, s/o N.L. & Lillie.
Cox, Infant	Aug.6,1919 - Jan.23,1920,s/o A.F. & L.L.Cox
J.W.	b. & d. May 4,1941, s/o Rufus & Lochiel Cox.
Davidson, Joseph	1811 - July 23,1889
Isabell	Mar.17,1814 - Sept.22,1888
Depew, Sarah Trevitt	July 26,1835 - July 2,1912,w/o Isaac L.
Isaac L.	Sept.29,1831 - Oct.26,1893
Buell W.	1861 - 1937
Mary Alice	June 4,1879 - June 28,1963
Robert W.	June 28,1861 - Oct.9,1949
Laura Rebecca	July 9,1866 - Aug.11,1942

Rock Springs United Methodist Church Cemetery, cont.

Depew, Ruby	Sept.17,1920 - June 30,1921
Paul	May 6,1922 - June 4,1923
Reba	July 10,1931 - Mar.8,1932
Roy H.	Sept.5,1885 - Oct.8,1918, s/o Dr.E.S. & Mariah Depew.
Mariah C.	Oct.4,1846 - Dec.7,1914, w/o Dr.E.S.Depew.
Dr. E.S.	Sept.15,1834 - Sept.18,1891
Guy M.	Sept.21,1887 - June 26,1889, s/o Dr.E.S.
Walter	1874 - 1942
Infant	Jan.13-16,1930, s/o Walter & Lola Depew.
Devault, Jesse C.,Sr.	Sept.18,1884 - Nov.4,1955
Lillie	July 2,1890 - Nov.29,1921, w/o J.C.Devault.
Reese D.	Nov.11,1875 - Feb.1,1929
Nancy Melvina	1845 - 1931
Orgie Milton	1878 - 1934
Elon H.	Feb.13,1928 - Aug.27,1955,TN Sq.US Navy WWII.
Eaton, Mary Byers	1877 - 1929
Flin, Nellie	June 20,1823 - no date
John W.	Oct.29,1828 - Mar.3,1892,
J.W. Flin & Emeline Carroll	mar. Jan.5,1856.
Frazier, E. Kenneth	Jan.25,1942 - Feb.16,1942
Freeman, Fieldon M.	1917 - 1965
Galloway, Etta Depew	Aug.3,1873 - Dec.21,1958
Sarah Elvina	Mar.5,1889 - May 1,1930
Hilton, Helen R.	1912 - 1948
Hite, T.Nelson	Apr.26,1856 - Mar.14,1913
Hood, John H.	July 10,1869 - Aug.31,1934
Hunt, Hannah Hite	Dec.11,1872 - June 14,1958
S.A.	1869 - 1943, Father.
Sallie E.	1880 - 19--, Mother.
Jones, James P.	no dates
Jonathan W.	July 18,1888 - Aug.3,1889, s/o J.P.& E.P.
Lady, Andrew Duncan	Apr.18,1902 - Oct.1971
Elizabeth Pauline	Mar.16,1866 - Feb.19,1932, mar.Nov.13,1903, J.D.Lady.
Milburn, Lillie May	Dec.25,1905 - Dec.22,1945
Huston D.	1892 - 1967
Moore, Margaret	Dec.29,1860 - Feb.16,1937
Overbay, N.J.Carroll	June 28,1880 - Feb.6,1908,w/o O.R.Overbay.
Pierce, Georgia Byers	Nov.17,1918 - June 19,1965
Poore, Roy Lee	1898 - 1965
Mattie J.	Aug.31,1869 - Oct.22,1956
Elbert P.	Sept.13,1870 -Mar.27,1955
Reeser, M.Alice	Jan.29,1870 - Sept.9,1897, w/o Dr.G.M.Reeser.
Infant	no date, inf/o G.M. & M.A.
Lillia Reva	no date, d/o G.M. & M.A. Reeser.
Rutledge, Sophie	July 2,1860 - July 18,1924
David	Aug.28,1856 - Jan.25,1909
Smith, Charley R.	1871 - 1934
Steadman, Reva Lee	Aug.9,1916 - Aug.10,1924
Leeta May	b. & d. July 25,1914
Lillie M.	Jan.15,1885 - Mar.28,1946
E.L.	Feb.12,1898 - Aug.29,1941
Sumpter, Robert L.	1910 - 1973
Sykes, Neta Marie	b. & d. Sept.19,1939,d/o Harold & Neta.

Rock Springs United Methodist Church Cemetery, cont.

Trevitte, George D.,Jr.	July 6,1906 - Dec.27,1951
Trivitt, Luther C.	Jan.6,1900 - Apr.14,1900
George W.	July 17,1876 - Dec.3,1943
Maggie A. McCulley	Sept.20,1870 - July 19,1902, w/o G.W.
Rachel L. Eads	Mar.28,1871 - Aug.1,1941
Vaughn, James Earl	1901 - 1968

Paperville Cemetery

Blevins, Stephen A.	Apr.5,1885 - Aug.1,1961
John H.	Oct.13,1874 - Apr.27,1948
William H.	June 24,1842 - Feb.24,1925,
	Pvt. Co.H.,4th Reg.Tn Inf. Vols. Union Army.
Jemima E.	Aug.31,1844 - Nov.19,1911, w/o William H.
Lillie E.	Nov.13,1881 - Mar.16,1895, d/o William H. &
	Jemima E. Blevins.
Booher, Sarah	Aug.13,1856 - Aug.14,1874
Margaret Evelyn Cumbow	Mar.11,1933 - Sept.6,1963
Margaret	no dates
David, Sr.	Nov.13,1781 - Apr.1,1841
David	July 1,1815 - June 5,1894
Susanna	Aug.7,1812 - Oct.17,1877, w/o David Booher.
Isaac	d. July 19,1838, aged 16 yrs.
Bowers, Infant	1948, inf/o James Bowers.
Broce, Joseph Ray	Jan.19,1895 - Aug.10,1976,m. May 19,1918.
Callie P.	Jan.29,1895 - no date,w/o J.R.
Armon Ray	Feb.21,1928 - Feb.23,1929
J.E.	1869 - 1936
Sallie E.	Aug.30,1872 - Sept.30,1913,w/o J.E.
Edna Kate	Sept.21,1897 - July 22,1898,d/o J.E.&S.E.
Bertha	Oct.4,1901 - Oct.17,1902,d/o J.F.&M.A.
Charlie P.	July 20,1897 - July 22,1898, s/o J.F.& M.A.
G.W.	Aug.17,1830 - Dec.3,1904
Amanda J.Lambert	Dec.24,1831 - Feb.29,1908
Burkhart, George	Oct.29,1775 - June 30,1852
Elizabeth	Sept.23,1779 - July 11,1850-
Bushang, Phillip	Feb.1807 - Apr.30,1859
William	June 10,1820 - Jan.15,1882
Mariah E.	Nov.12,1771 - Oct.12,1845
George W.	May 7,1793 - Feb.12,1852, War of 1812
Mary E.	Oct.8,1810 - May 31,1883
Sarah Pyle	July 29,1798 - Apr.6,1852
David	Aug.1767 - May 3,1827
David	Mar.3,1825 - May 23,1828,s/o G. & S.B.
Butler, John L.	d. Nov.20,1904, aged 56y8m13d.
Campbell, William Beatie	1853 - 1934
James	no dates
John Wallace	Oct.17,1856 - Dec.18,1929
Annie E.B.	Dec.1,1846 - Mar.8,1915
Capt. William B.	May 18,1817 - Dec.25,1886
Margaret E.	Apr.22,1823 - Sept.8,1872, w/o Capt.Wm.B.
Infant	Mar.12-15,1865

Paperville Cemetery, cont.

Carmack, ---	Sept.30,1873 - Jan.22,1906, w/o R.P.
Martin H.	1863 - 1944
Samuel V.	1873 - 1927
Watson J.	1891 - 1911
Infant	d.Sept.3,1846, d/o W. & H.E. Carmack.
John	June 18,1836 - Apr.5,1904
Mary C.R. Hagy	Dec.23,1838 - Jan.4,1924
Jacob S.	Aug.8,1830 - Nov.30,1904
Elizabeth J.	June 23,1838 - Aug.8,1929, w/o Jacob S.
Infant	d. Dec.12,1876, s/o Jacob & Elizabeth.
Childress,Henry Devault	1892 - 1978
Margaret Ella	1890 - 1974, w/o H.D.Childress.
Lou Willie	June 14,1882 - Aug.28,1964
William H.	1835 - 1928
Lucinda	1842 - 1923, w/o W.H.Childress.
Christian, Hazel R.	Aug.14,1852 - Dec.20,1952
James C.	1893 - 19--
Maude R.	1895 - 1972
James Earl	Mar.20,1914 - Apr.6,1965,Tec. 5 US Army WWII.
Paul Louis	Nov.27,1924 - June 29,1981, SF US Navy WWII.
Crumley, Addie W.	Aug.9,1863 - July 24,1885
Cumbow, William P.	Mar.1,1907 - Jan.28,1953
James Allen	Apr.5,1962 - June 4,1969
Denny, J.L.	Dec.18,1827 - Jan.25,1903
J.S.	Feb.8,1840 - July 23,1919,w/o J.L.Denny.
John W.	1858 - 1937
Mary E.	1862 - 1929
Leaton	Apr.15,1839 - Mar.31,1902, Cpl. Co.B 12 TN Cav.
Sarah A.W.	June 24,1839 - Sept.28,1895
Devault, Emma Childress	Jan.4,1866 - Sept.24,1944
Duncan, Adelia B.	Dec.20,1846 - Nov.17,1891, Mother of W.F.Jones.
Elbey, Charles H.	Sept.28,1905 - Dec.30,1975
Faris, Nannie	Oct.21,1858 - May 21,1886, w/o Jack Faris, d/o Lewis J. & Catherine Hise.
Frye, John C.	Jan.17,1856 - June 12,1938, mar. Sept.15,1888
Sarah Jane Weaver	Jan.10,1863 - Dec.15,1936
John H.	1895 - 1948
Fulcher, Little Sallie	Nov.1,1861 - Dec.1,1865
Gray, Moses	1836 - 1903
Sarah Catherine	1844 - 1931
Isaac	Sept.26,1800 - Apr.24,1876
Minnie Lee	1877 - 1958
J.A.	1844 - 1916
Sallie G.	1849 - 1924, w/o J.A.Gray.
Mary	Mar.29,1806 - June 1,1893
Greene, David H.	1872 - 1955
Elva E.	1883 - 1936
Grimes, John	Sept.27,1851 - Mar.11,1911
Stella N.	Dec.28,1897 - Dec.17,1900,d/o John & L.M.
Hackady, John M.	Nov.26,1856 - Oct.16,1928
Eliza J. Synder	Feb.28,1857 - Feb.19,1937,w/o John M.
Hall, Minnie	1909 - 1941
Hammer, ---	d.Sept.6,1856
Henderson, M.Maria	d. Aug.30,1858, aged 15y6m11d,d/o T.J.& S.R.

Hisey, Catherine	Oct.2,1822 - Sept.28,1899
George W.	June 1,1851 - Oct.1,1860
Jane	Nov.15,1853 - Apr.20,1886
Lewis J.	June 16,1817 - Oct.13,1875
W.K.	Killed Jan.1,1889, aged 22y6m19d.,
	Greene County.Steam Engine on stone.
Hobbs, Adam	Jan.12,1856 - Jan.21,1887
George Anna	May 11,1877 - Apr.18,1901, d/o A.D. & H.M.
Harriet M.	May 27,1834 - Apr.2,1917
Zella May	Nov.12,1880 - Oct.20,1899, d/o A.D. & H.M.
Hunigan, George B.	Oct.29,1918,Tn Pvt.339 Rifle Arty,88 Div.
D.C.	Aug.31,1881 - May 8,1900
Delilah Jane	1897 - 1932
Oliver H.	June 3,1844 - Apr.24,1922
Mary Sue Criner	May 3,1862 - July 11,1926, w/o Oliver H.
Charlie S.	1801 - 1804, s/o Oliver & Mary Sue.
Johnson, Getus	1917 - 1939
Theodore S.	May 6,1890 - Aug.22,1949
Hassie P.	June 6,1891 - Aug.1,1981, w/o Theodore S.
Jones, Angus G.	Jan.7,1927 - June 2,1982
Edith P.	May 7,1927
Charles W.	1896 - 1961
Bina Ragan	1902 - 1979
David Albert	Apr.23,1901 - May 11,1981,Pvt.US Army WWII.
D.F.	1875 - 1937
Floyd M.	1881 - 1936
Nancy C.	1886 - 1936
George	Aug.2,1867 - Nov.5,1933
V.A.	no dates
W.H.	July 14,1838 - Dec.24,1905
Norma R.	Sept.16,1925 - Nov.5,1969
Scott D.	June 12,1912 - Dec.9,1971, 174th Ord.Depot Co.
Lelia B.	Sept.21,1914 - July 3,1915
Ida E. Phipps	Dec.13,1874 - Feb.27,1953, w/o George Jones.
G.W.	no dates
Jessie Mae	1905 - 1983
Joseph Alrac	1883 - 1945
Anna Lee	1884 - 1965
Joseph C.	June 29,1840 - July 14,1916,
	Co. K., 28 Tn INf. CSA, 1861 - 1865.
Sarah Margaret	June 24,1848 - Dec.18,1917
Lambert, Johnie	June 10,1895 - Oct.13,1898,s/o T.T. & B.N.
W.M.	Aug.1889 - Oct.1903
Lathan, Jane T.	May 18,1842 - May 3,1916
Mary E.	June 20,1844 - June 2,1927
Elizabeth	no dates, w/o J.E.Lathan.
James E.	d. Oct.30,1844
Edward E.	Jan.27,1817 - Nov.23,1883
Sallie S.	June 8,1819 - May 11,1902
Edward G.	d.Feb.1,1845, aged 3y7m13d.
McChesney, Samuel	Mar.16,1776 - June 1,1841
Elizabeth E.	Dec.25,1775 - Dec.27,1859
Sarah W.	b. 1814, w/o Hugh McChesney.

McClelland, Henry Taylor	Sept.22,1891 - Sept.24,1892, s/o R.H.& H.C.
Infant	d. July 3,1886 , s/o J.H. & I.L.
Infant	d. Oct.1887, s/o R.H.& H.C.
John Edward	Nov.7,1889 - Sept.24,1892
Josaphine L.	Nov.15,1859 - Sept.11,1882, w/o J.H.
Marcie A.	May 21,1861 - July 6,1883
Mary E.	Feb.8, 1851 - Aug.9,1888, w/o B.S.
Philip C.	Apr.2,1882 - Mar.19,1888, s/o B.S.& Mary E.
Samuel O.	June 1,1888 - Oct.5,1888, s/o B.S. & Mary E.
Robert H.	Feb.15,1863 - Aug.9,1925
R.W.	Mar.20,1821 - July 27,1884
Dolly I.	Mar.10,1821 - Apr.20,1890
McGhee, Joseph E.	Oct.1,1849 - Dec.31,1912
Virginia P.	May 19,1861 - Dec.1,1954
Paralie	Mar.16,1877 - Oct.16,1964
Reed	1853 - 1924
Sarah Alice	1864 - 1933
Marks, ELizabeth	d. Jan.15,1895, aged 56yrs.
Mays, Etter Jane	Nov.21,1892 - Aug.29,1901, d/o W.A. & S.A.
Mattox, John J.	Oct.4,1826 - May 20,1885
Miller, Martin	Dec.9,1849 - July 15,1935
Sibena N. Roberts	Apr.15,1855 - Mar.31,1918
Mitchell, Abraham	July 4,1862 - Feb.12,1944
Sarah E.	July 14,1862 - Jan.13,1957
Orbin R.	Apr.22,1885 - Oct.2,1941, s/o Abraham & Sarah.
Robert E. Lee	1900 - 1962
Florida May M.	1894 - 1978
Mary Lee	Sept.15,1932 - Aug.11,1933, d/o Orbin & Ida.
Glina W.	Apr.4,1906 - Dec.17,1906, d/o A.& S.E.
Joseph	Oct.27,1895 - Sept.8,1896, d/o A. & S.E.
Mary Magdaline	June 22,1904 - July 30,1904, d/o A. & S.E.
Wilburne Verne	Apr.12,1883 - Sept.19,1905, s/o A. & S.E.
Moore, David D.	Oct.3,1890 - June 20,1892
James	Mar.3,1855 - Oct.15,1925
Neal, Emma Pauline	July 28,1930 - Mar.21,1934
John W.	1904 - 1974, mar. June 29,1929
Willie H.	1912 - no date
Newman, Annie E.	Aug.7,1924 - Mar.24,1978
Nutty, William	Feb.22,1802 - June 25,1867
Jane	Apr.20,1802 - May 14,1883
Martin M.	Mar.12,1832 - Dec.27,1913
Infant	b. & d. Aug.22,1889
James C.	Nov.21,1846 - Nov.9,1922
Sallie E.	Aug.22,1859 - no date
James	July 18,1888 - Oct.16,1888,s/o James C. & Sallie E. Nutty.
Oliver, Dorothy H.	1932 - 1979
Osborne, Lorenzo D.	1870 - 1936
Ollie E.	1871 - 19--
Peters, Infant	1906, s/o N.S. & wife Peters.
Phillips, Ira	1865 - 19--
Nancy Phillips	1860 - 1936
Phipps, Walter S.	Oct.7,1885 - Feb.29,1928
William A.	June 6,1854 - Aug.17,1927

Paperville Cemetery, cont.

Phipps, Eliza A.		Sept.9,1860 - Feb.22,1901
	R. Ricena Smith	July 21,1893 - Jan.9,1940
	George W.	1881 - 1967
	Emma M.	1906 - 1926, s/o George W. & Emma M.
	J.E.	1912 - 1914, s/o George W. & Emma M.
	James Claud	Oct.30,1889 - Oct.10,1935, Tn. Pfc Co.A. 3 Corps School, WWI.
	Johnie Martin	1932 - 1932, s/o Charlie & Mertie.
	John Zebedee	Jan.22,1881 - Oct.1,1933
	Mae Hunigan	Mar.16,1885 - Nov.27,1975
	Kyle Z.	1914 - 1917, s/o John & Mae Phipps.
	L. Benton	June 8,1851 - Feb.20,1931
	Mary Jane	Mar.24,1853 - Sept.27,1907
Poore, John Henry		1883 - 1931
	Corra Eller	1882 - 1975
	M.V.	Spet.14,1826 - Sept.17,1886
	Zack E.	Mar.13,1906 - Jan.5,1969
Quarles, Samuel D.		1898 - 1949
Rader, Elizabeth T.		Feb.21,1816 - Feb.11,1876
Ragan, Tilda M.		Mar.24,1866 - Mar.6,1936
	James William	July 7,1890 - Oct.8,1918,Killed in action, Argonne Forest Hill 180, Co.G 327 Inf.82 Div.
	June S.	1898 - 1969
	Martha S.	1896 - 1958, w/o J.W.Ragan.
	Ruth E.	1926 - 1935, d/o Martha Ragan.
Reed, John W.		May 1,1856 - Oct.14,1857, s/o T.P.& M.D.
Rutherford, Ryburn		Apr.22,1846 - Mar.2,1900
	Mary Ann Booher	Apr.2,1846 - Oct.30,1931
Sells, David B.		Jan.31,1822 - Mar.26,1823
	Isaac	May 17,1810 - Apr.4,1866
	James K.	no dates
	Samuel	no dates
	Sarah Buschong	d. Sept.1,1838, aged 44 yrs.
2nd wife, Cynthia S.		d. Apr.8,1872, aged 58 yrs.
Seneker, Elizabeth		Dec.8,1821 - Nov.10,1857
	G.B.D.	Jan.6,1845 - Feb.21,1860
	Infant	Spet.4-13,1870, s/o Jas. & Lanorah.
	James K.	June 6,1813 - May 28,1886
	Mary	Mar.16,1843 - Mar.29,1889
Simpson, Mary		Mar.9,1798 - Dec.4,1856,relict/o James C.
Smith, Henry C.		1891 - 1964
	Noah W.	Jan.5,1867 - June 19,1931
	Margaret Franklin	Nov.25,1858
	Thomas J.	Dec.22,1873 - Jan.11,1899
	Shadrach	Aug.2,1890 - May 7,1933
	Robert F.	May 14,1895 - July 5,1952
	Sallie W.	Apr.23,1854 - May 1,1905, w/o N.D.Smith.
Sproles, William C.		Dec.20,1908 - July 19,1945
	Sylvia E.	July 25,1914 - June 29,1966
Stewart, Frank L.		1885 - 1937
	Nora L.	1889 - 1938
Tolbert, Wm. Newton		1893 - 1946
	Clara Mae	1898 - 1982
	Ned T.	1866 - 1956
	Fronie E.	1870 - 1966

Paperville Cemetery, cont.

Vance, Marie R.	Nov.6,1922 - Dec.17,1922
Eldridge G.	Oct.21,1860 - Jan.29,1935
Martha E.	Nov.13,1860 - 1948
Earnest	Mar.22,1891 - Oct.7,1918, s/o E.G.& M.E.
Mary E.	Sept.22,1893 - July 4,1919, d/o E.G. & M.E.
James R.	Apr.25,1882 - Nov.30,1963
Rosa A.	Feb.12,1886 - Apr.26,1963
Marie R.	Nov.6,1922 - Dec.17,1922
Walker, Lenwood L.	1905 - 1971
Gladys H.	no dates
Wilson, Benjamin J.	Mar.30,1878 - May 21,1961
Alice H.	Dec.20,1880 - Dec.7,1973
Fred Allen	Dec.26,1918 - Sept.17,1966, Tn. Cpl. 370 Bomb Sq. AAF., WWII.
Rev. Lee Roy	1903 - 1937

Edgefield Cemetery

Carden, Eva Belle	Mar.25,1892 - May 3,1972
James A.	Feb.2,1888 - Mar.1,1970
Carroll, C.C.	1896 - 1974
Nell	Sept.9,1904 - no date
Clay, Nathan B.	1983 - 1983
Patricia Sue	1952
Baby Ella	1959
George Willard	Feb.17,1919 - Dec.10,1967
Walter Clarence	1915 - 1938
Cole, Elbert C.	1903 - 1969
Pansy G.	1904 - 19--
Cross, George N.	Dec.25,1900 - May 14,1982
Myrtle M.	July 8,1903
Campbell C.	1908 - 1976
Billie H.	b. & d. Mar.14,1934, s/o G.N.& Myrtle.
William Decatur	Feb.23,1873 - Dec.2,1956
Cora Alice	May 21,1878 - Aug.17,1962
Crowe, Fred F.	1903 - no date, father.
Mary B.	1902 - no date, mother.
Betty A.	1935 - 1985, daughter.
Crown, George D.	Jan.11,1871 - May 27,1930
Eulie	Feb.23,1867 - Aug.20,1941
Crowe, Carmel C.	1902 - 1977, mar. Feb.22,1924
Goldie R.	1905 - 1970
Frances Loraine	Nov.3,1924 - Aug.12,1929, d/o G.R.& Carmel.
Dryer, Edgar William	Feb.1,1894 - Apr.27,1962
Coose Hyatt	Oct.21,1895 - Dec.4,1966
Duncan, Janet Elizabeth	Oct.1,1960 - no date
Durham, Worley W.	May 3,1907 - Oct.22,1949
Fagan, Charlie D.	Nov.18,1884 - June 23,1953
Rotha J.	Feb.13,1881 - Sept.14,1957
Fitzgerald, Bige	Feb.1,1874 - Aug.2,1967
Fannie T.	July 9,1879 - Aug.7,1945
Worley	Jan.9,1898 - Jan.18,1984
Vergie	May 16,1901 - Nov.28,1964

Forrester, Dennis E.	Sept.30,1948 - Oct.20,1971,2nd Lt.
Frye, Buddy Lee	1979 - 1979
Crease	1882 - 1956
George	Aug.10,19-- - Jan.19,1982
Giesler, Infant	b. & d. Nov.24,1908, d/o E.V.&E.J.
Infant	b. & d. Apr.1,1910, s/o E.V. & E.J.
Infant	b. & d. Mar.20,1911, d/o E.V. & E.J.
Infant	b. & d. May 21,1912, s/o E.V. & E.J.
Infant	b. & d. June 4,1914, d/o E.V. & E.J.
Ernest J.	1886 - 1950
Etla V.	1885 - 1981
Goodman, Robert D.,Jr.	Oct.24,1934 - Jan.29,1979
Gouge, Michelle Louise	1983
Harden, Tony N.	1980 - 1980
Hale, Eugene L.	May 31,1898 - Nov.1,1977
Hall, James	Sept.12,1821 - Sept.17,1886
Elizabeth Snider	Dec.22,1818 - July 9,1883
Hall, Nathaniel	May 15,1857 - May 7,1944
Elizabeth Berry	Oct.4,1862 - Jan.22,1933
Jennie Volena	Nov.3,1900 - July 27,1901
Elizabeth	Feb.7,1849 - Oct.31,1919
Sarah Jane	Mar.8,1860 - Dec.31,1920
Esther Sandidger	Dec.2,1895 - June 4,1940, w/o Dannie Hall.
Dannie J.	Aug.19,1892 - Feb.26,1978
James Roberts	Oct.11,1851 - Mar.14,1893
Elizabeth	no dates
James	no dates
Billy	no dates
Harvey, Suzie Viola	Apr.8,1906 - Dec.19,1982
Hawk, Molly Crowe	June 4,1891 - July 6,1983
Hodges, Robert Gentry,Jr.	Jan.26,1948 - Nov.25,1968
Ella Jane	July 12,1886 - Jan.10,1966
Atlee	Mar.30,1888 - Oct.28,1957
Robert A.	May 15,1930 - Jan.30,1968,mar. Dec.8,1951.
Ellen E.	June 1,1928 - no date
Canada (Can)	June 27,1896 - June 23,1976
Ina Mae	Aug.10,1899 - Oct.9,1981
Hyatt, Samuel M.	Mar.4,1901 - Feb.7,1971
Bertha H.	May 23,1901 - no date
Hyder, Willie	1923 - 1979
Iva C.	1898 - no date
Henry A.	1896 - 1945
Johnson, Penny Teresa	May 24 1957 - May 25,1957
Kelly, Robert F.	Nov.29,1911 - Oct.11,1958
Viola Mae	Feb.25,1907 - Mar.30,1973
Luther H.	Dec.14,1891 - Apr.12,1971
Lizzie	1984
Lawson, Stanley G.	Oct.30, 1915 - Oct.10,1975
Mildred I.	May 8,1926 - no date
Leonard, Vollie	Mar.28,1872 - Feb.27,1938
Pearl Torbett	May 14,1873 - no date
Erma Evelyn	Jan.2,1900 - Aug.9,1945
McFarland, William H.	1890 - 19--
Emma (Dimple)	1906 - 1971

Martin, John P.	Nov.17,1885 - Nov.24,1966
Julia F.	Mar.27,1886 - Apr.18,1963
Glenn	1915 - 1984
Thelma S.	1921 - no date
Mellons, Thomas C.	Mar.1,1905 - Oct.1,1980
Effie H.	Oct.18,1901 - Apr.6,1982
George Henry	Spt.22,1923 - Dec.2,1980
Carrie Belle	Oct.28,1926 - no date
Milhorn, Reece Baylass	May 9,1880 - Sept.14,1961
Cordia Emma	Oct.22, 1891 - no date
Nelson, U.G.	1918 - 1978, mar. Oct.6,1939
June V.	1923 - no date
Oliver, John L.	1871 - 1957
Maggie W.	1886 - 1970
David W.	1873 - 1955
Delia S.	1878 - 1956
Robert L.	1901 - 1961
Vona M.	1901 - 1986
Paul P.	1986
Osborne, Paul James	1940 - 1942, s/o Wallis & Cleo
Payne, Janice S.	Sept.23,1940 - July 4,1982, d/o Ralph & Leota Snapp.
Perkins, Odis D.	1935 - 1975
Roberts, Sue M.	Mar.14,1901 - Sept.20,1973
Rutledge, George W.	1860 - 1948
Margrett Mock	1862 - 1955
Henry Lee	July 15,1935 - Apr.9,1953
Sanders, Linda Faye	Dec.9,1960 - Dec.10,1960
William B.	Oct.16,1889 - Apr.10,1982
Vena A.	Mar.25,1908 - no date
James Robert	May 9,1887 - Dec.9,1965) ch/o W.A.& M.H.
Mabel Hassie	Dec.12,1881 - Mar.3,1966,)
Saylor, George Wayne	1929 - 1076
George W.	1902 - 1961
Any Jane	1896 - 1959
Shipley, Robert Lee	June 17,1900 - Dec.3,1963
Nora G.	Aug.20,1898 - Dec.14,1967
Sluder, William L.	Aug.7,1906 - Nov.14,1947
Kathleen N.	June 18,1910 - no date
Sluss, Wesley I.	1886 - 1977
Lena R.	1903 - 19--
Smith, Jonathan Wade	Dec.7,1972 - June 3,1978
William Eli	1894 - 1971
Sally B.	1909 - no date
Snapp, Robert L.	1887 - 1975
Mattie Pearl	1886 - 1945
S.B.	May 10,1868 - Aug.27,1931
Katie Torbett	Dec.4,1884 - July 15,1944
Margie	d. 1985
James B.,Sr.	1875 - 1962
Bessie Williams	1885 - 1946
Stewart, Stephen A.	Feb.28,1879 - Mar.14,1961
Rena Lewis	Sept.21,1904

Edgefield Cemetery, cont.

Taylor, James E.	Oct.11,1900 – Dec.4,1963
Charlie P.	1897 – 1955
Mary E.	1896 – 1966
Thomas A.	1870 – 1956
Samuel L.	June 18,1904 – Nov.21,1951
Ina L.	Apr.19,1908 – no date
William	June 20,1893 – Nov.29,1976
Donna	June 29,1912 – no date
Clifford H.	Mar.3,1921 – Aug.16,1944
Tester, James O.	1918 – 1974
Bruce O'Dell	May 25,1922 – July 29,1944
George Washington	Sept.30,1880 – Feb.17,1946
Torbett, Hugh Millard	Mar.7,1883 – Nov.1,1960
Ollie Mae Hicks	Mar.6,1908 – no date
E. Claire	1885 – 1961
Mary P.	1912 – no date
Porter E.	1895 – 1985
Martha K.	1905 – 1946
Myrtle Velma	June 25,1901 – Jan.15,1948
George I.	1892 – 1968
Lela Mae	1905 – 19--
Harry W.	1915 – 1976
Trula M.	1910 – 1940
Eli Anderson,Sr.	1876 – 1961
Mary E. Fitzgerald	1882 – 1925
William F.	Jan.1,1843 – Dec.4,1919
D.A.	Feb.6,1841 – Aug.15,1924, w/o Wm. F.
Clifford B.	1902 – 1983
Pansy O.	1903 – no date
Voorhees, R. Stephen	July 20,1976 – Aug.5,1976

Latture Family Cemetery
Also known as the Wilson Family Cemetery.

Booher, Maggie Perkins	July 12,1893 – Nov.26,1926, w/o R.M.
Robert M.	1876 – 1950 (fhm)
Annie McClain	Apr.5,1884 – May 10,1917, w/o Robert.
Infant	Feb.19-22, 1904, s/o R. & A.C.
Brown, Jesse N.	June 13,1834 – Oct.15,1881
Cain, John W.	Feb.5,1871 – June 5,1871, s/o M.A. & S.J.
Margaret C.	Mar.23,1872 – Nov.21,1874, d/o M.A. & S.J.
Christena	Jan.29,1821 – Mar.30,1905, w/o Wm.Cain.
William M.	Oct.17,1822 – Apr.25,1873
A.B.	Oct.10,1825 – Sept.8,1910, mar. July 16,1854.
Margaret A. Hancher	July 25,1836 – Apr.17,1916
Frances	d. 1875
Cox, Nannie B.	Sept.5,1885 – no date
Robert S.	Feb.7,1871 – Jan.24,1955
James Jesse	July 25,1914 – Oct.1,1943
Infant	Feb.13,1912, s/o R.S.& N.B. Cox.
Denton, Mayme C.	1890 – no date
William J.	1883 – 1957
Chas.,Jr.	1935 – 1936, age 2 months.

Latture Family Cemetery

Denton, Infant	b. & d. Jan.2,1937, s/o J.E.& M.M.
Infant	b. & d. Apr.19,1938, s/o J.E. & M.M.
Nannie S.	Sept.24,1909 - Feb.18,1923
William H.	b. & d. Sept.29,1927
Sam	1877 - 1945
Mallie	1882 - 1959
Dixon, Lizzie L.	1890 - 1948
Dee	1889 - no date
Sam C.	1907 - 1960 (fhm)
Alexander	d. Apr.23,1941, aged 65y3m27d (fhm)
Martha E.	1849 - 1935
Mollie	1871 - 1938
Elsea, Howard Mahlon	Dec.9,1928 - July 30,1930
Folkner, Rebecca	1834 - 1918
Edna Ruth	d. Sept.22,1936, d/o G.H. & M.E.
Godsey, Ida Alice Snapp	July 23,1902 - Aug.7,1921, w/o S.A.
Groves, Edith B.	Feb.11-26,1933
Hancher, Elizabeth D.	d. Oct.11,1875, aged 74y2m, w/o Rev.Wm.
Huffamn, Dessie	1880 - 1956 (fhm)
I. Ray	1919 - 1941
Jackson, Thomas	Dec.19,1885 - Feb.17,1954
Louise J.	Jan.16,1863 - Sept.6,1953
Annis	Oct.8,1895
James, ---	d. June 11,1838, d/o A. & N.C.James.
James, ---	d. Oct.26,1839, s/o A. & N.C.James.
Mary E.	d. June 25,1844, d/o A. & N.C.James.
Latture, George W.	Jan.16,1851 - Jan.16,1929
Sallie A. White	Nov.2,1851 - May 20,1932
Mary G. Cox	Feb.29,1856 - Feb.19,1891
Cora F.A.	June 1, 1875 - Oct.18,1893
Mary Lou	Sept.10,1879 - Mar.26,1896
Daisy	Sept.4,1885 - Dec.8,1928
Daughters of G.W. & M.G. Latture.	
Latture, Infant	July 13,1894, s/o J.A. & F.R. Latture.
Ethel	May 22,1887 - Nov.29,1888, d/o J.A.& F.R.
James M.	Sept.16,1848 - Dec.14,1922
Annie E. Vance	Apr.15,1848 - May 12,1930
Olive Agnes	June 17,1892 - Aug.3,1930
Annie Helen	Mar.12,1890 - Sept.28,1924
William French	Nov.21,1911 - Feb.27,1931, s/o G.D. & S.E.
Ward W.	Jan.9,1914 - Aug.23,1922, s/o G.D.& S.E.
Mary Lou	Mar.20, - Apr.1,1877, d/o J.M. & A.E.
Willie T.	Nov.21,1874 - June 15,1886, only s/o J.M.& A.E.
Laura Lee	July 1,1878 - Dec.1,1894, d/o J.M.& A.E.
Nathan C.	1884 - 1943
Mary G.	Feb.29,1856 - Feb.19,1891, w/o G.W.
John A.	Nov.26,1855 - Apr.29,1936, mar.Feb.11,1879
Fannie R. Erwin	Feb.24,1858 - Oct.20,1931
John H.	Oct.1,-Nov.2,1920, s/o N.C.& B.E.
Infant	June 21,1925, s/o N.C. & B.E.Latture.
Joseph	Jan.18,1808 - Jan.25,1878
Margaret C.	Feb.29,1812 - May 23,1863,w/o Joseph.

Latture Family Cemetery, cont.

Children of Joseph & Margaret C.

Nannie J.	Mar.6,1853 - June 27,1878
2nd wife,Sarah Webb	Nov.16,1823 - Nov.28,1878
William H.	June 29,1837 - May 20,1862
Joseph D.	Nov.11,1841 - June 15,1865
Thomas A.J.	May 1,1846 - Jan.18,1870
McClain, Roy D.	Oct.26,1941 - June 8,1942, s/o R.K.& N.E.
Gaines Esti	Apr.14,1914 - Mar.28,1937
Robert Ray	Feb.27,1903 - Sept.20,1930
Wiley	Sept.3,1857 - June 8,1927
Mary C. Folkner	Feb.26,1861 - Aug.31,1927, w/o Wiley.
Andrew	May 3,1853 - Jan.7,1929
Christena	May 24,1853 - Jan.8,1925
Laura Mae	Spet.3,1917 - Aug.21,1929,d/o S.K. & I.L.
S.K.	Feb.24,1876 - Sept.25,1929
William Frank	Mar.3,1886 - Jan.31,1947
McLain, Mary M.	Mar.19,1819 - Feb.12,1858, w/o Thomas.
Plain Fieldstone	d. Nov.25,1874.
McMurray, Sylvester H.	July 30,1907 - Nov.18,1934
J.E.	Feb.22,1871 - Nov.30,1935
Mary A.	Mar.29,1876 - no date
Matherly, Elizabeth	d. Apr.10,1940, age 84y8m5d (fhm)
W.M.	1862 - no date
Miller, Evelina	d. Aug.31,1846, aged 54y1m25d.
Pannell, Frank Gaines	June 30,1854 - Aug.12,1925
wife, Louisa A. Cox	Mar.30,1861 - June 10,1919
E.M.	Sept.20,1898 - Aug.24,1933, s/o F.G. & Louisa.
Pendergrass, Rev.James A.	Mar.1,1840 - Feb.16,1927
Anas R. Rutherford	Aug.4,1847 - Sept.10,1926
Pendelton, Bayard	1877 - 1924
Kate Pendleton Newland	1880 - no date
Pope, John L.	1858 - 1940
Fannie E.	1864 - July 8,1948
Lillie M. Denton	Nov.27,1901 - Oct.21,1934, w/o C.E.Pope.
Elizabeth K.	Dec.31,1925 - Oct.10,1926, d/o C.E.& L.M.
Puckett, Mary Kate	child's grave, no dates.
Olinger, William	1853 - 1927
Louise Younce	1868 - 1939
Edward	1855 - 1930
Rosie McMurray	1906 - 1933
William Henry	1880 - Mar.3,1957
John J.	Mar.5,1855 - May 21,1920
Mary Ann	1839 - Dec.5,1906, w/o John Olinger.
John	Jan.16,1854 - June 2,1930
Shaffer, Billy W.	1948 - 1956
Shaver, John	Sept.27,1801 - June 10,1888
Jane L. Wilson	Sept.18,1806 - Nov.15,1877, w/o John
Snapp, Hattie M. Fulkerson	Dec.16,1885 - May 9,1943
Thomas N.	Feb.29,1857 - Apr.5,1924
Catherine A. Cain	Jan.25,1864 - no date
J.B.	Jan.12,1866 - Mar.29,1888, s/o A.L.G.& H.I.
Charles S.	Aug.26,1881 - Mar.15,1887, s/o A.L.G.& H.I.
M.M.	Spet.28,1871 - May 6,1888, only d/o A.L.G.

Latture Family Cemetery, cont.

Snapp, H.I.	June 9,1843 - Jan.24,1911, mar.Mar.26,1864
A.L.G.	May 7,1835 - Apr.23,1894, w/o H.I.
Robert Lee	1875 - 1945
Mary A.	1872 - no date
Stout, Ruby Denton	Aug.30,1912 - June 12,1937
Taylor, Robert L.	Oct.28,1895 - July 17,1898, s/o S. & M.M.
Martha White	Jan.17,1859 - Dec.29,1937
Samuel	July 9,1836 - Dec.23,1915
Martha	Apr.14,1837 - Feb.12,1877, w/o Samuel
James H.	Dec.10,1874 - Nov.1,1891, s/o S.& M.
Elbert S.	Feb.11,1867 - Dec.5,1872, s/o S.& M.
Eliza R.	Sept.25,1869 - Mar.9,1875, s/o S.& M.
Martha	Apr.14,1837 - Feb.12,1877, w/o Samuel.
Tibbs, William M.	1904 - no date
Margaret Elva	1921 - 1951
Whitaker, Lee	1892 - 1959
Kate	1897 - 1944
Ibba Catherine	d.Sept.16,1869, aged 54y4m4d, d/o Granville H. & Mary A. Whitaker.
Melissa J.	Dec.9,1853 - May 3,1898, d/o G.H.& M.A.
Rachel P.	May 14,1865 - May 23,1884, d/o G.H. & M.A.
Infant	d. Aug.17,1894, s/o A.G.& B.D.Whitaker.
J.T.J.	Apr.15,1859 - July 10,1920
Betty	1870 - 1936
Wilson, Margaret L.	1847 - 1907
W.W.	1868 - 1940
Bobby Lee	Sept.17,1928, infant.
Bobby Joe	1919 - 1922
Mary	b. July 22,1776, aged 67y3m15d, 2nd w/o W.W.
William	b. May 2,1768, aged 52y6m21d.

Beeler Cemetery

Anderson, Dr. Cam	aged 49 yrs.
Barr, Samuel E.	1854 - 1921
Beeler, Robert J.	Dec.18,1895 - Mar.16,1964
Booher, John E.	1856 - 1943
Goerge L.	1901, s/o G.W. & N.B.M.
Samuel J.	1888 - 1896, s/o G.W. & N.B.M.
Daniel V.	1856 - 1916
Darcus E.	1866 - 1936
Baxter	1899 - 1959
Ethel K.	June 16,1903 - Feb.28,1936, w/o B.F.
George W.	1858 - 1932
Nancy B.M.	1867 - 1931
Melton L.	Jan.21,1927, s/o J.B. & Bettie
Broce, Harvey H.	1844 - 1920
Ida A.	1854 - 1930
Burton, Amand F.	d/ Sept.11,1887, w/o W.H.Burton.
Carrier, Wm.Rice	1913 - 1944
Carter, John M.	Apr.2,1860 - Aug.21,1911
Amanda M. Hodges	Feb.2,1870 - Jan.21,1939, w/o John M.
John P.	Jan.1,1818 - Aug.20,1882

Beeler Cemetery, cont.

Carter, Martha F.	Apr.20,1832 – Feb.24,1889	
Areaner	Aug.21,1862 – Aug.5,1882	
Minnie Lee	Sept.21,1867 – Sept.21,1888	
Charley E.	Jan.1,1865 – Aug.20,1889	
Elvira C.	Feb.13,1883 – Mar.18,1950	
George P.	Sept.21,1873 – June 16,1938	
Albert Lee	June 12,1906 – Feb.28,1921	
Edna Lou	Spet.18,1913 – Jan.23,1939	
Collin, Chalmers E.	1872 – 1938	
Frances A.	1881 – 1933	
Margaret	1912 – 1924	
A.C.	1853 – 1937	
Colton, Clarence W.	Apr.22,1872 – Jan.27,1916	
Crumley, Cordelia E.	Jan.22,1870 – Dec.19,1888, w/o W.D.	
Freeman, Willard Ronnie	1940 – 1940	
Glover, Mary F. Carter	May 6,1857 – Mar.24,1891, w/o W.T.	
Hale, Susan Shoemaker	Mar.13,1890 – Dec.6,1921,w/o G.W.Hale.	
Hall, Lizzie Claud	Oct.26,1907 – Jan.19,1938	
Nannie Maud	Oct.26,1907 – Mar.17,1933	
Holden, Junior T.	1922 – no date	
Susie G.	1924 – 1979	
Howard E.	1893 – 1968	
Nellie V.	1893 – 1981	
Hopkins, Mahaley A.	Oct.1,1849 – Apr.5,1888	
Susan	June 5,1826 – Aug.8,1896	
John	Mar.16,1887 – Feb.16,1902	
Howell, John R.	Sept.27,1852 – Sept.5,1931	
Nancy R.	Feb.21,1850 – Mar.20,1927, w/o John.	
Hunt, Malinda B.	d. Mar.11,1898, aged 73 yrs.	
Kennett, L.V.	1871 – 1953	
Kidwell, Ada A.	Apr.24,1878 – Sept.19,1894, d/o W.H.& S.E.	
W.H.	Aug.5,1857 – Dec.12,1909	
Lambert, William C.	Nov.26,1903 – Feb.10,1971	
Laura G.	1877 – 1957	
Clarence Arron	1899 – 1933	
Margaret Tennent	1902 –1934	
Robert Hayden	May 8,1909 – Apr.13,1981	
Ruby L.	Sept.23,1933 – Sept.25,1933,d/o C.A.& M.	
James H.	1875 – 1935	
Large , Joshua P.	Jan.2,1861 – May 29,1887	
Annie E.	1868 – 1948	
McCracken, Margaret N.M.	Dec.31,1895 – Oct.1901	
Joseph D.	Dec.24,1897 – Dec.10,1921	
Samuel H.	1875 – 1947	
McCrary, Samuel	Aug.17,1815 – Aug.31,1878	
Lydia	Feb.22,1821 – May 21,1873	
George	June 29,1840 – Aug.11,1887	
Mary H.	Dec.24,1848 – Jan.11,1897	
Martin, John A.	1886 – 1933	
Emma L.	1888 – 1952	
Mills, Edward C.	June 16,1878 – Aug.11,1882, s/o E.F. & E.	
Catherine	Mar.8,1809 – Sept.3,1886	
E.F.	Jan.1,1837 – Apr.10,1906	
Elethe	Feb.9,1836 – no date	

Beeler Cemetery, cont.

Minnick, Etta	1862 - 1942
Peter, Daniel	Sept.3,1863 - Mar.16,1942
Peters,Ida F.	May 2,1873 - Oct.5,1893,w/o C.C.Peters.
Martha B.	Mar.23,1884 - July 11,1884
Martha E.	July 25,1852 - Mar.28,1884, w/o G.W.
John	June 29,1829 - July 20,1907
Mariah	Sept.26,1836 - Dec.29,1925, w/o John.
Joseph A.	May 24,1872 - Aug.18,1888, s/o J.A. & S.
Daniel	Nov.20,1815 - Aug.7,1893
Edward	Jan.28,1928 - no date
Gertrude	Dec.23,1939 - no date
Samuel E.	June 3,1880 - Apr.13,1957
Martha S.	Sept.25,1879 - no date
Mary R.	Aug.16,1818 - Nov.15,1893, w/o Isaac.
Isaac	Feb.24,1814 - Jan.4,1885
Phillip	Feb.20,1812 - Apr.2,1889
Martin L.	1847 - 1902
Sarah E.	1864 - 1935
James A.	1837 - 1927
Susan A.	1839 - 1910
Pleasant, Mollie J.	Dec.5,1869 - no date, w/o W.P.Pleasant.
Scott, James M. & Nanie J., Family:	
James M.	June 4,1848 - Nov.10,1921
Nannie J.	1860 - Nov.4,1917
John	1883 - July 13,1916, s/o James & Nannie.
Lillian E.	Feb.28,1915 - oct.16,1916, d/o C.W. & C.N.
Martin, Edna	Nov.14,1916 - Apr.16,1917
Wilbert	Apr.21,1913 - Apr.18,1917
Scott, Carl J.	June 5,1914 - May 4,1917, s/o B.A.& E.E.
Benjamin H.	May 15,1889 - no date
End of Scott Family.	
Sells, Emma Peters Kidwell	July 27,1862 - Jan.21,1937, w/o S.H.Sells.
Senter, Mittie Clayton	Dec.29,1877 - Feb.13,1879
Sharrett, Ossie L.	Mar.25,1886 - Aug.29,1945
David L.	Jan.3,1885 - Sept.12,1958
Shaw, Mary Grace	1866 - 1937
Shelton, Hugh	1928 - 1930
Shuttle, Charles M.	Jan.20,1873 - Feb.7,1951
Mary A.	Aug.12,1887 - Mar.7,1963
Smith, Peggie Jene	1941 - 1941
Stone, Wm.	Apr.19,1879, aged 69 yrs.
H.J.	d. Jan.27,1881, aged 63y2m.
Stophel, Susannah	d. Feb.11,1917, aged 80 yrs.
Swiney, Sarah C.	Dec.12,1844 - Mar.31,1909, w/o Noah.
Margaret F.	Mar.22,1887 - Sept.13,1897, d/o Noah & S.C.
Bessie Lee	Oct.14,1907 - Mar.29,1908, d/o A.L.& M.N.
John S.	1870 - 1949
Kate C.	1870 - 1962
Taylor, Bessie V.	Jan.5,1890 - Aug.11,1981
Treadway, Arthur A.	Nov.21,1907 - Apr.16,1983
Eva M.	Mar.25,1936 - no dates
Jacob B.	June 4,1864 - Mar.2,1951
Minnie Blevins	1879 - 1911, w/o J.B.Treadway.
Vance, Nancy Alice Peters	Aug.12,1867 - Mar.9,1937, w/o S.D.
Samuel D.	Aug.17,1859 - May 17,1928

Beeler Cemetery, cont.

Vance, William T.	1883 - 1971
Nora B.	1895 - 1969
Hugh D.,Jr.	Mar.23,1917 - no date
Lucille L.	May 7,1918 - June 23,1980
Jerry Hugh	Jan.15,1945 - Sept.4,1954
David Hugh	Nov.12,1888 - Mar.12,1973
Hattie M.	June 6,1892 - Feb.1,1973
Ralph E.	Infant, Oct.1956
Milton Lee	1883 - 1974, s/o D.R. & Elizabeth.
Children of D.R. & Elizabeth Vance:	
Vance, Joe	1881 - 1892
Bunk	1892 - 1892
Nannie	1896 - 1896
Vance, Elizabeth Booher	1860 - 1949, w/o David R. Vance.
Daniel Hadley	Feb.12,1920 - Aug.31,1920, s/o Lindsay & Hester Vance.
Soloman S.	Feb.18,1826 - May 25,1900
Sarah O.	July 10,1884 - Jan.24,1906
Weeks, Susan	aged about 78 yrs., m/o Wm.Weeks
Anna K.	1866 - 1940

Muddy Creek Baptist Church Cemetery

Akins, Rose	May 22,1876 - Nov.16,1942
Ashby, Joseph	Aug.20,1850 - Dec.14,1924
Sarah Willen	June 7,1859 - Jan.9,1930
Infant	inf/o J. & S. Ashby.
Anderson, Sarah Poe	May 20,1856 - Sept.3,1936, w/o J.B.
E.G.B.	1850 - 1851 (plain limestone marker)
Bays, David Eugene	Nov.24,1944, born not to live, s/o W.G. & Anna Bays.
Beard, Joshua M/N	d.---12,1843, aged --- ---.
Sarah	JAn.29,1817 - Nov.29,1900, w/o Jesse.
Jesse	Aug.30,1811, joined the Baptist Church Apr.9,1842, was made Deacon July 10,1843, & cont. faithful until death Aug.30,1863.
James M.	May 30,1850 - Aug.23,1882, erected by his brother, N.L. Beard.
A. Hiter	Aug.23,1820 - May 3,1874
Eliza E.	Mar.29,1820 - July 11,1898
Erskin D.	Nov.18,1868 - Sept.27,1891,s/o W.E.& N.P.
Nannie P.	July 2,1842 - Apr.11,1927
W.E.	Aug.10,1840 - Feb.8,1911
Bedwell, A.C.	1852 - 1939
S.A.	1860 - 19--
Bond, Nancy Hull	Dec.16,1835 - June 23,1902, w/o Nathan.
Bowery, Herman Lester	Apr.10-11,1945, s/o E.S. & J.M.
Bowman, Delia	Dec.21,1888 - Dec.5,1950
Broyles, Martha P.	d. Nov.17,1919, d/o E.W. & M.V.
Carlton, Sarah	Dec.12,1838 - Nov.13,1905, w/o Adam
Cartright, Carlyle F.	Apr.1,1895 - Sept.7,1898,s/o J.N. & A.E.
Cooper, James Polk	1844 - 1928
Susan Hicks	1851 - 1938
J.R.Brooks	Aug.4,1909 - Jan.2,1910, s/o J.N. & S.J.

Cooper, Sarah Jane	June 10,1869 -June 11,1945
John N.	Dec.18,1869 - July 13,1931
Cox, Henry P.	d.Mar.9,1891, age 20 & 23 d, s/o W.T.& M.D.
Rachael	Oct.28,1848 - Aug.18,1925, w/o Samuel R.
Samuel Rhea	June 2,1845 - Dec.2,1915
Cross, Julia A.Hart	Nov.17,1834 - Feb.25,1912
David H.	Oct.25,1826 - Feb.8,1886
T.Jones	Sept.23,1812 - Mar.27,1888
Polly	Sept.4,1826 - Feb.10,1889, 3rd w/o T.J.
Stella M.	1898 - 1900
Frank P.	1853 - 1898
Mary P.	1813 - 1901, w/o Elijah Cross.
Hesse	no date
Tessie	no date
Bessie	no date
Rev. Wm.K.	d.Oct.17,1893, aged 79y3m3d
Martha	Oct.5,1819 - Apr.2,1873, 2nd w/o T.J.
Elijah	Tn.Orderly Sgt. Shelby's NC Reg.,Rev.War.
Jacob G.	Jan.1,1840 - Aug.5,1896
Sallie E. Fleenor	July 9,1844 - June 20,1921
Henry W.	1875 - 1943
William C.	Feb.17,1851 - Feb.1,1931
Martha E.	Nov.3,1861 - Feb.23,1909
Fannie Rhea Spurgeon	Mar.25,1861 - Apr.10,1922, w/o C.B.Cross.
Carlton B.	Sept.9,1865 - Nov.24,1942
Davis, Bettie M.	June 25,1870 - June 17,1905, d/o T.A. & S.F.
Davidson, Nathan E.	June 11,1873 - Mar.26,1949
Deakins, Martha Hicks	Jan.3,1849 - Aug.31,1916
J.M.	Nov.5,1845 - Nov.9,1912
Margaret M.	1908 - 1958 (fhm)
R. Bruce	Apr.23,1875 - Feb.10,1900, d/o J.M. & Martha.
William J.	1870 - 1939
Mary E.	1875 - no date
W.B.French	Oct.6,1902 - Nov.4,1909, s/o J.W. & M.E.
Doan, Emmaline	Oct.2,1825 - Nov.5,1889, w/o Wm.Doan, Erected by O.B.Doan.
William	Jan.9,1812 - Mar.14,1886
E.D.	Apr.2,1853 - Dec.31,1913
Susan E. White	Aug.5,1856 - Oct.26,1907, w/o E.D.
Fickle, Anna May	May 16,1893 - Apr.21,1901
John Naff	July 11,1889 - died in Bakersfield, CA., July 6,1910.Children of S.B.& E.A.Fickle.
Ellen A.	July 24,1862 - no date
Samuel B.	Oct.18,1857 - May 2,1938
Cora Glenn	July 1,1883 - Oct.18,1908, d/o S.B.& E.A.
Ford, C.M.	Mar.29,1832 - Jan.29,1911
Frazier, Mary	Mar.20,1862 - Dec.6,1911, w/o John T.
Galloway, Mary D. Keen	Nov.13,1835 - Dec.10,1872, d/o James & Sarah.
Sarah	Nov.13,1795 - June 25,1870, w/o James
James	Feb.10,1792 - Oct.18,1855
Glover, Glenna M.	Apr.6,1925 - Apr.11,1925
Beatrice V.	May 9,1926 - May 19,1926
Howard Franklin	Dec.28,1909 - Feb.26,1910,s/o Edgar & Maudie.
Goodman, Patricia Ann	July 9-10,1946

Muddy Creek Baptist Church Cemetery, cont.

Gray, Nannie E.	Oct.13,1896 - June 16,1919,d/o E.S.& M.E.
Laura P.	Mar.10,1900 - June 1,1916,d/o E.S.& M.E.
Mary E.	1874 - 1913
Elbert S.	1872 - 1946
Anise Monteith	Sept.9,1849 - Apr.17,1930, w/o James.
James	Apr.20,1839 - Sept.16,1919
Elizabeth E.	May 21,1869 - July 30,1895, d/o James & Anise.
Hackney, James G.	1886 - 1932
Margaret	1888 - 19--
Hall, Caldonia S.	Nov.22,1842 - Jan.3,1869, w/o Wm.A.Hall.
Harr, J.Joseph	Mar.12,1845 - Apr.9,1913
Hicks, Ethel May	Oct.8,1903 - Nov.8,1918, d/o G.W.& C.A.
George W.	1861 - 1942
James A.	1869 - 19--
Anna N.	1879 - 1932
Robert T.	June 12,1880 - May 5,1955
Cora May	Feb.13,1887 - July 9,1890, d/o I.E.& L.C.
Rebecca R. Hull	Aug.15,1814 - Jan.13,1886, w/o Isaac
Myrtle	1880 - 19--
Marion	1872 - 1956
David	Feb.14,1873 - Dec.27,1939
Barbara A.	1851 - 1949
J.C.	May 19,1923 - Mar.31,1936
Roy B.	1903 - 1955
Mary Lida	1879 - 1950
Annie Emaline	1876 - no date
Abraham	Apr.19,1838 - Aug.20,1885
Celia Wagner	July 31,1835 - Dec.15,1924
Matilda E.	Dec.2,1859 - July 2,1909
Hull, William R.	Feb.28,1845 - Apr.7,1921
Margaret R.	May 15,1865 - Dec.13,1905, w/o Wm.R.Hull.
Elbert	Aug.6,1855 - Jan.6,1924
Olabeth	Dec.4,1911 - May 23,1917, d/o Elbert & Belle.
Mary A. Cook	Mar.5,1782 - Sept.2,1867,w/o Frederick Hull, A faithful member of the Pres.Church, Erected by dau., May.
Frederick	Oct.29,1777 - Nov.6,1867, A consistent member of the Evangelical Lutheran Church., Erected by his dau.,May.
Lucinda	July 5,1826 - July 25,1892, w/o Noah Hull.
Noah	May 29,1819 - Aug.17,1863
John C.	July 14,1842 - Sept.23,1910
D.E.	July 1,1851 - Oct.27,1855
Johnson, Mary	d.May 17,1815, aged about 60 yrs.
Philip	d.Jan.30,1839, aged 99y1m.
Edward	dates gone.
Jones, Sarah	1839 - 1908
William	Oct.18,1832 - Nov.9,1892
John W.	Apr.5,1857 - Aug.5,1934
Susan C.	Sept.15,1856 - June 27,1898, w/o John W.
Kuhn, Elizabeth	Sept.24,1798 - July 23,1890
Rev. Peter	Dec.1,1793 - Nov.15,1871, aged 77y11m14d., for 40 yrs. a faithful minister of the Baptist Church.

Leonard, G.M.	b. & d. 1932, d/o L.B.& Willie Leonard.
Ruby L.	b. & d. 1932, d/o L.B. & Willie Leonard.
G.W.	b. & d. July 25,1930, s/o L.B. & Willie.
J.H.	b. & d. Oct.16,1929, s/o L.B. & Willie.
Marie	b. & d. Mar.23,1928,d/o L.B. & Willie.
Lindamood, Nancy M.	Feb.18,1821 - June 23,1879, w/o William.
William	Apr.21,1811 - Mar.17,1883
McCoy, Sallie E.	Apr.5,1872 - Dec.5,1899, w/o C.H.McCoy.
Mrs. Laura B.	d. June 14,1936, aged 63y2m21d (fhm)
John B.	Oct.2,1868 - Apr.26,1917
Laura B. Cooper	Mar.24,1878 - no date,(she has 2 stones)
Infant	Jan.27-28,1907, s/o J.B. & L.B.McCoy.
Malone, James Clifton	Oct.20,1924 - Apr.23,1938
Afton	Feb.11,1923 - Jan.9,1924, s/o P.B.& M.H.
Millard, Samuel F.	Dec.27,1821 - May 7,1855
Catherine	Feb.18,1821 - Dec.7,1863
Mary E.	Feb.27,1849 - Dec.14,1914, w/o J.J.Harr.
Sarah J.	Dec.14,1850 - Jan.13,1873
Miller, Arrie Lee Hull	Mar.15,1907 - Dec.11,1927, w/o Joseph B.
Monteith, Willie H.	Aug.7,1870 - Sept.27,1870, s/o Geo. & Julian.
Infant	Nov.19,1872, s/o Moses & E.J.
Infant	Jan.14,1881, d/o Moses & E.J.
Elizabeth	Apr.29,1849 - no date
Moses	Sept.15,1847 - Aug.17,1913
Morrell, Elbert J.	1866 - 1931
Mary E.	1878 - 1937
Ethel Mae	Oct.27,1895 - June 18,1901, d/o E.J.& Bessie.
Morris, Elizabeth R.	d. Sept.12,1871, aged 40y6m7d, w/o A.W.
John M.	Oct.28,1854 - July 12,1888
A.W.	Nov.16,1830 - Feb.10,1907
Mary S.	d. Aug.14,1901, aged 70y7m5d,w/o A.W.
Neal, Ester B.	Sept.4 - Oct.27,1921, d/o T.C. & B.L.Neal.
Bertha C. Williams	Feb.27,1887 - July 10,1929,w/o T.C.
Thomas Cleve	July 31,1884 - Nov.24,1946
Lizzie Kate G.	Sept.18,1886 - no date
Infant	Apr.9,1914 - May 24,1914
Phillips, John W.	Aug.15,1891 - drowned on Mar.21,1895, s/o J.J. & R.E. Phillips.
Brady M.	May 27,1893 - Apr.15,1895, s/o John W.
Rowena E.	July 30,1872 - Oct.17,1898, w/o J.J.
Poe, Mollie R.	Aug.25,1845 - Oct.29,1898
Mary	Mar.10,1815 - Aug.26,1882, w/o E.D.Poe.
Elkanah D.	Nov.18,1818 - Mar.24,1892
Rader, James M.	Dec.10,1894 - Sept.16,1896, s/o W.M. & E.R.
Jacob A.	Mar.14,1894 - Sept.11,1896, s/o W.M. & E.R.
Martha S.	Dec.2,1889 - Spet.6,1896, s/o W.M. & E.R.
Rhea, Clara K.	Jan.4,1920 - Jan.17,1920
Rev.J.M.	May 9,1847 - Mar.29,1921
Elizabeth Smith	Nov.22,1857 - Feb.10,1930, w/o Rev.J.M.
John Fain	Yeoman 2nd Clas, US Navy, who died in line of duty, May 2,1926,Erected by loving shipmates.
J.N.	Oct.30,1889 - July 19,1912, s/o J.S. & M.A.

Muddy Creek Baptist Church Cemetery, cont.

Rhea, Joseph	1861 - 1906
Adeline	1868 - 1945
Rodgers, Mary E.	June 1,1823 - May 4,1892
Jesse R.	Aug.4,1835 - Aug.30,1902
Joseph	Apr.10,1827 - May 27,1889
Shipley, Martha E. Cox	Mar.27,1862 - Oct.17,1904, w/o J.T.
John K.	June 22,1836 - Mar.13,1915
Charles M.	Apr.19,1876 - Sept.22,1877, s/o J.K.& M.E.
Lena R.	Aug.24,1882 - July 26,1889, d/o J.K.& M.E.
Isena	July 26,1889 (plain limestone marker)
John P.	Oct.1,1904 - Sept.30,1905
Slaughter, Mary	Sept.4,1827 - Mar.7,1900, w/o Joseph.
John	Sept.16,1832 - June 30,1899
Smith, Addie Willing	July 3,1867 - Mar.25,1941
David Elbert	Apr.15,1871 - Apr.17,1939
Walter C.	June 22,1894 - Dec.8,1895, s/o D.E.& Addie.
James C.	Dec.22,1891 - Nov 5,1895, s/o D.E.& Addie.
Frances O.	July 29,1889 - Nov.18,1900, s/o D.E.& Addie.
Frances M.	Aug.27,1871 - May 26,1903
Joseph	1831 - 1901
Adline	1836 - 1924
Lillie	d. May 11,1878
Laura E.	Nov.16,1881 - Oc.t15,1901
Nancy J.	Apr.8,1850 - Oct.7,1898, w/o H.W.Smith.
Roy B.	Aug.5,1900 - Nov.10,1916, s/o H.W.& M.L.
Henry W.	Aug.1854 - Feb.1926
Rebecca P.	July 3,1854 - Jan.28,1926
J.A.	1893 - 1931
Lula J.	1932 - 1934
Alice E.	Oct.22,1864 - Dec.6,1939
W.T.	Nov.1,1854 - July 4,1928
John A.	Oct.17,1887 - Aug.4,1918, died in L.A.,Ca., Photo in stone, s/o W.T.& A.E.Smith.
Infant	Jan.27,1884 - Jan.28,1885, s/o W.T.& A.E.
Addie	Oct.12,1885 - July 2,1897, d/o W.T.& A.E.
Elbert S.	Sept.25,1851 - Dec.24,1921
Sarah C.	Apr.11,1850 - Feb.7,1892, w/o E.S.Smith.
Charles & William	b. & d. Dec.16,1923
Joseph D.	1865 - 1932
Cordelia F.	1867 - 1934
Bessie M.	1903 - 1953
Spurgeon, John E.	Apr.28,1856 - July 7,1863
Mary Ruth	Aug.15,1852 - Oct.20,1862
Thomas J.	June 15,1861 - Aug.30,1863, children of Elkanah & Mary Spurgeon.
Thomas Craft	Jan.23,1889, aged 62y9m13d.
John Rhea	Feb.2,1830 - Feb.3,1898
ELizabeth	d. May 19,1918, aged 88 yrs.
Susan	Oct.29,1833, the death date was between iron bands used to repair the stone, w/o J.E.
Spurgin, Olivia J.	Nov.15,1859 - Dec.3,1859, d/o S.P.& E.

Spurgin,	Ann	July 27,1801 - Apr.13,1856, w/o Joseph.
	Joseph	June 29,1796 - Dec.23,1872
	John	d. Mar.20,1803, aged about 30y1m13d.
	Elizabeth	d. May 6,1807/37?, aged about 83y2m19d.
	Tabitha	d. Apr.1831, aged 4y2m29d.
	Mary	June 6,1789 - Feb.17,1860, w/o John.
	John	Dec.20,1790 - Nov.30,1869, was ordained a Deacon of Muddy Cr.Bap.Church Oct.7,1831 & elected clerk, Oct.7,1837.
	J.A.	d. May 4,--80?
Stidham,	Baby	1945
	Arlie G.	1917 - 1944
	Ada Lee	1895 - 19--
	Thomas N.	1892 - 1944
Troxwell,	Bobby Gene	1944 - 1944, s/o W.C. & A.C. Troxwell.
	Andy	MAr.14,1879 - Apr.16,1949
Wagner,	Sudie E.	Nov.21,1897 - July 10,1924
	Barbra	Mar.12,1868 - Feb.8,1934
	Mike F.	June 1,1870 - July 10,1942
	Eleree	Jan.21,1890 - Nov.9,1896
	Mary	Nov.19,1836 - Sept.7,1918
	Martha Ellen	Oct.10,1864 - 1889, erected by M.T.Wagner.
Walch,	Donald Ray	1948 - 1946 (note error in date & spelling)
Walsh,	Norma Jean	1942 - 1942
White,	Benny K.	Jan.5,1895 - May 15,1896, s/o A.J.& M.J.
	Rebecca	Nov.25,1826 - June 27,1901, w/o T.W.
Williams ,	David T.	Oct.6,1872 - Oct.28,1888,s/o J.M.& E.G.
	Jerry M.	Nov.23,1840 - May 22,1909
	Elizabeth	July 30,1845 - July 23,1922, w/o J.M.
Yoakley,	Rosannah	June 16,1846 - Mar.25,1848
	Richard L.	Nov.30,1844 - May 1,1847
	Rebecca J.	Feb.8,1861 - Feb.19,1878
	Sarah E.	Apr.11,1863 - July 22,1863
	Infant	June 22-July 24,1858, s/o J.C. & M.A.

Wheeler Cemetery
Established in 1877

Akard,	David	July 15,1829 - May 18,1905/9
	Ellen	Sept.3,1883 - Apr.5,1911
	Clint	1881 - 1935
	Abbie	1886 - 1962
	Craft	1877 - 1923
	Mae	1879 - 1964
Arnold,	twins	1981 - 1981
Bachman,	Sarah Hoss	Mar.26,1846 - June 30,1925
Barker,	Carrie E.	July 17,1909 - Jan.28,1912, d/o J.W.& L.E.
Barnes,	Jessie Pearl	Jan.25,1911 - May 17,1913, d/o C.D.& L.C.
	Lydia Hathern Holt	June 4,1887 - June 17,1922, w/o C.D.
	Earl	Mar.9,1903 - Mar.23,1929
	Noah D.	July 3,1867 - Sept.5,1895
	Alice Hamilton	Jan.14,1870 - Mar.10,1901, w/o N.D.
	James	Jan.16,1844 - Mar.8,1917
	Mary A.	July 30,1846 - July 6,1928

Wheeler Cemetery, cont.

Barnes, David T.	1870 - 1949
Olena M.	1874 - 1971
Adam Stephen	1872 - 1938
Sue Bachman	1880 - 1949
Elbert F.	1882 - 1937
Bettie L.	1881 - 1955
George R.	Apr.29,1846 - Mar.15,1902
Sarah J.	July 30,1844 - July 12,1938
Fletcher A.	1873 - 1940
Alice L.	1872 - 1954
George Wright	Jan.2,1901 - Mar.19,1916, s/o A.F.& A.L.
Blalock, James	Aug.8,1853 - no date
Mattie Lane	July 1,1861 - Aug.8,1899
Bowman, Carrie Connor	Jan.1,1887 - July 21,1914
Theodore	July 16,1840 - Sept.18,1882
Margaret E.	Apr.3,1851 - Aug.4,1941
Browlee, Lena Jane	Apr.16,1902 - Apr.2,1940
Carter, Phillip Jackson	June 5,1831 - Oct.27,1916
Francis Lucinda	Aug.6,1833 - Dec.10,1927
Cartwright, John S.	Aug.1,1830 - Apr.7,1914
Barbara A.	Jan.31,1830 - Aug.19,1898
Fred	July 21,1869 - July 3,1907, s/o J.S.& B.A.
S.J.Yoakley	Sept.16,1881 - Feb.22,1909, w/o L.F.
Cash, Hannah C.	Sept.27,1894 - May 2,1900, d/o C.C.& O.E.
Infant	Apr.15,1898, s/o C.C.& O.E.
Charles C.	1867 - 1939
Ollivene	1866 - 1934/9
Coffman, William David	Dec.31,1907 - Mar.24,1908, s/o D.P.& N.A.
Roy Artimus	Feb.3,1913 - Oct.1,1916, s/o S.W.& C.V.
D.S.	Mar.19,1845 - June 13,1916
C.S.	Feb.10,1854 - Mar.25,1926, w/o D.C.
M.E.	Oct.21,1886 - Mar.30,1897
H.E.	Apr.21,1894 - Oct.20,1899
Cross, Allen B.	1919 - 1985
Gladys E.	1916 - 1983
Eliza	Apr.17,1824 - Oct.9,1912, 2nd w/o Rev.W.K. Cross, d/o Rev.Blake & Betsy Carlton.
Deakins, John H.	Oct.17,1860 - Aug.11,1884, s/o R. & Mary.
Richard	Nov.25, 1820 - July 5,1898
Mary E.	Sept.12,1819 - June 25,1898, w/o Richard.
Deck, Etta Barnes	1880 - 1920
Mary Lanetta	1907 - 1918
Infant	no date
Doane, Glenn Bernard	May 15,1920 - Nov.30,1921, s/o T.G.& D.S.
Durham, Betty	1863 - 1901
Feathers, Clarence Cleavland	Nov.1-29,1892, s/o W.J.& M.A.
William J.	Feb.24,1865 - Oct.1,1948
Margaret Ann Marion	Apr.23,1871 - Oct.30,1948
Fickle, Mary Eliza	May 27,1898 - Nov.30,1899, d/o S.B.& Ellen.
Ford, George W.	Oct.3,1861 - Feb.1,1933
James G.	Feb.10,1857 - Dec.31,1896
Sarah F.	Sept.24,1856 - Mar.6,1945
Mahala	Jan.22,1839 - Oct.15,1915

Wheeler Cemetery, cont.

Ford, Rebecca A.	1862 - 1938
W.A.	Dec.25,1858 - Jan.15,1925
Mary A.	Dec.2,1870 - Oct.26,1954
Gammon, Sunshine	1906 - 1907
James	1897 - 1898
Barbara Elizabeth	1875 - 1925
Robert Lee	1864 - 1961
Hale, George W.	July 27,1866 - Mar.31,1941
Minnie Z.	Feb.28,1881 - Sept.6,1950
Hamilton, Anthony G.	Jan.17,1841 - May 9,1910
Martha Ellen	Mar.20,1844 - May 18,1891,w/o Anthony G.
George E.	Sept.19,1859 - Apr.8,1893
Barbara E.	June 28,1867 - Sept.18,1950
George Opal	Sept.13,1891 - Feb.10,1963
Hawk, Valdrie D.	Oct.3,1895 - Sept.29,1918, in France.
J.N.	1862 - 1934
Harriet	1860 - no date
H.D.	Feb.11,1841 - July 5,1927
Sarah Emma Akard	Dec.31,1851 - Apr.17,1913
Infant	May 18,1893, d/o D.E. & L.C. Hawk.
Jessie	Apr.30,1846 - May 14,1921
Nannie J. Nighbert	Sept.19,1848 - Aug.3,1917
Thomas F.	May 15,1874 - Nov.18,1898, s/o Jessie & N.J.
W.I.	Sept.13,1843 - June 22,1919
Martha E.	Dec.1,1850 - Dec.23,1928, w/o W.I.Hawk.
Hawley, William Houston	no dates
Susan Gammon	no dates
Leogene	no dates
Hayes, Mary Elizabeth	Apr.15,1837 - July 12,1837, d/o W.T.& E.I.
Henry, Elbert E.	1899 - 1953
Mayme M.	1906 - no date
Kyle D.	Oct.27,1940 - Dec.29,1940
Mary Catherine	July 30,1942 - no date
William B.	1863 - 19--
Sarah J.	1866 - 1939
Hickam, Charlie C.	Feb.24,1892 - June 22,1949
William Wheeler	Feb.26,1898 - Dec.17,1898, s/o L.D.& E.
A.J.	OCt.13,1859 - Feb.25,1903
Sarah L.	Oct.29,1862 - Nov.27,1953
Eva Ruth	Aug.17,1900 - Feb.27,1927
Clyde Worley	Jan.9,1898 - Sept.16,1905, s/o W.O. & L.V.
Hodges, Bertha Ruth	Aug.25,1913 - Feb.15,1917, d/o James & Jemima.
Noah	May 19,1873 - June 11,1897
E.C.	Oct.1,1825 - Feb.11,1906
Ama Ruth	Apr.11,1907 - Mar.1,1927
Georgie Genevie	Mar.3,1918 - June 17,1919, d/o R.G.& M.F.
Hughes, James L.	Sept.5,1865 - Jan.23,1955
Julia E. Lacey	July 25,1871 - June 29,1941
Isley, William G.	Jan.24,1889 - Aug.15,1926
Roy A.	Dec.1,1890 - Feb.16,1920
Kidd, William J.	Feb.3,1859 - Feb.29,1932, m.Sept.18,1877,
Eliza Jane Tate	Jan.15,1860 - Sept.12,1915, w/o W.J.
A.A.	1879 - 1938
Margaret E.	May 12,1874 - July 30,1915, w/o A.A.Kidd.

King, E.W.	May 1,1822, s/o J.E. & S.M. King.
Orda M. Cox	Feb.9,1864 - May 3,1904, w/o S.S.King.
Lacy, Andrew J.	1841 - 1912
Sarah E.	1843 - 1919
G.T.	Sept.26,1873 - Apr.1,1893
Cleo	Oct.23,1884 - Nov.27,1903, d/o W.J.& Mollie.
Loggans, R. Jane	Apr.8,1866 - Oct.10,1897, w/o P.H. Loggans.
McDonnell, Michael S.	1907 - 1966
Ester	1907 - 1970
Marion, Lena Myrtle	June 3,1902 - Dec.13,1940
Matthew	Mar.17,1844 - June 14,1930
Cornelia E.	Oct.9,1853 - Feb.10,1904, w/o Matthew.
Abe	Aug.15,1881 - Oct.27,1962
Darth	Mar.19,1882 - 1975
Chester B.	Apr.1,1923 - Aug.14,1968
Tommy	Oct.14,1890 - Sept.25,1896, s/o J.F. & R.E.
Mashburn, M.Jane	May 19,1929 - Nov.23,1945
Milhorn, Andrew J.	Dec.24,1883 - Apr.7,1904
George W.	Aug.28,1840 - Dec.7,1926
Malissa H.	June 11,1839 - Aug.22,1923
Millhorne, Bessie Lee	July 21,1918 - Aug.30,1918, d/o J.M.& L.E.
Millhorn, William H.	1862 - 1930
Nora E.	1877 - 1951
Eldridge	d. 1982
William E.	June 18,1885 - Jan.31,1965
Jessie A.	Aug.16,1905 - Jan.21,1923
T. Ray	July 27,1897 - Jan.15,1930
Horace	b. & d. Nov.25,1884
M. Alice	June 18,1858 - May 18,1924
J.A.	Dec.28,1846 - June 14,1936
Minga, Nannie I.	1904 - 1986
Miller	Dec.28,1822 - June 1,1896
Elizabeth M.	Sept.19,1826 - July 16,1897, w/o Miller.
James M.	Apr.8,1906 - Sept.9,1908, s/o N.S. & E.
Noah S.	Jan.17,1863 - Mar.14,1922
Lizzie	June 22,1871 - Nov.24,1934, w/o Noah S.
Nell F.	1903 - 1957
John H.	1853 - 1933
E. Lou	1867 - 1908
Stella Willet	Feb.1,1905 - Sept.10,1905, d/o J.H.& E.L.
Margaret Sanders	1855 - 1935
Monteith, George W.	Feb.16, 1840 - Jan.2,1895
Julina	June 10, 1840 - Mar.21,1916
Noah B.	Dec.7,1872 - Dec.3,1896
Morrell, Rev. J.F.	Nov.17,1841 - Jan.9,1906
Susan C.	Apr.30,1848 - Aug.21,1929
Nidiffer, Mark L.	1872 - 1928
Mollie E.	1874 - 1947
Norris, Infant	b. & d. Jan.14,1891, s/o J.E.& L.A.
Lura Etta	Oct.13,1910 - Oct.27,1913, d/o H.W. & Ida R.
Pence, Samuel S.	1840 - 1925
Armetta J. Gammon	1861 - 1936

Wheeler Cemetery, cont.

Poore, William B.	Feb.21,1936 - Jan.21,1937
George A.	Oct.10,1937 - Nov.24,1937
Violet	Jan.1,1941 - Feb.12,1941, ch/o Allen & Iva.
Roller, A. Fleetwood	1885 - 1930
Noah T.	1861 - 1947
N. Orlena	1861 - 1935
Nell M.	1896 - 1980
A.H.	Sept.19,1826 - Mar.29,1900
Russell, Elizabeth	1854/64 - 1930
Rutherford, Willie J.	Nov.19,1867 - July 5,1905
Eliza	Dec.3,1877 - no date
Sanders, Abraham	July 19,1821 - Apr.10,1908
Jamima	Oct.6,1823 - May 1,1896, w/o Abraham
Johnnie F.	May 12,1889 - Aug.27,1890, s/o M.J.& M.J.
Jemima	Mar.20,1888 - Mar.23,1888, d/o M.J.& M.J.
Charlie & Stasy	b. & d. July 3,1885, ch/o M.J. & M.J.
Cordia F.	Sept.1,1886 - Jan.31,1906, d/o M.J.& M.J.
Mary Brooks	Feb.11,1898 - Oct.12,1912, d/o M.J.& M.J.
Jesse B.	1859 - 1914, m.Dec.25,1881
Margaret E.	1858 - 1915, w/o Jesse B.
M.J.	May 23,1862 - Feb.19,1942
Mary J.	May 4,1865 - June 1,1927
Sarah J.	Dec.8,1828 - June 18,1885
Saunders, Abram	1848 - 1927
Sarah	1856 - 1936
Sell, David Roscoe	Apr.30,1898 - Oct.26,1904, s/o G.W.& S.E.
Sarah Elizabeth	Nov.30,1866 - Aug.5,1916, w/o G.W.
Lewis A.	Jan.28,1902, aged 72y10m28d.
Barbara Ann	Mar.7,1834 - Dec.3,1909, w/o Lewis A.
Sherfey, Charles E.	1919 - 1949
Shirley, Sarah C. Ford	Sept.8,1858 - APr.6,1917, 3rd w/o J.T.
Smalling, Anna Mae	May 31,1909 - Aug.19,1909, d/o Chester & Mae.
Smith, John E.	1910 - 1910
Franics G.	1910 - 1912
John M.	1869 - 1910
Ellen B.	1872 - 1950
Stidham, Kelly	June 8,1884 - Oct.28,1887, s/o R.S.& S.J.
Reed S.	July 20,1856 - Mar.16,1928, m. Oct.25,1875
Sarah J.Durham	J n.12,1858 - Sept.25,1915, s/o Reed S.
Webb, Joyce	June 16,1933 - Nov.17,1933, d/o Thurman & Dimple Webb.
Wise, Nancy	1830 - Aug.12,1905
Wood, Jno. W.	Nov.17,1838 - Sept.18,1912
J. Manley	Jan.28,1884 - May 19,1957
Yoakely, Jessie C.	Dec.2,1820 - Mar.28,1891
M.A.	Apr.7,1822 - Mar.14,1901
Laura Ellen	d. Oct.12,1886, aged 17y2m8d, d/o W.F.& E.E.
W.M. "Doc"	Feb.5,1875 - July 21,1898, s/o W.F. & E.E., Mortally wounded in charge of San Juan Hill.
Bessie L. Millhorn	Apr.28,1891 - Feb.21,1921
W.F.	Oct.7,1843 - July 26,1919
Elizabeth F.	Apr.24,1848 - Dec.8,1927
King Frederick	1905 - 1923
Yokley, Benjimen Haskew	May 8,1855 - Nov.17,1937
Minerva Etta Barnes	May 7,1873 - June 21,1947

Old Methodist Cemetery

Barr, Lou Delpha	d.Sept.3,1933, aged 62y3m4d.
Bailey, Pollie M.	Sept.27,1877 - July 26,1916,w/o Robert M.
Brown, Thalma M.	Mar.16,1915 - Sept.26,1916, d/o H.C.& P.M.
Devault, James Miller	June 27,1828 - Feb.11,1914
Samuel P.	Jan.6,1868 - Aug.11,1918
Emert, Margaret	Jan.19,1828 - Dec.5,1904,m. Aug.1,1848.
Grim, Sophia	Feb.8,1819 - July 31,1845, d/o Wm.& Susan.
Jones, William E.	Apr.22,1832 - Aug.15,1893
Keller, Mollie Ann	Dec.27,1858 - July 7,1925, w/o J.W.Keller.
Lampson, Infant	b. & d. OCt.23,1856, d/o J.L.& M.F.
Lynn, Charles	July 14,1815 - July 27,1871
Ellen A.	June 27,1830 - Aug.3,1861
Charles	July 14,1815 - July 27,1871
Frances	Jan.4,1819 - May 21,1865
James C.	June 16,1844 - July 7,1861
Charles M.	Jan.9,1849 - Nov.5,1854
Hugh W.	Oct.17,1846 - Nov.18,1854
Joseph H.	June 15,1851 - Nov.1,1854
Frances Rhea	Feb.7-Apr.28,1929, d/o John & Nancy.
James	May 24,1801 - Feb.5,1840
John	Dec.17,1768 - Aug.20,1830
John	Nov.28-Dec.16,1834, s/o John & Nancy.
Joseph Rhea	Aug.15,1833 - Jan.3,1857, s/o John & Nancy.
Martha	1775 - Dec.27,1824
Nancy	Feb.25,1801 - Oct.7,1839
Neeley, Catherine	c.1752, Ireland - Aug.1828
Netherland, Ann	d. May 6,1827, aged about 35 y.
O'Brien, Sarah	d. Sept.24,1827, aged 14y10m28d., Coffin shaped iron slab on grave,listing date.
Parker, L.J.	Apr.5,1833 - Aug.30,1917
Smith, E.D.	Nov.7,1854 - Oct.13,1929
L.M.	Aug.15,1865 - July 1,1914, w/o E.D.Smith.
Willie	Oct.10,1887 - OCt.28,1895, s/o E.D.& M.L.
Walker, John Lynn	Oct.7,1856 - Oct.14,1859, s/o J.R.& M.A.
Wood, Rev. Phillip	July 12,1801, in Hollis,NH.,died Kingsport, TN., June 6,1856.Removed to East TN.,1827.

Shipley Cemetery

Adams, Albert D.	Jan.20,1910 - May 27,1977
Katherine E.	Sept.7,1915
Charles Henry	Apr.14,1912 - Nov.14,1946
Joe H.	1892 - 1949
Nancy Ann	1866 - 1936
Melvin W.	1895 - 1961
Preston Ray	Oct.19,1910 - June 9,1959
Addison, Billie Jo	Sept.10,1937 - June 14,1948
Margaret A.	June 7,1942 - Sept.26,1956
Akers, Ansel L.	1935 - no date
Wanda B.	1936 - 1965
Ansel L.,Jr.	1962, infant.
Infant	1958
Alford, Clifton	June 2,1906 - Sept.1,1906
Flosie D.	Apr.25,1910 - Nov.30,1910,d/o John & Mary.
Infant	b. & d. Aug.15,1892, s/o John & Mary.
James E.	Jan.14,1885 - May 29,1924

Shipley Cemetery, cont.

Alford, James L.	Feb.4,1910 - Dec.3,1968
Minnie L.	Sept.22,1928 - no date
John	Feb.13,1841 - Dec.5,1915
Louis B.	Jan.30,1928 - Mar.22,1929
Margaret E.	Dec.18,1882 - Dec.25,1908
Mary Florence	Mar.30,1888 - Sept.8,1976
Michael W.	May 8,1957
Oscar L.	1907 - 1976
Carmon R.	1907 - 1960
Sarah	Jan.24,1809 - June 23,1896
Sarah Ellen	Feb.28,1881 - Sept.19,1886, d/o John & Polly.
William E.	July 25,1901 - July 30,1934
Lizzie O.	May 21,1905 - Dec.21,1943
Worley T.	Jan.9,1913 - Aug.1,1973
Arnold, Clarence D.	Apr.3,1913 - Oct.25,1971
Ashburn, Milton	Aug.24,1906 - Nov.9,1985
Zelma	June 28,1920 - no date
Veva Louise	no dates
Barbe, Roy Lester	May 2,1905 - Nov.30,1975
Faye B.	Sept.19,1911 - Oct.28,1985
Baumgardner, Lesley J.	Jan.19,1923 - no date
Virginia M.	Nov.29,1921 - Aug.23,1981
Blevins, E.M.	Feb.28,1853 - Aug.28,1909
John M.	Nov.14,1801 - Nov.10,1875
John W.	Nov.30,1848 - Dec.2,1935
Margaret	Aug.15,1836 - Apr.22,1886, w/o Mathew.
Mary A.	Apr.15,1856 - Oct.13,1884,w/o E.M.
Mary Ann	Mar.20,1837 - May 16,1903
Maggie Booher	Jan.3,1848 - June 13,1911, w/o Mathew.
Matthew	Nov.4,1833 - June 6,1905
Robert R.	1895 - 1975
Bessie S.	1900 - 1972
Samuel D.	Nov.4,1847 - Oct.11,1924
Charlotte A.	Dec.29,1851 - Oct.23,1934
Spurgeon	1895 - 1955
Winnie	1895 - 1980
Susan Kathern	Feb.2,1860 - July 14,1945,w/o E.M.
Williams A.	Nov.17,1901 - Mar.10,1927
Herman W.	Feb.2,1926 - Apr.23,1928
Booher, Alice M.	1879 - 1950
Amanda Caldonia	Jan.19,1884 - Feb.27,1971
Bryan M.	Mar.3,1900 - Nov.21,1976
Charlie	May 10,1889 - Apr.6,1933
Clyde E.	1906 - 1976
Ethel M.	1916 - 1978
David Oscar	Mar.8,1903 - June 12,1965
David Samuel	1936 - 1972
Dexter T.	July 13,1903 - Dec.9,1976
Elzira B.	May 9,1863 - May 11,1918
Earnest H.	1904 - 1974
Henry C.	Dec.2,1893 - Dec.3,1959
MAry M.	Jan.16,1898 - no date

Shipley Cemetery, cont.

Booher, Henry N.	1886 - 1934
Eva O.	1886 - 1967
J.E.	1855 - 1916
Jacob M.	Apr.19,1883 - Aug.24,1975
Myrtle S.	Mar.10,1888 - Apr.27,1914
James W.	Jan.19,1884 - Mar.19,1974
Nancy R.	Feb.20,1887 - Nov.11,1946
James S.	July 24,1914 - no date
Virginia M.	Mar.3,1918 - Nov.30.1982
John E.	Sept.20,1936
Joesph S.	Oct.4,1888 - Oct.14,1966
Kenneth Allen	Oct.17,1967 - Dec.17,1983
Lionel D.	1913 - 1978
Louisa R.	1862 - 1950
M.Katheryn	1911 - 1985
Martin D.	May 23,1859 - Apr.7,1933
Mary M.	1888 - 1934
Sarah J.	1847 - 1944, w/o P.W.Booher.
Sidney P.	Aug.2,1900 - Oct.8,1966,m.Sept.19,1924.
Ava E.	Feb.15,1907 - Apr.18,1970, w/o Sidney P.
Sidney P.Jr.	Aug.28,1925 - Feb.3,1984
Walter E.	1890 - 1984
Lorena E.	1894 - 1971
William A.	1875 - 1937
William Charles	1861 - 1935
Barbara Ellen	1866 - 1936
Boughers, John S.	Dec.19,1895 - Aug.16,1979
Parris Marie (Peachie)	Feb.13,1961 - Apr.5,1962
Virginia Morton	Oct.30,1894 - Apr.3,1970, w/o John S.
Bouton, Andrew J.	1884 - 1970
Sylvia E.	1908 - no date
Clarence	1906 - 1969
Daniel A.	1862 - 1920
Elizabeth M.	1860 - 1940
Frances G.	1856 - 1932
James E.	Feb.11,1921 - Feb.2,1984
Addie L.	June 3,1921 - no date
Jennie E.	Aug.30,1861 - July 15,1924
John P.	1882 - 1964
Malissa J.	1885 - 1973
Holland C.	May 26,1918 - Mar.10,1974
William J.	Jan.1,1859 - May 5,1914
Rev.Wm. Tate	1889 - 1947
Bowers, Billy M.	1940 - 1940, s/o W.H.& Edna Bowers.
Cora N.	1903 - 1983
Dana	1901 - 1984
Louise	1906 - 1978
Ethel G.	Nov.17,1902 - Nov.28,1915,d/o I.L.& N.B.
Henry Abe	Jan.11,1886 - Jan.19,1976
Kate C.	July 24,1890 - Mar.12,1978
Isaac L.	1856 - 1941
Barsha N.	1866 - no date
Joe L.	1897 - 1974
Mela M.	1898 - 19--

Shipley Cemetery, cont.

Bowers, Mary R.	Feb.15,1904 - Aug.3,1905, d/o W.L.& M.L.
Tessie O.	May 6,1890 - Jan.24,1962
William H.	1911 - 1958
Edna V.	1920 - no date
William L.	1875 - 19--
MaryLou	1871 - 1949
Boyd, Alec	Mar.14,1861 - Mar.15,1946
Martha Jane	June 16,1888 - Apr.11,1961
Andrew W.	Oct.4,1845 - Aug.5,1915,Co.B,13th TN.,Calvary.
George F.	May 15,1888 - Apr.15,1982
Lottie P.	Feb.28,1905
George S.	Feb.9,1864 - Dec.7,1921
Mrs. George S.	1855 - 1930
J.M.	Nov.12,1853 - Nov.7,1861, s/o J. & Anna.
James Elmer	Aug.9,1925 - Nov.10,1926, s/o Alex & Jennie.
Joseph Charles	May 2,1928 - Nov.2,1929, s/o Alex & Jennie.
John W.	1884 - 1970
Anna M.	1908 - 1970
Margareta M.	Apr.13,1855 - Apr.21,1855, d/o J. & Anna.
Martha A. Carrier	Apr.14,1878 - Feb.6,1901, w/o R.A.Boyd.
Mary Anne	Aug.22,1888 - Mar.14,1915,d/o G.S.& S.A.
Mary E.	1866 - 1919
Mary L.	Mar.20,1845 - Mar.3,1905, w/o A.W.Boyd.
Nathan M.	Aug.29,1856 - Mar.27,1909
Nora	Feb.11,1897 - Jan.30,1900,d/o R.A.& Martha.
Ollie J.	Nov.15,1892 - Mar.5,1920,s/o G.S.& S.A.Boyd.
Omer C.	1916 - no date
Zilliah M.	1918 - 1973
Robert C.	1922 - no date
Altha R.	1923 - no date
Robert Gayle	1949 - 1950
Robert Ted	Feb.19,1925 - Apr.19,1975
Leola G.	Oct.23,1924 - no date
Roger Dale	1949 - 1966
Rosa M.	1888 - 1938
Bradley, Bertha L.	1910 - 1984
Donald Gilbert	Sept.21,1932 - May 3,1971
Jean Kitzmiller	Nov.12,1939 - no date
Brown, Dayton J.	Nov.7,1919
Maxine E.	May 26,1925 - Jan.30,1971
James C.	1917 - 1984
Ronald N.	1945 - 1971
Janice M.	1947 - no date
Buchanan, A.E. (Gene)	May 21,1934 - Oct.17,1962
Betty S.	Aug.18,1934 - no date
A.E. (Buddie)	Dec.27,1955
Oleta Joy	1930, d/o R. & Vilas Buchanan.
Roosevelt	1902 - 1933
Buckles, A.J.	Dec.26,1854 - Mar.5,1912
Arvil	1918 - 1918
Carl D.	Oct.5,1892 - May 27,1982
Ade E.	Oct.23,1898 - Oct.3,1983
David E.	1907 - 19--
Myrtle M.	1905 - 1939

Buckles, E.S.	1889 - 1932
Flora Albertie	Aug.29,1899 - Apr.8,1979
Floyd Burlie	Sept.28,1899 - Nov.15,1928
Harlen M.	Sept.20,1927
Gladys B.	Jan.21,1928 - Apr.12,1979
Holland J.	Mar.13,1892 - Nov.15,1965
Mary E.	Dec.27,1909 - Feb.10,1983
Homer H.	June 9,1886 - July 7,1965
John Henry	Feb.8,1860 - Oct.17,1943
Leone	1922 - 1923
Mildred M.	Nov.18,1867 - May 3,1939
Rebeca McGarry	Oct.2,1862 - Mar.19,1907,w/o A.J.Buckles.
Rebecca H.	Dec.28,1886 - Sept.30,1956
Robert	Dec.13,1825 - June 7,1920
Ruben P.	July 11,1858 - Sept.7,1918
Ruth	Sept.9,1895 - Mar.21,1919, d/o R.P.& Lenora.
Ruby Nell	1936 - 1938
Wallace R.	Apr.5,1913 - Dec.10,1974
Mattie B.	Feb.4,1921 - no date
William R.	July 10,1904 - July 13,1982, m.Oct.26,1926,
Virginia A.	Apr.17,1911 - May 11,1970
William W.	Aug.8,1866 - Apr.1,1928
Bunn, Silas C.	Aug.6,1906 - Sept.30,1978
Isabel G.	May 14,1907 - Jan.2,1975
Buskill, Charles	May 15,1920
Joseph R.	1888 - 1934
Calloway, Isham T.	July 23,1886 - Aug.13,1968
Campbell, Dr. Joseph L.	May 5,1870 - Feb.17,1934,m.Feb.6,1898
Cornelia B.	Nov.6,1881 - Dec.28,1964, w/o J.L.
Cardwell, Eugene Sr.	no dates
Carr, Flora Mae	1923 - 1978
Carrier, Betty Jane	Sept.5,1939 - Feb.21,1961
Bryan J.	Sept.23,1919 - Dec.25,1983
Josephine P.	July 12,1922 - no date
C.N.	1851 - 1931
Casaner	July 19,1893 - May 4,1913, w/o Noah.
Catharine	Oct.21,1847 - June 7,1907,w/o J.C.
Clarence	1904 - 1983
Ida S.	1920 - no date
Dewey A.	Oct.7,1919 - Mar.7,1972
Dorothy B.	Aug.16,1926 - no date
Dexter C.	Aug.20,1916 - Sept.11,1980
E. Arthur	May 22,1902 - May 22,1976
Fannie H.	Sept.12,1904 - Sept.21,1978
Edgar W.	1908 - 1940
L.Viola	1906 - 19--
Edna Belle	Oct.29,1925, infant
Lela Bell	Jan.28,1934, infant
Finley H.	1913 - no date
Ava Lucille Powers	1928 - 1968
Floyd L.	1907 - 1983
Addie H.	1911 - 1985
Frank T.	Mar.17,1883 - Nov.28,1933
Brookie E.	July 23,1883 - Feb.24,1912

Shipley Cemetery, cont.

Carrier,	George A.	1884 - 1933
	Pearl E.	1882 - 1933
	Haskel R.	1932 - 1965
	Betty	1932 - no date
	Henry S.	1881 - 1951
	Susie E.	1883 - 1953
	Hershel L.	Sept.7,1931 - Feb.11,1980
	Hugh	Aug.5,1899 - Jan.6,1964
	Mazie B.	June 6,1906 - Feb.12,1975
	Hughey J.	July 13,1917 - Nov.16,1960
	J.	Apr.25,1823 - July 13,1904
	J.A.	Apr.6,1845 - Feb.12,1910
	J. Calvin	June 10,1873 - June 7,1966
	J.W.	1927 - 1980
	J.Hugh	Nov.28,1859 - Mar.5,1916
	James Paul	Aug.5,1935 - May 22,1936
	Joe	Jan.15,1909 - Jan.26,1983
	Anna K.	Oct.4,1910 - Aug.12,1963
	John E.	Mar.17,1905 - Mar.4,1981
	Hudie J.	Mar.18,1906 - Dec.11,1986
	John F.	1876 - 1934
	Sallie A.	1876 - 1946
	John L.	1846 - 1932
	John M.	1877 - 1960
	Nora M.	1897 - 19--
	Jonathan C.	Apr.11,1931 - Sept.24,1975
	J.R.	Mar.23,1843 - Nov.30,1916
	Lawrence E.	May 21,1932 - July 8,1953
	Lester	1912 - 1967
	Katheryn	1915 - no date
	Luther C.	Apr.7,1913 - May 1,1971
	Margaret	1910 - 1972
	Mary A. Emmert	Aug.6,1880 - Nov.14,1923, w/o W.N.
	Mary Elizabeth	Dec.12,1856 - Mar.2,1948, w/o W.D.
	Noah I.	Dec.27,1893 - Sept.10,1978
	Emma M.	Nov.27,1894 - July 5,1981
	Odell	Aug.18,1912 - Sept.15,1912
	Paul J.	June 22,1908 - Sept.26,1986
	Ada K.	Aug.8,1914 - no date
	Robert E.	1928 - 1981
	Hannah E.	1926 - no date
	Robert Earl	Mar.22,1956 - Mar.23,1956
	Robert Burl	Mar.27,1956 - Mar.24,1956
	Robert Lee	Oct.6,1879 - July 23,1947
	Bertie Ellen	Dec.23,1879 - Aug.26,1950
	Roy T.	1905 - 19--
	Lennie O.	1903 - 19--
	Sarrahan	June 7,1852 - Apr.24,1887, w/o C.N.
	Stephen L.	Nov.17,1898 - Sept.7,1964
	Ada Mae	Dec.14,1903 - Apr.28,1981
	Thurman	1910 - 1968
	Alice H.	1924 - no date
	W. Carlie	1896 - no date
	Martha B.	1892 - 1983
	Delores	1923 - 1926

Shipley Cemetery, cont.

Carrier, W.D.	1848 - 1930	
W.J.	1929 - 1929, s/o W.N. & M.C.Carrier.	
William N.	1876 - 1974	
William P.	Dec.10,1872 - July 4,1961	
Lizzie O.	June 30,1875 - Nov.3,1957	
William T.	1907 - 1967	
Verlie W.	1910 - no date	
Worley	1901 - 1951	
Bertie	1904 - 19--	
Worley J.,Jr.	1935 - no date	
Edna L.	1941 - 1975	
Chapman, Anna Laura	1922 - 1965, w/o Samuel O.Chapman.	
Randy Lee	June 28,1974	
W.R.	1889 - 1968	
Lillie A.	1892 - 1978	
Combs, William B.	Apr.1,1841 - Apr.4,1905	
Cook, Henry B.	1909 - 1979	
Lillie M.	1910 - no date	
Jannett E.	Dec.12,1962 - Apr.25,1977	
Craig, John H.	Feb.10,1930 - Mar.18,1980	
Gladys M.	Aug.15,1928 - no date	
Crampton, Wilbert S.	1921 - 1980	
Rosa Lee	1931 - no date	
Crumley, G. Decator	1916 - 1930	
John W.	Aug.2,1876 - Mar.15,1917	
Malissa A. McGarry	Aug.9,1855 - Oct.9,1905, w/o D.Crumley.	
Culbertson, Elsie Mae	Dec.30,1932 - Nov.1,1981	
Infant	Apr.16,1954	
Dakin, Floyd G.	Oct.29,1869 - Dec.29,1920	
Sallie I.	Oct.25,1877 - Nov.30,1912, w/o F.G.Dakin.	
Denton, H.M.	Aug.14,1918 - no date	
Hazel L.	July 7,1918 - no date	
Early, Conley Freel	Feb.18,1909 - Sept.16,1972	
Jonathan Everett	1938 - 1984	
Ellis, J. Dannel	Aug.29,1838 - Oct.5,1909	
L.M.Blevins	July 31,1868 - Jan.13,1907, w/o J.W.Dodson & w/o J.D. Ellis.	
Martha Ellen	Dec.5,1843 - Mar.10,1882	
Elkins, Johnnie M.	June 2,1847 - Oct.2,1928	
Mary Odell	Aug.19,1849 - June 6,1906, w/o J.M.Elkins.	
Elswick, Cathern Hinkle	Apr.17,1852 - Feb.14,1911,w/o G.L.Elswick.	
Emmert, Catharine Morrell	May 15,1817 - Sept.11,1850, w/o Rev.J.B.	
Charles Fiander	1892 - 1954	
Frances Cleveland	1892 - 1968	
E. O'Dell	Apr.4,1913 - Apr.22,1974	
Louise A.	Feb.21,1918 - no date	
George F.	Nov.24,1849 - Dec.8,1899	
Rev. Jacob B.	Apr.25,1815 - Oct.8,1873	
John R.	1875 - 1931	
Margaret A.	July 4,1851 - Jan.24,1923, w/o G.F.Emmert.	
Mattie C. Crumley	Sept.7,1878 - Oct.2,1919, w/o J.R.Emmert.	

Shipley Cemetery, cont.

Ferguson, Lilly Mae	May 20,1908 - Feb.18,1975
Myrtle	Apr.16,1884 - Oct.21,1982
Fouch, Amanda	1925 - 1941
Gracie	1942 - 1942
James T.	1900 - 1960
Maggie E.	1903 - 1985
Frazier, W.D.	no dates
Jane	no dates
Fritz, Jake N.	Feb.10,1892 - Sept.16,1968
Maude L.	Apr.4,1902 - Aug.5,1951
John L.	Feb.15,1931 - no date
Marjorie	Oct.16,1933 - no date
Mildred E.	1972 - 1972
Thomas W.	May 11,1920 - no date
Beulah K.	Jan.11,1925 - no date
Geisler, Sallie	Sept.20,1882 - Sept.1,1904, w/o Walter.
Gentry, Eli	May 23,1873 - Jan.20,1931
Emma	Apr.14,1882 - Feb.12,1948
William D.	Apr.22,1905 - Aug.15,1975
Harriet E.	Aug.11,1909 - no date
Gibbons, Anna Mae	July 15,1893 - Mar.18,1985
Glover, Argie E.	Dec.15,1903 - Sept.16,1983
Maxie A.	June 5,1914 - no date
Goodwin, Robert H.	Nov.30,1900 - June 21,1927 (K.K.K.)
Grayboal, Clinton V.	Aug.20,1907 - July 25,1973
Gross, Daney Marvin	Mar.1,1927 - Mar.13,1927
Grubb, Andrew E.	1881 - 1960
Maggie P.	1890 - no date
D.S.	no dates
Guess, Robert Lee	Nov.3,1920 - Sept.4,1965
Guinn, Andrew Jackson	Oct.3,1922 - Mar.21,1984
Sarah Kate	1928 - no date
Cleveland M.	Oct.6,1900 - July 19,1965
Easter Q.	Mar.14,1905 - Feb.6,1978
J.D.	1929 - 1966
Jackie	Oct.4,1953 - July 24,1973, s/o Andrew & Sarah.
Nathan J.	June 6,1892 - Apr.6,1979
S. Venia	June 6,1900 - Dec.22,1961
William C.	Oct.7,1885 - Nov.28,1965
Texie Ann	Apr.11,1895 - July 6,1984
Guy, John Henry	Dec.29,1871 - Apr.7,1959
Joseph L.	1906 - 1987
Polly L.	Mar.1,1879 - June 24,1957
Hale, Andrew Franklin	Nov.10,1892 - Oct.20,1940
Judy Bell	1941 - 1943
R.L.	Aug.22,1869 - Feb.27,1908
Willie L.	Apr.30,1913 - June 10,1921
Harr, Omie Jean Dowell	1920 - 1962
Hartley, David H.	Nov.24,1905 - Nov.1,1985
Amanda E.	June 23,1907 - July 18,1981
Dewey E.	June 3,1937 - Feb.21,1978
Eunice	Jan.22,1882 - Feb.16,1963

Shipley Cemetery, cont.

Hayes, Armena	June 29,1898 - Aug.14,1918, d/o W.H.	
Belcon Jackson	July 3,1903 - Nov.23,1974	
Dave J.	Sept.23,1915 - no date	
Alene G.	July 30,1915 - Aug.27,1970	
Delcia	May 3,1914 - Apr.17,1927	
Florence	July 29,1892 - Apr.6,1893	
Infant	b. & d. Feb.8,1896, infant d/o W.H.& M.R.	
Jake	June 27,1888 - Mar.29,1958	
Fannie	Aug.1,1890 - Apr.9,1953	
James	Apr.19,1902	
Polly	Apr.20,1902	
Norman V.	Mar.25,1936 - May 10,1936	
Rebecca	Oct.9,1872 - Apr.23,1954	
Robert E.	Nov.27,1943 - Oct.26,1970	
W.H. (Pete),Jr.	Mar.7,1919 - no date	
Kate E.	Nov.26,1921 - no date	
William H.	Aug.27,1871 - June 30,1959	
Haynes, William E.	May 23,1911 - Mar.22,1979	
Hensley, Levi	June 24,1893 - Nov.15,1928	
Henson, Clay C.	Jan.10,1899 - May 24,1972	
Della P.	Aug.20,1905 - Dec.28,1974	
David J.	1896 - 1972	
Norma D.	1900 - 19--	
Edith G.	July 8,1894 - Sept.6,1984	
Infant	Aug.7,1958, s/o Odell & Louise Henson.	
Odell D.	Jan.24,1921 - Apr.20,1963	
Louise H.	Apr.2,1930 - no date	
Hicks, Avery Fonza	1877 - 1979	
Robert Lee, Sr.	June 22,1940 - Feb.24,1983	
Sarah L.	1882 - 1961	
Obed R.	Sept.18,1913 - Nov.15,1979	
William T.	1874 - 1969	
Hilliard, Charles B.	Apr.17,1883 - May 29,1897,s/o S.P. & E.C.	
Cora E.	Aug.30,1875 - July 6,1890, d/o S.P.& E.C.	
Ruby E.	Sept.22,1909 - June 6,1911,d/o R.E.& Elva.	
Silas P.	Aug.7,1850 - Dec.24,1920	
Elizabeth C. Musgrave	Mar.27,1845 - Jan.4,1911	
Hinkle, Cecil N.	Sept.23,1927 - July 10,1983	
Clyde E.	1926 - no date	
Dorothy	1928 - 1977	
David Clifton	Sept.24,1912 - May 31,1944	
George Dewey	Aug.31,1898 - Sept.23,1944	
Icyann	Apr.17,1845 - Mar.10,1891,w/o J.A.Hinkle.	
Jacob	Feb.8,1862 - Dec.13,1920	
James A.	Mar.19,1854 - Aug.24,1928	
John E.	Jan.26,1882 - Jan.20,1950	
Mary E.	July 23,1899 - Feb.12,1978	
John Ed.	Sept.26,1893 - July 7,1973	
Vesta M.	Oct.17,1896 - no date	
Jonathan H.	Feb.12,1963 - July 20,1977	
Joseph B.	Oct.12,1909 - Oct.6,1986	
Alma P.	Apr.10,1908 - Feb.27,1983	

Shipley Cemetery, cont.

Hinkle, Joseph W.	1885 - 1959
Lena C.	1880 - 1959
Henry	Jan.29,1907 - Jan.5,1975
Hattie	Feb.19,1906 - Nov.5,1978
Luther T.	Mar.14,1938 - Jan.26,1963
Clella R.	Feb.14,1938 - no date
Mary E. Pearl	1901 - 1938, d/o Jacob & Alice.
N.A.	no dates
Rebecca Alice	1875 - 1941, w/o Jacob Hinkle.
Rile P.	Dec.16,1891 - June 22,1894, s/o Jacob & Allis.
Toby	1918 - 1966
Hockett, Leslie E.	Apr.30,1913 - May 27,1974
Tim O.	Nov.29,1922 - Aug.9,1971
Hopkins, Beryl E.	May 30,1922 - July 18,1922
Charlie	1876 - 1958
Minnie	1877 - 1966
Floyd W.	May 29,1894 - Feb.23,1925
Floyd W.,Jr.	May 24,1921 - May 24,1921
James E.	July 19,1836 - Sept.14,1913
Leona Lou	May 14,1895 - Nov.21,1977
Pamela Jean	Mar.22,1972 - Jan.30,1986
Ross Evans	Aug.20,1900 - Jan.6,1936
Humphrey, Fred W.	1915 - 1965
Hugh Lewis	1940 - 1987
Joe James	June 20,1911 - May 7,1961
Lela D.	Sept.27,1888 - Nov.3,1972
Hyatt, Arthur	1888 - 19--
Bessie	1888 - 1960
George W.	1879 - 19--
Ellen M.	1879 - 1948
Johnson, Ivan E.	no date
Mary A.	no date
R.L.	Oct.8,1882 - Feb.26,1948
Jones, J.Reeves	1889 - 1966
Almeda M.	1894 - 1943
Keeling, Irene	no dates
Kinley, Stanley L.	June 18,1915 - Aug.12,1977
Knowles, JoAnn Morrell	June 3,1936 - Dec.10,1979
Lady, James Harold	1926 - 1976
Shirley R.	no dates
James R.	1894 - 1986
Margaret B.	1897 - 1975
Larimer, Albert A.	June 5,1895 - July 30,1927
Martha Odell	Feb.6,1894 - Nov.14,1967
Thomas A.	1920 - 1945
Larve, Richard A.	Nov.7,1945 - Sept.16,1966
Leedom, Donald Thomas	June 5,1953 - May 31,1981
Leonard, Eary E.	1916 - 1983
Vesta R.	1916 - no date
F. Grant	1918 - 1962
Mary Jo	1917 - no date

Shipley Cemetery, cont.

Hartley, L.D.	Mar.16,1877 - Dec.13,1922
Raymond C.	Oct.19,1934 - Dec.19,1979
Hashbarger, Betty Ann	Sept.2,1955 - Jan.24,1956
Rozane L.	1966 - 1968
Hatcher, C.M.	MAy 31,1886 - Dec.27,1930
James A.	1856 - 1924
Alice E.	1869 - 1937
Virginia Anna	Apr.11,1858 - Aug.20,1888, w/o J.A.
Leonard, Hubert C.	May 23,1932 - no date
Lillian K.	Mar.16,1931 - Feb.7,1972
William J.	1905 - 1964
Cora Lee	1910 - 19--
Lingerfelt, Cecil Wayne	1945 - 1946
Charlie Paul	Aug.17,1909 - Dec.25,1948
Fannie	1916 - 1933
Flora May	Mar.23,1913 - Feb.14,1941
Joe S.	1912 - 1963
Viola L.	1916 - 1985
Odell	May 18,1915 - Feb.9,1966
Lockner, Infant	1957 - 1957
Loudy, Hugh T.	1881 - 1965
Katherine	1886 - 1965
Love, Pearl	1900 - 1974
Lovett, Ralph Ellis	June 22,1926 - Apr.4,1964
Lunsford, E.L.	APr.18,1916 - Aug.9,1947
James	1884 - no date
Mary	1889 - 1947
Maiden, Bill M.	1900 - 1983
McClellen, Don	1939 - 1969
McCracken, Lawrence M.	Feb.10,1936 - Dec.15,1983
McGarry, Rev.Andrew B.	Feb.5,1827 - May 3,1869
Edward J.	Aug.16,1856 - July 19,1911
John	Mar.8,1801 - Aug.14,1878
John	Jan.3,1831 - Apr.30,1881
John A.,Jr.	1930 - 1931
John W.	Jan.3,1831 - Apr.30,18881
Margarett E.	Jan.24,1837 - Jan.19,1922,w/o J.W.
Martha Ann	Feb.8,1858 - MAy 29,1876
Martha Morrell	July 13,1792 - Aug.10,1866, w/o John.
Mollie C.	1856 - 1929
Nellie	Aug.30,1878 - Dec.31,1926, w/o R.J.
Robert J.	Jan.3,1907 - Jan.17,1962
Maude E.	July 24,1900
Sarah E. Hicks	Dec.22,1831 - June 4,1909, w/o Rev.A.B.
Melvin, Cornell	Jan.27,1911 - Nov.25,1983
Meredith, Stephen Edward	Mar.6,1924 - July 12,1984
Miller, Geneva Vorita	Oct.29,1933
Isaac F.	Feb.12,1884 - Feb.22,1966
Sarrah E.	May 28,1886 - July 24,1962
Silas E.	1900 - 1977
Roxie H.	1904 - 1987
William J.	Oct.16,1914 - Mar.17,1977
Minnick, Paul C.	d. no date
Nell E.	d. Feb.6,1975

Shipley Cemetery, cont.

Molyneux, George T.	1895 - 1929
Moore, H.Douglas	Nov.18,1944 - May 4,1969
Linda C.	Sept.19,1947 - no date
Rev. James	July 17,1909 - May 15,1982
Margaret R.	Oct.22,1911 - Mar.20,1976
Morrell, Albert N.	1900 - 1908
Andrew Johnson	1860 - 1941
Margaret	1868 - 1947
Bessie Bouton	Aug.19,1891 - May 10,1948
Bessie M.	d. June 26,1890, aged 14 days, d/o M.J.& M.B.
Brooks M.	Oct.3,1891 - Oct.7,1917
Charles R.	1919 - 1976
Mary E.	no dates
Connie Janette	Nov.8,1966
Sharon Lynne	May 17,1968 - Jan.16,1969,d/o David & Alice.
D.Edgar	July 19,1905 - June 13,1986
Rosa C.	Feb. 9,1906 - no date
Danny James	b. & d. May 11,1947
David P.	June 5,1858 - Jan.1,1930
Elizabeth	Nov.26,1863 - Nov.19,1962
E.L.	1900 - 1985
Lucille	1902 - no date
Edward E.	1927 - no date
Laura Mae	1927 - 1968
Eleanor S.	Mar.10,1914 - July 31,1977
Essie Woods	Mar.28,1887 - Nov.25,1978
Fred E.	Oct.4,1903 - Apr.19,1978
Beulah E.	Mar.18,1903 - no date
Frances E.	Dec.29,1925 - Jan.9,1928
G.A.	Oct.14,1864 - July 10,1930
Mollie A. Odell	June 17,1873 - Feb.10,1950
G.W.	1821 - 1909
Mary A. Bond	1825 - 1900, w/o G.W.Morrell.
Gary Wayne	June 1957
Gaston M.	1869 - 1939
Nancy Boyd	1867 - 1947
George R.	Nov.26,1920 - Jan.25,1983
George W.	1889 - 1928
Mary R.	1884 - 1945
Helen Louise	May 28,1926 - June 22,1926
Herbert Kent	1922 - 1922
Hobart W.	1921 - 1938
Howard Emmett	Dec.18,1929 - Mar.3,1983
Hubert A.	1910 - 1944
Isaac O.	Sept.24,1826 - Oct.25,1904
Mary Ann Peters	Feb.14,1833 - Sept.8,1868
J.	Oct.7,1782 - Jan.31,1863
J.N.	1852 - 1876
Capt. J.R.	Mar.23,1824 - June 7,1902
Jack Allen	1937 - 1945
James A.	Apr.4,1957 - July 21,1978
James Andrew	b. & d. May 1943
James A.H.	May 1,1944 - Aug.24,1857

Morrell, James L.	1907 - 1973	
John B.	Sept.21,1871 - Apr.4,1956	
John B.,Jr.	Feb.7,1927 - Mar.16,1927	
John C.	1901 - 1967	
Pauline O.	1908 - 1983	
John H.	May 23,1935 - May 15,1978	
John Mack	Apr.16,1895 - June 23,1975	
Jonathan I.	1857	
Joseph Mack	Jan.20,1929 - Jan.16,1980	
Lafayette	Aug.10,1896 - May 31,1910, s/o D.P. & E.	
Lanna May	1891 - 1918	
Lilly V.	1892 - 1929	
Louis R.	July 13,1906 - Dec.18,1985	
Arlene R.	Jan.5,1911 - Sept.17,1981	
M.Clifton	1912 - 1978,m. July 31,1947	
Wanda A.	1928 - no date	
Margaret Florence	1923 - 1924	
Mark Allen	1969 - 1969	
Mary P.	1908 - 1983	
Michael J.	May 28,1865 - July 9,1945	
Maggie Belle	May 29,1866 - Nov.11,1937	
Nathan G.	May 28,--- - Mar.28,----	
Nora C.	no dates	
Odie	1910 - no date	
Merle E.	1912 - no date	
Paul T.	Sept.1,1927 - May 16,1983	
Rebecca	Dec.15,1849 - Jan.25,1916,d/o Rev.T.M.& S.	
Rev. Robert J.	1895 - 1968	
Lillie C.	1899 - 1979	
Robert L.	Nov.23,1894 - Sept.12,1964	
Addie C.	Aug.23,1901 - Jan.28,1965	
Samuel	1808 - 1880	
Frances	1811 - 1880	
Samuel W.	1860 - 19--	
Mary F.	1867 - 1938	
Sarah	1884 - 1908	
Thomas	1886 - 1908	
Tracy	1968 - 1968	
Walter M.	Jan.25,1895 - Feb.21,1966	
Rebecca G.	Mar.18,1906 - Sept.20,1968	
William C.	Apr.17,1863 - Aug.18,1864	
William J.	1893 - 1968	
Myrtle M.	1895 - 1969	
Morton, Albert Stephen	Sept.19,1909 - Apr.11,1962	
Zelma	Mar.16,1915 - Oct.16,1973	
Jerry	Dec.25,1941 - Nov.19,1978	
Alice G.	June 2,1849 - June 17,1911, w/o N.D.	
Andrew A.	1867 - 1925	
Anna R.	1870 - 1932	
Clyde C.	Nov.5,1896 - Sept.29,1918	
E.M.	Mar.13,1886 - Sept.12,1965	
Ellen S.	Dec.23,1839 - Sept.19,1916	
G.W.	Dec.11,1843 - Apr.12,1916	
George W.	June 29,1906 - Oct.8,1971	

Morton, Icy		Apr.8,1821 - Feb.25,??,w/o Arthur.
	Ida Shipley	Dec.4,1903 - Jan.1,1985
	Jeanette	July 13,1912 - Sept.4,1975
	Jennie M.	Aug.29,1865 - Oct.31,1950, w/o N.D.
	Jonathan Morrell	1876 - 1965
	Marion Bullock	Jan.4,1884 - July 29,1982
	Martha A.	Oct.1,1847 - Feb.5,1933
	Mary Katharine	1878 - 1945
	Mary P.	June 16,1813 - Aug.13,1876
	N.D.	June 29,1849 - Mar.29,1925
	Robert W.	Mar.27,1894 - Apr.17,1915
	Roberta V. Craig	Aug.31,1873 - Mar.7,1961, w/o Stephen A.
	S.G.	d. May 1880
	Samuel A.	May 16,1910 - no date
	Samuel George	Jan.12,1884 - Apr.12,1980
	Stephen A.	Aug.5,1873 - Dec.19,1961
	Thomas	May 11,1881 - Dec.11,1957
	Wayne	Jan.7,1906 - Nov.20,1977
	William S.	1873 - 1926
	Jennie L.	1875 - 1970
Mottern, George Andrew		1914 - 1981
	Mary Alice McGarry	Dec.19,1852 - Apr.15,1895,w/o S.S.Mottern.
	Mattie A. Odell	Mar.16,1894 - Mar.9,1925, w/o A.G.Mottern.
Mullennix, Mollie		Apr.29,1869 - Feb.23,1935
Myers, Earl J.		1926 - no date
	Ida Bowers	1916 - no date
Neal, Jimmy C.		1951 - 1977
Nelson, James D.		Sept.22,1892 - Jan.1,1963
	Walter Claude	July 6,1919 - Sept.22,1975
Odell, Albert E.		Sept.24,1911 - Aug.2,1970
	Blanche P.	Apr.1,1915 - Apr.13,1984
	Alice Crumley	May 7,1854 - Oct.16,1876, w/o Isaac Odell.
	Amne Millard	Mar.25,1817 - Dec.29,1893, w/o Andrew.
	Andrew	Oct.17,1815 - Jan.30,1865
	Andrew O.	Jan.19,1876 - Sept.14,1971
	Blanche M.	June 15,1927 - Aug.18,1928
	Catherine H.	Aug.4,1827 - Nov.27,1882,w/o Daniel.
	Cecil A.	Oct.22,1924 - Apr.26,1969
	Clemantine	1873, d/o Wm. & Martha Odell.
	D. Herman	Oct.10,1907 - June 2,1969
	Daniel	Aug.20,1823 - Apr.28,1906
	Daniel,Sr.	Oct.20,1795 - Dec.29,1879
	Daniel T.	Mar.8,1879 - July 5,1961
	Dixie Mable	Dec.18,1920 - Dec.18,1920, d/o W.F.Odell.
	Eliza J.	May 1, 1851 - Nov.8,1879
	Ella L.	Jan.1,1882 - Sept.30,1957
	Ezekiel P.	Mar.24,1832 - Oct.1,1857,s/o Daniel & Francis.
	F. Preston	1887 - 1927
	Finley	Aug.1884 - Oct.1943
	Lillian	June 1886 - Mar.1971
	Francis	Aug.3,1799 - July 31,1858,w/o Daniel,Sr.
	George Andrew	Nov.8,1910 - Apr.29,1970
	George D.	1880 - 1956
	Lucretian	1882 - 1912
	George W.	Sept.29,1835 - Nov.3,1843,s/o D.& F.

Odell, George W. Oct.21,1914 - Mar.23,1959
 Gladys M. Apr.24,1904 - Dec.22,1947
 Hattie 1891 - 1973
 Hettie 1877, d/o Wm. & Martha Odell.
 J.D. Jan.14,1881 - Aug.27,1952
 J.L. "Jake" 1882 - 1939
 James Wiley 1885 - 1953
 Joe Lee July 11,1921 - Apr.11,1960
 John Edd June 23,1872 - Feb.2,1936
 John M. Aug.14,1851 - June 2,1922
 Johnnie A. May 15,1895 - no date
 Isabelle B. Nov.28,1897 - Feb.15,1976
 Ida Belle Aug.17,1889 - Mar.4,1958,d/o Isaac &
  Nancy Shipley Odell.
 Ida Morton 1902 - 1947
 Infant Mar.6,1895, s/o W.J. & M.C.Odell.
 Infant b. & d. Aug.17,1905,d/o J.D.& E.L.
 Infant b. & d. Oct.1,1915, s/o A.C.& S.A.
 Isaac Mar.30,1852 - Oct.10,1927
 Leila M. 1890 - 1963
 Lydia J.Shipley Morrell Apr.8,1862 - May 1,1917
 Maggie M. Dec.31,1878 - Jan.11,1953
 Margaret 1855 - 1931, w/o D.W.D.Odell.
 Margaret E. Longacre Feb.14,1847 - Mar.3,1906, w/o T.F.Odell.
 Martha Mar.16,1839 - Dec.27,1843,d/o D. & F.
 Martha A. Jan.5,1876 - Feb.24,1879, d/o W.J.& M.C.
 Martha Nell 1919 - 1920
 Mary Ella Morton Mar.2,1879 - Dec.20,1924, w/o John E.
 Mary L. Apr.1,1878 - July 16,1879, d/o W.J.& M.C.
 Mary Louisa Sept.13,1856 - Oct.14,1861, d/o Andrew &
  Amney Odell.
 Nancy Shipley Feb.13,1855 - Dec.22,1928,w/o Isaac.
 Preston,Jr. 1920 - 1985
 Oscar T. Mar.10,1891 - OCt.26,1895, s/o W.D.& M.J.
 Ralph Sept.19,1911 - Jan.7,1917,s/o J.D.& E.C.
 Ruby Lynn Oct.21,1916 - Dec.1,1916, d/o Willie &
  Mattie Odell.
 Sallie d. Apr.17,1919. aged 68 yrs.,w/o Thomas.
 Samuel L. June 21,1850 - Dec.23,1856
 Sarah May 31,1855 - Mar.12,1897, w/o J.M.
 Sarah Morton Mar.2,1876 - May 31,1966
 Thomas Mar.21,1858 - Oct.12,1928
 Thomas Dehart Apr.13,1908 - June 29,1932
 Thomas M. June 9,1820 - Dec.16,1956,s/o D.& F.
 Thomas M. Oct.6,1845 - Sept.21,1912
 Thomas F. Aug.22,1847 - July 6,1921
 Thurman P. Feb.5,1907 - July 7,1973
 W.D.W. Mar.10,1854 - Nov.12,1912
 W.H. Apr.24,1882 - Mar.7,1908
 W.J. Aug.10,1853 - May 31,1903
 M.C.Crumley Mar.9,1852 - Apr.16,1922

Shipley Cemetery, cont.

Odell, William	1844 - 1918
Martha E. Longacre	1853 - 1890
William A.	1901 - 1960
Thomas A.	1901 - 1915
W. Leander	Aug.10,1909 - June 17,1978
B. Eileen	June 18,1918 - no date
William Leander	Apr.21,1883 - Nov.20,1896, s/o T.F.& M.E.
Willie M.	Nov.25,1887 - Oct.2,1932
Mattie A.	Sept.4,1887 - Feb.2,1973
Willie S. McGarry	no date
Osborne, Andy	Sept.15,1861 - July 2,1929
Arthur B.	Aug.2,1935 - Jan.16,1936
Glen William	Jan.27,1920 - Dec.13,1958
James Finley	1901 - 1973
Mollie Alice	1901 - no date
Roby	1873 - 1958
Annie	1880 - 1970
Owen, Leslie Booher	Mar.2,1927 - June 16,1967
Preston R.	Jan.7,1935 - Oct.29,1983
Randall P.	May 23,1949 - July 17,1977
Patrick, D.R.	1878 - 1935
Dorothy Edna	Nov.4,1909 - May 10,1911,d/o D.R.& R.M.
Eliza	1851 - 1939, w/o Thomas Patrick.
Ellen	Dec.28,1835 - Aug.22,1904
L.D.	Apr.15,1844 - July 4,1926
Matilda Howard	Jan.12,1878 - Sept.10,1921, w/o D.R.
Payne, Anna Lee	1928 - 1976
Peaks, Joseph T.	no dates
Pearce, Sylvia Mae	Dec.8,1920 - Feb.9,1975
Peters, Pleasant H.	Sept.17,1862 - Sept.26,1917
Petro, Edna Boughers	May 23,1918 - Feb.6,1964
Phillips, Della	Feb.10,1903 - Oct.29,1973
Pickel, Calvin H.	1896 - 1978
Dellmer L.	Oct.1,1922 - July 28,1984
Ruby E.	1900 - 1981
Sandra Sue	Feb.8,1958 - Dec.1,1978
Richard A.	June 19,1954 - Feb.21,1981
Sanford L.	Apr.12,1905 - June 28,1981
Bertha R.	Aug.17,1907 - no date
Poore, Howard Henry	May 31,1908 - no date
Ardith Campbell	Sept.27,1909 - no date
Potts, Arthur	1868 - 1938
Harriet	1873 - 1931
Carmen A.	Apr.11,1901 - Sept.14,1985
Charles Edgar	1894 - no date
Douglas	b. & d. Nov.27,1926, s/o F.L.& G.A.
Ferdinand	May 22,1835 - Aug.6,1901,b.Birmingham,Eng.
Fred L.	Sept.19,1896 - Feb.20,1986
James O.	1922 - 1943
Julia E.	1919 - 1978
Mary Kate	1897 - 1970
Rachel	Dec.3,1845 - July 23,1918,w/o Ferdinand, b. Birmingham, England.

Presnell, Infant	July 16,1962 - July 16,1962
Vernadeen Barbe	Feb.3,1907 - Nov.15,1972
Price, Edd B.	Mar.29,1914 - Apr.20,1971
Sarah W.	Aug.24,1913 - no date
Estel V.	1915 - 1976
Delpha C.	1920 - no date
Ramey, William R.	May 22,1900 - Dec.19,1978
Eula L.	May 20,1916 - no date
Rice, Ernest	Jan.20,1904 - no date
Burcha M.	Feb.13,1908 - May 25,1969
Everett	1892 - 1962
Rosa B.	1893 - 1978
Florence Almeda	b. & d. July 25,1930, d/o Ernest & Burcha.
J.L.	OCt.22,1929 - Nov.13,1984
Nellie A.	1896 - 1949
Richardson, Billy B.	Apr.9,1934 - Aug.1,1974
Burcha M. Odell	Jan.17,1889 - Apr.19,1976
Clarence	Sept.17m1898 - Feb.9,1909
Hollin Harvey	Aug.18,1888 - Aug.28,1930
J. Hugh	July 3,1904 - Jan.3,1981
Maggie B.	Feb.27,1904 - no date
Jasper L.	1906 - 1947
James R.	1872 - 1937
Rebecca J.	1800 - 1960
Joe L.	Oct.15,1901 - Mar.21,1963
Austin S.	July 23,1911 - Feb.10,1973
John A.	1867 - 1939
Elizabeth E.	1878 - 1955
Robinson, Helen	1947 - 1947
Daniel	1959 - 1959
James David	Aug.8,1955 - June 10,1974
James R.	1964 - 1964
Roe, Austtin	Dec.18,1894 - Dec.13,1951
Infant	1893, s/o J.L.& Addie W. Roe.
Rogers, Barbara Jean	1951 - 1952
James F.	Aug.25,1902 - Dec.7,1976
Susie M.	Dec.10,1906 - July 1,1976
Roberta June	June 13,1960 - Sept.9,1960
Rosenbalm, Jessie Sanford	June 4,1907 - Dec.31,1971
Jessie Eugene	Apr.27,1932 - Oct.13,1986
Rutledge, Infant	no dates,d/o G.W. & M.E.Rutledge.
Sampson, Paul D.	1915 - 1970
Ruby S.	1922 - no date
Shipley, Ada B.	1887 - 1970
Adam R.	Mar.29,1897 - Oct.23,1982
Alice N.	Jan.5,1907 - Jan.19,1986
Anna Laura	Dec.15,1890 - Nov.12,1910,d/o J.M.& M.E.
Daniel Lafayett	June 12,1900 - July 15,1902, s/o J.M.& M.E.
Daniel O.	1859 - 1907
Anne Hatcher	1859 - 1932
James	Mar.10,1829 - Mar.16,1891
James E.	Dec.23,1897 - Jan.15,1957
James & Arthur	1925
Edna	1921 - 1922

Shipley Cemetery, cont.

Shipley, John M.	Feb.27,1864 - May 20,1944	
John R.	Jan.20,1937 - Dec.12,1936	
Joseph W.	May 6,1926 - Feb.7,1984	
Lena J.	1892 - 1965	
Martha	Jan.4,1853 - Feb.18,1919	
Mary E.	Aug.22,1892 - Apr.6,1968	
Mary Eveline	May 29,1857 - June 21,1885	
Mollie W.	May 16,1864 - Feb.8,1925	
Phillip	1885 - 1952	
Phillip Andrew	Apr.10,1867 - Oct.1,1883	
Ruth Louisa	Nov.15,1894 - Feb.26,1899, d/o J.M.& M.E.	
Ruth Jane	Nov.15,1830 - Nov.2,1906	
Sarah C.	Aug.5,1851 - Apr.22,1925	
William Dedrick	Dec.1,1889 - Dec.24,1889, s/o J.M.& M.E.	
Simmons, Robert L.	1856 - 1954	
Minerva M.	1854 - 1929	
Sluder, John,Jr.	Oct.1,1926 - Dec.8,1983	
Smith, Archie W.	Mar.8,1922 - June 4,1974	
Lou Etta	Aug.4,1919 - no date	
Charles R.	1873 - 1957	
Della Emmert	July 21,1879 - May 11,1924,w/o Isaac L.	
Earl H.	1923 - no date	
Charity E.	1930 - 1983	
Emma B.	1882 - 1979	
Infant	Dec.22,1948, s/o Herbert & Ruby Lynn Smith.	
Infant twins	1961, Ronnie Dean & Donnie Gene.	
James S.	1897 - 1970	
Lilliam D.	1891 - 1976	
Karen L. (Sissie)	Aug.23,1965 - June 6,1984	
Ricky Lee	Aug.15,1957 - Jan.1,1974	
Ronald E.	Apr.26,1940 - Oct.23,1982	
W.O. (Smitty)	1909 - 1973	
Bertha M.	1916 - no date	
Wayne	Aug.1,1921 - Jan.21,1970	
Smithson, Addie S.M.	Sept.7,1909 - Aug.20,1910	
Alda	1910 - 1912	
Arthur N.	1892 - 1969	
Anna J.	1893 - 1969	
Daniel F.	1906 - 1972	
Mary L.	1911 - no date	
Edgar L.	May 10,1914 - Feb.18,1937	
George H.	Oct.20,1912 - Oct.20,1982	
Dot E.	Mar.31,1922 - Oct.18,1983	
Harmon	Dec.27,1931	
Daniel	Mar.1,1931	
James L.	1879 - 1958	
Nora B.	1881 - 1929	
J.C.	Nov.21,1924	
Cleda E.	Mar.12,1930 - Oct.12,1978	
J.Fred	1913 - 1973	
Helen J.	1921 - no date	
James S.	Jan.18,1912 - June 17,1976	
Nell F.	Feb.4,1912 - no date	

Shipley Cemetery, cont.

Smithson, Jessie M.	May 26,1895 - Dec.12,1941	
Nora M.	Mar.16,1896 - Oct.23,1948	
John A.	Aug.31,1928 - Nov.12,1928	
Infant	Sept.21,1921	
John M.	Apr.10,1867 - Dec.27,1929	
Ida L.	May 16,1874 - Mar.27,1963	
Joseph S.	July 26,1914 - Feb.27,1947	
Lester W.	1917 - no date	
Lettie M.	1927 - 1967	
Lissie	Feb.29,1879 - June 6,1935	
Margaret E. Shipley	Sept.28,1849 - Mar.15,1934,w/o S.D.	
Mary Louise	Sept.23,1923 - Nov.21,1923	
Norman F.	1936 - 1971	
Bonnie L.	1941 - no date	
Robert	July 13,1938 - Aug.21,1938	
Gordon	Sept.4,1933 - Mar.5,1934	
S.Brooks	Jan.5,1908 - June 3,1983	
Blanch C.	July 30,1918 - Aug.29,1982	
S.D.	Jan.10,1845 - Oct.11,1931	
Samuel L.	Jan.31,1899 - Apr.28,1964	
Eva B.	Oct.30,1900 - Jan.27,1956	
William Jennings	1897 - no date	
Elizabeth Bullock	1898 - 1983	
Snyder, Tena M.	1965 - 1965	
Tewana M.	1965 - 1965	
Starbuck, Earl	1913 - 1975	
Starr, Kenneth R.	Apr.5,1926 - Aug.29,1976	
Stophel, Abram C.	1865 - 1915	
Eliza J.	1870 - 1948	
Charles A.	1883 - 1928	
Louvenia	1887 - 1929	
Claude E.	1921 - 1945	
David D.	Nov.12,1893 - Dec.24,1941	
Dallas O.	Dec.23,1902 - Nov.12,1979	
Thelma M.	July 28,1908 - no date	
Caroline J.	Mar.31,1949 - Apr.1,1949	
Edward C.	1930 - 1946	
Elkanah	Feb.5,1859 - Aug.12,1940	
Mary Alice	July 20,1867 - Dec.17,1943	
Ellen Irene	May 30,1896 - Jan.18,1923	
Floyd W.	1904 - 1980	
Ada M.	1901 - 1986	
George L.	1898 - no date	
Mary R.	1900 - 1965	
George L.,Jr.	Feb.16,1923 - Feb.19,1923,s/o G.L.& M.R.	
Gordon F.	Dec.17,1925 - Aug.28,1977	
Katherine Alma	Sept.18,1892 - Jan.9,1977	
L.M.	Mar.30,1852 - Aug.21,1930	
Leander	1898 - 1973	
Lizzie B.	1888 - 1967	
Malissa Mahaffey	Dec.8,1861 - Jan.18,1923	
Marie Bellamy	Oct.6,1913 - no date,w/o G.L.Stophel.	
Myrtle G.	1903 - 1934	
Nellie M.	1901 - 1949	

Shipley Cemetery, cont.

Stophel, Sallie E.	1886 - 1957
Tiffany J.	1986 - 1986
William C.	Jan.4,1892 - Apr.23,1940
William Elkanah	Apr.5,1933
Strouth, David E.	1914 - 1968
Cathyrn T.	1920 - 1986
Grady P.	July 16,1946 - Feb.18,1980
Taylor, Carnell A.	Mar.11,1901 - May 31,1962
Amanda E.	July 16,1909 - no date
Eugene E.	May 9,1899 - no date
Gennie H.	Apr.29,1900 - Aug.9,1966
Rev.J.V.	d. Apr.28,1906
S.E.	Aug.22,1870 - Oct.19,1940
Jess S.	Apr.29,1908 - Feb.25,1968
Joe	May 15,1907 - June 26,1980
Carrie B.	May 26,1908 - no date
John E.	Jan.16,1882 - Apr.10,1967
Lizzie	no dates
Lula A.	June 15,1876 - Apr.5,1912
Lydia	Oct.5,1874 - Mar.18,1950
Sarah E.	Oct.28,1883 - Jan.2,1971
Tommy J.	Aug.11,1958 - June 3,1981
Thomas, Eugene Claude	Nov.25,1908 - Aug.28,1977
Nell E.	1913 - no date
G. Elizabeth	1949 - no date
Jean Carrier	May 5,1943 - Nov.10,1973
Edna	Dec.2,1906 - Jan.29,1925
Rev.J.V.	d. Apr.28,1906
S.E.	Aug.22,1870 - Oct.19,1940
Marie Glynden	June 29,1912 - Dec.19,1912
Mary E.	1881 - 1959
W.C.	1882 - 1924
Trent, Alice	June 8,1908 - Oct.18,1931,w/o Curtis.
Turner, Easter C.	May 21,1893 - Apr.20,1975
Vance, R.C.	Aug.1,1932 - July 20,1972
Vinson, Nellie G.	Mar.13,1908 - Mar.9,1936, w/o Henry A.
Voorhees, William R.L.	Feb.28,1958 - Nov.22,1974
Walling, Dora A.	July 7,1885 - Aug.5,1969
Henry Jackson	Jan.20,1878 - Dec.21,1952
L.J.	Age 46y10m2d.
Warren, Rev. H.C.	Jan.19,1848 - May 23,1900
H. Eli P.	May 23,1885 - Mar.5,1915, s/o H.C. & S.J.
Martha Jane	Sept.2,1871 - Feb.24,1891
Sarah Elliott	Dec.19,1847 - Dec.12,1891
Virginia T.	Nov.13,1873 - Nov.6,1891
Watson, Rev. Kenneth C.	Apr.19,1950 - Aug.29,1985
Weaver, Ben H.	1908 - 1977
Thelma B.	1914 - no date
Whitaker, Lisa Coletta	Apr.30,1959
White, Adam Lee	Apr.12,1912 - Dec.6,1961
Alice Carrier	Oct.24,1868 - Apr.9,1945, w/o S.H.
Alleta	Oct.17,1927 - Oct.20,1927, d/o W.G. & Hester.
Benjamin F.	d. June 26,1893
Martha C.	d. Nov.26,1888
Bertie B.	June 15,1886 - Aug.24,1962

Shipley Cemetery, cont.

White, Bill C.	1908 – 1975
Charles H.	May 17,1941 – Nov.7,1941
Charlie O.	May 7,1911 – no date, m.Nov.6,1932
Lola L.	Feb.20,1915 – Sept.30, 1976, w/o Charlie O.
J.D.	Sept.1857 – Nov.1924
J.G.	Jan.21,1879 – Jan.2,1901
Joe F.	Sept.27,1912 – Nov.1,1969
Murphy P.	Mar.3,1888 – Nov.11,1958
Robert S.	1880 – 1953
Lula M.	1885 – 1973
Sallie Elizabeth	May 22,1889 – Aug.26,1968
Sam R.	1916 – 1955
Anne B.	1925 – 19--
Samuel B.	Oct.25,1909 – Oct.8,1968
William J.	Nov.23,1885 – Sept.22,1929
Williams, Gary Eugene	Apr.1,1983 – May 15,1983, s/o Gary & Karen.
Wilson, Betty Ruth Glover	Apr.18,1941 – Sept.29,1982
Wise, Billy William	1951
Bob T.	Dec.10,1925 – no date
Bonnie M.	Mar.13,1931 – no date
Infant James Lee	March 1960
Margaret Pearl	Nov.6,1951 – Apr.11,1963
William H.	Jan.7,1895 – July 7,1964
Wix, Carson L.	Sept.20,1910 – Aug.25,1985
Wright, Samuel	1854 – 19--
Louisa	1850 – 1928
Wyatt, Clint	1910 – 19--
Lucille M.	1912 – 19--
Wynes, Jevia Lisa	Oct.16,1971 – Dec.19,1976

Blountville Cemetery
Incomplete listing, broken stones, illegible stones. I combined 2 versions
of this cemetery plus what I had done. There are alot of discrepancies.

Akard, E.D.	1854 – 1925
Lydia Gunning Spurgeon	1857 – 1923
Herman	June 9,1890 – Feb.25,1905, s/o E.D.& L.G.
Allison, Ellen R.	Dec.24,1845 – July 2,1897, w/o R.B.
Francis	date illegible.
J.S.S.	Apr.25,1818 – Nov.4,1912
Mattie Taylor	Mar.21,1824 – May 25,1914, w/o J.S.S.
R.B.	Dec.12,1842 – Aug.27,1883
Allen, Fannie A. Gammon	May 20,1845 – June 23,1870, w/o Robert.
Anderson, Delilah Amanda	1849 – 1888
Eliza Powell	1854 – 1896
Eliza Telford	1822 – 1879
Elizabeth F.	Nov.17,1852 – Feb.5,1915, d/o Audley & Margaret P. Rhea Anderson.
George Rutledge	1821 – 1902
George William	May 12,1887 – Jan.15,1906,s/o W.S.& H.Ella.
Infant	stone broken/no dates/s/o Wm. & Jane.
Infant	d. Oct.25,1842, s/o George & Eliza A.M.
James	May 8,1886(?) – July 25,1916, s/o R & Winnie.
James E.	Aug.3,1856 – Apr.30,1904, s/o W.R. & L.

Blountville Cemetery, cont.

Anderson, Jane/Joan		Nov.2,1802 - Dec.27,1852, s/o William.
	Jane P.	Sept.26,1828 - Apr.5,1904, w/o A.Anderson.
	Jane R.	Dec.6,1829 - Mar.6,1856
	Henry	Jan.5,1807 - Dec.24,1851
	Infant	Sept.19,1851 - Oct.4,1851, d/o A.J.& M.P.
	Maggie	July 25,1862 - May 9, 1895, d/o W.R.& L.
	Margaret P.Rhea	Nov.19,1832 - May 18,1909, w/o Audley.
	Nancy M.	Apr.28,1833 - Jan.26,1852, w/o Henry.
	Nancy R.	May 17,1824 - May 16,1859, w/o Henry.
	Robert I.	Nov.25,1853 - Dec.8,1901, s/o W.R.& L.
	Robert R.	June 6,1834 - Dec.6,1913
	Sarah A.	d. July 11,1838, d/o E.B. & E.E.
	Samuel	May 7,1845 - Feb.9,1849
	Samuel Rhea	Aug.20,1869 - Feb.8,1923, s/o Robert & Winnie.
	William	Oct.2,1796 - Feb.25,1863
	William R.	Feb.15,1821 - July 23,1902
	Winnie	Sept.14,1834 - Aug.29,1914
Athens, Mae		Sept.13,1841 - Dec.16,1849
Bachman, Cornelia E.		Apr.18,1818 - June 25,1877, w/o Enoch K.
	Enoch K.	d. July 8,1881, aged 67y7m22d.
	George Kelney	Sept.23,1853 - Sept.3,1861, s/o E.K.& C.E.
	Jane	Feb.7,1805 - May 27,1874
	John	d. Aug.7,1851, aged 1y4m10d.,s/o E.K.& C.E.
Bailey, B.B.		1853 - 1920
	Cyrus	Apr.17,1818 - July 15,1888
	Elizabeth J.	May 3,181- = May 1894, w/o Cyrus Bailey.
	Emily	Oct.18,1890 - Sept.13,1894, d/o Cyrus & Eliz.
	Ethel G.	June 21,1888 - Sept.13,1894, d/o J.C. & L.G.
	Lola C. Moore	June 3,1869 - Aug.4,1917, w/o J.C.
Ballard, Sallie		d. Jan.8,1934
Barger, C.Elsea		b. July 11,1884 - ?, w/o Samuel R.Barger.
	Harry Spurgeon	Mar.26,1914 - June 1,1914
	Mary M.	June 2,1862 - Nov.27,1888, w/o John Barger.
	Samuel R.	d. July 17,1918
Barr, Joseph		Feb.20,1884 - Oct.20,1915
	Susan Grosswell	Oct.3,1827 - Sept.27,1918
	Mary A. Comer	Feb.14,1868 - Dec.18,1900, w/o Samuel.
Bathis, Nancy E.		1856 - 1930
Baumbardner, Alice T.		July 15,1845 - Dec.23,1893
	E.D.	May 27,1857 - Sept.23,1906
	Freddie L.	Apr.20,1891 - Aug.8,1891,s/o E.D. & M.E.
	Fredrick L.	Sept.27,1806 - Apr.5,1879
	Edna M.	Sept.1,1816 - July 4,1872
	Mrs. M.M.	186- - Nov.10,1900, Bristol, TN.
Beard, Adelia Cole		Aug.13,1868 - Dec.8,1916
	George W.	Dec.4,1841 - Sept.10,1901
Bickley, Joseph D.		Apr.24,1854 - Dec.20,1893
Birdwell, Jane		Jan,16,1807 - July 6,1877
Blackburn, Ada E. Large		1836 - 19--, w/o N.M.Blackburn.
	N.M.	1822 - 1931
Blackmore, Robert		d.Jan.23,1835, aged 69 yrs.
Blevins, Sarah E.		Sept.23,1863 - May 6,1936, m. Sept.14,1882.
	Mrs. W.P.	---- - 1933

Blountville Cemetery, cont.

Bodwell, Edward L.	d. July 8,1890, aged 26y.,s/o James & E.G.
Elizabeth Gooch	d. Feb.16,1903, aged 75y., w/o James Bodwell.
James	d. Nov.8,1897, aged 81y11m19d.
Boring, Henry Perry	Oct.9,1867 - Aug.25,1859,s/o Rev.J.B. & L.A.
Boyd, Landon Earl	d. Aug.22,1819, s/o Henry C. & Lavina Boyd.
Brown, Rev.Abel J.,D.D.	Mar.27,1817 - July 13,1894, ordained Minister
	of Evang. Lutheran Church, 1836.
Charles Augustine	Sept.4,1856 - Sept.2,1918
Emily Tester	Nov.8,1826 - Mar.30,1901, w/o Dr.H.S.Brown.
Erakine	Sept.4,1896 - Feb.11,1906
Mabel	July 17,1901 - Jan.24,1906
Buckeller, Mary	d. Mar.27,1883
Calloway, Mary Gay	Oct.12,1803 - June 5,1896, w/o Abram.
Campbell, James H.	Apr.1,1812 - Dec.20,1880
Carmack, Catherine	May 14,1815 - June 4,1870, w/o W.T.Carmack.
Mary A.	June 30,1860 - Mar.18,1915, d/o W.R.& L.S.
Carr, John Lee	July 21,1856 - Feb.10,1923
William	Apr.20,1880 - Mar.15,1903/8
Casteel, G.K.	Jan.25,1835 - Oct.26,1884
J.G.	June 14,1880 - July 13,1881, s/o G.K.& S.J.
Casteel, John R.	Dec.27,1854 - Dec.4,1916
Cate, Katie M. Rader	Aug.3,18-7 - Mar.27,1920, s/o S.B.Cate.
Ralph T.	May 4,1900 - Aug.5,1913
Rev. T.L.	1862 - 1921, Monument by Bluff City,
	Chinquopin Grove & Blountville Baptist Churches.
Chambers, Rev. J.K.	Nov.7,1896, aged 46y3m1d.
Martha	1875 - 1948
Clay, Minnie	Oct.28,1865 - Oct.13,1881
Cleek, Vernon R.	Jan.10,1827 - July 1,1927
Cole, J.A.	Mar.29,1834 - Mar.28,1905
Martha Deck	Mar.8,1837 - July 19,1899, w/o J.A.Cole.
Mary Pearson	Oct.3,1903 - Oct.25,1923, d/o J.F.& M.G.
Mattie C.	Jan.8,1876 - June 30,1910,w/o A.F.Cole.
Roena Alma	1885 - 1890, d/o H.I.& Amanda G.Cole.
Converse, Elizabeth	d. Jan.5,1883, J.B.& Eva D. Converse.
James B.	1844 - 1914
Cox, ? E.	Oct.24,1843 - June 9,1939
J.H.	Feb.6,1855 - July 15,1915
Ada B.	July 20,1837 - Nov.27,1915
Isaac	1813 - 1880
Elizabeth Hamilton	1815 - 1900
James	June 5,1810 - Jan.24,1897
Jessie J.	Oct.6,1837 - Nov.26,1901
Margaret	Feb.18,1836 - Apr.1,1915
Margaret	Mar.17,1809 - May 19,1891, w/o James Cox.
Martha	no date, d/o Isaac & Eliza H. Cox.
Mary E.	July 13,1836 - Feb.20,1900,w/o Samuel E.Cox.
Nancy E.	Feb.7,1833 - Apr.23,1848
Rachel	Aug.27,1806 - June 10,1869, w/o John H.Cox.
Samuel E.	Feb.17,1834 - July 15,1911
Sarah	1836 - 1863, d/o I. & E. Cox.
Crawford, Cornelia Elizabeth	June 14,1881 - Jan.7,1903
Frances A. Bachman	Sept.30,1851, w/o S.H.Crawford.
Dr. John R.	Mar.16,1830 - May 21,1891
Mary E. Bachman	Apr.29,1842 - Nov.22,1923

Blountville Cemetery, cont.

Crawford, Thomas H.	d. Aug.21,1884, s/o S.H.& F.A.
Cross, Esther E. Cagle	Feb.20,1838 - Jan.12,1913,w/o G.P.Cross.
Jesse P.	Sept.1832 - July 28,1896
Joseph D.	Aug.4,1876 - Sept.20,1905, s/o Jesse P.
Mattie E.	Dec.15,1873 - Apr.11,1909, d/o J.P.& E.E.
Robert Wayne	1931 - 1933
Thomas Jones	no dates, s/o T.J. & R.J.
Crumley, W.L.	Jan.25,1839 - Oct.29,1894
Cummings - Monument -	consort of J.S.Cummings & d/o S.& T.Evans, b. Jan.14,1847, m.May 15,1866, d.Sept.5,1867, at the age of 23y 7m 22d.
Deadrick, Laura L.	Feb.4,1864 - Mar.2,1885, w/o J.D.Cox.
Deckard, Martha	illegible.
Denny, Bettie Powell	Apr.28,1860 - Jan.21,1901,w/o L.H.
J.E.	July 28,1840 - Jan.21,1860
Capt. L.H.	Mar.7,1834 - July 9,1920
Margaret	Feb.20,1803 - June 10,1884, w/o John.
Mary A.	Jan.17,1825/8 - Nov.8,1891/4, c/o L.A.
Derry, N.B.	no dates
M.A.	no dates
Gen. James H.	d. aged 36y, oldest s/o Wm. & Elizabeth Buried in Shelbyville, TN.
Mary Ann O'Brien	d. Feb.12,1892, aged 58y.,d/o Geo.Bushong, w/o William Bruce Derry.
Robert Eakin	d. Feb.14,1892, aged 62y.,s/o Wm. & Elizabeth Allison Derry.
William	c. 1767, Londonderry, Ireland, emigrated to U.S. c.1787.,d. Blountville,Feb.6,1845,aet73.
William Bruce	Feb.9,1892, aged 69y., s/o Wm. & Elizabeth.
Doan, George	Dec.20,1782 - Apr.13,1861
Dove, J.W.	Feb.2,1869 - Feb.11,1925
Susan A.	Dec.6,1858 - Sept.12,1924
Almina	Sept.13,1823 - June 1,1905
James G.	Dec.5,1854 - Mar.19,1904
Droke, S. Ella	June 23,18--.
Dulaney, B.L.	Apr.9,1813 - Sept.23,1859
Ben	1815 - 1959
Ben Love	Mar.23 - June 11,1880, s/o Dr.N.T.& Pauline.
Dr.Charles M.	1868 - 1938
Edna	d. Jan.7,1825, aged 20y.
Dr.J.E.	June 17,1830 - Sept.8,1877
J.Eugene	1875 - 1903
John C.	1911 - 1936
Katie Snapp	inf d/o Dr.N.T.& Pauline Dulaney.
Jonathan	inf s/o Dr.N.T. & Pauline Dulaney.
Willie	inf s/o Dr.N.T. & Pauline Dulaney.
Margitia Rhea	b. 1872 -
Margaret	d. Feb.19,1843, aged 64 y., w/o Dr.E.R.
Margaret Louise	18-5 - 1925
Mary C.	Sept.25,1806 - Jan.29,18--.,w/o Wm. R.
Mary H.	d. May 12,1838, aged 17y4m16d.,Benjamin L.
Dr.N.T.,Sr.	1834 - 1910
Pauline Davis	1845 - 1934

Dulaney, Rebecca	1825 - 1870, w/o Ben Dulaney.
Robert E.	Dec.3,1837 - Aug.29,1869
Dr. W.A.	1840 - 1934
Dr. William	1831 - 1881
William R.	Apr.2,1800 - May 4,1860
Eanes, Mrs. Emma W.	1857 - 1932
Robert P.	June 27,1844 - Sept.25,1881
Thomas B.	Oct.10,1834 - May 23,1906
Earhart, Charles	1864 - 1932
Charles Henry	Sept.16,1906 - Feb.22,1907,s/o J.H.& S.F.
Etta Powell	1866 - 1935, w/o Charles.
George J.	d. June 1,1856, s/o J.T.& M.T.
Infant	d. Nov.30,1910, s/o J.P.& S.A.
John Sidney	Mar.9,1906 - Aug.8,1907, s/o J.P.&S.A.
John T.	Mar.31,1826 - Mar.23,1896
Joseph Preston	18-9 - 1935
Margarite Preston	June 23,1836 - Feb.5,1913, d/o R.R.& S.G. Rhea, w/o J.T.Earhart.
Mary Ball Powell	1870 - 1920, w/o Robert R. Earhart
Mollie Roller	July 21,1901 - Nov.6,1904
Robert R.	1863 - 1915
Easley, Robert W.	Mar.13,1841 - Nov.11,1898
Samuel	Sept.16,1916 - Dec.19,1916, s/o W.D.& E.R.
Elsea, Elbert S.	Oct.19,1828 - July 2,1892
Hiram J.	Aug.22,1895 - July 12,1896, s/o E.S.& Mary.
Laura J.	Feb.6,1863 - May 29,1925
Melvin I.	Mar.23,1859 - Aug.5,1888
Melvin J.	Aug.11,1880 - Dec.11,1919,on C.& D. R.R., near Cincinnatti,Ohio,s/o M.L.& Laura.
Nancy W. Shipley	Jan.24,1831 - June 13,1901,w/o Elbert S.
Zera E.	Aug.25,1891 - July 29,1892, d/o E.S.& Mary E.
Ensor, Jane A.	Dec.6,1852 - Nov.10,1866, d/o Dr.J.J.& Amanda
Erwin, Harry Buford	Jan.21,1899 - June 11,1900,s/o W.F. & K.R.
William Thomas	Feb.2,1856 - Aug.8,1900
Evans, Elizabeth G.	Sept.14,1805 - Mar.11,1890
Ellen A.	d. Sept.10,1857, d/o Wm.D & Fanny D.Evans.
Fannie	d.Sept.7,1882,aged 76y6m15d,w/o Samuel.
Fannie D.	d.Mar.8,1854, aged 26y.,w/o William D.Evans.
M.F.D.	Nov.2,1819 - Feb.17,1894
Samuel	1770 - 1842, m.1800 to Margaret.
Samuel	d. May 3,1881, aged 77y7m14d.
Fain, Alice Ann Spurgeon	Mar.11,1858 - Nov.1,1902,w/o Will H.Fain.
Caroline Virginia Bickley	Feb.7,1842 - Dec.3,1916,w/o Gen.John Fain.
Eleanor	Jan.19,1788 - Nov.15,1861w/o John R.Fain.
Elizabeth	Dec.28,1789 - Apr.9,1853
John	Dec.20,1835, at Eden's Ridge - Oct.17,1898, Bristol, TN.,m.Dec.17,1857,s/o Thomas & Rachel Anderson Fain.
John R.	Jan.4,1778 - Apr.18,1869
Will H.	May 24,1842 - Feb.2,1897
Farmer, John	June 12,18-- - ?
Mary Elizabeth	May 19,18-0 - Feb.23,1934 ?
Feathering,Robert B.	Jan.30,1879 - Feb.1,1932
W.H.	Mar.23,1850 - Aug.20,1921

Blountville Cemetery, cont.

Fickal, Robert Thomas	1886 - 1899, s/o D.S.Carr & L.A.Fickal.
Fickle, Robert P.	Dec.14,1822 - Nov.23,1895
Mary E.	Sept.27,1831 - May 9,1894
Ford, David	d.Dec.1915, age 31 yrs.
Elizabeth A.	Jan.14,1847 - Oct.22,1928
Galloway, John M.	d. June 15,1825
Mary Cox	Oct.12,1803 - June 5,1896
Gammon, Ann R.	July 24,1848 - Nov.12,1862
Ann Rebecca	June 10,1850 - Nov.19,1850, d/o William & Rebecca M. Gammon.
Frank M.	Spet.12,1889 - June 13,1910, s/o M.H. & S.W.
George F.	Aug.19,1817 - June 11,1888
Lavina	d. Nov.20,1873, aged 49y1m9d,w/o George F.
Mary Emma	July 3,1842 - Aug.2,1859,d/o G.F.& L.
Nancy A.	Feb.28,1818 - Feb.3,1837
Richard	Apr.5 - Apr.12,1836, s/o Wm. & Rebecca.
William	Nov.6,1807 - June 7,1874
Rebecca	Sept.8,1814 - Mar.21,1863
Glover, Bessie R. Rhea	Jan.18,1833 - Dec.8,1918, m. May 12,1904, Henry A. Glover.
Elizabeth H.	Nov.8,1831 - May 17,1893, w/o Samuel
Samuel	d. July 13,1912
Gott, Sarah J. Elsea	Oct.21,1848 - Sept.15,1927, w/o John L.
John L.	Feb.27,1839 - Oct.6,1912
Hall, ?	d. Jan.10,1838, d/o M.A. & Ellen Hall.
Bettie Mae	Sept.5,1882 - Oct.7,1903, w/o W.R.Hall.
Johnny	Oct.29,1913 - Nov.6,1917
W.A.	Mar.16,1841 - May 3,1921
Hamilton, Eliza	1815 - 1900
Elizabeth	Feb.19,1790 - Feb.14,1856,w/o John B.
John B.	Feb.16,1796/8 - Oct.21,1862
Harban, ELizabeth	d. Oct.24,1855, aged 30y6m6d, w/o William.
Harr, Ada Paine	d. Mar.26,1882
Elizabeth	Jan.20,1812 - Jan.2,1896, w/o John Harr.
Elizabeth J. Allison	May 19,1844 - Feb.15,1912,w/o Dr.W.D.Harr.
John	June 28,1817 - Apr.5,1873
John D.	Apr.4,1857 - Aug.14,1934
Maggie Rhea White	Oct.12,1856 - Oct.5,1926
Lela Lee	1884 - 1933
Miss Lena Mae	1882 - 1943
M. Alice	Nov.30,1869 - July 15,1891, d/o Wm.& M.H.
Dr. William D.	Apr.12,1809 - Apr.18,1927
Wm. M.	Nov.17,1839 - Apr.5,1873
Hawk, Mollie M.	1878 - 1908
Haynes, Emma J.	d.Aug.10,1852, aged 1y, d/o M.E.Haynes.
M.P.	Mar.2,1832 - Apr.20,1867,m.Sept.1850,w/o W.D.
Margaret	d. Sept.20,1852, aged 24y4m10d,w/o Matthew.
Matt T.	Jan.28,1826 - Sept.30,1861
Will	June 28,1826 - Sept.30,1832
Hensley, Thomas	d. Sept.10,1931, aged 19y.
Hicks, Ann	Nov.25,184- - Sept.3,1920
Rebecca	July 31,1848 - Feb.18,1911, w/o A.M.Hicks.
Hoss, Russell	b. Sept.29,1785, Buckingham, VA.d.June18,1856.
Houser, Lydia C.	Apr.20,1851 - Jan.18,1915

Blountville Cemetery, cont.

Houts, Lula Mae	Aug.12,1911, aged 41y8m14d.,w/o Rev.T.J.
Hughes, James Rhea	Oct.29,1898 - Dec.14,1906,s/o J.& D.R.
Katy	1812 - 1860
Humphreys, Alice	b. 187-, w/o George Humphreys.
George	1876 - 1936
Irvin, Elizabeth	d. May 18--, age 6-yrs.
John,Sr.	d. Feb.24,1824
Margaret	May 17,1796 - Sept.14,1821
Thomas	Mar.20,1798 - Sept.19,1827
James, Infant	no date, d/o W.W.& M.E.James.
Mary E.	Apr.10,1818, Abington, VA,-Dec.3,1857, Blountville, TN.,w/o William W.James.
Jones, Alice Rhea	July 4,1882 - Feb.16,1934,w/o E.T.Jones.
C.M.	1866 - 1934
Mrs. C.M.	1870 - 1934
Kenny, Hance H.	Dec.11,1806 - June 21,1878
Jennie P. Fickle	Oct.13,1864 - Dec.1,1920,w/o E.B.Kenny.
Mary V.	June 26,1901 - Sept.30,1922
Robert L./R.	May 16,1864 - Jan.13,1890
Kidd, Beatrice D.	Aug.24,1923 - Nov.2,1927,d/o W.M.& Etta.
Etta	Sept.13,1897 - ?, w/o W.J.
C.O.	Dec.31,1867 - Oct.1,1909
Kuhn, Gerald D.	d. July 31,1858 (?), aged 34y4m18d.
Lindamood, Priscila	Dec.18,1819 - June 20,1858, w/o Will L.
Rachel	illegible.
Long, Beulah M.	1888 - 1943
Hattie M. Martin	Jan.1,1827 - Dec.3,1912, w/o John P. Long.
Lawson A.	May 6,1858 - Sept.1,1905
Nancy A. Galloway	Jan.19,1860 - Feb.27,1934, w/o L.A.Long.
Lynn, Charles A.	Feb.17,1852 - Oct.27,1917
Dorothy T.	d.Sept.28,1927, aged 27y11m4d.
Joseph S.	Feb.18,1897 - Feb.9,1910,s/o C.A. & S.E.
Mary Edith	July 15,1916 - Jan.16,1918
Sallie E. Cox	Apr.15,1864 - May 31,1909, w/o Charles A.
McClellan, Adeline	Mar.17,1825 - Oct.21,1901
George Edward	d. 1829
Col. George R.	Sept.3,1816 - Jan.11,1904
Nannie	Aug.8,1849 - Apr.24,1859
Sadie Murray	Aug.15,1859 - Jan.13,1922,w/o S.L.
Samuel L.	1858 - 1930
Sue Looney	d.1915, d/o S.L.& J.D.
Willie	Nov.10,1854 - May 15,1859,s/o G.H.& A.
McMillin, R.H.	18-- - ?
W.G.	1863 - 1932
Alice V. Snodgrass	Aug.17,1872 - Mar.30,1898,w/o R.H.
Virginia	Oct.9,1870 - Sept.20,1896
Marsh, Robert	Sept.13,1831, aged 57y3m23d.
Massengill, Infant	b. & d. Jan.21,1895,s/o H.H.& M.A.
Cecil	May 27,1886 - May 28,1889, s/o H.H.& M.A.
Ernest	b. & d. May 28,1890, s/o H.H. & M.A.
John David	Sept.22-29,1887, s/o H.H.& M.A.
Dr.John G.	May 11,1844 - Jan.8,1919
Josephine Evans	Mar.2,1849 - Sept.6,1934, w/o Dr.J.G.
Maggie A. McClellan	Mar.30,1858 - Sept.11,1934, m. Sept.19,1880 to Henry H. Massengill, b. June 8,1853.

Massengill, Margaret	18-- - 1851 ?
Massey, J.J.	d. June 24,1925
Mauk, Millard H.	May 22,1905 - Mar.15,1930
Mary Rebecca	Dec.16,1901 - Oct.19,1913]ch/o E.F.& E.H.Mauk.
Enfield (dau)	Aug.14,1903 - Sept.4,1903
Millard, Cordelia	Sept.9,1868 - June 28,1869,d/o J.D. & S.B.
Jesse M.	Dec.16,1850 - Jan.19,1853,s/o J.D.& S.B.
Joel D.	May 21,1817 - Jan.6,1884, m.Jan.25,1849,
	h/o Sallie B. Feather.
Levi Richard	Nov.6,1861 - Oct.25,1916, s/o J.D.& S.B.
Louise	July 15,1859 - Jan.3,1860, d/o J.D.& S.B.
Mary E.	Mar.10,1857 - Jan.26,1922
Rachel E.	Sept.30,1862 - Dec.20,1865, d/o J.D.& S.B.
Sarah B.	d. July 28,1825, w/o J.D.Millard.
Theodisia M.	Aug.20,1866 - Aug.22,1867, d/o J.D.& S.B.
Miller, Bessie Mae	Nov.5,1892 - Apr.11,1893, d/o J.D. & A.R.
Dr. D.M.	Feb.15,1840 - Jan.8,1911
David Garrison	June 7,1879 - Apr.25,1884, s/o D.M.& E.M.
Edna M.	Jan.19,1847 - May 4,1928, w/o Dr.D.M.
Graham	date illegible
Margaret	Dec.10,1871 - May 15,1872, d/o Richard & Susan.
Mary E.	Mar.10,1857 - Jan.26,1923
Richard	July 11,1878 - Jan.28,1913
Dr.Robert R.	Oct.25,1865 - Sept.15,1890
Abraham	Aug.9,1809 - Oct.30,1846
Milsaps, Celia E.	Aug.22,1874 - July 14,1931
J.W.G.	Jan.10,1853 - June 22,1920
Margaret Green	Jan.15,1851 - Jan.13,1929,m.June 27,1875.
Mullenix, Martha E.	1853 - 1913, w/o A.F.
N.B.	1858 - 1921
William	1821 - 1888
Ruth	1833 - 1919
Neal, Elizabeth S.	Mar.26,1821 - Mar.29,1855, w/o William B.
Joseph M.	Nov.21,1917 - May 19,1919, s/o N.C.& Mae.
Newland, Ella Hicks	Dec.16,1861 - July 17,1896, w/o W.M.
Infants	5 illegible stones.
Laura Parrot	Jan.16,1822 - Sept.2,1912,m.Dec.4,1890,W.H.
Mabel Eugene	Apr.8,1911 - July 27,1911
Mary Frances	Jan.2,1910 - Jan.9,1910
W. Milburn	Mar.10,1847 - Jan.26,1908
Parker, Robert	d. Nov.6,1918, aged 75y.
Lucinda M.	d. Feb.28,1920, aged 69y.
Parrott, Dr. William	dec.3,1815
L.V.	Dec.3,1815
Mary B.	Dec.3,1815
Margaret	Dec.3,1815
Henry J.,M.D.	1838 - 1927
Esmerelda Sells	1854 - 1938
Mollie A.	Nov.1,1844 - Feb.15,1874,w/o Dr.H.A.
D.William	d. Dec.3,1815, aged 32y1m5d.
Mollie	1815 - 1894, d/o Dr. Parrott.
Rufus	1801 - 1809, s/o Dr. Parrott.
Willie Kelly	1815 - 1894, d/o Dr. Parrott.
Dr.W.M.A.	1867 - 1899

Blountville Cemetery, cont.

Pearson, Miss Alice	aged 67y.
Amanda McMinn	1872 - 1911
Mary White	w/o William Pearson.
Dr. McMinn	1863 - 1927
Sidney H.	Nov.14,1883 - Sept.18, 1894
William R.	1821 - Mar.2,1900
Peoples, Frederick Lee	May 26,1895 - Oct.16,1918, Corp. in France.
Joseph Sterling	1851 - 1936
Catherine Barnes	1871 - 19--
Phillips, Clarence	1896 - 1904
Ellen H.	July 21,1841 - Dec.8,1886, w/o N.J.
Phillip Perry	1892 - 1894, s/o W.M. & R.A.
Rebecca	1852 - 1937, w/o N.J.
Pickens, Margaret Sturm	Apr.4,1813/9 - Apr.11,1896
Powell, Edna Roller	Aug.1,1830 - Mar.15,1911, w/o John
George David	Jan.15,1856 - Oct.23,1857, s/o John & Marg.
Jacob C.	Mar.30,1851, aged 57y5m.
John	Mar.29,1816 - Jan.16,1874
Margaret Ann	Nov.20,1853 - Mar.12,1859
Thoams Jefferson	Mar.8,1858 - Mar.10,1859,s/o John & Margaret.
Violetta Anne	d. Nov.31,1854, aged 7y6d.,d/o Joseph & Marg.
Rader, Calvin Lynn	d. Apr.24,1890, aged 71y.
Dorcas	d. July 10,1892, aged 85 yrs.
Peter	Sept.3,1880 - May 11,1869
Reeve(s), Adaline M.	Mar.25,1847/9 - July 6,1887, w/o Dr.N.H.
Ellen Snapp	Apr.13,1881, aged 5y27d,d/o N.H.& A.M.
Mattie Haynon	July 28,1808, aged 9m24d.,d/o N.H.& A.M.
Rhea, Alfred Carter	Oct.11,1838 - May 16,1869,s /o J.D.& E.J.
Ann Maxwell	d. Feb.22,1827, aged 22y1m26d.,w/o Samuel.
Elizabeth B.	Oct.22,1836 - Sept.12,1851,d/o J.D.& E.J.
Elizabeth J.	Feb.10,1814 - Apr.22,1857, w/o J.D. Rhea, d/o Alfred M. Carter & Elizabeth W. Winder.
Elizabeth Earhart	Dec.25,1835 - May 26,1919
Francis E.	Dec.11,1832 - Nov.4,1870
J.E.	Apr.5,1833 - Aug.19,1856, m. May 21,1856
John	1753, Ireland - May 27,1832
John I.	May 24,1869 - Apr.12,1933
John William	Sept.23,1880 - Oct.27,1882, s/o J.M.& E.
Joseph	Dec.12,1830 - Aug.13,1909
Magnolia C. Lindamood	Dec.6,1889 - Apr.9,1910,m.Samuel W.Rhea,Jr., Dec.25,1909.
Margaret R.	June 10,1920 - May 12,1925,d/o J.J.& Retta.
Martha	Dec.22,1810 - Nov.4,1878
Morman	d. May 1926
Nancy	d. Jan.25,1856, aged 76y., w/o Samuel Rhea.
Ruth E. Rockhold	Jan.17,1837 - June 30,1902,w/o John H.Rhea.
Sallie H. Irwin	Jan.26,1848 - July 30,1901, w/o Samuel.
Samuel	d. Dec.11,1848, aged 74 yrs.
Samuel	d. May 7,1863, aged 68 yrs.
Samuel W.	June 12,1841 - June 15,1927
Susan	July 17,1803 - Dec.11,1820,w/o Joseph C.
Theodoric B.	June 21,1833 - Nov.15,1868
Robert	May 6,1890 - Oct.6,1902
Robert P.	d. Mar.26,1881, aged 78y6m9d.
Sarah	Mar.5,1817 - Feb.18,1874, w/o Robert P.

Blountville Cemetery, cont.

Rhea, Sarah G.	June 27,1803 - July 20,1874, w/o R.P.
Sarah Sells	1848 - 1934
Rhea, Monument	Samuel A. Rhea, d. at Ali-Shad,Persia, Sept.2,1865, aged 38y. His son,Robert Leighton,b.May 21,1865,d. at 1 yr.
Rhea, William	b. Jan.30,17-- ?
William	Nov.8,1834 - June 13,1853, s/o J.D.& Eliz.
Robeson, Amanda	May 30,18-0 - May 10,1872
Nancy C.	Apr.2,1853 - June 22,1899, d/o Rev.Wm., w/o H.P.Robeson.
Rev. William	June 28,1832/22 - May 29,1905
Robinson, Lorick W.	June 22,1868 - July 4,1868
Rogan, Catherine	Apr.11,1813 - Jan.2,1848, w/o Rev.Daniel.
Little Rosa	Mar.6,1873 - Aug.28,1873, d/o Ed.& Isadore.
Rogers, Ellen Shumaker	July 24,1828 - Dec.19,1910, m.Jan.18,185-, Jacob Rogers.
Infant	Aug.17,1922, d/o W.A. Rogers
Jessie J.	Apr.7,1864 - Jan.9,1893
Joseph	d. May 29,1926, aged 71y.
Mary E.	1869 - 1933
Sarah C.	d. Nov.16,1931, aged 71y1m13d.
Susan Shumaker	Mar.22,1833 - Dec.3,1910, m. Oct.27,1854, James Rogers.
William G.	Oct.1,1855 - July 17,1907
Rutledge, Anna S.	d. Nov.1834, aged 70 yrs.,w/o Gen.George.
General George	1755 - 1813, Revolutionary Soldier.
John G.	not legible.
Matilda W. Rhea	Apr.5,1833 - May 21,1856, w/o William G., d/o Col.J.D. & E.R.Rhea.
Rutter, Sallie Belle	1865 - after 1911, w/o R.B.Rutter.
R.B.	1859 - 1920
Schoolfield, L.E.	Sept.16,1812 - July 15,1891
Seneker, John E.L.	1848 - 19--
Oliver H.	July 14,18-3 - Oct.9,1918
Short, Callie Hill Floyd	July 25,1872 - Mar.28,1905
Sudie T. Miller	Dec.22,1875 - Nov.21,1900, w/o C.F.Short.
Shumaker, Lavenia S.	1851 - 1886
Smith, Charles W.	July 20,1875 - Sept.29,1891,s/o E.S.& Eliza E.
Elizabeth	Sept.11,1841 - May 18,1900, w/o E.S.Smith.
F.M.	July 25,1828 - May 13,1902
Henry Luther	June 22,1824 - Nov.21,1887, s/o E.S.& L.E.
Homer	Nov.27,1908 - Dec.28,1910, s/o E.S.& L.E.
Jacob	Jan.22,1821 - Jan.12,1896
Jane S.	July 22,1830 - Mar.28,1883, w/o Jacob Smith.
John L.	Dec.30,1816 - Sept.4,1871
Lousie	Nov.19,1829 - May 12,1909, w/o F.M.Smith.
Louis	Jan.31,1907 - May 13,1907, s/o H.H.& F.M.
M. Adolphus	Dec.1,1858 - May 9,1904
Margaret E.	d. June 21,1856, aged 24y.,d/o Jacob.
Mary	July 15,1793 - May 7,1851, w/o John J.
Mary Louise White	July 4,1861 - Nov.29,1921, m. Dec.23,1880, M.A.Smith.
Mrs. N.A.	1889 - 1931
Nathaniel	Jan.6,1871 - Jan.6,1926, s/o E.M. & Louisa.
Robert F.	Feb.8,18-0 - Feb.23,1934

Smith, Thomas	1874 - 1895
Victoria Kinney	July 26,1866 (?) , m.Sept.18,1865, w/o Robert Smith.
Snapp, Ella H.	May 3,1868 - Jan.14,1897
Ellener R.	d. Aug.21,1850, aged 48 yrs.,w/o Jacob K.
George H.	Nov.182- - 1855
?	d.1828, age 1y10m.
James P.	Aug.3,1824 - June 30,1901
Magdalene	July 22,1767 - Nov.22,1855
Margaret	d.1828, aged 12y.
Snodgrass, C.W.	Mar.5,1862 - May 12,1917
Elizabeth C.	May 15,1844 - June 22,1910, w/o W.J.
H.W.	Mar.22,1866 - Nov.4,1935
Wm. J.	June 1855 - Aug.1933
Spangler, Bettie J.	May 26,1860 - May 3,1933,w/o J.J.Spangler.
J.J.	Nov.6,1861 - June 3,1920
John W.	Sept.19,1882, s/o J.J.& R.J.
Sproles, ?	Mar.8,1882 - Mar.1,1905, s/o D.C.& L.G.
Charles L.	Nov.8,1887 - Nov.25,1928,s/o D.C.& L.G.
Spurgeon, Elizabeth C.	May 23,1839 - Oct.6,1860, w/o Samuel Spurgeon.
Dr.George W.	d.Feb.25,1885, aged 48y10m9d.
Margaret	June 12,1844 - July 2,1891, w/o Dr.G.W.
Spurgin, Nora Kate	Dec.13,1873 - Nov.19,1881, d/o M.E.& S.J.
Statzer, Nannie A. Smith	Oct.10,1891 - June 27,1919,w/o Dr.J.C.
Sturm, Frederick	d. June 27,1874, aged 70y8m24d.
Margaret P.	d.Sept.7,1848, aged 57y.,w/o W.Strum.,d/o Samuel & Nancy Rhea.
Martha D.	Jan.6,1823 - July 11,1896, w/o Frederick.
Robert Baxter	d. June 16,1872, aged 25y1m25d.,s/o F. & L.
Taylor, Willie	Mar.1,1852 - May 31,1889s/o W.G.& E.O.
Thomas, Hortense	Feb.9,1877 - May 22,1877, d/o Jacob & Mattie.
Infant	d. Dec.1,1883, d/o M.L. & E.H.
Jacob	no dates
Mary McClellan	1852 - 1929, w/o Jacob Thomas.
Paul	Mar.6,1881 - Jun 27,1887, s/o J. & M.P.
Tipton, A.B.	Oct.8,1794 - Mar.2,1865
Margaret Snapp	Nov.23,1793 - Aug.10,1886
Torbett, J. Kennedy	Apr.6,1863 - Sept.9,1888, m. Dec.24,1885, H.V.Seneker
James	d. June 30,1882 - Aged 57y10m5d.
Vance, Elizabeth	1830 - 1917
Laura E.	1829 - 1928 ?
White, Elizabeth J.	Apr.24,1845 - June 5,1921,d/o O.N.& S.B.
Ellen Yost	Aug.22,1857 - Oct.8,1927
Ida Rogers	Apr.6,1855 - Apr.6,1913
Maggie Rhea	Oct.12,1856 - Oct.5,1926
Mattie	Jan.22,1935, aged 42yrs.
T.W.	Aug.7,1843 - Jan.20,1926
Wiley, Col Robert M.	d. July 16,1882, aged 56y7m3d.
Williams, G.A.	July 22,1837 - Apr.22,1910
Infant	July 9,1912, s/o J.T.& M.E.
Maude Norvell	Dec.10,1875 - July 14,1912
Stewart	1874 - 1913
J. Thorn	June 18,1870 - Jan.7,1934

Blountville Cemetery, cont.

Williams, W.A.	Nov.19,1847 - Jan.8,1925
Witcher, D.A.	Feb.18,1856/66 - July 7,1903
Myrabel Rhea	May 23,1872 - Dec.2,1920,w/o D.A.Witcher.
J.R.	Oct.15,1901 - Dec.6,1918,s/o Dan & Myra.
Wolfe, Mary E.	1877 - 1934
Yost, Mary Fain	Mar.12,1860 - Jan.30,1891, w/o W.K.Yost.
W.K.	stone broken.
?	no dates, s/o W.K.Yost.

New Bethel Presbyterian Church Cemetery

Alexander, Leda	1972 (fhm)
William P.	July 16,1916 - May 18,1965
Milidean W.	Aug.29,1921 - no date
Alison, Carl I.	Sept.10,1872 - Sept.22,1963
E. Edra	Apr.18,1911 - July 19,1965
John Burton	July 11,1904 - Apr.9,1947
Mildred K.	Mar.17,1912 - Apr.30,1958
N. Lester	Sept.17,1880 - Jan.29,1962
Nora K.	Jan.22,188- - Feb.25,1964
Phillip Gail	July 22-25, 1937, s/o Lionel & Jessie.
Robert Calvin	Aug.4-6,1942, s/o John B. & Mildred W.
Robert J.	Dec.14,1839 - Feb.24,1914
Catherine E. Sawyers	Apr.1,1865 - Feb.9,1931
Robert J.	1889 - 1958
Florence W.	1893 - 1960
Allison,Benjamin F.	1845 - Apr.8,1877
Mary Elizabeth	1854 - Apr.20,1882
Finly	d.1833, aged 59y1m5d.
Susannah	d. Feb.1831, aged 52y21d.
Frank	d. 1922, aged 25y., WWI.
George Washington	b. Jan.9,1812, s/o Capt.Jack.
J.M.	May 14,1857 - Oct.5,1910, s/o Joseph Allison, 1798 - 1872.
Jesse	d. June 25,1880, aged 78y4m13d.
Clementina Shell	d. May 5,1845, aged 21 yrs.
Capt. John	d. Feb.2,1832, aged 74 yrs.
John R.	Sept.21,1848 - Feb.7,1910
John, I	illegible, very old.
Susannah	illegible, very old.
Joseph	Dec.9,1798 - Sept.5,1872
Artie Mingle (wife)	Oct.10,1818 - July 17,1890
Martha	b. Nov.13,1793, d/o Capt.Jack Allison.
Mattie Daniel	Nov.22,1851 - Feb.24,1924
Mrs. Robert	1865 - 1931, 2nd wife.
Robert	Confederate Soldier.
Robert Milton	Dec.29,1876 - Apr.20,1887
Anders, D.S.	Mar.27,1925 - Dec.5,1933
Anderson, Eli	Feb.2,1829 - 1900
Edney	1829 - 1872
William R.	Dec.18,1803 - Oct.18,1871
Elizabeth Warren	1807 - 1896
Baker, Charles Cecil	1904 - 1944

Barlett, Sam R.	Jan.6,1891 - Oct.28,1967
Cordie R.	Apr.3,1875 - no date
Barnes, Isaac W.	Nov.21,1905 - no date
Ila Ruth	Oct.29,1904 - Aug.7,1964,m. Oct.30,1926.
Vickie Lynn	b. & d. Feb.2,1955, d/o Harold & Dorothy.
Beck, William	1903 - 1975
Isabella	1913 - no date
Berry, Rev.Bro. J.Andrew	1864 - 1905, Presbyterian Minister.
John H.	Dec.26,1831/4 - Apr.21,1906
Sarah J. (1st)	Mar.28,1826 - Dec.15,1872
Lucretia (2nd)	June 26,1837 - Aug.17,1915
Black, Annabel Scott	June 30,1920 -
Stanley Shaffer	Nov.26,1907 - Nov.2,1979
Blevins, Ailenic Sells	1904 - 1946
Boling, George R.	Apr.3,1918 - Nov.11,1968
Bond, Mary Rhea	1816 - 1888, w/o George Bond.
Boring, James Wesley	Apr.12,1844 - May 10,1906
Martha Jane	1852 - 1936
Rev. Washington	d. Aug.19,1954, aged 34y.
Elizabeth	Sept.15,1828 - Oct.11, 1892
Bowman, Carl D.	1905 - 1976
Zella R.	1906 - no date
Boyington, William	1895 - 1957
Margaret	1885 - 1972
Brainard, David L.	Jan.2,1881 - Oct.25,1964
Elizabeth W.	June 29,1886 - Dec.8,1966
Britt, Delia Hicks	Mar.26,1884 - Oct.7,1956
Broyles, Wilsie M.	Aug.23,1913 - May 21,1967
J.T.	July 3,1907 - Apr.7,1952
Brumitt, Pauline Sell	Mar.14,1903 - no date
Elbert K.	July 27,1898 - Sept.5,1964
Campbell, James	1832 - 1906
Carr, Allie M.	Nov.10,1946 - Feb.27,1947
Charles S.	Mar.18,1908 - Sept.19,1958
Clarence Wendall	1923 - 1980, aged 56y.
Mrs. Dean	Apr.30,1923 - Feb.26,1980
Earl Gentry	1916 - 1979, TEC 5, US Army, WW II.
Earnest B.	1913 - 1979
Ida Mae E.	1917 - no date
George S.	May 18,1909 - July 4,1969
Margaret L.	Aug.26,1923 - no date
J.Elbert	Aug.30,1898 - no date
Wilma Annie	June 9,1896 - Mar.19,1955
James Earl	July 23,1914 - Mar.3,1962, Tn HQ & Co. 20 Inf.
Mary E.	Aug.18,1883 - Jan.4,1959
Worley B.	July 24,1882 - July 14,1954
Clark, Gilbert N.	Sept.10,1892 - Dec.25,1944
Clay, Fannie	Mar.9,1869 - Nov.24,1924
John R.	Aug.14,1834 - May 17,1913
D.A. Bishop	Feb.14,1832 - Aug.4,1910
Cole, Isaac	Apr.9,1892 - Mar.13,1963
Robert M.	1876 - 1952
William	1890 - 1972
Lucy H.	1900 - no date

Collins, Ambrose	no date, Confederate Soldier.
Arthur C.	1900 - 1960
Helma McCrany	1908 - 1935
J.T. (Jessie)	1861 - 1932
James	Apr.18,1839 - Aug.18,1916, Confederate Soldier.
Elizabeth	1844 - June 23,1896
Jim	July 2,1909 - Mar.14,1968
M.C.	1869 - 1931
Mary (Mother)	Oct.28,1872 - no date
Elizabeth B. (dau)	Aug.7,1904 - Nov.29,1934
Ordia	Oct.10,1884 - Mar.24,1967
Valentine	d. Oct.25,1927, age 81 yrs.,Conf.Soldier.
William	May 20,1871 - Oct.2,1941
Cox, Charles M.	1877 - 1956
Roxie Berry Warren	1877 - 1956
Cretsinger, Dora	Aug.21,1874 - Aug.30,1935
Herman	1947 - 1948
Mary Ann	Feb.24,1810 - June 6,1908
Sylvia King	May 11,1941 - Aug.28,1958
W.B.	illegible
Cross, F.M.Hall	Dec.31,1942, d/o D.N.& H.S.Hall.
Georgia Mae	July 30,1905 - Aug.26,1948
Infant	b. & d. Apr.9,1939
Infant	b. & d. Feb.15,1936, s/o W.R. & Georgia.
Cunningham, Arthur H.	1895 - 19--
Lucy S.	1898 - 1964
Jeanette	Oct.13,1925 - no date
Claude H.	Apr.4,1923 - Jan.29,1980
Davenport, Clifford O.	May 2,1905 - Feb.21,1961
Gladys R.	May 12,1905 - no date
Davidson, Andrew	no dates, Confederate Soldier.
Andrew J.	1878 - 1956
Eliza E.	1899 - 1975
Arthur F.	1901 - 1974
Gentry	b. & d. 1945
Henry C.	Aug.31,1880 - Nov.28,1954
J. Alfred	Dec.26,1910 - May 21,1955
James J.	Jan.13,1882 - Apr.21,1969
Lila M.	Mar.10,1891 - June 15,1959
Joseph Martin	Oct.6,1875 - Sept.21,1963
Myrtle Gertrude	Apr.11,1903 - no date
Robert	1931 - 1937
Shirley Jon	May 29 - Sept.4,1953, d/o Paul & Dorothy.
Delp, ?	Oct.1,1962, d/o Lester & Nancy Delp.
DeVault, John Wesley	d. July 25,1954
Phitna P.	d. Nov.2,1959
Dotson, Annie Whitaker	Sept.30,1872 - Jan.5,1968
Dunn, Janet	Mar.14,1931 - Nov.1,1935
John H.	1876 - 1933
Lucy Ann	1874 - 1946
Durham, William Paul	May 24,1914 - May 10,1963
Dyer, John A.	1843 - 1903, Confederate .
Mary M.	1843 - 1906
William	Sept.14,1796 - Sept.14,1832

New Bethel Presbyterian Church Cemetery, cont.

Fagan, Cora B.	Aug.10,1874 - June 29,1965	
Delmar C.	Mar.19,1910 - Jan.18,1965	
Onnie C.	Jan.11,1910 - 1979	
Grover Perry	1908 - 1955	
W.R.	Oct.31,1882 - Jan.14,1952	
Pluma A.	Mar.4,1892 - Nov.16,1951	
Woodrow (Rounder)	Oct.16,1918 - Aug.5,1977	
Frye, Daisey	1888 - 1968	
Lee	1911 - no date	
Fulmer, Elizabeth White	Oct.12,1787 - Sept.10,1882, w/o John Fuller.	
Galloway, Ethel Warren	1893 - 1977	
Gantt, Sue King	Aug.2,1937 - Nov.11,1976	
Giesler, Gertrude Almorde	Jan.15,1896 - Feb.22,1928, s/o Willie P.	
Henry David	1871 - 1951	
Lena M.	Dec.8,1904 - Mar.9,1965	
Willie P.	Nov.24,1892 - May 19,1959	
W.R.	1847 - 1930	
Edna King	1851 - 1929	
Goodman, Charolett Ann	Oct.3,1944 - Oct.15,1969	
Hubert Lee	June 21,1904 - Apr.14,1956	
Trula Mae	Mar.5,1901 - Apr.20,1968	
Graybeal, Lester S.	July 6,1893 - ?	
Lula Ellen	Feb.19,1896 - Sept.16,1951	
Milton	Jan.25,1881 - Jan.6,1944	
Rena	Nov.24,188- - no date	
Green, Fred A.	June 25,1892 - Apr.15,1973	
Susan E.	May 9,1889 - Apr.21,1966	
Gregg, Abraham	Sept.19,1790 - Sept.21,1876	
Jannett	1796 - Jan.22,1851	
James	d. 18--	
James, Jr.	d. 1866, aged 65y.	
Jannett	Oct.1788 - Feb.15,1828	
Mary M.	June 22,1809 - Nov.18,1881	
Col. Nathan	Aug.5,1835 - July 5,1894	
Catherine	Oct.29,1843 - Jan.26,1902	
Rachel	Dec.13,1813 - 1894	
Sarah	1823 - 1876	
William	Feb.22,1836 - Mar.7,1894	
Gross, Addie	Dec.10,1861 - Sept.25,1943	
Alfred F.	1822 - 1902	
Julia A.	1830 - 1904	
Alfred & Julia	Their children: Corda, Roy, Beulah, Lillian, Vesta, Clifford, Blanche, Glenna, Atlee, Lida, Claude, Retha, & Virgie.	
David A.	1853 - 1930	
Louisa Britt	1855 - 1924	
Jacob, I	d. 1790	
Jacob, II	d. MAy 21,1872	
Mary P.	no dates, d/o Alfred Gross & Julia A. Woods.	
Robert F.	Nov.4,1859 - Feb.5,1939	
Victoria Hughes	Mar.11,1862 - Dec.23,1940	
Hall, Andrew Jackson	Nov.6,1830 - Dec.23,1903, Union Soldier.	
Mary Ann Wilson	May 24,1835 - Sept.20,1901	
B.E.	d. Aug.7,1948, s/o D.N.& H.S.Hall.	
David N.	Dec.12,1853 - June 26,1899, Confed. Soldier.	

New Bethel Presbyterian Church Cemetery, cont.

Hall, Harriet S.	Apr.19,1842 - Jan.21,1921
Mattie Leonard	1878 - 1945
Maude R.	Feb.14,1885 - Jan.8,1970
Hamilton, J.H.	Sept.10,1855 - June 14,1941
Nancy H. White	Feb.22,1856 - Sept.26,1929
Lula Mae	Sept.7,1890 - Aug.1,1891, d/o J.H.& N.H.
Hampton, Dwain J.	Apr.4,1915 - no date
Harris, E.B.	1888 - 1960
Harvey, Andrew J.	1875 - 1939
Sena M.	1880 - 1939
Hubert E.	Jan.4,1907 - Aug.25,1949
Lina King Dishner	Jan.20,1906 - July 29,1977
Hawley, Nora E. King	1862 - 1914
Haws, Virginia Mae	Apr.22,1924 - Dec.19,1949
Hensley, K. Sylvester	1906 - 1980
Maggie A.	1906 - no date
Hickman, Mrs.	1925 - 1973
Hicks, Charles L.	Nov.21,1892 - Apr.11,1919, Pvt., WW I.
Wade	1951 - 1973 ?
Audrey	?
E.Edgar	1884 - 1961
Lizzie W.	1899 - no date
Michael	no dates
Meigs	1923 - 1973
William Isaac	July 13,1880 - Feb.27,1958
Sarah Bridges	June 4,1892 - Feb.28,1958
Himes, Christopher	d. Jan.27,1860, aged 45y.
Hodge, ?	no stone, s/o John & Rebecca Mears Hodge.
Anderson R.	Mar.21,1850 - July 13,1917, s/o Joseph & Margaret Rhea Hodge.
Francis	d. MAy 27,1855, aged 87y5m16d.
Martha Ferguson	no date
Francis, I	d. 1798
Capt. Francis, III	May 15,1799 - June 2,1863
Priscilla King	d. Aug.2,1857, aged 55y.
James Madison	May 12,1844 - May 31,1926, Confed.Soldier.
Lucinda Gross	no stone (1843-1908)
Joseph	Aug.2,1811 - May 13,1901
Mary (1st wife)	d. Mar.27,1848
Margaret Rhea (2nd wife)	Dec.9,1818 - MAr.13,1895
Josiah	d. Feb.12,1876, aged 74y11m3d.
Lucinda Torbett	d.Aug.12,1873, aged 68y.
Benjamin Clifton	June 4,1896 - May 20,1962
Bessie Harvey	Dec.24,1897 - May 17,1944, s/o J.J.
Carl A.	June 23,1884 - Dec.14,1922
Creed F.	1869 - 1955
Nancy Bertie	1880 - 1958
Eliza Ann	Apr.1,1865 - June 12,1950
Henry J.	1892 - 1960
Ina M.	1891 - 19--
Homer H.,Jr.	Nov.26,1917 - Jan.23,1950
John C.	1839 - 1923
J.C.Q.	Aug.7,1833 - July 15,1923
James A.	1870 - 1956
Addie O.	1868 - 1952

New Bethel Presbyterian Church Cemetery, cont.

Hodges, James J.	1878 - 1964
Lura B.	1875 - 1941
Lola B. Prude	Mar.13,1894 - Apr.16,1927
Nora	Oct.1888 - -----
Homsher, Fannie Sells	Apr.13,1871 - Aug.11,1949
Hughes, Daivd	d. June 19,1849, aged 92y.
Anna	d. May 17,1838, aged 75 yrs.
David M.	Nov.11,1838 - Mar.15,1862, Confed.Soldier.
Franklin H.	Nov.25,1920 - Mar.12,1979,TEC 5,US Army WWII.
Henry	d. Aug.28,1874, aged 43y., Union Soldier.
Hiram	1832 - 1907
Mary	1829 - 1880
Mary Bowers	June 12,1836 - Dec.10,1880
Robert	d. June 2,1852, aged 60y4m26d.
Elizabeth	Oct.11,1797 - Oct.15,1878
Roy W.	1888 - 1962
Carrie E.	1897 - 19--
Samuel D.	Dec.26,1825 - Mar.22,1897
Thaddeus C.	Nov.15,1863 - June 12,1945
Julia A. White	Apr.11,1864 - Jan.13,1938
Thomas	May 27,1788/98 - Mar.21,1862
Minerva McFarland	Dec.13,1813 - Nov.25,1851
Thomas R.	Oct.18,1830/32 - June 30,1887
Humphrey, J.B.	June 5,1915 - June 24,1973
Mary Lee	July 13,1919 - Dec.29,1965
Lawrence J.	Aug.8,1948 - Aug.16,1968,TN.Cpl.Co.B.,46 Inf., 196 Lt.Inf. Vietnam BSM-PH.
Robert O.	Apr.2,1914 - Oct.31,1971,TN Pfc,US Army WWII.
Hyatt, Alvin	Aug.22,1926 - Oct.6,1966
Cora	July 24,1903 - Jan.1,1960
Herman D.	1909 - 1978, S1,US Navy, WW II.
Lawrence	Mar.23,1906 - Jan.18,1964
Minnie	Mar.16,1873 - Nov.16,1941
Nick	1875 - 1947
Paul	1903 - 1977
Ralph	1910 - 1971
Georgia	1913 - no dates
Isley, J. Joe	1939 - 1968, m. Dec.8,1965,
Ida Jane	1938 - no date, w/o J.Joe.
J.Logan	Aug.2,1910 - Aug.6,1966
Jamey V.	Dec.12,1907 - no date
Linda Jane	1938
Jamison, Gertrude	Sept.28,1886 - June 18,1968
Jeter, James W.	Feb.18,1849 - Apr.21,1912,MasonicEmblem.
Will N.	May 22,1888 - Nov.1,1972
Clarcia J.	Feb.6,1910 - Sept.23,1960
Johnson, Charles H.	Oct.2,1889 - May 9,1976,TN Pvy.157 Depot Brigade WW I.
Ted L.	June 19,1913 - no date
Emily S.	Jan.31,1918 - May 24,1974
W. Hiram	1891 - no date
Viola Poe	1892 - 1974
Jones, Pompey Demon	1875 - 1964
Nannie Emiline	1880 - 1942
Ruby Sells	1907 - 1942
William A.	1890 - 1977

New Bethel Presbyterian Church Cemetery, cont.

King, Arden L.   May 28,1901 - Sept.7,1971
     Daisey B.   Jan.15,1905 - no date
     Carl A.   1886 - 1966
     Mary Faye   1894 - 1952
     David Giesler   Jan.9,1877 - Jan.21,1964
     wife   Nov.21,1879 - Feb.19,1947
     E.R.   no date, s/o Isaac C. King & Susan S.Dyer.
     E.Rutledge   d. 1925, aged 80 yrs.
     Elizabeth Jane Hodge   1850 - 1900, w/o J.A.King.
     Elizabeth Jane   Sept.29,1866 - Jan.23,1938, w/o Marion King.
     George A.   1934 - 1974
     Henry Birton   Jan.29,1882 - July 11,1961, m. Dec.24,1901.
     Eva Sue   Aug.21,1881 - July 13,1969, w/o H.B.
     Infant   Feb.18,1951, d/o Lynn & Georgia.
     James Anderson   May 16,1852 - June 26,1931
     James Marion   1860 - 1933
     John   Sept.4,1860 - May 19,1910
     John   Spet.18,1837,a ged 79yrs.
     Sarah   May 31,1782 - Mar. 6,1853
     Lafayette   Feb.14,1853 - May 12,1929
     N. Adeline Giesler   Nov.30,1856 - June 22,1926
     Lavina   d. June 10,1852, aged 53y5m21d.
     Noah G.   May 23,1904 - Jan.23,1977
     Roy A.   1879 - 1959
     Mary A.   1878 - 1939
     Sallie Ellen   Aug.6,1893 - Jan.11,1942,w/o W.A.King.
     Sarah Etta   July 5,1859 - June 14,1902
     Thomas   d. June 18,1847, aged 93 yrs.
     Ann   aged 66y.
     Verblin P.   June 11,1900 - Oct.7,1918, Pfc 1st Class, Co. F., 117 Inf., WW I.
     Cpl. Weldon William   Oct.9,1922 - May 19,1949, killed in service, Fort Bragg, North Carolina.
     William   May 25,1798 - Apr.28,1866, Mexican War 1847.
     Sarah   d. 1853, aged 52 yrs.
     William   Sept.28,1828 - Oct.21,1900
     Mary Emily Hodge   no dates

New Bethel Presbyterian Church Cemetery, cont.

Lane, Nora Boring	Mar.30,1881 - Jan.31,1922
Patton T.	May 13,1884 - July 24,1957
Latture, Jacob	July 25,1825 - Jan.12,1883
Mary Ann	May 24,1829 - July 31,1870
Lawson, Thomas W.	Feb.5,1905 - no date
Stella S.	Sept.7,1904 - Dec.19,1975
Leonard, John	July 15,1836 - May 3,1910, Union Soldier.
Logan, Susannah	d. Apr.9,1833, aged 18y., w/o William B.
Love, John	1907 - 1970
Elizabeth	1914 - no date
Kenneth F.	Sept.6,1940 - Apr.1,1946
McClellan, Samuel	May 10,1820 - Dec.9,1904
McKamy, Nancy	Mar.29,1842 - Sept.18,1906
George E.	1899 - 1961
Hermia B.	1904 - 1978
George	no dates, Confederate Soldier.
George W.	1847 - 1900
M.Jane	1848 - 1919
Mary Catherine Hodges	1839 - 1920, w/o Robert McKamey.
Robert	1834 - 1908, Confederate Soldier.
Rufus Burton	Sept.17,1874 - June 10,1938
Mary Catherine	Feb.7,1881 - Nov.13,1951
William T.	1910 - 1973
McKinley, Isaac	d. Apr.19,1818, aged 79y., Corp.John Dunn Co., Co.D.,9th Tn Cavalery.
William	aged 83 yrs.
Madron, Minnie M.	Sept.14,1884 - May 6,1957
Malone, Jennie King	Apr.27,1899 - Mar.30,1962
Penny Renee	May 5,1965 - Oct.9,1965
Mason, A.J.	May 30,1872 - Feb.17,1957
Anna B.	Sept.24,1891 - Oct.13,1969
Fred L.	1915 - 19--
Ora K.	1921 - 1974
Infant	d. Aug.20,1912, s/o & d/o A.J.& Annie Mason.
Meadows, E.M.	Mar.12,1823 - Aug.18,1903
Ida Catherine	Feb.16,1869 - Dec.24,1938
Mary Mills	Oct.29,1899 - June 2,1970
William C.	June 6,1887 - Aug.17,1948
Millhorn, Joe J.	1879 - 1954
Lena B.	1887 - 1972
Samuel T.	1877 - 1940
Bertie Rose	1882 - 1958
R. Alyward	1890 - 1948
Mills, B.F.	1874 - 19--
Bertie Hamilton	1880 - 1935
Bennie	1897 - 1979
Cuzzella Mae	Aug.23,1901 - Oct.13,1946
James P.	Feb.17,1868 - Feb.9,1942
Mary Hodges	Nov.4,1858 - Aug.14,1929
Minga, John A	May 21,1882 - May 11,1964
Cora E.	Apr.14,1886 - Aug.11,1966
Mingea, David M.	July 9,1867 - June 15,1938
Amanda M.	Mar.9,1879 - Oct.14,1935
Moore, James J.	1901 - 1969
Gracie H.	1911 - 1978

New Bethel Presbyterian Church Cemetery, cont.

Morgan, Walter J.   no date, Co.6,19C Inf. Spanish-Am. War.
Morris, Charlie C.   1884 - 1963
       Nora A.   1885 - 1971
       James Norman   May 20,1859 - Nov.8,1936
       Barbara Ellen   Nov.11,1853 - Nov.1,1936
       Ephream B.   Sept.3,1895 - Apr.28,1958,
                           Tn. Pvt. Co.C.,383 Inf. WW I.

Odell, Helen A.   1877 - 1954
Oliver, Howard   July 22,1913 - Mar.13,1977
       Martha   May 24,1913
       Hubert   Dec.16,1879 - July 11,1952
       Ida Williams   July 28,1873 - Feb.17,1964
       Isaac B.   July 7,1876 - Mar.23,1936
       Lula   Apr.14,1871 - Jan.12,194-
       James M.   June 9,1830 - Apr.17,1914
       Mary   1840 - 1924
       James Wesley   Jan.28,1866 - Jan.28,1925
Pennel, James Monroe   1888 - 1956
Pickens, Abraham   no dates,Confederate Soldier.
        Clancy O.   June 14,1887 - Oct.19,1968
        Anna Bell   Mar.10,1913 - no date
        Martha   1821 - 1878
Poe, Ida   May 6,1865 - Nov.12,1955
    Milburn   1847 - 1913, Confederate Soldier.
Ramsey, Mose Berry, Sr.   Feb.14,1861 - July 31,1948
        Martha Ellen Glenn Feb.20,1865 - Nov.11,1953
Range, Allen   1927 - 1957
       John M.   1879 - 1945
Raybon, William A.   1898 - 1968
        Nora M.   1900 - ----
Reed, Mae   Apr.12,1896 - Aug.8,1967
Rhea, Sue   Feb.19,1843 - July 19,1882,w/o W.R.Rhea, Jr.
      William P.   Aug.20,1804 - Dec.5,1861
Riley, James R.   Feb.7,1792 - Aug.17,1869
       Elizabeth   Dec.19,1809 - Aug.7,1956
       Permelia A. King Warren 1844 - 1907, w/o J.T.Riley.
Roberts, Curtis   1919 - 1976
         Fannie O.   1928 - no date
Rose, Jacky   no dates, Union Soldier.
      Worley M.   1904 - 1974
      Sarah M.   1899 - no date
Sanders, Elizabeth D. Allison 1853 - 1896m w/o J.H.Sanders.
Sandres, John H.   unmarked, Confederate Soldier.
Scott, Annie Belle   Nov.28,1875 - June 25,1937
       Ida Elizabeth   May 31,1870 - Sept.24,1948
       John   d. 1839, aged 59y.
       Mary Allison   no dates
Scott, John M.   Aug.9,1818 - Apr.17,1877
       John Milton   Dec.7,1872 - Dec.19,1960
       Roxanne May   Jan.21,1890 - Nov.18,1976
       Robert F.   Feb.9,1824 - Dec.29,1883
       Mary Jane Hodge   1835, w/o R.F.Hodge.
       Susannah Allison   b. May 8,1792, w/o Samuel, d/o Capt.
                          Jack Allison.
       William Monroe   Aug.27,1862 - Aug.1,1926

Seehorn, Harriet N.	Aug.10,1834 - Jan.1,1880, w/o Dr. J.W.
Sells, A.D.	1911 - 1935
Cora	1883 - 1928
Ella Mae	Mar.21,1912 - Oct.13,1973
Harriet	1867 - 1940
Howard W.	1908 - 1966
Elsie C.	1910 - no date
Landon	no date
William C.	July 1i,1873 - Oct.24,1935
Ollie B.	Nov.17,1882 - Jan.4,1962
Shell, Clementine	no dates
Sheperd, James K.	1974 - 1980
Shipley, David	Sept.22,1878 - Nov.4,1957
Matilda Frances	Mar.25,1878 - Jan.11,1937
Dela Besheba	Aug.30,1903 - Oct.27,1905
George W.	1895 - 19--
Bertha M.	1905 - 19--
J.C.	Oct.22,1873 - Dec.9,1942
Elizabeth Giesler	Nov.19,1877 - Feb.28,1938
James	no dates, Union Soldier.
James V.	1923 - no date
Ruth H.	1924 - 1976
James Walter	Mar.26,1897 - Sept.20,1959
John	no dates, Union Soldier
Lola Jane	Sept.30,1885 - Nov.22,1948,w/o H.C.Davidson.
Lula Alice	Feb.18,1905 - Oct.21,1909
Mary Frances	Dec.4,1911 - Nov.26,1927
Perry W.	Feb.21,1916 - Dec.31,1966
Dorothy V.	July 23,1916 - Dec.31,1966
Smalling, John N.	Nov.23,1869 - June 10,1950
Dora H.	July 2,1865 - Feb.2,1932
Ranken	Oct.26,1900 - Sept.27,1978
Mar Mingea	no dates
Smith, Charles H.	1921 - 1979
Dora B.	Jan.14,1870 - May 14,1944
Iva Lindamood	June 22,1902 - Dec.10,1933
John H.	Dec.20,1861 - Nov.29,1904
Lucille	Jan.11,1931 - July 8,1932
Snapp, J.M.	Aug.25,1890 - Mar.7,1958
Myrtle Houston	Nov.7,1892 - Feb.6,1935
Phyllis Dean	Mar.9,1934 - Aug.19,1949
R.L.	June 3,1845 - June 2,1896
Dorothula J.	Sept.7,1844 - Nov.15,1927
Raymond H.	Sept.13,1907 - no date
Trula Dean	Apr.17,1912 - Oct.26,1978
Spurgeon, Gertrude Alison	Nov.1,1860 - Nov.29,1957
Thomas, William St.John	Aug.24,1918 - Nov.12,1977,PFC US Army WWII.
Elizabeth Hodges	July 3,1921 - no date, w/o William.
Torbett, Allen	Aug.4,1802 - Apr.26,1855, Mexican War.
Fred Lucinda	1904 - 1953
George Martin	1859 - 1930
J. Franklin	1849 - 1909
Virginia G.	1850 - 1926
James	d. 1855

New Bethel Presbyterian Church Cemetery, cont.

Torbett, John	1820 - 1902
John A.	Feb.3,1849 - May 28,1923,Confederate Soldier.
Julie E. Smith	1850 - 1888
Joseph	d. 1839
Sarah	d. 1853, aged 76y.
Lawrence K.	July 4,1949 - July 6,1949
Martha J.	1833 - 1888
Samuel W.	Sept.14,1852 - Mar.7,1933
Sarah E.	Nov.5,1861 - Jan.22,1928
Walter Clyde	Dec.2,1902 - June 16,1970
Jennie Mingea	no dates
I.G., The Unknown Traveler	d. 1790
Ward, Conley J.	Apr.19,1904 - no date
Mary Lou	Aug.14,1890 - Sept.30,1964
Warren, Claude J.	June 8,1896 - Jan.27,1948
George C.	1886 - 1953
Lela O.	1886 - 1964
Mary I.	1900 - 1901
S.K.	1876 - 1940
Katie	1872 - 1917
William E.	Jan.19,1843 - Dec.7,1807
Wexler, Daniel B.	May 24,1825 - Apr.19,1898
Elizabeth G.	Sept.23,1824 - Oct.15,1895
David F.	Feb.21,1860 - Oct.3,1864, s/o D.B.& E.
Edwin C.	Nov.14,1884, s/o E.B.& L.L.
Henry B.	Dec.29,1886 - Jan.17,1968
Lila Lea King	1890 - 1951
Infant	b. & d. JAn.23,1892, inf/o E.B.& L.L.
John M.	no date, s/o D.B.& E.Wexler.
Samuel L.	Dec.22,1857 - Sept.26,1862, s/o D.B.& E.
Whitaker, Abe L.	1856 - 1919
Ann C.	1857 - 1931
Fred T.	1928 - 1972
Anna L.	1932 - no date
Helen E.	18-- - 19--
Jess J.	1894 - 1956
Nannie Z.	1890 - 1965
Joe	1884 - 1950
Bessie	1893 - no date
John W.	Aug.20,1884 - Jan.25,1969
Eva Mae C.	June 27,1893 - no date
June	1900 - 1976
Howard T.	July 15,1919 - July 17,1962, TN Pfc 301 MP ES Cart, CD Co. WW II.
Mabel	1910 - 1952, d/o R.B.Whitaker.
Mattie E.	18-- - 19--
Nanie K.	1873 - 1954
Paul	Feb.9,1907 - Oct.20,1950
R.E. (Ruff)	Jan.28,1877 - Mar.28,1966
T.L.	July 11,1928 - Sept.23,1938
Walter C.	Sept.8,1900 - May 26,1965
William	Aug.26,1874 - Nov.26,1946
Ethel	July 21,1885 - Feb.8,1953

New Bethel Presbyterian Church Cemetery, cont.

White, Adam	Sept.3,1789 - Aug.10,1873	
Mary	Dec.7,1783 - Mar.23,1819	
Charles A.	Apr.14,1881 - Aug.5,1935	
Effie Rose	Apr.12,1886 - Feb.13,1954	
Herbert D.	Jan.30,1895 - Nov.16,1968	
I.J.	June 29,1898 - no date	
James	illegible.	
Mary	Dec.7,1783 - Mar.23,1819	
Jay S.	Jan.5,1820/9 - May 21,1897	
Sarah	Apr.20,1829 - Jan.28,1893	
John	July 15,1754 - Aug.25,1796	
Ann	July 15,1763 - Apr.10,1817	
Norman M.	Oct.14,1876 - June 14,1947	
Ada Z.	May 23,1875 - Feb.23,1971	
Wilson, Charlene L. "Dumpy"	Mar.14,1945 - Nov.29,1964	
Forest "Frosty"	1911 - 1974	
Winebarger, Jonas	1864 - 1946	
Bertie T.	1886 - 1941	
Wolfe, Creed F.	1845 - 1906, Confederate Soldier.	
Kate Maxwell	1852 - 1882	
Melissa W.	1861 - 1935	
Woods, David	d. Jan.23,1872, aged 66 yrs.	
Jane Alexander	d. Nov.17,1970	

Morrell Cemetery

Bare, Dewey M.	1899 - 1970	
Flora F.	1900 - no date	
Jerry E.	Nov.3,1949 - June 25,1955,s/o M.& M. Orville.	
Hage H.	Feb.14,1898 - Jan.2,1973	
Howard	June 12,1926 - Jan.5,1929,s/o D.M.& F.O.	
Barnett, Dave	1881 - 1940	
Maggie	1883 - 1960	
Berry, James R.	1930 - 1958	
Alona L.	1930 - no date	
Booher, J.L.	1862 - 1955	
Noah C.	1895 - 1965	
Ethel B.	1898 - 1959	
Brown, Ned R.	1926 - 1985	
Bryan, James Landon	Nov.9,1920 - Dec.26,1984	
Buckles, Emmett C.	1896 - 1965	
Oda L.	1903 - 1978	
Guy A.	Jan.1,1914 - Feb.27,1957	
James O.	Nov.10,1887 - Jan.14,1952	
Jennie M.	Feb.10,1895 - no date	
Paul L.	June 10,1920 - May 3,1958	
Tompkin	Sept.18,1927 - Feb.22,1974	
Bullock, Estel Ray	1950 - 1974	
Mary Duglas	1947 - no date	
Johnny Earl	1963 - 1987	
Minnie P.	1854 - 1926	
Oscar	1924 - 1979	
Rhoda Ann	Nov.27,1887 - Dec.14,1961	
Samuel T.	Dec.19,1851 - no date	
Susan R. Masengill	Feb.24,1856 - May 23,1931	
Tom	1906 - no date	
Bertha S.	1907 - 1981	
Carr, Anna Lee	Dec.24,1924 - Feb.26,1975	
Corintha M.	1945 - 1947	
Eugene	Mar.1,1927 - Dec.11,1983	
Herman	1924 - 1925	
Jack	Aug.30,1927 - Oct.27,1976	
Kenneth Loyd	May 20,1937 - Nov.21,1984	
Minnie	Jan.7,1923	
Naomia	1922 - 1925	
Noah F.	1893 - 1955	
Lena M.	1894 - 1965	
Mitchell P.	Nov.6,1900 - May 21,1955	
Sula Mae	Nov.3,1901 - Mar.12,1949	
Odd	1901 - 1961	
Corintha	1900 - 1982	
Sinia Lyons	June 15,1873 - Sept.1,1958	
Carter, Floyd J.	1915 - no date	
Edna I.	1917 - 1966	
Chappell, Augusta G.	1892 - 1980	
Roy L.	Feb.22,1919 - Dec.6,1972	
Walter E.	1898 - 1976	
Cross, Barbara Jean	1937 - 1937	
Infant	June 4,1933, s/o Paul & Lillie Woods Cross.	
Cyphers, Amos Lawrence	May 29,1902 - Aug.21,1968	
Myrtle Wilma	July 28,1908 - Mar.5,1980	

Morrell Cemetery, cont.

Davenport, Babette "Betty"	Oct.11,1920 - Apr.27,1986
Dempsey, Bertha N. Moore	1905 - 1983
Charlie C.	1875 - 1944
Bessie E.	1881 - 1946
Gerstell C.	Nov.22,1914 - Sept.29,1978
James S.	1881 - 1953
Sallie R.	1883 - 1957
Sameul D.	Nov.27,1906 - July 4,1944
Denton, Charlie C.	June 14,1897 - Mar.13,1985
Melvinia Lee	July 15,1902 - July 18,1983
Pamela J.	1956 - 1957
Paul R.	1935 - no date
Amma Lee	1937 - 1984
Duffrain, Virginia D. Shipley	1930 - 1961
Ellis, Florence Evelyn	May 30,1928 - Nov.30,1930,d/o Dave & Minnie.
Fagans, "Bun"	1895 - 1961
Sallie	1895 - 1959
Fair, Infant	d/o C.C.Fair
Fleenor, Raymond I.	May 29,1900 - Aug.12,1983
Eva M.	Apr.23,1902 - Dec.16,1975
Fox, Frank M.	Apr.2,1910 - Sept.14,1970
Lida B.	Sept.8,1913 - no date
Friesland, Baby	July 31,1934
Glover, G.V.	Aug.2,1856 - June 12,1928
Harriet E.	Apr.15,1856 - May 23,1954
Godsey, Charlie	Oct.9,1886 - Oct.12,1969
Charlie Lee	Dec.4,1920 - May 18,1957
Junior	June 8,1946 - Oct.26,1963
Lucy J.	Apr.23,1902 - Oct.5,1973
Goodwin, Michael Dwayne	Oct.24,1965
Ray W.	1909 - 1981
Mildred H.	1915 - no date
Hendrix, Mack Cody	Jan.25,1907 - Mar.30,1982
Ruth Irene	May 15,1914 - no date
Hicks, Carrie	1883 - 1886
Charles L.	1904 - 1966
Mary W.	1910 - 1972
Elbert	b. 1864
Rev.Elbert H.	Nov.4,1872 - Jan.14,1941
George L.	Sept.5,1871 - Jan.5,1931
Molly M.	Dec.25,1872 - Dec.23,1932
Gilbert	1828 - 1902
N.D.	1843 - 1911
John	1874 - 1874
John L.	Feb.6,1882 - Jan.10,1965
Blanche C.	Apr.6,1894 - Feb.7,1977
Maggie May	1881 - 1881
Marion S.	May 8,1879 - Jan.28,1949
Ollie V.	Apr.2,1884 - July 18,1963
Matilda	1866 - 1888
Mary E.	1879 - 1880
Ruth	1866 - 1887
Rev. W.H.	Aug.22,1851 - Sept.11,1930
Anne Frazier	July 11,1853 - Jan.11,1932

Morrell Cemetery, cont.

Hodge, Harry Frank	Feb.6,1924 - Dec.27,1978
Houston, Bertha W.	1888 - 1968
Hyatt, Arthur	Mar.10,1883 - Nov.1,1963
Rona	Feb.9,1882 - Nov.14,1944
George	Sept.17,1921 - Oct.14,1980
Hazel	Dec.24,1915 - July 21,1918,d/o A.H.& R.E.
Ida	Sept.28,1912 - July 11,1912, (as they appear on stone), d/o A.H.& R.E.Hyatt.
Samuel	Jan.27,1910 - July 6,1912,s/o A.H.& R.E.
Jessee, Bobby	1935
Baby	1940
Jones, Clyde Lewis	Oct.6,1918 - Aug.29,1982
Martha Alice	1928 - 1976
John W.	1965 - 1965
Lane, Major Clinton	Nov.27,1870 - Aug.23,1928
Jennie Thornton	Dec.6,1889 - May 21,1948
Leonard, Charles Ray	Jan.30,1949
Lilly, William L.	Mar.25,1868 - Apr.28,1950
Lyons, Elbert	July 14,1892 - Jan.16,1964
Martha Alice S.	Sept.21,1892 - May 2,1926
McAninich, Carrie L.	Sept.4,1900 - Sept.10,1982
Malone, John	1926 - 1953
Masengill, Donna Cheryl	Oct.11,1948 - Feb.21,1952
George E.	Jan.7,1891 - Dec.24,1979
Margaret P.	May 17,1898 - no date
Paul	Apr.16,1915 - July 20,1916, s/o S.W.& L.C.
Bill	Nov.6,1898 - July 11,1976
Ollie	June 28,1904 - no date
Blanche	1889 - 1958
Clyde R.	1898 - 1954
F.D.	1925 - 1930
James C.	Mar.8,1917 - Oct.13,1969
Lillie W.	1890 - 1930
Messimer, Allen	Mar.4,1914 - July 21,1931
Donn Gene	Mar.19,1957 - Jan.17,1984
James	no dates
William H.	July 2,1870 - Sept.14,1949
Carrie S.	Nov.1,1882 - Jan.29,1941
Milhorn, Laura Chappell	d. June 4,1979, aged 86 yrs.
Miller, John Ervin	Apr.16,1918 - Feb.26,1981
Minton, Jerry Dean	Oct.9,1943 - July 22,1972
JoAnn	Nov.15,1948
Larry B.	Jan.11,1919 - Sept.20,1986
Moffitt, George E.	July 27,1925 - Aug.30,1986
Moore, "Coonie" C.	Jan.1,1926 - Aug.13,1982
Morrell, Auburn L.	Feb.8,1889 - Oct.10,1955
James A.	Sept.10,1915 - Feb.12,1967
James K.	Sept.21,1852 - Feb.15,1905
Jennie Odell	Jan.10,1880 - Apr.22,1962
John E.	Nov.15,1880 - May 12,1960
Lena May Busby	b.Lawrenceburg, TN.,Jan.2,1898, d.Bluff City, TN, Apr.22,1950.
Leona N.	1906 - 1935

Morrell Cemetery, cont.

Morrell, Ludie Carr	May 14,1899 - Feb.15,1926
Martha	Mar.24,1822 - June 3,1907
Mary Carrie	1893 - 1916
Melvin M.	1878 - 1928
Rebecca Ann	June 23,1856 - July 25,1923
W.H.	1891 - 1973
Morris, Robert T.	July 30,1907 - Mar.9,1977
Golda A.	Sept.29,1912
Peeks, James C.	1909 - no dates
Viola L.	1912 - 1973
Robert Lee	Mar.30,1866 - June 1,1950
Sarah L.	1875 - 1967
Perry, Grant	Feb.26,1900 - May 16,1973
Jennie Carr	Oct.25,1879 - Mar.11,1955
John A.	Feb.2,1875 - June 13,1956
Nannie Mae	Dec.21,1902 - Dec.26,1985
Pierce, Dorothy M.	1925 - 1986
Rasnick, James A.	1907 - 1960
Ethel S.	1910 - 1977
Reece, Luther C.	Feb.22,1915
Evelyn J.	May 25,1924 - Nov.27,1981
R. Floyd	1890 - 1977
Maggie M.	1894 - 1969
Rhodes, Michael S.	Feb.17,1969 - Feb.24,1982
Rhymer, Millard M.	1894 - 1975
Etta Lee	1915 - 1984
Rumley, Frances L.	Dec.1,1946 - no date
George E.	Oct.13,1921 - May 7,1973
Herman	Dec.3,1946 - no date
Herman, Jr.	June 11,1968 - June 12,1968
James C.	1870 - 1951
Laura B.	1892 - 19--
Ray	Jan.17,1939 - Mar.19,1983
Georgia L.	Dec.17,1938 - no date
Vickie D.	1967, d/o Herman & Frances Rumley.
Sams, Clarence W.	Aug.24,1916 - no date
Ruby J.	Apr.8,1930 - no date
Lee	Apr.1,1887 - Aug.5,1975
Mattie	Oct.15,1892 - May 23,1983
Nina Ellen	Oct.23,1926 - June 6,1977
Ted	Jan.15,1939 - Mar.6,1939
Scalf, Ernest W.	1917 - 1981
Frances S.	1920 - no date
Shankle, Howard J.	Aug.6,1917
Eunice	Jan.5,1912 - Mar.30,1916
Isaac F.	Sept.17,1874 - July 12,1956
Margaret Shipley	May 3,1878 - Feb.8,1942
Shipley, Adam	Apr.11,1834 - July 5,1904
Adam L.	Feb.13,1881 - Aug.19,1955
Mamie E.	Mar.15,1886 - Oct.15,1960
Agenes Morrell	Nov.24,1828 - July 17,1870,w/o Adam Shipley.
Anna Pearl	Apr.20,1890 - Nov.8,1964
Betty G.	1872 - 1953
Caroline	1858 - June 6,1916, w/o E.C.Shipley.

Morrell Cemetery, cont.

Shipley, Claria V.		Feb.21,1910 - Aug.27,1924
	E.C.	1856 - 1928
	Fairy E.	July 30,1919 - July 29,1931
	Floyd T.	Nov.4,1911 - July 22,1917
	Fonda Smith	Apr.12,1907 - Apr.8,1937,w/o L.D.Shipley.
	Georgia A.	aged 13 months, s/o A.D.& M.E.Shipley.
	Hester A.	May 4,1894 - Nov.4,1897, d/o E.C.&C.
	Jerry E.	Sept.8,1941 - Apr.22,1942
	John M.	Jan.25,1865 - Feb.10,1944
	Mary E.	Jan.18,1872 - Aug.15,1959
	Landon D.	Oct.12,1904 - Apr.18,1947
	Margaret E.	Aug.31,1849 - Jan.12,1932
	Melvin T.	1897 - no date
	Sarah B.	1905 - 1968
	Phillip Andrew	Oct.4,1883 - May 19,1945
	Amie Stout	Oct.14,1895 - Aug.14,1968
	Samuel E.	Jan.5,1920 - Oct.3,1960
	Thurman A.	Dec.9,1878 - Aug.2,1957
Slagel, Rose Bullock		Jan.6,1909 - Jan.31,1948
Stanfield, Alice Woods		July 3,1868 - Jan.7,1928
	John Franklin	Nov.8,1865 - Mar.4,1929
	Susie Crussell	Sept.20,1892 - Mar.26,1976
	William Levi	May 28,1894 - Aug.16,1975
Stout, Harvey		May 28,1934 - Jan.6,1987
	Shirley D.	Dec.27,1942 - no date
Warren, Paul A.		1908 - 1984
	Georgia M.	1915 - no date
Weaver, Dave H.		1854 - 1921
	Etta J.	1872 - 1944
Webb, Arlie D.		May 29,1903 - Apr.29,1978
	B.W.	1851 - 1925
	Mary S.	1862 - 1938
	Bruce D.	1895 - 1957
	Pearl L.	1905 - 1987
	Carl G.	June 16,1890 - Mar.3,1945
	David Lynn	Apr.2,1965 - Apr.2,1965
	Edgar G.	1919 - 1940
	Glenn C.	1898 - 1898
	Launa	1898 - 1898
	Velvie W.	June 10,1895 - May 5,1983
Williams, Betty Shipley		May 29,1931 - Oct.16,1979
	Clarence	Nov.4,1890 - June 15,1913
Woods, Andrew Jackson		Mar.15,1883 - Jan.7,1964
	David Alexander	Nov.11,1861 - Feb.5,1930
	Eldredge	1912 - 1945
	Conley	1918 - 1936
	Frank P.	Nov.25,1853 - Jan.4,1919
	Hester	Aug.6,1869 - Feb.26,1937,w/o David Alexander
	Maggie Bell	Jan.6,1884 - Sept.6,1938
	N.W.	Apr.28,1880 - no date
	Margaret H.	1860 - 1916
	Myrtle Alice	Mar.28,1887 - June 5,1956
	Myrtle M.	1891 - 1892
	Walter	Mar.10,1878 - Nov.11,1959
	Pernelopa Shelton	Mar.14,1878 - Apr.12,1950
	Walter Eugene	1909 - 1929

Holston Grove Luthren Church Cemetery

Akard, Thomas V.	1850 - 1923
Sarah King	1853 - 1929
Charles, David	1886 - 1936
Mary Marion	18-- - 19--
DeVault, Mary I. Deakins	Sept.3,1855 Mar.15,1928, w/o H.D.
H.D.	Sept.2,1855 - Apr.4,1931
Eliza J.	Spet.20,1835 - Apr.16,1928,w/o M.W.
M.W.	Jan.28,1832 - Mar.12,1912
Haskin, Leon J.	Aug.13,1893 - Aug.8,1946
Jones, Jacob L.	1828 - 1912
Hugh	1875 - 1928
J. Ed.	June 18,1874 - Oct.16,1944
Laura	no dates
Lindamood, Infant	July 5-6,1922, s/o G.N. & B.A.Lindamood.
Curtis Kyle	d. 1917, s/o G.N.Lindamood.
Ruth E.	June 13,1929 - June 14,1929,d/o G.N.& B.A.
Loudy, Mary F. Droke	1850 - 1936, w/o George W. Loudy.
George W.	1834 - 1920
Malone, Mary E.	July 8,1860 - Dec.12,1936
W.G.	Nov.16,1846 - Dec.30,1928
Payne, Joseph L.	1848 - 1925
Dorthula C.	1850 - 1936
Phillips, Mrs. Maggie Akard	d. Nov.8,1951, aged 76y
Noah D.	1867 - 1951 (fhm)
Bessie Mae	July 22,1901 - Feb.4,1918, d/o N.D.& E.M.
Shaver, Margaret Lee	d. Apr.14,1911, d/o A.D.& J.E.
Josie E.	Oct.14,1882 - Sept.30,1935
John E.	1850 - 1927
Eliza C.	1845 - 1922, w/o John E. Shaver.
Reece B.	d. APr.20,1857 (fhm), aged 72y16d
Infant	d. Mar.20,1945, s/o John & Ruth Shaver.
Webb, Harold D.	1912 - 1915, s/o M.B.& M.E. Webb.
Mike B.	1889 - 1918
James D.	1854 - 1907
Elizabeth	1859 - 1936

Surname Index

Adams - 39,63,109,150
Addison - 150
Aiken - 54
Akard - 47,94,145,170, 198
Akers - 150
Akins - 140
Albright - 119
Alexander - 181
Alford - 150,151
Allen - 63,170
Alison/Allison - 170,181
Allmon - 94
Andarson/Anderson - 48,63,94,117,
            137,140,170,171,181.
Andis - 39
Anney - 39
Archer - 39
Arnold - 2,50,58,59,63,145,151
Arrants - 63,109
Ashburn - 151
Ashby - 140
Athens - 171
Atkins - 9,58
Austin - 63
Ayers - 94
E.G.B. - 140
L.E.B. - 140
Bachman - 24,63,145,171
Bacon - 112,120
Bailey - 24,117,150,171
Baird - 63
Baker - 11,40,63,181
Bales - 94
Ball - 19,94
Ballard - 171
Barbe - 151
Bare - 1,26,63,193
Barger - 54,55,171
Barker - 18,145
Barlett - 182
Barnes - 112,145,146,182
Barnett/Barnette - 26,39,40,63,
            93,193.
Barr - 12,47,48,94,137,150,171
Barrett - 50
Bartle - 63
Bates - 63,64
Bathis - 171
Baumgardner - 151,171
Bays - 19,140
Baxley - 26
Beach - 64
Beaman - 120

Bear - 2,48
Beard - 19,64,140,171
Bebber - 53
Beck - 182
Bedwell - 140
Beeler - 137
Beidleman(s) - 15,94
Bell(e) - 19,117
Bellamy - 59,64
Belton - 15
Bennett - 64,117
Bentley - 59
Benton - 50
Berry - 13,39,64,182,193
Bickley - 171
Birdwell - 64,171
Bishop - 19,59,64,94
Black - 64, 182
Blackburn - 171
Blackmore - 171
Blair - 64
Blakely/Blakley/
Blakeley - 112,119,120,124
Blalock/Blaylock - 64,146
Blankenship - 64
Blevins - 7,15,19,40,94,120,
            126,151,171,182.
Bodwell - 172
Boling/Bolling - 26,40,64,182
Bolton - 47
Bond - 24,113,140,182
Booher - 7,40,46,53,54,55,61,
            94,95,109,124,121,134,
            137,151,152,193.
Booker - 16
Boone - 16
Boring - 172,182
Boughers - 152
Bouton - 16,39,64,152
Bowen - 95
Bowers - 5,19,64,126,152,153
Bowery/Bowry - 7,39,95,140
Bowling - 26
Bowman - 39,140,146,182
Boy - 13,64,65
Boyd - 39,50,120,124,153,172
Boyer - 117
Boyington - 182
Bracken - 120
Bradley - 65,117,153
Bragg - 50,51
Brainard - 182
Brawley - 2
Bray - 19
Breden - 95

Brewer - 15
Brickey - 59
Bridwell - 55
Britt - 182
Broce - 126,137
Browlee - 146
Brown - 2,5,16,19,25,65,96,116,
        134,150,153,172,193.
Broyles - 39,65,95,96,140,182
Brumit(t) - 65,182
Bruner - 113
Brushingham - 60
Bryan - 26,65,193
Bryson - 65
Buchanan - 26,40,153
Buckeller - 26,172
Buckles - 7,39,65,96,153,154,
          193
Buckner - 65
Bullis - 55
Bullock - 96,193
Bunn - 65,154
Burkey - 109
Burkhart - 126
Burnett (e) - 19,65,109
Burton - 137
Bush - 65
Bushang/Bushong - 96,97,126
Buskill - 154
Butler - 126
Byers -124
Byrd - 48
Cable -97
Cagle - 1,19,20
Cain - 134
Callahan - 65
Calloway - 154,172
Calton - 117
Campbell - 20,53,65,97,121,126,
           154,172,182.
Campton - 2
Cannon - 66
Canter - 26 66
Carberry - 113
Carden - 131
Cardwell - 154
Carico - 13
Carlton - 140
Carmack - 127,172
Carmody - 66
Carr - 1,27,41,60,66,154,172,
       182,193.
Carrier - 11,13,16,20,26,41,
          66,67,97,137,154,
          155,156.

Carriger/Carrieger - 27,67
Carroll - 27,37,113,121,124,
          131.
Carter - 48,59,67,121,138,146,
         193.
Cartright/Cartwright - 27,140,
                       146.
Carty - 16
Cash - 146
Cassidy - 46
Castell - 172
Castle - 2
Cate - 172
Catron/Catlon - 67,124
Caudill - 11
Cawood/Caywood- 40,67,97,121
Cecil - 117
Chamberlain - 67
Chambers - 109,172
Chapman - 97,156
Chappell - 193
Chase - 51,113,120
Childress - 113,124,127
Christian - 127
Clark - 47,48,51,67,97,111,
        112,113,182.
Clay - 131,172,182
Cleek - 25,47,172
Clinton - 67
Church - 3
Clyce - 2
Cloud - 2 6
Coates - 51
Coffey - 15,16,20,40
Coffman - 146
Cole - 5,11,37,41,48,97,131,
       172,182.
Coletrane - 2
Collin(s) - 16,20,37,51,67,68
Colton - 138
Comb(es) - 4,11,13,26,27,40,
           68,97,156.
Conkin - 51,52
Converse - 172
Cook - 68,97,156
Coolsby - 68
Cooper - 58,140,141
Cope - 68
Copehaver - 97
Cornett - 40
Cosler - 18
Cotter - 37
Cowan - 9,68,97

Cox - 11,27,40,52,55,68,112,
    113,114,116,117,120,124,
    134,141,172,183.
Crabtree - 68
Craig - 156
Crampton - 156
Crawford - 52,54,68,119,120,
    172,173.
Cretsinger - 182
Crockett - 68,97
Croft - 97
Cross - 1,4,5,6,10,20,26,37,
    68,97,114,131,141,146,
    173,183,193.
Crouch - 112
Crout - 11
Crow(e) - 27,68,131
Crowder - 68
Crown - 131
Crumley - 40,41,68,97,98,127,
    138,156,173.
Culbertson - 156
Cummings - 173
Cunningham - 183
Curtis - 69
Crusenberry - 16
Crussell - 37,68,69
Cumbow - 127
Cyphers - 193
Czoka - 69
Dailey - 8
Dakin - 156
Dalton - 109
Danner - 27
Darchrity - 2
Daugherty - 11
Davenport - 121,183,194
Davidson - 59,109,124,141,183
Davis - 20,60,69,98,141
Deadrick - 173
Deakins - 141,146
Dean - 11,41,69
Deck - 7,18,146
Deckard - 173
Delaney -9,69,98
Delp - 183
Dempsey - 69,194
Denny - 69,127,173
Denton - 12,36,38,69,70,134,
    135,156,194.
Depew - 52,117,121,124,125
Derry - 173
DeVault/Davault - 2,10,117,125,
    127,150,183, 198
Dickens - 98

Dickson - 70,98
Dillard - 47
Dillow - 117
Dishner - 2,3,8,54,70
Dixon - 55,135
Doan(e) - 70,140,146,173
Dodd - 70
Dodson - 7
Dollar - 58
Donigan - 70
Dooley - 18
Doss - 70
Dotson - 183
Dove - 173
Dowell - 70
Doyle - 20
Droak/Droke - 6,46,47,48,70,
    173.
Dryer - 131
Duffrain -194
Dugger - 98
Dulaney - 173,174
Duncan - 27,52,61,114,127,131.
Dunn - 27,41,70,183
Durham - 131,146,183
Dutton -70
Dyche - 70
Dyer - 183
Dykes - 52,109
Eades/Eads - 13,27,70,71,121
Eakins - 55
Ealey - 27,41,71
Eanes - 174
Earhart - 174
Early - 71,156
Easley - 117,121,174
East - 20
Eaton - 71,125
Edwards - 71
Elbey - 127
Elkins - 98,156
Elliott - 71
Ellis - 1,27,156,194
Elsea - 135,174
Elswick - 156
Emerson - 98
Emery - 71,150
Emmert - 16,20,71,121,156
Ensor - 174
Erwin - 55,174
Evans - 174
Ewing - 71
Fagan(s) - 131,184,194
Fain - 50,71,174
Fair - 119,194

Faison - 71
Faris - 127
Farley - 41
Farmer - 117,174
Farthing - 41
Fauver - 71
Faw - 71, 72
Feagins - 98
Feathering - 174
Feathers - 16,72,98,146
Feazell - 72
Fenner - 72
Ferguson - 112,114,117,157
Ferriter - 7
Fickal/Fickle - 141,146,175
Fields - 59,98
Fine - 98
Fink - 112,114,121
Fitzgerald - 131
Flanary - 52
Fleenor - 13,16,20,72,109,110,
        121,194.
Fleming - 16,72,110
Flin - 125
Floyd - 60
Folkner - 125
Ford - 25,55,72,114,119,122,
      141,146,147,175.
Forrester - 132
Foster - 13,111
Fouch - 157
Foust - 72
Fowler - 27
Fox - 194
Frazier - 60,72,125,141,157
Freeland - 72
Freeman - 59,72,125,138
Friebel - 72
Friesland - 72,194
Fritz - 157
Frye - 27,127,132,184
Fugate - 15
Fulcher - 127
Fulkerson - 117,118
Fulmer - 184
Gagaway - 119
Gaines - 25,46
Galliher - 98
Galloway/Golloway - 49,55,72,
 98,99,118,122,125,141,175,184.
Gammon - 53,72,99,147,175
Ganit - 84
Garland - 20
Gardner - 28
Garrett - 28,29,99

Geisler - 38,73,157
Gentry - 43,73,157
George - 61
Gerstle - 73
Gibbons - 47,157
Gibson - 47,54,73,114
Giesler - 73,132,182
Giles - 73
Gilley - 73
Gilliam - 59
Gilreath - 73
Glover - 9,20,21,27,28,37,42,
        60,61 73,99,138,141,
        157,175,194.
Gobble - 28
Goddard - 99
Godsey - 21,73,135,195
Goff/Gott - 8,175
Goforth - 48
Golden - 114
Goldstein - 99
Good - 73
Goodman - 2,21,131,141,184
Goodson - 21
Goodwin - 73,99,157,194
Gorley - 21
Gorman - 73
Gouge - 131
Gray - 99,127,141
Graybeal - 11,42,184
Grayboal - 157
Green(e) - 28,41,47,73,99,
        127,184.
Greenlee - 99
Greenway - 5,73
Greeson - 99
Greer - 28,58,110
Gregg - 1,184
Gregory - 58
Grier - 110
Griffith - 21,73
Grills - 122
Grimes - 127,150
Grimsley - 74
Groseclose - 47,99
Grose - 61,99,157,184
Groves - 135
Grubb - 157
Guess - 157
Guffey/Guffy - 157
Guinn - 157
Gunning - 50
Guthrie - 73
Guy - 157
E.F.M.H. - 114

Hackady - 127
Hackney - 142
Haga - 12,21,54,111
Hakes - 25
Hale - 132,138,147,157
Hall - 74,127,132,138,142,175,
      184,185.
Hamblin - 47
Hamilton - 16,48,74,110,147,
      175,185.
Hammer - 74,127
Hammond - 59
Hampton - 74,127
Hancher - 49,135
Hansford - 74
Harban - 175
Harden - 132
Hargis - 118
Harkleroad - 21,74,75
Harman/Harmon - 29,43,75
Harr - 24,46,47,49,157,175
Harrigan - 75,100
Harris - 185
Harshbarger - 114,160
Hart - 21,29
Hartley - 43,157,160
Harvey - 132,185
Hatcher - 43,100,160
Hauk - 55
Hawk - 75,100,104,132,147,175
Hawkins - 61,75
Hawley - 55,147,185
Haws - 185
Hawthorne - 21,100
Hayes/Hays - 21,43,55,100,147,
      158
Haynes - 158,175
Hempton - 21
Henderson - 110,127
Hendricks - 43
Hendrickson - 55
Hendrix - 75,76,194
Henley - 21,76
Henry - 76,147
Hensley - 158,175,185
Henson - 7,43,76,158
Herron - 118
Hickman - 21,25,52,55,76,111,
      114,147,185.
Hicks - 6,10,13,16,21,22,29,
43,48,50,60,100,142,158,175,194.
Hill - 100
Hillard - 58
Hilton - 114,125
Hinkle - 29, 122,158,159

Hisey - 128
Hite - 118,119,120,122,123
Hobbs - 12,76,128
Hockett - 159
Hodge(s) - 29,76,77,132,147,
      185,186,195.
Holden - 138
Holley - 77
Holt(s) - 4,6,20,49,56,77
Homsher - 186
Hood - 77,118,123,125
Hopkins - 11,29,100,110,138,159
Horner - 53,100
Hoss - 175
Hostrawser - 22
Hoover - 37
Houser - 100,101,175
Houston - 13,77,195
Houts - 176
Howard - 15,77
Howell - 138
Hudson - 22,118
Huffman - 29,28,135
Huggins - 101
Hughes - 15,101,147,176,186
Hull - 49,77,142
Hulse - 115
Humphrey/Humphreys - 13,77,159,
      176,186
Hunigan - 128
Hunt - 54,77,123,125,138
Hutchins - 48,77
Hyatt - 1,16,43,77,132,159,186,
      195
Hyder - 62,77,132
Ingle - 123
Inscho - 77
Irvin - 176
Isbel - 118
Isley - 56,147,186
Jackson - 48,116,123,135
Jacobs - 77
James - 77,135,176
Jamison - 186
Jarrett - 29
Jarvis - 77
Jenkins - 11,29,30,43,77,78,
      101
Jennings - 60
Jessee - 195
Jeter - 6,186
Jobe - 52
Johns -22
Johnson - 60,78,128,142,159,
      186

Johnston - 22,78
Jones - 2,4,10,16,22,29,37,43,
  58,59,78,101,110,111,115,118,
  123,125,128,142,150,159,176,
  186,195,198
Jordan - 48,101
Justice - 29,78
Kastner - 30
Kaylor - 30
Kaywood - 78
Keeling - 159
Kelly - 132
Kennett - 138
Kenny - 176
Kensinger - 78
Kesner - 101
Kestner - 123
Ketchum - 22
Ketron - 78
Keys - 48
Kidd - 147,176
Kidwell - 138
Kincheloe - 112, 115
King - 2,8,11,22,30,37,78,101,
  123,148,187
Kinley - 159
Kinney - 107
Kirkpatrick - 78
Kishpaugh - 123
Knowles - 159
Kuhn - 30,142,176
Kyte - 78,101
Lacey - 123,148
Lady - 112,115,125,159
Lambert - 22,78,128,138
Lamberth - 56
Lamkins - 47
Lampson - 150
Landers - 79
Lane - 10,31,49,60,61,101,
  188,195
Large - 138
Larimer - 159
Larkin - 60
Larve - 159
Lathan - 128
Latture - 79,135,136,188
Laughter - 101
Lawson - 132,188
Ledford - 6
Lee - 79
Leedy - 115
Leedom - 159
Lemons - 54

Leonard - 4,8,20,31,79,101,
  132,143,159,160,188,195.
Lessley - 48
Lewis - 3,31,101
Light - 52,118
Liley/Lilley - 1,5,36,79,195, 9
Linderfelt - 12
Lingerfelt - 43,79,160
Lingerfile - 31
Lions - 79
Lipps - 79
Lisenby - 123
Little - 79
Littleford - 79,101,102
Litz - 118
Lockhart - 123
Lockner - 160
Logan - 188
Loggans - 148
Lomg/Long - 176
Longacre - 110
Loudy - 160,198
Love - 79,160,188
Lovelace - 79
Lovett - 160
Lowrie - 31
Lucas - 52
Luck - 110
Lunsford - 160
Luttrell - 22
Lynn - 25,50,150,176
Lyon(s) - 30,31,43,79,80,
  102,195
McAninich - 195
McBroom - 80
McCall - 102
McChesney - 128
McClaney - 1
McClellan(d) - 24,80,102,128,
  160,176,188
McCluer - 47
McCorkle - 102
McCoy - 143
McCracken - 138,160
McCrary - 16,18,115,138
McCrory - 102
McCulley - 115
McDonald - 115
McDonnell - 148
McElyea - 31
McFall - 62
McFarland - 132
McDavid - 60
McGalamary - 80
McGarry - 160

McGhee - 129
McKamey - 80,188
McKinney - 12,44,80,81,188
McLain - 136
McLaney - 1
McLaster - 22
McMackin - 62
McMillin - 22,176
McMurray - 136
McNeill - 102
McNew - 5 8
McNutt - 22
McQueen - 44
Madgett - 102
Madison - 81
Madron - 188
Mahady - 18
Mahaffey/Mahoffey - 38,81
Maiden - 160
Main/Maine(s) - 32,36
Malone - 4,6,16,17,37,38,81,
        143,188,195,198
Manes - 81
Manis - 22
Mann - 2,102
Marion - 81,148
Marks - 129
Marley - 81
Marsh - 102,176
Martin - 5 8,115,123,133,138,139
Masengill/Masengale/Massengill -
    62,82,115,176,177.
Mashburn - 148
Mason - 102,188
Massey - 177
Mast - 82
Matherly - 115,136
Matthews - 82
Mauk - 38,82,177
May/Maye/Mayes - 30,31,44,58,
                69,116,129.
Mayne - 30,50
Mattox - 129
Meadows - 22,188
Melear - 52
Mellon - 133
Melvin - 160
Meredith - 102,160
Messimer - 195
Metzger - 82
Milburn - 125
Milhorn/Millhorn(e) - 4,82,102,
            103,133,148,188.
Millard - 14,82,83,102,110,
        143,177.

Miller - 3,7,12,14,17,22,32,
    38,83,102,110,129,136,143,
    160,177,195.
Mills - 22,83,84,138,188
Millsap - 31,103,17
Miner - 52
Minga/Mingea - 52,148,188
Mink - 37
Minnick - 14,84,139,160
Minton - 31,195
Mitchell - 103,115,129
Moffet - 195
Molyneaux - 161
Monroe - 22
Montgomery - 32,103
Monteith - 143,148
Moody - 25,31,84,115,118,123
Moore - 2,22,53,54,103,115,
    125,129,161,188.
Morefield - 123
Morgan - 17,84,189
Morelock - 52
Morell/Morrell - 4,6,14,17,48,
    61,84,85,103,143,148,161,162,
    195,196.
Morris - 10,44,85,110,143,
    148,161,162,195,196.
Morton - 103,162,163
Morse - 32,103
Moser - 17
Moss - 85
Mottern - 3,31,32,44,85,163
Mullenix - 52,163,177
Mullins - 52
Murphy - 85,103
Murry - 85
Myers - 32,85,163
Nave - 44
Neal - 17,22,85,129,143,
        163,177
Necessary - 56,85,
Neeley - 150
Neil - 47
Nelms - 3,47
Nelson - 32,85,103,110,133,163
Nepella - 3
Netherland - 2,18,150
New - 120
Newland - 18,177
Newman - 85,129
Newton - 44,85,112
Nichels/Nichols/
Nickels/Nuckols - 44,45,56,
                85,86
Nidiffer - 32,148

Norris - 59,148
Nutty - 129
Oldfield - 61
Odell - 17,22,45,61,86,103,163,
        164,165,189.
Offield - 9,103
Oler - 118
Olinger - 136
Oliver - 10,86,103,129,133,189
Ollis - 53
Osborn(e) - 7,58,53,129,133,165
Overbay/Overbey - 22,53,118,125
Owen(s) - 22,23,86,165
Painter - 17
Pannell - 136
Parker - 150,177
Parks - 86
Parrott - 177
Patrick - 104,165
Patterson - 87
Patton - 2,15,49,60,87
Payne - 133,165,198
Peaks - 32,104,165
Pearce - 165
Pearson - 178
Peeks - 196
Peltier - 3
Pemberton - 61
Pence - 148
Pendergrass - 136
Pendleton - 136
Pennel - 189
Pennington - 87
Peny - 45
Peoples - 104,178
Peregoy - 9
Perkey - 12
Perkins - 133
Perry - 61,87,104,118,123,196
Peterman - 12
Peter(s) - 9,87,104,129,139,165
Peterson - 87
Petro - 165
Phelps - 23
Phillips - 23,37,58,53,59,87,
           104,129,143,165,178,198
Phipps - 18,104,129,130
Pickens - 115,119,178,189
Pickel/Pickle - 165
Pierce - 47,125,196
Pierson - 87
Pile - 61
Pippin - 32
Plank - 87
Pleasant - 139

Pless - 12
Plummer - 104
Poe - 32,143,189
Poore - 59,125,130,149,165
Pope - 49,136
Posten - 123
Potter - 12,58,116,117
Potts - 165
Powell - 2,3,119,178
Prater - 87
Presnell - 1,7,166
Preston - 87,104
Price - 104,166
Profit/Profitt - 1,9,104
Puckett - 87,136
Pulliam - 25
Pyle - 32
Quailes - 104
Quarles - 130
Quillen - 123
Quisenberry - 23
R.L.R. - 7
Rader - 14,104,130,143,178
Ragan - 130
Rainey - 56
Ramey - 166
Ramsey - 105,123,189
Range - 189
Rankin - 87
Rasnick - 196
Ray - 23
Raybon - 189
Rayl - 25
Redfain - 87
Reece - 45,87,105,196
Reed - 32,87,130,189
Reedy - 87
Reeser - 125
Reeve(s) - 87,178
Repass - 87
Reynolds - 87
Rhea - 87,105,111,143,144,
       178,179,189.
Rhodes - 62,196
Rhymer - 23,196
Rice - 166
Richard(s) - 32,33,45,88,105
Richardson - 7,20,33,88,105
Richmond - 87
Riddle - 88
Riden - 88
Riggs - 115,116,123
Rigsby - 116
Riffey - 105
Riley - 14,33,45,88,105,189

Ringley - 105
Ritchie - 88
Roark - 45,88
Robeson - 123,179
Roberson - 2,33
Roberts - 23,88,133,189
Robertson - 62
Robinson - 56,116,166,179
Roe - 88,89,111,166
Rogan - 2,179
Rogers - 4,45,62,105,166,179
Rohr - 62
Roller - 25,57,149
Rose - 189
Rosenbalm - 9,23,53,62,166
Ross - 23
Royston - 14,33,105
Rumley - 196
Rush - 58,59,89
Russell - 149
Russum - 10
Ruth - 23
Rutherford - 105,119,125, 58
            130,149
Rutledge - 37,50,89,105,106,
            133,166,179.
Rutter - 179
Ryan - 12
Ryden - 89
Ryder - 59
Rymer - 106
P.J.S. - 8
P.L.S. - 8
St.John - 8
Salts - 89
Salyer - 49
Sames/Sams - 12,35,61,89,
            106,196
Sanders - 60,133,149,189
Savage - 89
Saylor - 133
Scalf - 34,196
Schoolfield - 179
Scott - 89,106,139,189
Sedgley - 106
Seehorn - 190
Sell(s) - 89,111,130,139,
            149,190.
Seneker - 8,46,106,130,179
Senter - 139
Shaffer - 3,139
Shankle - 196
Shanks - 116
Sharp(e) - 90,106
Sharrett - 139

Shaver - 18,136,198
Shaw - 139
Sheets - 34
Shell - 90,190
Shelley - 23,90
Shelton - 23,60,111,139
Shepard/Shephard - 90,190
Sherfey - 112,116,120,149
Shields - 106
Shipley - 38,57,61,116,133,
            144,166,167,190,
            196,197.
Shirley - 149
Shoecraft - 23
Shoemaker - 112
Shore - 45
Short(t) - 120,179
Shumaker - 179
Shuttle - 139
Sigman - 34
Silver(s) - 23,90
Simerly - 45,106
Simmons - 116,167
Simpson - 130
Sims - 90
Sine - 87
Sisk - 23
Sizemore - 123
Sizer - 106
Slaughter - 49,90,106,123,144
Slagel/Slagle - 35,112,197
Sloan - 106
Sluder - 117,133,167
Sluss - 133
Smalling - 9,90,149,190
Smiley - 123
Smith - 4,5,6,14,23,24,33,34,
    37,45,47,49,53,50,90a,91,107,
    116,125,130,133,139,144,149,
    150,167,179,180,190.
Smithson - 167,168
Snapp - 47,133,136,137,180,190
Snodgrass - 23,180
Snow - 107
Snyder - 58,107,168
Soboleweski - 90a
Spahr - 8
Spangler - 180
Spary - 35
Spears/Speers - 60,90a,116,123
Sproles - 90a,130,180
Spurgeon/Spurgin - 90,144,
                145,180
Stafford - 90a,107
Stanfield - 35,38,197

Stanford - 116
Stanley - 90a
Staples - 90a
Stapleton - 90a
Starbuck - 168
Starr - 168
Statzer - 23,180
Steadman - 23,116,125
Steel(e) - 54,112
Stepp - 45
Stevens - 34
Stewart - 38,58,90,112,130,133
Stidham - 145,149
Stine - 90a
Stokes - 90a
Stone - 8,59,90a,139
Stophel - 7,45,53,139,168,169
Stout - 23,53,90a,107,137,197
Strouth - 23,107,169
Stuart - 62
Stufflestreet - 12
Sturm - 180
Suesong - 57
Sumner - 47
Sumpter - 125
Sutter - 45
Swanner - 34
Sweeney - 14
Swiney - 14,139
Sword - 5
Sykes - 125
Tate - 90a
Taylor - 7,18,23,35,90a,107,
  111,119,134,137,139,169,180.
Teague - 3
Tedrow - 123
Terry - 91
Tester - 35,37,91,134,9
Thacker - 91
Thomas - 91,107,111,169,180,190
Thompson - 91,107,119
Tibbs - 137
Tinsley - 91
Tipton - 180
Tittle - 91
Todd - 91
Tolbert - 45,130,190
Tollie - 35,91
Torbett - 91,134,180,191
Townsend - 35
Trail - 17
Treadway - 139
Trent - 169
Trinkle - 23,24
Trivett(e) - 91,126

Troxwell - 145
Trusler - 107
Turner - 45,91,169
Upchurch - 2,91
Vance - 45,46,91,107,108,131,
           139,140,169,180.
Van de Vort - 108
Van Hoy - 108
Vanover - 58,91
Vanzant - 119
Vaughn - 47,119,126
Vaught - 91
Vickers - 91
Vinson - 169
Vires - 108
Voorhees - 134,169
Waddell - 91
Wagner - 91,119,145
Walsh/Walch - 145,146
Waldron - 91
Walker - 91,131,150
Wallace - 92
Walling - 169
Wampler - 108
Ward - 24,92,119,191
Warren - 91,108,169,191,197
Washington - 15,92
Washow - 92
Wassom - 14,15,36,92
Waterman - 25
Waters - 12
Waterbury - 3
Watkins - 53,116
Watson - 35,36,92,169
Weaver - 17,24,108,109,169,197
Webb - 6,10,17,46,61,92,149,197,198
Webster - 24,36,58
Weeks - 140
Wells - 92,116
Welsh - 49,57
Wenny - 46
Wexler - 119,191
Whillock - 111
Whitaker - 92,137,169,191
White - 1,4,24,58,92,109,145,
          169,170,180,192.
Whitlock - 93
Widner - 24
Wilburn - 17
Wiles - 93
Wiley - 180
Wilkerson - 109
Willard - 112,119
Williams - 93,145,170,180,
           181,197.

Willaimson - 93
Willis - 109
Wills - 2
Wilson - 1,25,36,49,5 8,60,109,
            131,137,170,192.
Winebarger - 192
Wisdom - 15
Wise - 109,149,170
Wishon - 93
Witcher - 93,109,181
Witt - 93
Wix - 170
Wolf(e) - 17,62,181,192
Wolford - 46,49,54
Wood(s) - 36,59,61,93,111,149,
            150,192,197.
Woodring - 46
Woolf - 62
Worley - 15,17,93
Worsham - 93
Wright - 93,170
Wyatt - 24,5 8,59,93,170
Wynes - 170
Yakley - 53
Yamashiro - 94
Yoakley - 25,145,149
Yonce - 57
Yost/Youst - 94,181
Zimmerman - 119

Charles - 198
Hashen - 198
Lindamood - 4,6,79,143,176,198

www.ingramcontent.com/pod-product-compliance
Lightning Source LLC
Chambersburg PA
CBHW080237270326
41926CB00020B/4275